D0776912

Strictly Confidential: The Private Volker Fund Memos of Murray N. Rothbard

Edited by David Gordon

Foreword by
Brian Doherty

LvMI
MISES INSTITUTE

Strictly Confidential: The Private Volker Fund Memos of Murray N. Rothbard

Edited by David Gordon

Foreword by
Brian Doherty

LvMI

MISES INSTITUTE

© 2010 by the Ludwig von Mises Institute and published under the Creative Commons Attribution License 3.0. *http://creativecommons.org/licenses/by/3.0/*

Ludwig von Mises Institute
518 West Magnolia Avenue
Auburn, Alabama 36832
mises.org

ISBN: 978-1-933550-80-0

Table of Contents

Foreword

I never met Murray Rothbard.

Because I am the author of *Radicals for Capitalism: A Freewheeling History of the Modern American Libertarian Movement,* that was highly unfortunate. More than any other person, Murray Rothbard *was* the modern American libertarian movement.

Intellectually, he was the most prolific and active advocate and scholar for the ideas and concerns that most vividly mark libertarianism as a distinct tendency and movement; he brought together Austrian economics, natural-rights ethics, anarchist politics, and a burning interest in history   in the actual facts of the intellectual heritage of antistate thinking, and of how and why in specific incidents governments oppress and rob the bulk of the populace.

Institutionally, he helped form or worked closely with every significant libertarian group or organization from the 1940s to the 1990s, from the Foundation for Economic Education to the Volker Fund, to the Institute for Humane Studies, to the Libertarian Party, to the Center for Libertarian Studies, to the Cato Institute to the Ludwig von Mises Institute.

Every other significant libertarian thinker was personally influenced by him or felt obligated to grapple with him where they disagreed, from Leonard Read to Robert Nozick.

When it comes to modern American libertarianism, Rothbard was the Man. That I was not able to meet him and get his fresh words into my book is my greatest regret associated with it.

This does not mean that my book was not shaped by Rothbard's words or interpretations. He was also the most prolific and thoughtful theorist of institutional and movement libertarianism. From the 1950s to the 1990s, he wrote on where the movement had been, where it was going, and what he thought it needed to do. He left hundreds of thousands of words of great insights on these matters, words that are sometimes general and theoretical and often—especially in the pages of his great 1968–84 journal, *Libertarian Forum*—precise and personal.

As a researcher into libertarianism, I was greatly fortunate to have not only his many, many published essays, columns, and interviews to rely on for Rothbard's thoughts and actions; the Mises Institute, the repository of Rothbard's library and papers, granted me wide-ranging access to his heretofore unpublished memos, essays, and letters. These documents are a treasure well beyond my comparatively parochial needs in researching my book. They are a joyful alternative career of Rothbard's writings and research, and as such inherently one of the most valuable (and most fun) intellectual resources of the past century.

David Gordon—probably the only man around who knows as much about as much as Rothbard did when it comes to the historical, philosophical, and economic background of libertarianism—has compiled this new book of letters, memos, and reviews from Rothbard on the value—and often on the libertarian bona fides—of dozens of thinkers and books that came to the attention of the Volker Fund and Volker-associated groups such as the National Book Foundation, which helped promote and publish libertarian-friendly scholars and scholarship in an age when it was welcome almost nowhere.

The readers of this book—and of editor Gordon's introduction—will find out for themselves in the best way possible the scope of what Rothbard accomplishes here. There are useful and rich nuggets covering every aspect of Rothbard's intellectual project, starting with his bold call for the necessity of a pure and unsullied *libertarian* set of institutions and activists.

I was most delighted to notice subtle little throughlines that help remind the reader of Rothbard's perspicacity (his consistent recognition of the not-to-be-forgotten distinctions between the modern libertarian and the modern conservative or right-winger) and of the disciplined humane concern that could almost be said to constitute the heart of Rothbard: his recognition, from the War of 1812 to the Cold War and every war in between (no matter how beloved by historians nowadays), that the monstrous crime of state-launched murder and rapine and destruction so blithely called "war" has been the greatest enemy not only of life but of American liberty.

Rothbard wrote a wonderful four-volume history of colonial America, published as *Conceived in Liberty*. His fans have long wished he had managed a full-on history of America. He never had the time to do so.

But in this volume's bravura centerpiece, disguised as a simple book-review memo of George B. DeHuszar and Thomas Hulbert Stevenson's *A History of the American Republic*, we have in essence at least the outline or study guide to one. It's a marvelously detailed step-by-step discussion of the primary points, personalities, and controversies in American history that should most interest the historian who loves liberty. How I wish someone could add more meat to this already strong and imposing skeleton of an American history. Alas, the man who had the knowledge and stamina and proper perspective to do so left us in 1995.

I never met Murray Rothbard. Likely you didn't either. But most especially in this book—because of its immense range, its private purpose, and its easy and wide erudition—you are meeting the man at his finest: impassioned, funny, learned, brilliant, unfoolable, relentless. I advise you to read this with pen and notebook in hand. Rothbard is going to teach you so many things, in so many unforgettable formulations, that you are going to want to take note of them; just as Rothbard, in his decades of staggering reading and thinking, took notes for us, and passed on his insights tirelessly.

That benefit accrues now not just to his friends and colleagues who sought his advice on matters libertarian in years gone by, advice solidified in these memos; thanks to Gordon and the Mises Institute, that benefit is for the ages.

Writing from the 2010 perspective of the "Ron Paul Revolution," the first mass-political movement to make a splash in America in our times—a movement clearly animated by Rothbardian style and ideas about currency, war, and the evils of the state—I believe the ages will more and more note Rothbard and his message. And the world will be a better place for it.

Brian Doherty
Los Angeles, California
March 2010

Introduction

The recent publication of *Rothbard versus the Philosophers*, edited by Roberta Modugno, brought to many readers' attention a not very well-known aspect of Murray Rothbard's work. His vast published output did not exhaust his writing. To the contrary, a large number of important items had never been published. Many of these were reports on books and conferences that Rothbard wrote while he worked for the William Volker Fund, which during the late 1950s and early 1960s was the principal American foundation supporting classical liberalism. Professor Modugno drew from Rothbard's papers, housed at the Mises Institute, several of these unpublished reports.

Strictly Confidential continues the project that Modugno has so ably begun. It presents over forty new items from the unpublished papers. These range over political theory, history, economics, foreign policy, and literature. We begin, though, with a confidential memo, "What Is to Be Done?" which Rothbard prepared for the William Volker Fund. The Leninist echo in the title is not accidental. In this memo, Rothbard addresses an issue that concerned him throughout his adult life: how can a libertarian society be created? He thought that the Volker Fund should not view itself as just another conservative organization. Instead, it should favor a militant strategy that emphasized aid to scholars fully committed to a radical libertarian ideology. Libertarianism is a system of belief that in many respects is revolutionary rather than conservative.

The radical nature of Rothbard's libertarianism becomes clear when we turn to the section on political theory. He thought that classical liberals who favored limited government had not fully thought through their position. If the market was desirable and government intervention bad, why need there be a government at all? In "Are Libertarians 'Anarchists'?" he asks whether libertarians who accept his view about government should designate themselves by a very controversial word. (In the years after this article was written, he became much less ambivalent about this word.)

Another item in this section is of fundamental importance. One of the major conservative political theorists of the 1950s and 1960s was Willmoore Kendall, a teacher of William Buckley, Jr. at Yale and a senior editor of *National Review*. Unlike most conservatives, Kendall thought highly of Jean-Jacques Rousseau and his "general will." American conservatism, he argued, reflects the "deliberate sense of the community." Kendall was entirely ready to endorse suppression of civil liberties if a public consensus that met his conditions supported this. Rothbard subjected this view to merciless criticism, arguing that Kendall's principle would justify the Crucifixion.

Rothbard could make little of another figure much in favor among the conservatives of the time: Eric Voegelin. His skeptical remarks on a panel devoted to Voegelin's work contrast with almost all other studies of him. I well remember Rothbard's asking me in puzzlement what Voegelin might have meant by a "leap in being."

Rothbard's criticism was of course not confined to assaults on conservative thinkers. He found little use for Charles Black's attempt to create a political myth to elevate the Supreme Court in the public's estimation. Here Rothbard foreshadowed a theme prominent in his last years: he sympathized with populism and deplored attempts by an elite to justify government. Of course, as his critique of Kendall makes clear, he did not support populist suppression of rights. The point, rather, is to what extent in the American system one should place weight on the Supreme Court to protect these rights.

The section on history demonstrates, if proof were needed, Rothbard's remarkable knowledge of both historical events and historiography. In his long report on George B. DeHuszar and T.H. Stevenson's *A History of the American Republic*, Rothbard shows his incredible command of details perhaps better than anywhere else, through his constant challenges to the authors.

At the time Rothbard was in graduate school at Columbia University, the most influential American historian was Charles Beard. His famous *An Economic Interpretation of the Constitution* led many to think that Beard was a Marxist, and Rothbard addresses this issue in a carefully reasoned essay. Among contemporary historians and economists interested in an economic interpretation of history, Douglass North is probably much more studied than Beard. Rothbard did not rate him highly, and in an early review of him raises criticisms that he never retracted.

In Rothbard's brand of libertarianism, revisionist history occupied a prominent place. In order to promote a peace-loving foreign policy, it was essential to revisit the propaganda version of events used to embroil America in war. In this connection, his review of Paul Schroeder's *The Axis Alliance and Japanese-American Relations, 1941* is especially valuable. Rothbard discusses in detail Schroeder's contention that the Roosevelt administration pursued a belligerent rather than conciliatory policy in the months before Pearl Harbor. Rothbard accepts Schroeder's thesis but holds that he does not go far enough. He also viewed with critical sympathy William Appleman Williams's revisionist general survey of the history of American foreign policy, *The Tragedy of American Diplomacy.*

It comes as no surprise that Rothbard regarded highly Alexander Gray's *The Socialist Tradition.* Gray was entirely clear that socialism was a fatal error; and he skewered all the icons of socialist theory, Karl Marx foremost among them. But his praise for Gray is mixed with criticism. Gray, carried away by his animus toward the socialists, often indulged in personal ridicule.

Though the struggle against bad economics was of crucial importance for Rothbard, the battle had to be waged in a correct fashion. For this reason, Rothbard did not report favorably on the anti-Keynesian pamphlet *Keynes at Harvard,* which during the 1960s attracted much attention among conservatives. The pamphlet cited the communist-front records of many prominent Keynesians. Rothbard thought that these affiliations did not affect the validity, or lack thereof, of Keynesian theory.

What was a better way to answer Keynes? The answer to this question takes us naturally to the next section of *Strictly Confidential*. Even before he was fully acquainted with Austrian economics, Rothbard had formulated penetrating criticisms of Keynesian economics. He was influenced here by the classroom lectures of one of his main professors at Columbia, Arthur Burns. Rothbard wrote a detailed account of these criticisms, which he endeavored to publish in his friend Frank Chodorov's journal *analysis*. Unfortunately, Chodorov thought that the material was too technical for his audience: it is a brilliant internal criticism of the Keynesian system and deserves wide circulation.

The principal critic of Keynes among Austrian economists was Henry Hazlitt; and in a letter included here, Rothbard expresses his esteem for Hazlitt's work. He was pleasantly surprised at the theoretical depth in *The Failure of the New Economics*; while he realized that Hazlitt was a brilliant economic journalist, he had nevertheless underestimated him. Rothbard also admired Lionel Robbins's *The Great Depression*. Its Austrian account of the crash influenced his own *America's Great Depression*. Robbins later repudiated his own book, but Rothbard saw no need to follow Robbins in this mistake.

Rothbard's opposition to Keynes is hardly surprising, but the ostensibly free-market Chicago School fared not that much better in his eyes. The reason for this does not lie entirely in the deviations of its various members from complete *laissez-faire*. To the contrary, he had far-reaching theoretical objections to the Chicago approach. In particular, he opposed the unrealistic nature of assumptions that Chicago economists incorporated into their models. In Rothbard's opinion, correct economics must not allow convenience in mathematical manipulation to trump the truth of one's assumptions. Otherwise, science abandons theoretical rigor.

The Chicago School admired Irving Fisher, but Rothbard, in a paper included here, rejects the centrality of Fisher's famous equation of exchange. He found Benjamin Anderson's *The Value of Money* only slightly more congenial, although he was not in entire accord with Anderson's theories.

I should like to call particular attention to Rothbard's review of Lawrence Abbott's *Quality and Competition.* This is a neglected book, but Rothbard thought that its notion of "quality completion" struck at the heart of the imperfect-competition theories of Joan Robinson and E.H. Chamberlin. Rothbard used Abbott's theory in *Man, Economy, and State.*

As mentioned earlier, Rothbard regarded a peaceful foreign policy as imperative. We should, in his view, return to the traditional American doctrine of nonintervention. In taking this position, Rothbard stood in polar opposition to the *National Review* Right. This group favored an aggressive policy directed against international communism. Frank S. Meyer, a senior editor of *National Review,* took belligerent policy to an almost unimaginable extreme. He favored preemptive nuclear war against Soviet Russia. Meyer, who was a friend of Rothbard's, professed his allegiance to classical liberalism and a limited state. In a long analysis of Meyer's position, perhaps his most important theoretical statement on foreign policy, Rothbard maintains that one cannot consistently combine libertarian economic policies with international belligerence.

A brief concluding section shows us his taste in literature. In response to an inquiry, he lists his favorite novels. It is apparent from his essay on "Romanticism and Modern Fiction" that he could have become a literary critic, had he been inclined in this direction.

Rothbard was a true polymath, and one looks forward to future volumes that allow us even further access to his many contributions.

I am very grateful to B.K. Marcus, Nathalie Marcus, and Judy Thommesen for their painstaking editorial work on this book.

David Gordon
Los Angeles, California
2010

I. Setting the Stage

Rothbard's Confidential Memorandum to the Volker Fund, "What Is to Be Done?"

July 1961

To: F.A. Harper, George Resch

STRICTLY CONFIDENTIAL

It is the thesis of this memorandum that the problem of tactics and strategy for advancement of the libertarian-individualist cause is at a critical crossroads, a crossroads in the historical development of this stream of thought, transcending even the important problems of establishing a possible libertarian institute, or of deciding how to rechannel educational funds from various blind alleys into which they have fallen. Many of us have devoted a great deal of time to advancing and developing libertarian and individualist thought itself, into rendering it consistent, deepening and rediscovering its implications, etc. But none of us has devoted time to thinking about a theory of strategy and tactics for advancing the cause of this doctrine, and it is therefore to this end that this paper is modestly offered. We need more than any other single thing a fruitful dialogue and research into this whole problem. This is not to say, of course, that a development of libertarian thought itself should be neglected.

Editor's note: all information with brackets [ ] has been added for clarification.

Toward A Theory of Revolutionary Strategy

I am here using the shock term "revolution" not in the sense of violent, or even nonviolent revolution against the State. I mean by "revolution" the effecting of an ideological revolution in the framework of ideas held by the bulk of our fellow men. We are, in this sense, revolutionaries—for we are offering the public a radical change in their doctrinal views and we are offering it from a firm and consistent base of principle that we are trying to spread among the public. (Largely, this comprehensive system is "libertarian," i.e., the pure libertarian system, or, as a step to that, the *laissez-faire* system. But it also encompasses other aspects of "individualist" thought. An example is the good work that Volker and its Council of Basic Education have been doing against progressive education. As libertarians solely, we have no quarrel with progressive education, privately offered. But as individualists and rationalists, as people who want to see individual intellectual excellence and moral principles fostered in society, we favor intellectual, as opposed to "progressive," education.)

Here we stand, then, a "hard core" of libertarian-individualist "revolutionaries," anxious not only to develop our own understanding of this wonderful system of thought, but also anxious to spread its principles—and its policies—to the rest of society. How do we go about it?

I think that here we can learn a great deal from Lenin and the Leninists—not too much, of course, because the Leninist goals are the opposite of ours—but particularly the idea that the Leninist party is the main, or indeed only, moral principle. We are not interested in seizing power and governing the State, and we therefore proclaim, not only adhere to, such values as truth, individual happiness, etc., which the Leninists subordinate to their party's victory.

But from *one* aspect of Lenin's theory of strategy we can learn much: the setting forth of what "revolutionaries" can do to advance their principles, as opposed to the contrasting "deviations from the correct line," which the Leninists have called "left-wing sectarianism" and "right-wing opportunism." (In our case, the terminology would be reversed, perhaps: "left-wing opportunism" and "right-wing sectarianism.")

The sectarian strategists (e.g., the current Trotskyite sects) are those who pass out leaflets on street corners, state their full ideological position at all times, and consider any collaboration in halfway measures as "opportunist," "selling out the cause," etc. They are undoubtedly noble, but almost always ineffective.

The opposite "deviation" is "opportunism": the willingness to collaborate with any halfway measures or organizations, and, in effect, to abandon the true principles in the name of gradualist advance, "realism," "practical life," etc. These are the *real* sellers-out of the revolution, and they almost always, in historical Leninist experience, end by turning "reformist" and abandoning—in fact and later even *de jure*—their revolutionary principles. These people are ignoble, and, if they are at all effective, they are *not* effective in the proper, revolutionary direction.

On the "Right," we have had plenty of experience with the opportunists. If we were forced to choose, surely self-respect would demand the "sectarian" course; the "opportunist" is, by his nature, "liquidationist" of true principle. But I believe that there is a third, "centrist" course—certainly hard to find in practice, but the broad outlines of which can be sketched, and then perhaps used as a guide for our future activities. This "middle way" (Ugh! How I hate that concept!) may, for convenience, be dubbed "centrist" or "Leninist," and it runs, I believe, roughly as follows:

Our objective is, of course, to advance our principles—to spread libertarian-individualist thought (from now on to be called "libertarian" for short) among the people and to spread its policies in the political arena. This is our objective, *which must never be lost sight of.* We must, then, always aim toward the advancement of libertarian thought, both in its creative development, and its spread among the intellectuals and eventually the "masses." This is the ultimate essence of our aim, this advancement of the "hard core" of libertarian thought and libertarian thinkers. The group of totally libertarian thinkers is, in short, the "hard core" or the "cadre" of the broadly libertarian or quasi-libertarian movement.

Second, bearing this objective in mind, we should work on the "lower levels" of thought and action toward a "Fabian" advance of libertarian objectives. In this way, the hardcore man, the "militant" libertarian, works to advance not only the total system, but all steps *toward* that system. In this way, we achieve "unity of theory and practice," we spurn the pitfalls of base opportunism, while making ourselves much more effective than our brothers, the sectarians.

Let us turn to a hypothetical example (purely hypothetical). Suppose one or two hardcore libertarians join some Organization for Repeal of the Income Tax. In working for OFRIT, what does the hardcore libertarian accomplish?

(1) In the very act of agitating for repeal of the income tax, he is pushing people in the direction of repeal and perhaps eventually bringing about repeal—which, in itself, is a worthy, if limited, libertarian objective. In short, he is advancing the cause of libertarianism *in the very act* of advancing the cause of income tax repeal. Thus, everything he does for OFRIT, being *consistent with* the ultimate libertarian objective helps advance that objective, and does not betray it.

(2) *In the course* of this work, the hardcore libertarian should try to advance the knowledge of both the masses and his fellow OFRIT members, toward *fuller* libertarian ideals. In short, to "push" his colleagues and others toward the direction of hardcore libertarian thought itself. (In Communist-Leninist terms, this is called "recruiting for the Party," or pushing colleagues at least some way along this road.) The hardcore man is working for his idea on two levels: in a "popular" or "united" front for limited libertarian goals, and to try to influence his colleagues as well as the masses in the direction of the total system. (This is the essence of the much-misunderstood Leninist theory of "infiltration.")

The effective centrist avoids the pitfalls of "opportunism" by keeping the objective firmly in view, and, in particular, by *never acting in a manner, or speaking in a manner, inconsistent with the full libertarian position*. To be inconsistent in the name of "practicality" is to betray the libertarian position itself, and is worthy of the utmost condemnation. (I would say here, by the way, that I think that Baldy [F.A.] Harper has been remarkable in hewing to this "strategy" of consistency with libertarianism in all of his writings.)

In the name of practicality, the opportunist not only loses any chance of advancing others toward the ultimate goal, but *he himself* gradually loses sight of that goal—as happens with any "sellout" of principle. Thus, suppose that one is writing about taxation. It is *not* incumbent on the libertarian to always proclaim his full "anarchist" position in whatever he writes; but it *is* incumbent upon him in no way to praise taxation or condone it; he should simply leave this perhaps glaring vacuum, and wait for the eager reader to begin to question and perhaps come to you for further enlightenment. But if the libertarian says, "Of course, some taxes must be levied," or something of the sort, he has betrayed the cause.

Examples of "opportunist liquidationists" recently: the host of so-called "anarchists" who went around telling all their friends that good old Dick Nixon is "really a libertarian"; or, in the same campaign, Professor William H. Peterson's revolting letter to the *New York Times contra* Galbraith, in which he said that, of course, there must be some "public sector," but that this must be "balanced." (Presumably, Galbraith's suggested size of the public sector was not "balanced"? And just what is your *criterion* for balance, Mr. Peterson?) (This does not mean that I believe *any* support for Nixon or Kennedy was necessarily liquidationist; it is the absurd reason given—"Dick Nixon is really a pretty good libertarian"—that I am talking about. I do think, however, that most of the libertarians for Nixon were being, in effect, liquidationist in their outlook.)

As an example of a sectarian approach, I would cite the strategic view of Mr. Leonard Read, who believes that all one need do is to stay away from specifics, keep repeating over and over that liberty is a good thing and the number of ingredients that the free market puts into a pencil, keep advancing yourself, and the world will beat a path to your door. Setting aside the problem of specifics and generalities, I think that this view of strategy—*only* self-improving, never trying to influence others—is nonsensical, that it will get nowhere, particularly get nowhere in diffusing the influence of the hard core. For one of the reasons behind the idea of "infiltration" is that we can probably never hope to have everyone a hardcore man, just as we can never hope to have everyone an intellectual. Since the hard core will always be relatively small, its influence must be maximized by giving it "leverage" through allied, less libertarian "united fronts" with less libertarian thinkers and doers.

To restate my view of the proper strategy: we must, first and foremost, nourish and increase the hard core; we must, then, try to diffuse and advance principles and action as far as possible *in the direction of* hardcore doctrines. To abandon the hard core is liquidationist; to abandon all hardcore leverage upon others is to remain sterile and ineffective. We must combine the two elements; we must, in short, nourish and develop a hard core, which will then permeate and exert leverage upon others.

As I will make clearer later on, I think the outstanding weakness of the programs of Volker-Earhart in recent years—which have been magnificent in their impact—and the weakness of Mr. Kenneth Templeton's theory of "infiltration" is that, while a broad base of "right-wing" intellectuals has been developed and nourished, it has been done to the neglect of the vital task of building up the hard core. There can be no successful "infiltration" or "permeation," unless there is a flourishing hardcore nucleus that does the infiltrating. But more on this anon.

To answer the vital question, "What is to be done?" it is necessary (1) to set forth the theoretical framework for a theory of libertarian strategy; and (2) to engage in a brief historical analysis of the data of the current case—to see where we are and how we have gotten that way. Having treated the first problem, let us now turn to a historical analysis of the libertarian movement in the United States since World War II.

From the Depths: World War II and After

Certainly, the period of World War II was the nadir of libertarian thought in America. (One of the reasons why I am personally optimistic about libertarianism is that I became a libertarian during this absolute trough period.) Anyone with libertarian inclinations felt himself completely isolated and alone; he believed that he was the only one remotely of such views. This period was preeminently the period of *isolation* for the libertarian. I was one of two students on the entire Columbia campus "to the right" of Harry Truman, and others of my generation felt the same way. There was, in short, no movement; there was, in particular, no open center for a libertarian to go to, to "enter the movement," to find congenial and like-minded thinkers, etc.

(I am going to stress, again and again through this memo, the importance of an "open center" for hardcore men. For one way to develop a hardcore man, is gradually—through, in my hypothetical example, working in OFRIT, then gradually being moved to a more "advanced" position. But *another* and important way is an open center where someone who is already a hardcore or near-hardcore man, can find his way and enter. This is one of the functions of an open center—and one of the reasons, again, why the Communist Party always wants to maintain an "open Party" *as well as* infiltrating groups, etc.)

So the dominant fact of this era was isolation for the libertarian. Here and there, in the catacombs, unbeknownst to us struggling neophytes, were little, separated groups of people: In Los Angeles, Leonard Read, Orval Watts, and R.C. Hoiles began to move toward a libertarian (or quasi-libertarian) position in the L.A. Chamber of Commerce, reprinting Bastiat, establishing Pamphleteers, Inc. At Cornell Agriculture School, F.A. Harper and several students of his were developing a libertarian view. Albert Jay Nock and a few right-wing Georgist disciples advanced their theory, Nock publishing *Memoirs of a Superfluous Man*, Frank Chodorov, having been fired as director of the Henry George School, establishing his superb "little magazine," *analysis*. Nock gained a post as book reviewer for the National Economic Council, and was succeeded by another independent and isolated libertarian thinker, Rose Wilder Lane. Garet Garrett, having been ousted in the left-wing palace revolution at the *Saturday Evening Post*, established a quarterly *American Affairs* at the National Industrial Conference Board, under the benign eye of Dr. Virgil Jordan. Isabel Paterson, brilliant and cantankerous, resigned from her column at the *Herald-Tribune* to publish her great work, *God of the Machine*.

These, in the World War II years, were the tiny, isolated currents struggling to be heard. This was Phase I of the libertarian movement in this era: "In the Depths." (I should add that Ludwig von Mises, unhonored and unsung, was eking out a pittance at the NYU School of Business.) There were, of course, older mass-influencing publications with generally "right-wing" views (much more so than today): the Hearst Press, the NAM, etc., but these could hardly function as leaders of thought or as bases for growth of a movement. And they were hardly libertarian.

Phase II: The Founding of FEE

With the formation of the Foundation for Economic Education in 1946, the libertarian movement turned a corner and began its postwar renaissance. FEE can be attacked on many, many counts—and I have done my share—but one achievement it can be proud of: it gathered together the many isolated and loose strands of the libertarians, and created that crucial *open center* for a libertarian movement. It not only disseminated libertarian literature; it provided a gateway, a welcoming place, for all hitherto isolated and neophyte libertarians. It launched the movement.

This great feat of FEE in launching the libertarian movement is testimony to the enormous need for a functioning "open center" for libertarians. For not only did this open center provide a channel and gateway for people to enter the libertarian ranks; not only did its agitation convert some and find others; it also, by providing an atmosphere and a "center" for like-minded students of liberty, provided the atmospheric spark for rapid advance from old-fashioned *laissez-faire* to 100 percent liberty on the part of much of its staff and friends. In short, FEE, by its very existence, exerted an enormous multiple leverage in creating and advancing and weaving together the strands and people in the libertarian cause. For this may it always be honored!

Leonard Read it was, of course, who performed this feat, and he drew together at or near FEE the various strands of the movement: Harper and his students from Cornell; the Los Angeles group; Herb

Cornuelle, who had been converted to liberty by the almost legendary unknown figure "Red Miller" of a Detroit municipal government service; Frank Chodorov, etc. And FEE, from the very beginning, devoted itself to the task not only of spreading its ideas, but also of finding and developing hardcore (at least hardcore according to its lights) libertarians. I believe it safe to say that virtually every libertarian in the country found his way into the ranks through FEE, and that almost every leading libertarian was, at one time or another, connected with FEE staff.

The Decline of FEE

Yet, with its achievement recorded, FEE must be set down as a tragic failure when we consider what it *could have* accomplished. It could have been a great center for libertarian thought; its members had the potential. But this potential was crippled—largely by the limitations, intellectual and otherwise, of Leonard Read. Read, in the last analysis, molded FEE in his own image, which is not writ very large.

Hardly appreciative of scholarship or of the conditions of free inquiry and research, Read stifled the scholarly and creative productivity of everyone on his staff—to the extent that all of the capable people, one after another, were forced to leave. FEE publications were increasingly pitched toward housewives, rather than scholars, which immediately tossed away the importance of the "pyramid of influence" from intellectual to mass. The advance of purer libertarian thought was not only discouraged by Read but bitterly attacked.

But housewives, in their turn, are not very interested in the construction of a pencil or the tale of a shirt; they are rather interested in specifics in evaluating Barry Goldwater or the problem of federal aid. The FEE literature in sticking to generalities—and low-grade generalities at that—fell between two stools and has therefore lost influence both among the intellectuals and among the "mass base."

Leonard Read, observing this process of flight from FEE of its capable members, has rationalized the process as one of "training" libertarians and then sending them off to better things, thus functioning as a "high school" of liberty. He thus ignores the fact that it could have been a lot more. But a "high school" it still is, and probably its most useful functions *now* are to influence and attract *beginners* in liberty—especially, indeed, high school students—and to still act as a gateway into the libertarian movement. But it is a gateway only and not in any sense a libertarian center any longer; so the question still remains: gateway to what I need not dwell here on the overriding importance of the intellectuals and scholars in forming a libertarian cadre. For the filiation of ideas and influence works as a pyramid, from the highest-level intellectuals to lower levels, from graduate school to college, from treatise authors to journalists, on down to the housewife and man in the street. In this pyramid, one scholar is worth a thousand housewives, in the matter of influence, import, etc. (For more on the importance of intellectual filiation and influence, cf. the memorandum, "Suggestions for a General Research Program for the Volker Fund," Rothbard to Richard C. Cornuelle, April 3, 1954.)

Even Claude Robinson has recognized that the trouble with the "right wing" is that it has willingly financed a great deal of mass-influence propaganda directed to the average voter, while neglecting its scholars; the result has been, inevitably, not only a failure of scholarship to grow, but a lack of influence on the average voters themselves. No group, for example, acted with more energy on the mass base directly than the old Committee for Constitutional Government, and with no results whatever.

Another danger which the history of FEE and other right-wing organizations tells us: the tendency for the fellow who can obtain money to be in control of policy, and the corollary tendency to begin to trim the output of the organization to what will attract the money. When the latter happens, the gathering of money begins to become the end, not the means, and the organization begins to take on the dimension of a "racket."

Phase III: The Emergence of the Volker Fund Concept

A new and vital turning point in the postwar libertarian movement was the emergence of the Volker Fund program. Originated by Harold Luhnow of the Volker Fund, it was brought to fruition by Herbert

Cornuelle, and successors Richard Cornuelle and Ken Templeton. William Volker himself had always stressed the importance of grants to individuals, rather than organizations. The Volker Fund concept was to find and grant research funds to hosts of libertarian and right-wing scholars and to draw these scholars together via seminars, conferences, etc. Funds would be granted for projects that would advance libertarian thought; seminars would draw together right-wingers and permeate them with libertarian ideas.

In this new phase, with its crucial emphasis on scholarship and research, the Volker Fund has succeeded remarkably well. Libertarians have been found and nurtured, and libertarian allies in specific fields (e.g., recreation, water supply, and a host of others) arrayed together in informal "popular front" activity. Indeed, the whole Volker Fund activity may be considered a vast, informal, scholarly "popular front" operation. In addition, it has created successful formal "fronts," such as the Council for Basic Education or the National Book Foundation, for specific activity along specific lines.

On the other hand, the Earhart Foundation program, structured along similar lines, has been less successful, primarily because the Volker grantees have been those whose *preponderant* impact has been libertarian, taking their major fields into consideration, whereas Earhart grantees have been virtually everyone to the right of Walter Reuther, and the Earhart Foundation has thus reflected an abandonment of "centrist" strategic thinking in an "opportunist" and liquidationist direction. Thus, when Earhart sponsored A.F. Burns's series of lectures at Fordham some years ago, the net effect of this was to grant funds for A.F. Burns to shift his business leaders *further to the left* than they already were: a particularly disastrous example of the poor strategy of embracing almost everyone who is not an out-and-out socialist.

In addition to individual grants and seminars and symposia, the Volker Fund has also done excellent work in sponsoring such influential graduate school professors as Mises at NYU and Hayek at Chicago, and awarding fellowships for study with these men. Here, too, is an approach toward a policy of nurturing a hard core.

(As an example, by the way, of the importance of individual scholars and their influence, virtually every libertarian or even economist in the country has been a student of either Ludwig von Mises, Frank Knight, or F.A. Harper.)

Current Problems

The FEE has been in existence for fifteen years; the new Volker Fund program for over ten years. Not only does this length of time make a reassessment necessary, but other problems have emerged that make the present time an important crossroads. First, the building up of the "popular front" Volker list has reached its maximum impact. Summer seminars and conferences have begun, inevitably, to repeat their members; and the bulk of the members there have been "libertarian" in only the vaguest manner.

In short, the Volker Fund list consists largely of individual scholars who are vaguely sympathetic with libertarian or "conservative" aims, with others scattered through who more and more approach the hard core. There is little more that can be accomplished through *widening* the list; the time has come for a *deepening* of that list.

With the popular front having reached its widest functioning extent, problems and gaps have increasingly emerged in the fund program. And the biggest of these gaps is *the failure to build up a hard core*. I mentioned before about Ken Templeton's theory of "infiltration" that for successful infiltration, there must be a strong hard core which functions as a nucleus, a center from which the infiltration emanates. There is not, and has not been, such a hard core. Without a strong hardcore center, the "infiltration" process inevitably leads *not* to the "revolutionary" goal of exerting leverage on less-advanced persons, *not* to drawing new members into the hard core, *but to the weakening and dissolving of the hard core itself*.

The failure to nurture a strong core means that those who are inclined to be hardcore libertarians, as they work and act constantly "in the field" with their "united front" allies, *begin to lose their own hardcore libertarian principles*. Acting in the world, acting "practically," then, is all very well, but doing so without a strong hardcore nucleus means the eventual loss of principle, it means a surrender to liquidationism and "opportunism." This is bound to happen when the hard core is not nurtured and made strong, and *it has happened increasingly* over recent years. It happens when a William Peterson begins to shape farm programs for a Dick Nixon, or prattles about "balance" in the "public sector"; it happens when a Richard C. Cornuelle insists on acting "positively," on cracking down on "negative thinking" about the government, on hopelessly trying to compete with the government in financing the ends that the Left decides to set for society. (Who can more abundantly and amply finance a Left-set goal such as a "college education for every man," or "palaces for old people"? The government, or a private welfare outfit?)

In World War II, as I said before, the danger and despair of the individual hardcore libertarian was his isolation. Now, in 1961, with the libertarian and right-wing movements seemingly flourishing and growing apace, on scholarly and more popular levels, he is, once again, increasingly in danger of being *isolated*. Except this time, the danger is less apparent and more insidious. For it is the danger of the hardcore libertarian being swamped by a growing mass of "conservative" and right-wing thinkers.

Although libertarians, under first FEE and then Volker aegis, grew in number and influence, a reversal has begun to set in, a reversal caused by a confusion of everyone on the Right, a growing erasure of the important lines that separate the hardcore libertarian from the "conservative." The result of exclusive emphasis on popular-front work, has meant that a buildup of the "Right" in general, has diluted the hard core, made the public, and the Right itself, increasingly unaware of the crucial *differences* between a hardcore libertarian and a plain conservative. With FEE no longer taken seriously as a center, and with Volker not having provided such a center, the hardcore libertarian movement—the essence and the glory of what the struggle is all about—is in danger of dying on the vine.

Thus, any given Volker Fund seminar will have only one or two hardcore men to a dozen "confused" conservatives. This is inevitable, given the numerical weakness of the hard core. But, if there is no hardcore center, no firm, well-nourished nucleus, the hardcore men will have little influence on the conservatives who heavily outnumber them; hardcore strength itself will be diluted and vanish; and the whole purpose will be lost.

Furthermore, the Volker Fund program of giving grants to professors *where they are* begins to suffer from precisely the same set of problems. This, too, is a popular-front activity. Here, too, one libertarian professor at the University of Keokuk will remain, forever, one libertarian professor at the University of Keokuk. Being isolated at his university, he will have little or no influence. Outnumbered by the faculty colleagues, he will be held up to ridicule by faculty and students alike as an isolated "crackpot." He will, then, generate no influence, as he will be isolated and cut off from productive interchange with fellow hardcore men (especially since those he may meet at summer seminars will be generally much less clearly libertarian than he himself), and he will therefore eventually lose his libertarian drive, if not his libertarian principles themselves.

The increasing danger of the "swamping" of the libertarian intellectual—which itself is inherent when the hard core is not nourished, fostered, and brought together as a nucleus—has been enormously redoubled by the transformation that has been effected in the right wing itself. This transformation, led by the theoreticians of *National Review,* has transformed the Right from a movement that, at least roughly, believed first of all in individual liberty (and its corollaries: civil liberties domestically, and peace and "isolation" in foreign affairs) into a movement that, on the whole, is opposed to individual liberty—a movement that, in fact, glorifies total war and the suppression of civil liberty; it also glorifies monarchy, imperialism, polite racism, and a unity of Church and State.

The Right having increasingly taken on this tone and complexion, it is all the more vital for the libertarian movement to be dissociated from, rather than allied with, the bulk of the right wing. The chief trouble now with the theory of the "popular front" is that this "front" has been largely infected with enemies of, rather than friends of, liberty. Fortunately, the Volker Fund's own program suffers much less than others (Earhart, Richardson, etc.) from this problem, because the fund's concentration has been on economists, who, in their capacity as economists (Chicago School, etc.) have been, at least on net balance, proponents of liberty. But in any other field but economics, the danger is grave indeed.

The present parlous state of the "right wing" makes imperative, in my view, a negative approach to any fund involvement with "direct action" organizations of the Right: this means not only such directly political organizations as the Young Americans for Freedom but also such organizations as the Intercollegiate Society of Individualists, which has, increasingly, been playing hand-in-glove with the right-wing drive for war and "anti-Communism." And even though there is opportunity for a philosophic synthesis, in some respects, between libertarians and conservatives (e.g., the addition to libertarianism of natural law, moral principles, etc.) there is no real opportunity for a political synthesis.

(Even philosophically, conservatism has so many things wrong with it that an attempt at synthesis distorts the real nature of conservatism: as it must overlook the conservatives' hostility to personal liberty, drive toward war, reverence for a theocratic state so long as it be "traditional," support for colonial imperialism, opposition to reason, etc. And here I want to go on record as regretting my own recent article in *Modern Age*, as distorting the nature of conservatism by dwelling almost exclusively on its favorable features.)

Needless to say, any support for such organs as *National Review* is contraindicated, and this extends even to the much better organ, *Modern Age*. I have come to the conclusion that, for libertarian thought to survive, a sharp break with "conservatism" must be undertaken, and even the new, improved *Modern Age* is too riddled with conservatism to be satisfactory. The time is too late for such a popular front.

I think it important to state what I am not advocating. I am most certainly not advocating that the Volker Fund drop its great program of aid to individual scholars. This superb conception needs to be continued and expanded. But there needs to be, in addition, much greater concentration on nourishing a hardcore libertarian center. I am sorry to say that at this point, I have no concrete panacea to offer. *What form* this nourishment should take is still unclear. I believe that a scholarly libertarian institute, on the postgraduate level, a counterpart to the Institute for Advanced Study, would be the ideal solution. The idea would be to gather together leading libertarian scholars, to have permanent and also temporary staffs (the latter via fellowships), etc. This would not be degree granting, and thus would avoid the enormous pitfalls faced by any graduate school operation such as [Hans] Sennholz's "American School of Economics."

Failing the considerable amount of funds required for such an advanced study institute, there are other partial steps that could be taken which could eventually lead into an institute. One libertarian has suggested a counterpart of the Social Science Research Council, which would channel grants, create seminars, perhaps someday found an institute or society of alumni fellows, etc. Another suggestion is to have a sort of libertarian counterpart of the Mont Pelerin Society, with annual papers read, a scholarly journal, etc. Certainly, one modest step would be to expand the number of Volker Fund–supported professors, with fellowships to students, as is now being done in the case of Mises and Hayek.

This would not, of course, provide much of a libertarian center, but it would at least stimulate fellowships for studying under good people. The problems of the present program are (1) that Mises is teaching at a business school, with the result that his students are almost all low level, and when they graduate they do not teach or do research and thus do not have the "leverage effect" which is the main purpose of furthering intellectual work. It is important to have programs established in the liberal arts departments rather than in schools of business, which are looked down upon by the intellectual world anyway and often with good reason. (2) Hayek's Social Thought program is in an "offbeat" department which, rather than integrating all humane disciplines, teaches very little and makes almost no demands on the students; further, the result of this is that a Ph.D. from Social Thought carries little or no academic weight.

I am sorry that I have no further concrete suggestions to offer. My thesis can be summed up as saying that in this crossroads in the history of libertarian movement it is vital to de-emphasize drastically popular fronts with the conservative "Right," to nourish and construct the hardcore libertarian movement with some form or forms of nucleus or center, and to emphasize libertarian scholars and intellectuals primarily, and, if more direct action is desired, libertarian publicists and workers exclusively. The big danger to the libertarian movement now is a swamping by a rapidly growing (on intellectual and "practical" levels) conservative movement that presents more of a threat to liberty than a support. The great task facing us is the rescue of the libertarian movement from this danger.

II. Political Theory

1. Are Libertarians "Anarchists"?

(date unknown)

To: Aubrey Herbert

The libertarian who is happily engaged expounding his political philosophy in the full glory of his convictions is almost sure to be brought short by one unfailing gambit of the statist. As the libertarian is denouncing public education or the Post Office, or refers to taxation as legalized robbery, the statist invariably challenges: "Well, then are you an *anarchist*?" The libertarian is reduced to sputtering "No, no, of course I'm not an anarchist." "Well, then, what governmental measures *do* you favor? What *type* of taxes do you wish to impose?" The statist has irretrievably gained the offensive, and, having no answer to the first question, the libertarian finds himself surrendering his case.

Thus, the libertarian will usually reply: "Well, I believe in a *limited* government, the government being limited to the defense of the person or property or the individual against invasion by force or fraud." I have tried to show in my article, "The Real Aggressor" in the April 1954 *Faith and Freedom*, that this leaves the conservative helpless before the argument "necessary for defense," when it is used for gigantic measures of statism and bloodshed.

There are other consequences equally or more grave. The statist can pursue the matter further:

If you grant that it is legitimate for people to band together and allow the State to coerce individuals to pay taxes for a certain service—"defense"—why is it not equally moral and legitimate for people to join in a similar way and allow the State the right to provide other services—such as post offices, "welfare," steel, power, etc.? If a State supported by a majority can morally do one, why not morally do the others?

I confess that I see no answer to this question. If it is proper and legitimate to coerce an unwilling Henry Thoreau into paying taxes for his own "protection" to a coercive state monopoly, I see no reason why it should not be equally proper to force him to pay the State for any other services, whether they be groceries, charity, newspapers, or steel. We are left to conclude that the pure libertarian must advocate a society where an individual may voluntarily support none or any police or judicial agency that he deems to be efficient and worthy of his custom.

I do not here intend to engage in a detailed exposition of this system, but only to answer the question, is this anarchism?

This seemingly simple question is actually a very difficult one to answer in a sentence, or in a brief yes-or-no reply. In the first place, there is no accepted meaning to the word "anarchism" itself. The average person may *think* he knows what it means, especially that it is bad, but actually he does not. In that sense, the word has become something like the lamented word "liberal," except that the latter has "good" connotations in the emotions of the average man.

The almost insuperable distortions and confusions have come both from the opponents and the adherents of anarchism. The former have completely distorted anarchist tenets and made various fallacious charges, while the latter have been split into numerous warring camps with political philosophies that are literally as far apart as communism and individualism. The situation is further confused by the fact that, often, the various anarchist groups themselves did not recognize the enormous ideological conflict between them.

One very popular charge against anarchism is that it "means chaos." Whether a specific type of anarchism would lead to "chaos" is a matter for analysis; no anarchist, however, ever deliberately wanted to bring about chaos. Whatever else he or she may have been, no anarchist has ever deliberately willed chaos or world destruction. Indeed, anarchists have always believed that the establishment of their system would eliminate the chaotic elements now troubling the world. One amusing incident, illuminating this misconception, occurred after the end of the war when a young enthusiast for world government wrote a book entitled *One World or Anarchy*, and Canada's leading anarchist shot back with a work entitled *Anarchy or Chaos*. The major difficulty in any analysis of anarchism is that the term covers extremely conflicting doctrines. The root of the word comes from the term *anarchos*, meaning opposition to authority or commands. This is broad enough to cover a host of different political doctrines. Generally, these doctrines have been lumped together as "anarchist" because of their common hostility to the existence of the State, the coercive monopolist of force and authority. Anarchism arose in the nineteenth century, and since then the most active and dominant anarchist doctrine has been that of "anarchist communism." This is an apt term for a doctrine which has also been called "collectivist anarchism," "anarcho-syndicalism," and "libertarian communism." We may term this set of related doctrines "left-wing anarchism." Anarchist communism is primarily of Russian origin, forged by Prince Peter Kropotkin and Michael Bakunin, and it is this form that has connoted "anarchism" throughout the continent of Europe.

The principal feature of anarchist communism is that it attacks private property just as vigorously as it attacks the State. Capitalism is considered as much of a tyranny "in the economic realm" as the State is in the political realm. The left-wing anarchist hates capitalism and private property with perhaps even more fervor than does the socialist or Communist. Like the Marxists, the left-wing anarchist is convinced that the capitalists exploit and dominate the workers, and also that the landlords invariably are exploiting peasants.

The economic views of the anarchists present them with a crucial dilemma, the *pons asinorum* of left-wing anarchy: how can capitalism and private property be abolished, while the State is abolished at the same time? The socialists proclaim the glory of the State and the use of the State to abolish private property—for them the dilemma does not exist. The orthodox Marxist Communist, who pays lip service to the ideal of left-wing anarchy, resolves the dilemma by use of the Hegelian dialectic: that mysterious process by which something is converted into its opposite. The Marxists would enlarge the State to the maximum and abolish capitalism, and then sit back confidently to wait upon the State's "withering away."

The spurious logic of the dialectic is not open to the left-wing anarchists, who wish to abolish the State and capitalism simultaneously. The nearest those anarchists have come to resolving the problem has been to uphold syndicalism as the ideal. In syndicalism, each group of workers and peasants is supposed to own its means of production in common and plan for itself, while cooperating with other collectives and communes. Logical analysis of these schemes would readily show that the whole program is nonsense. Either of two things would occur: one central agency would plan for and direct the various subgroups, or the collectives themselves would be really autonomous. But the crucial question is whether these agencies would be empowered to use force to put their decisions into effect.

All of the left-wing anarchists have agreed that force is necessary against recalcitrants. But then the first possibility means nothing more nor less than Communism, while the second leads to a real chaos of diverse and clashing communisms, that would probably lead finally to some central Communism after a period of social war. Thus, left-wing anarchism must in practice signify either regular Communism or a true chaos of communistic syndics. In both cases, the actual result must be *that the State is reestablished under another name*. It is the tragic irony of left-wing anarchism that, despite the hopes of its supporters, it is not really anarchism at all. It is either Communism or chaos.

It is no wonder therefore that the term "anarchism" has received a bad press. The leading anarchists, particularly in Europe, have always been of the left-wing variety, and today the anarchists are exclusively in the left-wing camp. Add to that the tradition of revolutionary violence stemming from European conditions, and it is little wonder that anarchism is discredited. Anarchism was politically very powerful in Spain, and during the Spanish Civil War, anarchists established communes and collectives wielding coercive authority. One of their first steps was to abolish the use of money on the pain of a death penalty. It is obvious that the supposed anarchist hatred of coercion had gone very much awry. The reason was the insoluble contradiction between the antistate and the anti-property tenets of left-wing anarchy.

How is it, then, that despite the fatal logical contradictions in left-wing anarchism, there are a highly influential group of British intellectuals who currently belong to this school, including the art critic Sir Herbert Read and the psychiatrist Alex Comfort? The answer is that anarchists, perhaps unconsciously seeing the hopelessness of their position, have made a point of rejecting logic and reason entirely. They stress spontaneity, emotions, instincts, rather than allegedly cold and inhuman logic. By so doing, they can of course remain blind to the irrationality of their position.

Of economics, which would show them the impossibility of their system, they are completely ignorant, perhaps more so than any other group of political theorists. The dilemma about coercion they attempt to resolve by the absurd theory that crime would simply disappear if the State were abolished, so that no coercion would have to be used.

Irrationality indeed permeates almost all of the views of the left-wing anarchists. They reject industrialism as well as private property, and tend to favor returning to the handicraft and simple peasant conditions or the Middle Ages. They are fanatically in favor of modern art, which they consider "anarchist" art. They have an intense hatred of money and of material improvements. Living a simple peasant existence, in communes, is extolled as "living the anarchist life," while a civilized person is supposed to be viciously bourgeois and un-anarchist.

Thus, the ideas of the left-wing anarchists have become a nonsensical jumble, far more irrational than that of the Marxists, and deservedly looked upon with contempt by almost everyone as hopelessly "crackpot." Unfortunately, the result is that the good criticisms that they sometimes make of state tyranny tend to be tarred with the same "crackpot" brush.

Considering the dominant anarchists, it is obvious that the question "are libertarians anarchists?" must be answered unhesitatingly in the negative. We are at completely opposite poles. Confusion enters, however, because of the existence in the past, particularly in the United States, of a small but brilliant group of "individualist anarchists" headed by Benjamin R. Tucker. Here we come to a different breed.

The individualist anarchists have contributed a great deal to libertarian thought. They have provided some of the best statements of individualism and anti-statism that have ever been penned. In the *political* sphere, the individualist anarchists were generally sound libertarians. They favored private property, extolled free competition, and battled all forms of governmental intervention. Politically, the Tucker anarchists had two principal defects: (1) they failed to advocate defense of private landholdings beyond what the owner used personally; (2) they relied too heavily on juries and failed to see the necessity for a body of constitutional libertarian law which the private courts would have to uphold.

Contrasted to their minor political failings, however, they fell into grievous economic error. They believed that interest and profit were exploitative, due to an allegedly artificial restriction on the money supply. Let the State and its monetary regulations be removed, and free banking be established, they believed, and everyone would print as much money as he needed, and interest and profits would fall to zero.

This hyperinflationist doctrine, acquired from the Frenchman Proudhon, is economic nonsense. We must remember, however, that "respectable" economics, then and now, has been permeated with inflationist errors, and very few economists have grasped the essentials of monetary phenomena. The inflationists simply take the more genteel inflationism of fashionable economics and courageously push it to its logical conclusion.

The irony of this situation was that while the individualist anarchists laid great stress on their nonsensical banking theories, the political order that they advocated would have led to economic results directly contrary to what they believed. They thought that free banking would lead to indefinite expansion of the money supply, whereas the truth is precisely the reverse: it would lead to "hard money" and absence of inflation.

The economic fallacies of the Tuckerites, however, are of a completely different order than those of the collectivist anarchists. The errors of the collectivists led them to advocate virtual political communism, while the economic errors of the individualists still permitted them to advocate a nearly libertarian system. The superficial might easily confuse the two, because the individualists were led to attack "capitalists," whom they felt were exploiting the workers through State restriction of the money supply.

These "right-wing" anarchists did not take the foolish position that crime would disappear in the anarchist society. Yet they did tend to underestimate the crime problem and as a result never recognized the need for a fixed libertarian constitution. Without such a constitution, the private judicial process might become truly "anarchic" in the popular sense.

The Tucker wing of anarchism flourished in the nineteenth century, but died out by World War I. Many libertarian thinkers in that Golden Age of liberalism were working on doctrines that were similar in many respects. These genuine libertarians never referred to themselves as anarchists, however; probably the main reason was that all the anarchist groups, even the right-wingers, possessed socialistic *economic* doctrines in common.

Here we should note still a third variety of anarchist thought, one completely different from either the collectivists or individualists. This is the absolute pacifism of Leo Tolstoy. This preaches a society where force would not even be used to defend person and property, whether by State or private organizations. Tolstoy's program of nonviolence has influenced many alleged pacifists today, mainly through Gandhi, but the latter do not realize that there can be no genuinely complete pacifism unless the State and other defense agencies are eliminated. This type of anarchism, above all others, rests on an excessively idealistic view of human nature. It could only work in a community of saints.

We must conclude that the question "are libertarians anarchists?" simply cannot be answered on etymological grounds. The vagueness of the term itself is such that the libertarian system would be considered anarchist by some people and archist by others. We must therefore turn to history for enlightenment; here we find that none of the proclaimed anarchist groups correspond to the libertarian position, that even the best of them have unrealistic and socialistic elements in their doctrines. Furthermore, we find that all of the current anarchists are irrational collectivists and therefore at opposite poles from our position.

We must therefore conclude that we are *not* anarchists, and that those who call us anarchists are not on firm etymological ground and are being completely unhistorical. On the other hand, it is clear that we are not *archists* either: we do not believe in establishing a tyrannical central authority that will coerce the noninvasive as well as the invasive.

Perhaps, then, we could call ourselves by a new name: *non*archist. Then, when, in the jousting of debate, the inevitable challenge "are you an anarchist?" is heard, we can, for perhaps the first and last time, find ourselves in the luxury of the "middle of the road" and say, "Sir, I am neither an anarchist nor an archist, but am squarely down the *non*archic middle of the road."

2. In Defense of Demagogues

(date unknown)

To: Aubrey Herbert

For many years now, demagogues have been in great disfavor. They are not sober; they are not respectable; they are not "gentlemen." And yet there is a great and growing need for their services.

What, exactly, have been the charges leveled against the demagogues? They are roughly three in number. In the first place, they are disruptive forces in the body politic. They stir things up. Secondly, they supposedly fail to play the game in appealing to the base emotions rather than to cool reason. From this stems the third charge: that they appeal to the unwashed masses with emotional, extreme, and *therefore* unsound views. Add to this the vice of ungentlemanly enthusiasm, and we have about catalogued the sins of the species demagogue.

The charge of emotionalism is surely an irrelevant one. The problem of an ideology is not whether it is put forth in an emotional, a matter-of-fact, or a dull manner. The question is whether or not the ideology is correct. Almost always, the demagogue is a man who finds that his ideas are held by only a small minority of people, a minority that is apt to be particularly small among the sober and respectable. Convinced of the truth and the importance of his ideas, he sees that the heavy weight of public opinion, and particularly of the respectable molders of this opinion, is either hostile or indifferent to this truth. Is it any wonder that such a situation will make a man emotional?

All demagogues are ideological nonconformists and therefore bound to be emotional about the general and respectable rejection of what they consider to be vital truth. But not all ideological nonconformists become demagogues. The difference is that the demagogue possesses that quality of mass attraction that permits him to *use* emotion to stir up the masses. In going to the masses, he is going over the heads of the respectable intellectuals who ordinarily guide mass opinion. It is this electric, shortcut appeal, direct to the masses, that gives the demagogue his vital significance and that makes him such a menace to the dominant orthodoxy.

The demagogue is frequently accused by his enemies of being an insincere opportunist, a man who cynically uses certain ideas and emotions in order to gain popularity and power. It is almost impossible, however, to judge a person's motives, particularly in political life, unless one is a close friend. We have seen that the sincere demagogue is very likely to be emotional himself, while stirring others to emotion. Finally, if a man is really an opportunist, the easiest way to acclaim and power is to play ball with the ruling orthodoxy, and not the opposite. The way of the demagogue is the riskiest and has the least chance of success.

It is the fashionable belief that an idea is wrong in proportion to its "extremism," and right in proportion as it is a chaotic muddle of contradictory doctrines. To the professional middle-of-the-roader, a species that is always found in abundance, the demagogue invariably comes as a nasty shock. For it is one of the most admirable qualities of the demagogue that he forces men to think, some for the first time in their lives. Out of the muddle of current ideas, fashionable and unfashionable, he extracts some and pushes them to their logical conclusions, i.e., "to extremes." He thereby forces people either to reject their loosely held views as unsound, or to find them sound and to pursue them to their logical consequences.

Far from being an irrational force, then, the silliest of demagogues is a great servant of reason, even when he is most in the wrong. A typical example is the inflationist demagogue—the "monetary crank." The vast majority of respectable economists have always scoffed at the cranks, without realizing that they are not really able to answer his arguments. For what the crank has done is to take the inflationism that lies at the core of fashionable economics and push it to its logical conclusion. He asks, "If it is good to have an inflation of money of 10 percent per year, why isn't it still better to double the money supply every year?" Only a few economists have realized that in order to answer the crank reasonably instead of by ridicule, it is necessary to purge fashionable economics of its inflationist foundations.

Demagogues probably first fell into disrepute in the nineteenth century, when most of them were socialists. But their conservative opposition, as is typical of conservatives in every age, never came to grips with the logic of the demagogues' position. Instead, they contented themselves with attacking the emotionalism and extremism of the upstarts. Their logic unassailed, the socialist demagogues triumphed, as argument always will conquer pure prejudice in the long run. For it seemed as if the socialists had reason on their side.

Now socialism is the fashionable and respectable ideology. The old passionate arguments of the soapbox have become the tired clichés of the cocktail party and the classroom. Any demagogy, any disruption of the apple cart would almost certainly come from the individualist opposition. Furthermore, the State is now in command, and whenever this condition prevails, the State is anxious to prevent disruption and ideological turmoil. Demagogues would bring in their wake "disunity," and people might be stirred to think for themselves instead of falling into a universal goosestep behind their anointed leaders. Furthermore, individualist demagogues would be more dangerous than ever, because they could now be equipped with rational arguments to refute the socialist clichés. The respectable statist Left, then, fears and hates the demagogue, and more than ever before he is the object of attack.

It is true that, in the long run, we will never be free until the intellectuals—the natural molders of public opinions—have been converted to the side of freedom. In the short run, however, the only route to liberty is by an appeal to the masses over the heads of the State and its intellectual bodyguard. And this appeal can be made most effectively by the demagogue—the rough, unpolished man of the people, who can present the truth in simple, effective, yes emotional, language. The intellectuals see this clearly, and this is why they constantly attack every indication of libertarian demagoguery as part of a "rising tide of anti-intellectualism." Of course, it is not anti-intellectualism; it is the saving of mankind from those intellectuals who have betrayed the intellect itself.

3. Willmoore Kendall, Lectures on Democratic Theory at Buck Hill Falls[1]

September 1956

Kendall's lectures may be analyzed in two parts: (1) his discussion of the layman and the expert and (2) his discussion of freedom of thought.

---

[1]   Editor's note: Kendall's book *The Conservative Affirmation* (Henry Regnery, 1963), in particular chapter 6, "Conservatism and the 'Open Society'," is quite similar to what Rothbard is criticizing.

(1) Kendall, it should be said from the first, is revealed here as a very keen and stimulating thinker, incisive, and with a sharply radical spirit, i.e., with a propensity to dig to the roots of issues without fear or favor. He has a knack for sharply posing the right questions so that whether you agree or disagree with him, you have learned something from him. (I know it is a cliché that you always learn something from an opponent in argument, but actually you do only rarely, so this, I think, is a tribute.)

At the outset I should mention the charm of Kendall's picture of the liberal; it is a muted hint of his *National Review* column on the liberal machine, depicting a smug, quasi-conspiratorial but in a very fashionable way, ruling "power elite" with velvet gloves and democratic rhetoric. It is a description that strikes me as being quite accurate and reflects Kendall's radical temper.

Kendall's posing of the critical problem for democracy of the expert vs. the layman and his textual analysis of Mill are excellent. The only seriously misleading picture is the brief implication that Rousseau was a kind of Thomas Jefferson figure—a small-town democrat— ignoring the very vivid totalitarian mystique of Rousseau's. Be that as it may, Kendall develops very neatly, from Mill and on the basis of Mill's successors, how the Left has developed the doctrine of rule by an elite of bureaucrat-intellectuals within the form of ultramajority rule. Kendall's position is essentially that of a prodemocrat who is attacking the usurpation of power by this bureaucratic elite, an elite that has attained this power by virtue of its claim to the privileges of expertise.

There are numerous keen insights given off along the way: the recognition, for example, that the intellectual elite gets away with it by amalgamating values to pure knowledge of existential facts, by forgetting about values and then slipping their own in; the Millian confusion between intellect and morals; the insight that proving that the masses are incompetent does *not* prove the experts competent, contrary to "liberal" doctrine; the distinction between expertises. On the other hand, I do not go along with all of the criticism of the "roster" technique; it seems to me perfectly legitimate to say that the top few are significantly better than the rest, without worrying about the bottom few who are really terrible.

Still, when all these virtues have been recorded, we are left with the question: what is Kendall's solution to these problems; what is his alternative to the present system that both he and we consider evil? On the layman-expert issue, there is the hint of alternative solutions. There is an indicated possible preference for the "Rousseauan" route: if the problems of the modern world are so "complex" that bureaucratic rule is needed, then get rid of the complex modern world and get back to simpler rule. Is this a Röpkean call for back-to-handcrafts? Kendall doesn't say. But right here I would note that Kendall fails to make a crucial distinction: between the complexities *necessary* to an advanced modern economy and the complexities of *government* that arise from attempts to regulate and rule this economy. If he made this distinction, he could become a libertarian without calling for peasantry and crafts.

However, for Kendall this is an aside; his major solution seems to be to hammer home the distinction between fact and value, to convince everyone that experts are only experts on facts and scientific laws, while every citizen should choose final policy on the basis of which means will lead to his ends. The majority would then rule because while, admits Kendall, there is an intellectual elite, there is not a *moral* elite. As he cites Rousseau, the "general will" is right— provided it has all the facts.

Yet Kendall's attempted solution leaves all the critical questions unanswered and many of them even unasked. He does recognize that he has left unanswered the problem of what to do if the experts deliberately lie to the people in order to manipulate and control them. To this, he calls for experts to rate the experts so that the people will know what's going on, but he also recognizes that for this task *experts* themselves are needed, so who will supply this information?

There are other crucial issues that Kendall doesn't seem to recognize at all. *First,* he assumes that morally, everyone is equal and therefore the democratic census can decide. Why? Why is there not a "moral roster," even though a separate one from an "intellectual roster"? In short, Kendall's own theory of democracy seems to be erroneous because it is a *moral* one, i.e., he thinks majority rule and census-democracy a good in itself, presumably because of some such moral equality. But this is not justified. As far as I am concerned, both the democratic mass and any sort of an aristocratic elite can be bad. There is very little *moral* argument for democracy. *Second*, Kendall does not explore why it is that it is precisely in *government* that the expert-layman problem becomes important. Why don't we worry about such problems on the free market? Nobody worries about people being ruined or ruled by their accountants. The answer is that on the market (a) people are free to choose whatever experts they please, and also free to try to run their affairs without experts; experts never rule them, they only sell their services for money; (b) on the free market, laymen have the test of concrete success to help them decide what experts to patronize. The architect that builds the fine, sturdy house is the one who gets the customers flocking to his door. The market provides continuous testing of experts. In government, however, the expert-laymen relation is turned from harmonious cooperation into caste warfare because the experts are permitted to loot the masses and give them orders. And, further, because of this disjunction between position and revenue, from testable merit, there is no reason why these governmental experts should be efficient, i.e., why they should be experts at all. Indeed, they will be efficient *not* at providing the governmental service, whatever it may be (post office, foreign intercourse, etc.), but at organizing robber gangs to bludgeon the populace into yielding them more money and power—i.e., they will be most efficient at coercion.

Third, there is a critical moral question here not mentioned by Kendall: experts for what? On the free market, every expert is voluntarily paid and performs a service voluntarily desired. But what of the expert criminal? Are we to exalt him just because he is an expert? In short, Kendall fails to make the crucial distinction of what the experts are used for—if they are experts in crime, then we don't want them around. Further, if some or all governmental activities are really essentially criminal activities, then the *less* expertly they are conducted, the better off we all are.

I would like to add parenthetically another problem with Kendall's solution: that it takes high *intellectual* qualities, which the masses admittedly do not possess, to get them to realize the distinction between fact and value!

As for Kendall's broader position, he gives only one small clue; early in the work, he says that the current liberals are conducting a revolution against the "traditional philosophy and religion of the West." Now, here I must register a protest. I am tired of hearing this phrase. What is this "traditional philosophy and religion"? There is no single tradition of the West, and it's about time we realize this. The history of the "West" (West of *what* by the way?) is a history of the actions of millions of men and the thoughts of highly diverse thinkers; there is the tradition of the Inquisition and the tradition of the Enlightenment; of feudal warfare and of barbarian invasions; of religious wars to the knife; of the liberal (the true liberal) revolution of the seventeenth, eighteenth, and nineteenth centuries; of the divine right of kings; of mercantilism and of *laissez-faire*; etc., etc. Religiously, there have been Catholics, Protestants of all sects, Jews, and even atheists and Jacobins. All these are now tradition. All these now-traditions were themselves "revolutions" against the previous order when they were first introduced. So where do we go from here? Nowhere. For if this is Kendall's positive position, it is no position at all.

(2) Freedom of thought

In this section, on freedom of thought, Kendall does a very curious thing. He very neatly shows that the "clear and present danger" criterion is not at all libertarian, as the leftists imply, but an escape clause that permits the State to punish free expression; and he also shows that the current liberals, while professing (though not as often as he thinks) the "simon-pure doctrine" of absolute free speech, make all sorts of convenient exceptions—pornography, etc. (He might have added segregationists who "incite to riot.") But instead of attacking current liberal doctrine, he leaves them to pursue a lengthy and savage attack on the simon-pure doctrine, i.e., on pure libertarianism. Of course, he believes that free speech should not be restricted for light and transient causes, but his attack is leveled with relish against personal liberty. In short, Kendall is not, in this part, attacking the liberal machine; he is attacking M.N. Rothbard, R.C. Cornuelle, etc. Naturally, I find it hard to refrain from curses.

In the first place, Kendall is clearly correct about Socrates's doctrine in the *Crito*. Socrates is clearly here a statist of the first rank, and any overeager libertarian who may have concluded that the *Crito* is a libertarian tract could hardly be in greater error.

Next, Kendall scoffs at the "simon-pure liberal" who, while talking about seeking Truth, never believes that man has found it. In short, he assumes that the libertarian case rests on the proposition that truth can never be found, so that we better keep all paths open so that at least error will be minimized. (This is actually the position of H.F. Phillips, which is why I called him Kendall's *alter ego*. Actually, while this is the position of modern leftists, positivists, and pragmatists, it is emphatically not my position or that of other simon-purists and it was not the position of Mill in *On Liberty*, as a careful reading will show. E.g., Mill: "If the [suppressed] opinion is right, [mankind] is deprived of the opportunity of exchanging error for truth; if wrong, they lose, what is almost as great a benefit, the clearer perception and livelier impression of truth produced by its collision with error."[2] (Actually, while Truth can be and has been attained, it can also be *added to* and refined as time goes on, but this is not a necessary condition to holding that absolute freedom of opinion should prevail.) Consequently, since belief in Truth is by no means inconsistent with absolute freedom (in fact, in the deepest sense—in the Truth about the conditions necessary to the development of human nature—it is the only consistent system), it is not devastating to be told by Kendall that Socrates was not a positivist-pragmatist.

---

[2] John Stuart Mill, *On Liberty* (Longmans, Green, and Co., 1921), p. 10. Editor's note: Rothbard's original citation was to a different edition.

Whoever wrote the footnotes on page 85 was absolutely correct: Kendall's statement that Socrates's death was "inevitable," according to Plato, because of the chasm between his truth and the other Athenians, is belied by Kendall's other point about the closeness of the majority who delivered the verdict. (For some obscure reason, Kendall seems to think that it weakens the libertarian argument against the Assembly because it only had a small majority for the sentence.)

Kendall highly overdraws the case when he stresses Socrates as being essentially religious, and that Socrates arrived at truth by revelation and not discovery. It was precisely the difference between the Socratic Revolution and the pre-Socratic philosophers that Socrates asserted that man can find the truth about ethics and the other problems of philosophy by the use of his reason, in contrast to the utilitarian-pragmatist attitude of the Sophists. God is of course mentioned frequently, but not to the extent that Socrates can simply be called a religious prophet.

Now, here I want to shift from commenting on Plato and Kendall's interpretation, to Kendall's own position on the Socrates question, which is clearly implied on pages 91 ff. Namely, that the Athenians had three choices to make: (1) eradicate Socrates, which they did; (2) change their way of life, i.e., adopt Socrates's proposed "revolution;" or (3) "tolerate" him, *either* because no truth can be known, or because he is harmless. Notice how the dice are loaded, especially on alternative three. There is another ground, completely unmentioned by Kendall, for permitting revolutionaries to speak: the ground that freedom to express and hear opinions, whatever they are, is itself not only good for the nature of man, but the highest political end. Kendall says that the Athenians *cannot* adopt alternative two. (Actually, of course, alternatives two and three are by no means mutually exclusive; they could adopt both.) Why? Because they believe in their existing way of life. Therefore, they *cannot* accept the new. But why *cannot*? Despite Kendall's obvious horror of revolution—*any* revolution—revolutions have been successfully conducted in the past, ways of life have been changed. If they have been accomplished from time to time, why not in Athens?

Kendall concludes that it was right for the Assembly to kill Socrates; not only right but their bounden duty. Socrates was subversive; he was influential; and therefore the thing to do was to stop him before he really became a threat. If they had refused to do so, they would have deserted their way of life: "they in effect endorse his revolution." Now, I submit that this is nonsense and dangerous nonsense at that. If the Athenians were so damn committed to their way of life, they had little to worry about; and if Socrates were really becoming a threat, then they no longer were particularly committed to their way of life. In short, if 90 percent of Athenians were orthodox, and 10 percent Socratic revolutionaries, then, if the 90 percent are deeply committed, they have nothing to worry about, since the "revolution" can only take place if most of their number are converted, and such conversion is hardly likely if they are so passionately committed. On the other hand, if they are worried—and Kendall intimates that they are so worried—because they are afraid that enough of their number will be converted until say, 55 percent of the Athenians will become Socratics (or even more) and the revolution effected, then at least 45 percent of the Athenians must not be passionately committed, must be in danger of seceding to the enemy. But if that is the case, Kendall is *not* defending the right and duty of the majority to suppress a minority; he is defending the right and duty of an actual *minority* to suppress a possible majority. If, in sum, there are at the present time 45 percent passionate orthodoxes, 45 percent waverers, and 10 percent Socratics, clearly the waverers won't want to suppress that which they feel they might someday convert to (and if they *do* persecute, they are clearly *not* being responsible—they are instead being irrational, on anybody's count). Therefore, Kendall, the professed champion of all-out majority rule, in effect, the champion of the *duty* as well as the right of pure majoritarian despotism over anyone whom it claims challenges its "way of life," is *really* advocating *minority* despotism over the majority. I personally am passionately opposed to *all* despotism, majority or minority, but Kendall is here hoist with his own particular petard. It should, indeed, be made absolutely clear that Kendall is *not* simply saying what he is obviously trying to justify—the persecution of Communists and Nazis—he is also saying that *any* challenge to a way of life should also be treated in the same way. Logically, this would mean, for example, that a society devoted at some point of time to the use of powdered wigs, has the right—*and* the duty—to *put to death* anyone who presumes to advocate going without these wigs. For Kendall's way of life includes not only politics, but also philosophy, and all values. And if some poor Britisher should try to introduce cricket in this country, and he started earning a following—*however small*—Kendall should logically proclaim the bounden duty of the present passionately committed majority to put to death (literally) the unfortunate cricketer, who is now menacing their passionately held value.

See what is implied here in all of its grisly starkness. Kendall is *not only* saying that the champions of Truth have the right and duty to suppress Error, lest it threaten them. He is saying much more, though that would be bad enough. He is saying that any majority, so long as it *thinks* what it believes is true, has the right *and duty* to suppress any differences, even if these differences are *really* true. In other words, as long as a majority of men are sincere, they have the duty of annihilating any dissenters. *Even*, states Kendall expressly and fearlessly, if the dissenter were God himself (p. 94)!

There is no need for me to explain that this philosophy is the reverse of libertarian; it is not only that; it is *the* philosophy of savage tyranny, baldly and cogently expressed. It is the Enemy.

Setting aside the temptation to wax emotional over this, let us explore some more of Kendall's inconsistencies—even on his own terms. One problem he has is that if erroneous people also have the right and duty to suppress the Truth, how in the world will the Truth become known? As Mill said, there is no automatic guarantee that Truth will triumph; truth must be discovered, it must be argued, it must be discussed, it must win men's minds. How will it do so if it is killed at birth? If Socrates represents truth (and let us assume so for our purposes) how will Socraticism ever develop? And how could

Christianity ever have developed? Kendall forgets that *every* major social change came about, and necessarily so, through an ideological revolution. Those things that he now reveres as "tradition" were once themselves revolutionary. Why doesn't Kendall discuss the Christ question? If he did, he would have to conclude that the Romans should have killed Christ and persecuted the Christians (if Christianity was not subversive of the old order and way of life, what was it?) and that the Romans only erred in not extirpating Christianity thoroughly and ruthlessly enough. Is he prepared to say this? Is he prepared to say that if the Romans had had their Willmoore Kendalls to advise them, Christianity would not now exist, and Willmoore Kendall would have been, and should have been, a Roman pagan and not a Christian?

Not only would a Kendallian society be a savage despotism, with no individual freedom worth mentioning; not only would Truth be suppressed as much as error; but also it would be frozen into a static, completely unchanging mold. Kendall, in short, is the philosopher of the lynch mob. His hand is there to smash the first machines that opened the Industrial Revolution; he is there at the Inquisition; he is there to liquidate all advocates of any change. But see the inconsistency: since every new social change of importance is subversive of the old order and disturbs people's peace of mind for a while, Kendall must keep going back and back, since every society originated in a social revolution against some preceding society. In short, Kendall's ethical doctrine must lead straight back to where? To the era of the caveman. Only the most primitive tribes exemplify the Kendallian ideal and they alone; for they remain changeless, ruthlessly suppressive of any dissent, and consequently eternally static. *And* if all societies in the past were guided by a Willmoore Kendall, *that* is the level mankind would have remained at—barely above ape level. The first inventor of fire, the first inventor of the wheel would have been torn to pieces, and all succeeding dissenters and disturbers of the peace as well.

If Kendall has set forth the philosophy of tyranny cogently, we see that philosophy leads to the end of civilization and most of the human race—in short, the death principle. That is why I say that the

Kendallian doctrine is the Enemy of all that you and I hold dear, and all that is best for the nature of man.

Kendall, of course, does not think of himself in this light, but rather of a sensible savior of democracy from the subversive encroachments of Communists and Nazis. But actually, his principles when logically analyzed, lead straight to what I have described. It is all very well for Kendall to picture himself as adviser to Germany in 1928, as he saves the Weimar Republic by killing Hitler; but he neglects to picture himself adviser in Germany in *1938*, a time when his beloved community was passionately pro-Hitler. At that time, he would have had to counsel the duty of Germany to murder all *anti*-Nazis, who then would have been the subversive revolutionaries against the values of the community. And so we return to the Kendall regression—the eternal exterminating: the anti-Nazis in 1938, the Nazis in 1928, all Republicans in 1922, and so on back to the Visigoths.

(Kendall asks: shall we save Socrates or the Weimar Republic? There is no question how the libertarian will answer—to hell with the Weimar Republic!)

Kendall brilliantly sees that we have been engaged in a vast swindle: that our society has *taught* freedom of speech to us, but has, in fact, under such phony guises as "clear and present danger," persecuted opinions which the majority have found uncongenial. He would bring coherence to the situation by eliminating the contradiction. How? By ceasing to teach the merit of free speech. In short, we profess ideals of liberty, but we find that we're persecutors, so let's not confuse matters; let's stand up foursquare for persecution.

Kendall proceeds to add to his other inconsistencies and confusions two further ones. In fact, he commits the very sin he had neatly exposed long ago in Part I: the confusion of fact and value. He makes this confusion in two ways. First, he states that it is an empirical fact that people will simply *not* tolerate opinions radically different from theirs, and since they will not, it is wicked to teach simon-pure freedom. But even granted this "fact" (and I am very dubious—it seems to me that the persecution of Communists in the postwar years has been caused almost wholly by people *believing* that the Reds are a clear and present danger, and that, if Kendall convinces them otherwise, they would disappoint him by leaving the Commies alone as they did before World War II when Communist rhetoric was far *more* radical than today), it is illegitimate for Kendall to infer from this that this condition is *good*. People may be a bunch of murderers; that is no reason to say therefore murder is *good*. Second, he states—without any proof—that the simon-pure doctrine is unworkable, unhealthy, insane, etc., because no "society" could work if it practiced it. Every society has a "way of life," "values," etc. Here, we have a further confusion. What is this "society"? Like most other political theorists, Kendall offers no definitions. "Society" is not an independently existent entity; it is simply a shorthand label for a certain pattern of interpersonal relations. Now the point is that to have an existent society, no particular set of values, customs, ways of life, etc., are necessary. A society *can* exist which has an absolute principle: simon-pure liberty. Kendall waves this possibility away, but if such a society did exist, then Kendall or anyone else who attacked free speech would then be attacking a fundamental tenet of that society, and therefore would be doing evil on Kendall's own grounds. (And note: if our society, as Kendall concedes, *teaches* the simon-pure doctrine, may we not say that society holds this as one of its values, and therefore that Kendall is himself an evil subverter by coming around to attack it?) For "society" can exist among Christians, atheists, pants-pressers, or libertines. It can exist on old Athenian principles or Socratic principles. There are only two relevant ideal types of social patterns: the pattern of voluntary contractual interrelation, and that of hegemonic, coercive interaction. A can interact with B, in other words, in either of two ways: by free gift or exchange—voluntarily—or by coercion. And these are *all* the relevant alternatives. Now, if a society is voluntarist and contractual, this freedom will develop the personality of each and permit that great growth of living standards that makes modern civilization possible, that raises us up from the caveman. If the society is markedly coercive, not only will it stunt each individual's development, it will plunge humankind back to primitive living standards and not permit any maintenance of civilization.

We see that in the profoundest sense, then, liberty is necessary to a viable social order. In that case, Willmoore Kendall's suggested rule by the bayonet is disintegrative of "society" rather than its salvation. Simon-pure freedom, rather than destroy society, would usher in the best possible type of society. Further, it is not necessary to social relations for A and B to have the same values, as Kendall thinks; they can have as many different views as they want, and trade between them will still be profitable to both.

Kendall's final analogy between public discussion and the "scientific discipline" of the "academic community" is obvious nonsense. There is no pre-narrowed field, and, above all, the "academic community" is a voluntary club, making its own rules, while the general "community" rules by the bayonet. Further, since when is the "academic" orthodoxy the custodian of truth? We would be in a sorry way indeed if, guild-like, our academic bureaucracy could use force to suppress dissentient economists or political scientists—a sorry state for Truth, and, incidentally, a sorry state for Willmoore Kendall who earlier has inveighed against the "academic bureaucracy." (One wonders: if you call the academicians a "community," do they become good and revered, and if you call them a "bureaucracy," do they become fair targets, and, by the way, what is the difference?) I would also add that Kendall will have a hard time enforcing "good manners" (which don't always hold in the academic community either) on the public at large, which is not notorious for it; and, by the way, how would Kendall and the few other mannered elite go about imposing these manners by bayonet on the often unmannered masses? Democratically? The best answer on manners comes again from Mill, who points out that it is the majority who has the power, who should be exhorted to good manners, and not the few radical dissidents.

How now do we sum up the political philosophy of Willmoore Kendall? I have been treating it in this overlong memo in some detail because of the cogency of his presentation, the keenness with which he poses basic questions, and the fact of being a seeming star on the right-wing firmament, giving lectures at Buck Hill Falls. I sum up by repeating, advisedly, that Kendall is the philosopher *extraordinaire* of the lynch mob. As John Stuart Mill put it so well: "The propounder of a new truth, according to this doctrine, should stand, as stood, in the legislation of the Locrians, the proposer of a new law, with a halter round his neck, to be instantly tightened if the public assembly did not, on hearing his reasons, then and there adopt his proposition."[3] Read that great speech in Ayn Rand's *Fountainhead* as Roark explains that the great creators, the great individualists, were always met with hatred and persecution by their fellow men, who in the end benefited from them. Kendall is the eternal enemy of the Roarks, the enemy of liberty—a brilliant enemy, a cogent enemy, an honest enemy, a swell guy with an enormous capacity for Scotch, but an enemy nevertheless.

We should now face the question: how does Kendall differ, say, from Russell Kirk and the "new conservatives"? Why is he anti-Kirk, as he is reputed to be, even though both of them unite in being opposed to free speech and Mill's *On Liberty*? Answer: there is great difference between them. Kirk is the philosopher of old pre–Industrial Revolution, High Anglican England, the land of the squire, the Church, the happy peasant, and the aristocratic bureaucratic caste. He is essentially and basically antidemocratic. Kendall, on the contrary, is, as I have said, the patron of the lynch mob—he is an *ur*-democrat, a Jacobin impatient of any restraints on his beloved community. He hates bureaucracy, but not as we do, because it is tyrannical; he hates it because it has usurped control from the popular masses. He is the sort of person whom the [Clinton] Rossiter-[Peter] Viereck "new conservatives" are combating, for they are trying to defend the existent rule of the leftist bureaucracy against any populist mass upheaval. So they—the leftists—have shifted from mob whippers to soothing conservatives.

And here we come to the cosmic joke, the final contradiction that is Willmoore Kendall. Kendall's chief *bête noire* is revolution, and yet he fails to see that the revolution *was*. The leftists are in the saddle, have been for over two decades. *Therefore*, it is Kendall who

---

[3] John Stuart Mill, *On Liberty* (Longmans, Green, and Company, 1921), p. 16. Editor's note: The Locrians were a tribe in ancient Greece.

is now the revolutionary, the disturber of the peace, the guy outside the pale. The community, Kendall's saint, likes Ike, follows Walter Lippmann, etc. On Kendall's *own* premises, Sherman Adams should put Kendall to death this instant. So, Kendall's philosophy leads not only to death and destruction in general, but to his own death and destruction in great particular!

How is it that Kendall, an astute political analyst and chronicler of the liberal machine, can have made such a whopping mistake? How can he commit the Reece Committee fallacy that his views are in the majority *now* when this is palpably incorrect?[4] I submit that Kendall *can* work his way out of this contradiction in one way. This way is connected with a question that has been cropping up in my mind for a long time: in what way is Kendall a "right-winger"? If he is a Jacobin, a lyncher, a Keynesian, etc., in what way is he a "rightist"? The answer seems to be: in one way only—he wants to kill Communists. Outside of this, I fail to see any "rightist" view. And perhaps he has convinced himself, as other rightists have done, that the "community" *wants* to kill Communists, here and abroad, and they are being prevented from doing so by the liberal machine. I deny that the majority wants to kill Communists, but at least it is a plausible hypothesis. But I submit that if this is Kendall's only essential difference from, say, Arthur Schlesinger, Jr., I will put my nickel on Schlesinger, for, on net balance, Kendall is less libertarian than he. (It is possible, of course, that there are *some* libertarian views that Kendall holds, but if so, no one has been able to point them out to me. Of course, he *is* a Christian, which may increase his "right-wing" credentials, but not his libertarian ones.)

This leads me, at long last, to the question of what has happened to the Right in the last decade. It has grown but it has also decayed in quality by becoming confused, and confusing itself with wicked

---

4   Editor's note: B. Carroll Reece (Rep. Tennessee) chaired the Congressional Committee to Investigate Tax-Exempt Foundations. The 1954 report of this committee claimed that many foundations were biased toward a one-world state. The "fallacy" is the view that most people shared the committee's disapproval of the major foundations.

doctrine. A dramatic contrast can be shown, for example, in taking a very early issue of *Plain Talk*—I think late 1946—and noting a moving article by Edna Lonigan, "I Taught Economics." There, at the very beginning of this postwar flowering of the "radical Right," Lonigan wrote of her experiences as a wartime college teacher. The climax came when she converted some pro-Commies in the class, after arguing with them all term for individual liberty, by giving them Mill's *On Liberty*. In those days, the Right was small, but we were libertarian. We all fought for individual liberty, and battled majority as well as elitist tyranny of all types. And now, when we find Mill's *On Liberty* discussed today—ostensibly by "rightists" also, what do we find? Kirk and Kendall, each from his own point of view blatantly attacking liberty—and who is there to challenge them on the Right? This is the tragedy of this decade.

How did this change happen to the "Right"? How did they change from pro-liberty to pro-tyranny without noting the difference? I submit because of a change in spirit from being a conscious minority to being almost, at least, in the majority in the country. And this came about from a switch in emphasis in doctrine. It came about from increasing stress on the Right on the twin issues of Communism and Christianity. Since the bulk of the populace has become converted to anti-Communism in this decade, the rightist can give up the burdens of being a lonely minority, by forgetting about libertarianism and stressing only Red-baiting. The same thing happens when the completely irrelevant issue of Christianity crops up; by arrogating to itself the Christian, or more, the theist mantle, the Right can again join a majority. So this is what has happened. The journalists write about the iniquities of Moscow, and the "philosophers" talk about the Christian tradition.

It seems to me that to advance libertarianism, therefore, we should cut ourselves off completely, and even attack the Christian Red-baiting Right, which has become the evil exponent of tyranny that we note today. Red baiting and religion mongering should be exposed for the red herrings that they are, and shelved to concentrate on the prime issue: liberty vs. tyranny.

4. Review of Charles L. Black, Jr., *The People and the Court: Judicial Review in a Democracy*

March 24, 1961

To: Mr. Kenneth S. Templeton
William Volker Fund
Burlingame, California

Dear Ken:

Charles L. Black, Jr., *The People and the Court, Judicial Review in a Democracy* (Macmillan, 1960) falls into the category of book that is so biased in a left-wing direction that it is interesting for hitting on some of the crucial problems in its area, problems which most works miss. Black's jurisprudential views are biased in the left-wing direction on almost every issue: he favors the broadest of broad construction of the powers of government, *except* on such issues as freedom of speech, warrants for arrest, etc., of the Bill of Rights, where he joins the current "left wing" in favoring strict prohibitions on government.

Professor Black tries to avoid the obvious charges of inconsistency against his position by a clever sophistry: that, in both cases, he *really* favors broad construction—for he favors broad construction of government *powers* in the Constitution (e.g., the Commerce Clause, the "necessary and proper" clause, etc.), and also favors broad construction of the specific limitations on government (e.g., the First Amendment).

The complete sophistry of this supposed broad constructionism, however, is fully exposed when we find that Black emphatically *does not* apply such "broad" limits on government to those parts of the Bill of Rights that deal with *property* rights, e.g., "due process." Here, Black calls the late-nineteenth-century *laissez-faire* interpretation of due process not broad but "wild" and "fantastic."

Black's position is all the more self-contradictory when he totally ignores the fact that the broad, absolutist version of the First Amendment, as Professor Leonard W. Levy has shown in his seminal work *The Legacy of Suppression*, was itself a new construction by the later Jeffersonians (Wortman, St. George Tucker, etc.) and not part of the original meaning of the Founders. If, then, the theory of substantive due process was a totally new construction, then so is the absolutist version of the First Amendment, which ignores the original doctrine of "seditious libel."

Actually, from a libertarian point of view, broad construction of *limits* and strict construction of *powers* of government are perfectly compatible, since both conceive of the Constitution as imposing drastic limits on government power—preferably confining it to defense of person and property. However, the libertarian can make an even stronger case even within the constitutional domain itself.

First, if the Jeffersonian theory of strict construction of *powers* is adhered to, then there is no need for broad construction of limits since government powers would be drastically limited anyway. And, in my opinion, the Jeffersonian strict construction theory of the "necessary and proper" clause is obviously the meaning most appropriate to the text: "necessary" always means, in logical discourse, those steps that are truly essential and not just what some congressmen think to be conducive to the final result.

Black, of course, simply deprecates the Jeffersonian view. (Also, for example, the power to regulate "commerce" obviously should only be applicable to actual trade, so that, e.g., shipping and navigation are properly exempt from federal regulation, etc.)

Black also tries to uphold the disgraceful *Brown v. Board of Education* decision as not at all unprecedented; he sneers at states' rights, praises the New Deal as essential, etc.

So far, there is nothing of intrinsic interest here. The interest comes from Black's insight into the ambivalent functions of the system of judicial review, which he defends at length against the Frankfurter, etc. doctrine of "judicial restraint." For Black is perhaps the first since Calhoun to realize that judicial review is not simply a welcome *check* on government power. More important is the function of judicial review in *validating*, in legitimatizing, government power, and in inducing the public to accept it.

De Jouvenel, in his *On Power,* points out in excellent fashion that, in the history of political thought, time after time a concept originally designed to *limit* and *check* the State was turned by the State into an instrument to give it legitimacy and moral approval in the eyes of the masses. Thus, the "Divine Right of Kings" was originally designed to *limit* the power of the king through making him adhere to generally accepted divine law; the kings, of course, turned it into a very convenient divine stamp of approval on every act of the rulers.

Similarly, parliament was originated as a representative organ of the people *against* the king—to withhold supply until grievances were redressed, etc. Parliament was later turned into an absolute instrument of rule *over* the people in its own right, etc.

Now, judicial review, beloved by conservatives, can of course fulfill the excellent function of declaring government interventions and tyrannies unconstitutional. But it can *also* validate and legitimize the government in the eyes of the people by declaring these actions valid and *constitutional.* Thus, the courts and the Supreme Court become an instrument of spearheading and confirming federal tyranny instead of the reverse. And this is what has happened in America—so that the Constitution itself has been changed from a limiting to an aggrandizing and legitimizing instrument.

Professor Black's contribution here is to see and understand this process. In effect, he is telling his fellow étatists, "why do you carp and criticize the Supreme Court for its few, and, in the long run, ineffectual, checks on government power? Much more important is the continual process by which the Court, *ever since John Marshall,* has performed the extremely important function of validating aggrandized government in the eyes of the people."

Black, of course, hails this process. Black also shows in his historical summary, that not only did this validating process begin with the aggrandizement of John Marshall, but it also continued on in the supposedly restrictive and *laissez-faire* courts, such as Taney, and the post–Civil War courts where the slow, steady, massive validation of government power proceeded quietly, while public hullabaloo was concentrated on the few occasions when the Court balked. Further, continues Black, these few occasions in themselves were often valuable in giving the public the *impression* that the Court is an impartial and, therefore, valid legitimizing body.

Black, interestingly, says this about the special American need for legitimization: in a country such as England or France, where parliament reigns supreme and absolute, then there is no question raised in the minds of the masses about legitimacy; everyone simply assumes such legitimacy. But the United States was set up as a limited government, and given the originally sovereign states, etc., it could *only* have begun as a strictly limited government. But if everyone knows that government is limited, then for every extension of government power, people may believe that the government is acting unconstitutionally and hence illegitimately. It is therefore particularly important, writes Black shrewdly, for a *limited* government to convince and cajole people that it is acting with legitimacy—so that even the most hostile critics of its actions will, down deep, accept the government itself.

Herein lies the particular function of the Supreme Court. Black recognizes that it is illogical to have the State itself—through its Supreme Court—be recognized as the final and sole judge of *its own* (State) actions, but, says Black, what is the alternative? The Calhoun alternative? The Calhoun alternative (Calhoun saw this whole problem with beautiful clarity) was nullification, interposition, movements toward unanimity principles, etc., but Black instantly rejects this sort of route as leading to an anarchic negation of the national government itself. Therefore, aside from such ultimately superficial measures as keeping an "independence" or quasi-independence for the judiciary, all this is really only a trapping to convince the public, in almost mystical fashion, that the State has somehow transcended itself as best it can. Professor Black may complacently put his faith in this "something of a miracle" (p. 42) of government being a judge in its own cause (this is reminiscent of Jim Burnham's reference in his recent book to the "miracle" of government), but others of us may have different ideas.

The book—and the author, therefore—are whole-hearted celebrants of aggrandized national statism. Its interest for me is in discussing the crucial issue of legitimacy, from, however, a biased and distorted point of view. The book emphasizes for me, however, a point that I am making in an article in the forthcoming *Modern Age*: that the Constitution, regarded as an attempt to limit government, was one of the most noble attempts at limiting government, curbing the State, in human history—but that it has failed, and failed almost ignominiously. One reason for such failure, as Calhoun predicted, is the monopoly Supreme Court. At any rate, this failure points up the necessity of other, new, more stringent means of limiting and curbing government power.

5. Review of Leon Bramson, *The Political Context of Sociology*

June 20, 1962

Dr. Ivan R. Bierly
William Volker Fund

Dear Ivan:

Dr. Leon Bramson, *The Political Context of Sociology* (Princeton University Press, 1961) is an important book on several levels. On a purely "tactical" level, it is refreshing to see the sociologists—the professional debunkers of the ideas of others by reducing them to "ideology" and to other factors—have their own ideas and ideologies turned against them: in short, to see the "sociology of knowledge" turned against the sociologists.

More important is Bramson's positive critique and historical analysis of the development of modern sociology and its "conservative" antecedents in the first half of the nineteenth century. One of the most important neglected truths in the history of modern political theory is emphasized by Bramson: that modern left-wing and socialistic theories *grew out* of nineteenth-century conservatism, which adumbrated theories of holism, organicism, the "community," the group as superior to the individual, statism against *laissez-faire,* a fixed, hierarchically ordered society, etc.

This doctrine of conservatism originated as a reaction against the ideals of the Enlightenment and eighteenth-century liberalism and *laissez-faire,* which had brought to the world the ideas of liberty, industrial progress, separation of church and state, individualism, reason, equality before the law, etc. It was in reaction to this that the originators of conservatism such as Bonald, de Maistre, Hegel, etc., attacked classical-liberal and industrial society as being "atomistic," as "disintegrating" the helpless individual, etc., and called for a "reintegration" of the individual in the group and the community, a reestablishment of organicism, the "whole man," the State, hierarchical order, militarism, mystical irrationalism, etc.

Bramson shows that the original "socialists" were directly derived from this reactionary wave: e.g., Comte and Saint-Simon, who both wished to restore stagnation, hierarchy, and status from the period from which the Enlightenment had dethroned them. Karl Marx was more of an eclectic, as Bramson shows. From the classical liberals, Marx took an at-least-proclaimed devotion to humanism, reason, industry, peace, and the eventual "withering away of the State"; from the conservatives, however, he took much more, including an idealization of the feudal period, an opposition to individualism on behalf of favored classes and the whole collective society, a determinist belief in laws of history, and the charge that liberal division of labor and the free society "alienated" the laborer from his work, "atomized" the individual, etc.

Since these were the founders of sociology, it is no surprise that, as Bramson indicates, sociology in itself, in its inherent concentration on the group or holistic society as against the individual, is innately anti-individualist and anti-(classical) liberal. As Bramson says, "A consideration of the anti-liberal aspect of sociology brings into sharp relief the links between a reactionary like de Maistre, who idealized the feudal order, and a radical like Marx, who visualized a new industrial order." We can, incidentally, see these links also in the writings of *partisans* of such links: e.g., Karl Polanyi's *The Great Transformation* or R.H. Tawney.

The second important contribution of Bramson's work is, in his later chapters, the critique of the current left-wing attack on modern "mass society" or "mass culture," which Bramson shows to be derived from the nineteenth-century conservative *and* socialist attacks on "the atomization of the individual" due to modern capitalism and individualism. While the current critics attack not only capitalism but *industrialism* as well—and thus implicitly call for a return to some sort of agrarian-communal ideal—these critics are basing their theses not, as they claim, on social science, but on their own arbitrary valuations and romanticizing of all other times but the present.

The same criticisms are also present to a large degree in current "conservative" criticisms of mass culture, although the leftists are more explicitly anticapitalist in their absolving of the masses and pinning all the blame on the (capitalistic) mass media, which, through television, advertising, etc., "manipulate" the masses. Bramson has a good defense of mass culture in this respect, showing that even recent sociological work shows that individuals are as much—if not more—influenced by their friends and acquaintances than by mass media, and showing the arbitrary value judgment underlying the criticisms. He cites some apparently very interesting articles on this by Edward Shils and Raymond Bauer.

In his later chapters, Dr. Bramson is not quite as sure-footed as in the earlier. Thus, while in the early chapters, Bramson forthrightly and explicitly defines "liberal" as classical liberal, someone advocating individual liberty, in his later discussion of twentieth-century views, Bramson covertly shifts his meaning to use it in the vague modern sense of people interested in pragmatism, flexibility, openness, etc., which of course allows for a great deal more statism and loss of rigor in opposing it.

Further, he is a little too glib in linking the *current* conservative and the socialistic critics of "mass culture." Some of those cited (e.g., Dwight Macdonald) are simply people who dislike the cultural tastes of the masses, and Bramson tends to slide into the position of *equating* such a "cultural aristocratic" position with a *political* one: i.e., with charging that the person believes in rule of society by an intellectual elite. Cultural criticism and advocacy of statism are two different things, and Bramson tends to confuse the two too readily.

Bramson's biggest failure is the deficiency in his positive position, which, inevitably, weakens his criticism of the conservative-socialistic sociology, which he clearly opposes sharply. This is a *philosophic* failure, for Bramson believes that there is no such thing as social science at all, that there is no such thing as true objectivity in social inquiry, that *all* statements, even cause-and-effect and factual, rest on philosophical value-premises, and that *all* value-premises are arbitrary.

In short, Bramson is an ethical relativist, and an epistemological relativist as well.

For (a) it is *not* true that social science and its conclusions rest on value judgments; much of it does not. Only *political or ethical* conclusions (and judgments) rest on value judgments. The demonstration that price control causes shortages, for example, rests on no value-premises whatever; but the *conclusion* that price control *should not* be imposed is a policy judgment, which *rests on* ethical theories as well as on the economic law just mentioned. (E.g., the ethical principle that it is bad to cause shortages in this way.)

And (b) it is *not* true, as Bramson believes, that all value judgments and ultimate ideological positions are as good as any other, and that the choice is purely an arbitrary one. Some ethical doctrines or ideological positions are objectively and rationally good and some are bad. Bramson rejects the pure positivist separation of facts and values, but he also brusquely dismisses the natural-law connections between them; to Bramson, natural law is a static, and therefore antiliberal, search for "order," although he gives it almost no attention.

Bramson is therefore left with the jettisoning of any social science whatever and with the conclusion that the whole enterprise is an "art" based on arbitrary values. While we may applaud Bramson's own choice of some sort of vaguely liberal values, we can hardly be *convinced* of them by this sort of irrationalist procedure.

While Bramson's positive position is weak and unimportant, however, the value of the book is in his tracing of the strong linkage and affinity between conservative and socialist thought, joining together in the pseudoscience of sociology and in their common hatred and opposition to individualism and *laissez-faire*. Certainly the weaknesses, and probably also the strengths, of Bramson's book may be partially attributed to the evident influence on the author of the historian Louis Hartz.

6. Review of Charles Percy Snow, *Science and Government*

July 23, 1962

Dr. Ivan R. Bierly
William Volker Fund

Dear Ivan:

Charles Percy Snow, *Science and Government* (Harvard University Press, 1961) is a justly famous little book to which Sir Charles has just written a pamphlet "Appendix" (which I have not read) in answer to his critics. On the surface, the book is simply a chatty, well-written story about a series of conflicts about military science in the English government, before and during World War II, between two formidable protagonists: Sir Henry Tizard and F.A. Lindemann. Snow describes the points at issue and points a few moral lessons. But the book is justly well known because the issues at stake—for many of which Snow unfortunately does *not* point to the moral—are close to the heart of some of the most important issues of our time.

There is no doubt about the fact that, as far as the concrete instances of the story go, Snow is right: Tizard was consistently right and Lindemann consistently wrong. Tizard—backed up by virtually all the scientists who were let in on the issues involved—was all for the development of radar in air defense; Lindemann rejected this for inane schemes of his own. Tizard and the other scientists favored sharing of radar secrets with the United States before the war; Lindemann, passionate for "security and secrecy," was opposed. And finally, Lindemann had a great faith in a policy of massive strategic bombing of Germany, while Tizard and some fellow scientists were strongly opposed—and were proved right after the war. Two side morals from these instances are the futility of secrecy in science and the folly (as well as the wickedness) of the policy of strategic bombing in World War II.

Secrecy applies here at several levels. The British military tried fiercely to cling to the "secrets" of radar, when, at the very same time, their counterparts in the United States, Germany, and Soviet Russia were *also* clinging to *their* comparable "secrets." Science is an inherently international and cosmopolitan development, and this cannot be thwarted by censorship and the bayonet. Snow unfortunately does not make the case as strong as he might. He denies—in the face of his own evidence—that secrecy represses the growth of science.

The other important aspect of secrecy is that these decisions— life-and-death decisions for the country and even the world—were made by only a handful of men and made without giving the public a chance to participate. And yet Snow, while recognizing the secrecy and closed-closet nature of these decisions, does not really oppose the system. He is not at all concerned, apparently, with the violation of democracy involved; for how can members of the public make decisions about issues about which their government keeps them deliberately in ignorance? By what right, furthermore, does a govern- ment keep secrets from its taxpayers? Yet Snow, too secure a member of the "Establishment," presumably, to worry about such matters, can think of only the most picayune of reforms—which involve, paradoxically, more scientists in government and more government encouragement of science. (More on this below.)

In the instance of strategic bombing, Snow makes an important contribution to World War II revisionism (despite himself, since he admits that he is and was an ardent believer in the crusade against Germany in World War II). For he shows that the barbaric policy of strategic bombing of civilians was launched by the British (thus confirming [F.J.P.] Veale) when the Germans and the Russians had no interest in strategic bombing whatever; and, further, that this policy was pushed through by Lindemann over the opposition of scientists such as Tizard and [P.M.S.] Blackett, in a wave of patriotic fervor and the emotional denunciation of Tizard as a "defeatist."

Lindemann, a pseudoscientist with the unquestioning and fanatical devotion and support of Churchill, estimated that strategic bombing would be ten times as effective as it proved to be (even Blackett and Tizard, who opposed the strategic bombing program as military folly, overestimated by 100 percent the extent of bombing damage that would occur).

There is also the interesting revelation that the Lindemann strategic bombing program was not at all interested in selecting military or strategic targets for bombing (it was impossible to select them properly anyway), but was deliberately and solely aimed at killing the maximum number of civilians, and therefore concentrated on the dense and crowded housing of the poor and the working class.

The real moral of the story, which Snow refuses to draw in any such broad terms, is the folly of government intervention in science. One forceful quasi-charlatan gets the ear of a leading politician (Churchill), and the whole scientific policy of the government must swing into line. But it is more than a problem of one man, to which Snow tries to limit the problem. It is the general problem of science distorted and perverted by government—by politicians and by the bureaucracy alike.

The moral that Snow himself tries to draw—in short, more scientists in government and more government promotion of science—is precisely the reverse of the conclusion that emerges from an impartial survey of Snow's facts. But Snow, who cannot conceive of a world where government and science are separated, cannot draw such conclusions. Withal, this is a highly stimulating book.

7. Report on the Voegelin Panel

(date unknown)

Professor W.F. Albright

My critique of the Voegelin Panel is rather handicapped by the fact that I have not read the three volumes of the Voegelin *magnum opus*,[5] especially since much of the debate centered on an interpretation of what Voegelin's political position is.

Professor Albright's paper was an interesting and straightforward technical-historical criticism of Voegelin's work. Voegelin's philosophic position, said Albright, is a blend of Hegelianism, Lutheran Augustinianism, and existentialism. (If true, this bodes ill, for all three of these philosophies must be looked on askance, especially the first and third.) For Hegel's *Geist*, Voegelin substitutes "Order" as the "meaning of history."

Voegelin is better than Hegel, said Albright, because Hegel's *Geist* is realized through the dialectic by the State, whereas for Voegelin, it is not. On the other hand, Voegelin definitely combines the religious and the political in history. For the dialectic, Voegelin substitutes the mysterious concept of the "leap in being," which is supposed to have occurred in Greece and in Israel, which Albright identifies as a questionable variant of St. Augustine's "leap of faith." Albright then cogently attacked existentialism as essentially unhistorical and arbitrary. Then Albright placed Voegelin as a better historian than Toynbee, but I got the distinct impression that this would not necessarily have to be a compliment.

The bulk of Albright's paper was devoted to a historical critique of Voegelin's historical and empirical data, of which I am not competent

---

[5]   Editor's note: Eric Voegelin originally conceived *Order and History* as a six-volume examination of the history of order. The first three volumes, *Israel and Revelation*, *The World of the Polis*, and *Plato and Aristotle*, were published in 1956 and 1957. The fourth volume, *The Ecumenic Age*, did not appear until 1974. The fifth and final volume, *In Search of Order*, appeared posthumously in 1987.

to judge the validity. The gist of the criticisms is that Voegelin is not quite abreast of recent ancient-history scholarship. Specifically, there are three criticisms. First, that Voegelin adopts the "pan-Babylonian" theory of such historians as [Alfred] Jeremias, holding that the early Babylonians had an elaborately developed astrology and cosmology. This, says Albright, has been completely discredited by recent scholars who have shown that Babylonia only had a developed astrology in the second century BC.

Secondly, Voegelin follows the German school of Israel historiography, headed by [Albrecht] Alt, [Martin] Noth, and [Gerhard] von Rad, and neglects the current American and Israeli school based largely on archaeological discoveries and linguistic analysis (e.g., John Bright, *History of Israel*), all of which, as well as literary analysis, show that monotheism goes back to early Israel. Furthermore, these evidences show that while Israeli literature had monotheist sentiment from the tenth century BC, Northern Syrian literature had monotheism in the fourteenth century BC. Early Hebrew law extends back before Moses (thirteenth century BC), and back, indeed, to fourteenth-century-BC treaties of Syria (see researches of [George E.] Mendenhall.)

Thirdly, Voegelin neglects the findings that Greek science (e.g., Hesiod) was based on earlier Hittite and Phoenician influences, which the Greeks rendered in more systematic and abstract form.

Albright ended with praise, but with the pointed remark that empirical and rational methods are best for the historian, not idealism and existentialism (which Voegelin is supposed to be blending).

Professor Thomas I. Cook

Cook began, as did all other speakers, by praising Voegelin's erudition. He then said that he was going to devote his paper to attacking Professor Voegelin as "dangerous," "erroneous," and "subversive," and, in fact, as "the great enemy."

Voegelin argues, said Cook, that a proper political order requires the rule of those who understand and are a "part of" "ultimate reality." This understanding of ultimate reality can only be achieved by some sort of "leap in being," after which this understanding of ultimate reality is supposed to be imposed on the rest of society. When this rule is not imposed, society is in decline.

Voegelin adopts Plato's totalitarian *Republic* as his model of the political order that can stem a social decline. This is the good rule of the good State. But, said Cook in libertarian fashion, *when* has there *ever* been a true and good State? And, furthermore, *how* are these philosopher-rulers to be selected? How are they to be known? For these rulers are to arrive at their understanding of the required political order, not simply by reason or dialectic, but by some sort of intuition and grace. Voegelin, Cook agrees, is opposed vehemently to any *this-worldly* elitist order of government (and from this, clearly, stems Voegelin's opposition to the secular empires and secular states that he sees built by the "gnostic" spirit).

On the other hand, Voegelin *does* want an elite to rule who "truly know" and "truly understand" by some sort of intuitive, mystic means that transcend human reason. Furthermore, Voegelin implies that everyone, all of us, who do not have this mystic grace are "incompetent," in error, outside of the pale, not political scientists, and not fit to participate in political decisions.

Cook charges that this sort of doctrine permits no sort of *polis* to develop, because there can be no real, rational communication between the inspired elite and everyone else. Cook reminds Voegelin that politics is concerned not with the transcendent but with finite man and his relationships, and that the proper method of arriving at a political order is by reason. The basic concern of the State or *polis* should be, not "the good life," but *good lives*—i.e., the emphasis should be individualistic, not on the collective State.

In short, the political order should enable people to achieve the fulfillment of the potential of each individual, without having *one ought* imposed upon all of them. In this connection, Plato—Voegelin's model—is the great enemy that political science must combat. Our job, in politics, is to be materialist and empiricist. Our job, *in politics* (though not necessarily elsewhere, I take it) is to provide the maximum enabling means to allow diverse types of persons to develop their potentialities to their diverse maxima. The emphasis of politics is life on this earth.

As against the emphasis of human reason as used in the world, Voegelin emphasizes the intuition, the "leap in being" of an elite, whose doctrine of a transcendent good must be followed and accepted by the rank and file, else society is lost.

From this paper, I think we can conclude, first, that Professor Cook's instincts are libertarian, that he favors individual liberty and development of each person in freedom, and that he believes in human reason as the way to arrive at political decisions. He is certainly correct in attacking elitist rule of a group of supposedly inspired prophets, and in attacking the authoritarianism and statism of Plato.

Cook's own political views, as far as they can be gleaned here, seem to be in the right direction. The only real question, then, is whether his interpretation of Voegelin's position is correct. There was controversy about this, and the question is in doubt (and we will consider this more closely in our critique of Voegelin himself). To me, however, the fact that Voegelin takes Plato's *Republic* as his model is extremely disquieting and certainly lends credence to the "totalitarian" view of Voegelin.

I think it should be mentioned here that Professor Cook's interpretation of Voegelin is paralleled by that of the great ancient-history scholar Moses Hadas.[6] By "order," says Hadas, Voegelin means authority, by "transcendent" he means not only God but a human theocratic elite. History, for Voegelin, means God primarily; the enemy for Voegelin is the Enlightenment. And the inspired, transcendent elite is supposed to rule the rest of society.

Not only Plato's *Republic* but also his even more totalitarian *Laws* are the actual exemplars of Voegelin's preferred "leap in being." Hadas asserts that Voegelin praises the "noble lie" or "big lie" of Plato, that this is a proper action for the rulers to use, and that the rulers' interpretation of eugenic mating is right because "true order of the spirit cannot be realized in community unless supported by eugenic

---

6   See Moses Hadas, review of *Order and History*, by Eric Voegelin, *Journal of the History of Ideas* 19, no. 3 (June 1958): 442–44.

election of right bodies."[7] Voegelin praises the Nocturnal Council of the *Laws* which is to enforce laws against impiety, and since *all* the laws are sanctioned by religion, this means all laws, period.

Voegelin praises "the life and problems of the *polis*"—which Hadas interprets, perhaps with exaggeration, as a secret police.[8] Hadas concludes that Voegelin's "order" rests upon the rule of a supposedly divinely inspired elite, close to the Hellenistic theory that the ruler is *nomos empsychos*—"law incarnate." This was the basis for the authoritarianism of the Roman emperors and combated by the "gnostics" of the eighteenth century. Hadas concludes by saying— again, perhaps with exaggeration—that "leap in being" amounts, in the last analysis, to fascism.

In the discussion period from the floor, I asked Professor Cook whether he deduced Voegelin's authoritarianism merely from Voegelin's emphasis on God and the transcendent (as various defenders of Voegelin, including Frank S. Meyer, had intimated) or whether he had other reasons. Cook replied that he had other reasons, and that he himself would like very much for Voegelin to clear up the ambiguities of his work that led Cook to interpret Voegelin in this manner.

Professor Eric Voegelin

In general, I was frankly not very impressed with Voegelin's ratiocination in discussion. Thus, one of Voegelin's chief arguments was that assuming the existence of God is the only *scientific* course for the historian, since so many peoples have believed in God. This seems to me one of the weakest arguments for the existence of God I have heard in a long time. Secondly, his major argument against a secular world empire (or rather an immanentized religio-political empire— i.e., pagan or "gnostic") is that such an empire can only include in its community the people now living; it *cannot* include the dead and

---

7   Voegelin, *Order and History*, 3:119, quoted in Hadas, review of *Order and History*, p. 443.
8   Voegelin, *Order and History*, 3:265, quoted in Hadas, review of *Order and History*, p. 444.

the unborn, which Christianity can include. This is perhaps the weakest argument against a secular State rule that I have heard in a long time. I fail to see how the dead or the unborn can be fitted into any sort of order in this world, much as they might be a vital force in some other world.

In reply to Albright, Voegelin acknowledged a fundamental difference of opinion. He, Voegelin, believes that each civilization (Greek, Israeli, Babylonian, etc.) was self-built and uninfluenced by the other or earlier civilizations. Any similarity of culture, therefore, was only coincidence and not because of outside influence.

Voegelin asserted that while all men begin equal under God, they are unequal in their accomplishments. This is certainly true, but we are still left with the question of how much power Voegelin would give to his elite. Voegelin pooh-poohed the fears of Cook by saying that the U.S. Constitution hopes to elect people by merit, not by lot (the truly democratic thing), and then has beneficial checks and balances on these rulers. If *this* is all that Voegelin's "elitism" amounts to, this would be fine, but I have my doubts. The question is: is Voegelin cloaking his true position before this potentially hostile American audience.

Voegelin denied he was an existentialist and also joined in attacking existentialism as unhistorical. (However, the term "leap in being" is clearly taken from the existentialist Heidegger.)

After Cook had answered my question by saying that he had hoped that Voegelin himself would clarify his political position, Voegelin took the floor to say that he means that the elite should rule by *persuasion* merely, and that people would follow by being persuaded. Again, *if* this is true, Voegelin's political position would be fine (although I would still take grave exception to his exclusive emphasis on the transcendent, on intuition, and his attack on "gnostic" this-worldly emphases). However, I have my doubts, *especially* in view of Voegelin's admittedly taking the definitely despotic Plato as his model.

Frank Meyer took the floor to challenge Cook and to defend Voegelin as really laying the groundwork for freedom, in attacking absolute secular rule, and in harmonizing or balancing the transcendent and the real world—which balancing Frank obscurely finds as the only (???)[9] basis for freedom! Neither Voegelin nor Cook commented on Frank's statement, however.

There is a tendency on the Right to believe that any political philosopher who repeatedly invokes God and attacks secularism is, *ipso facto*, some sort of libertarian. I believe that Frank has fallen prey to this fallacy. I think it significant that Voegelin made no comment on Frank's remarks and did *not* take the opportunity to say that he really believed in freedom. I never heard Voegelin use the term "freedom" or "liberty" at all.

On the other hand, Frank admitted to me in conversation that Voegelin is a disciple of Plato. Since Plato is clearly pro-despotism, Frank concluded that Voegelin must be mistaken in his interpretation of Plato, that he must think of Plato as some sort of libertarian, etc. I cannot accept this interpretation since surely any eminent scholar such as Voegelin realizes the totalitarianism of Plato's politics.

The verdict is not conclusively in, but it seems to me that Voegelin must be approached with a great deal of skepticism, until the allegedly libertarian basis of his thought becomes a lot clearer than it is now. His devotion to Plato indicates the exact opposite than libertarian.

---

9   Editor's note: The parenthetical question marks are Rothbard's own.

III. History

1. Marxism and Charles Beard

April 1954

An evaluation of the extent of Marxist ideas in the work of Charles A. Beard is an extraordinarily difficult task. Due to his remarkably prolific output over the years, and the changes that took place in his ideas, I can do no more here than indicate some of the points that would be significant in any full-scale attempt to evaluate Beard's writings and influence as a whole.

In the first place, it cannot be denied that Beard was an out-and-out socialist. His socialism was of the nationalist variety, garbed in the trappings of complete central planning. Beard was one of the major and more extreme prophets of the New Deal, at least in its "domestic" sphere. A glance, for example, at chapter 13 of his *Open Door at Home* (New York, 1935) indicates clearly and definitely his collectivist proposals. Probably his chief difference from other rabid New Dealers was his consistency in advocating tariffs and exchange control.

Beard's *political* views are not at issue here, however, but rather his view of history as related to the Marxian view. Perhaps the best way of approaching his views of history is to consider his famous *An Economic Interpretation of the Constitution of the United States* (1913) and his new introduction to the revised edition of 1935. Beard states in these pages that when he approached American history in 1913 there were three dominant interpretative schools in American history. One, which he rather sneeringly referred to as the belief in divine guidance peculiarly granted to America, was, he asserted, typified by George Bancroft; the second was the "Teutonic" belief in the peculiar genius of the Anglo-Saxon race, typified by the Englishman [William] Stubbs; and the third were those pure fact-grubbers who merely presented a series of facts, without explanation.

He was particularly disgusted with the consequently prevailing view of the Constitution among historians as a quasi-divine instrument. Beard claims that his famous economic interpretation was inspired not by Marx, as many historians had charged, but by James Madison's famous Federalist No. 10. Beard quotes a passage from Madison which more or less sums up his new orientation:

> So strong is this propensity of mankind to fall into mutual animosities, that . . . the most frivolous and fanciful distinctions have been sufficient to kindle their unfriendly passions and excite their most violent conflicts. But the most common and durable source of factions has been the various and unequal distribution of property. Those who hold and those who are without property have ever formed distinct interests in society. Those who are creditors, and those who are debtors, fall under a like discrimination. A landed interest, a manufacturing interest, a mercantile interest, a moneyed interest, with many lesser interests, grow up of necessity in civilized nations, and divide them into different classes, actuated by different sentiments and views. The regulation of these various and interfering interests forms the principal task of modern legislation. . . .

This concept of clashes of economic interest was applied to the struggle over the Constitution by Beard, and later to other problems, including the whole sweep of American history in the *Rise of American Civilization* (1927). In his works, his use of economic interest was on a class basis, as has been indicated, and stressing the distinction between the propertied and the nonpropertied, although like Marx before him, he was forced to use various subdivisions, such as the "capitalist" (money and securities) interest as opposed to the "landed" interest, and, particularly, the creditors as against the debtors.

In defending himself against the charge of Marxism, he agreed that his position was similar to Marx in the matter of class conflict and history, but asserted that Marx, in this case, was also following in the Madison tradition. In particular, Beard cited as in this "economic interpretation" tradition the seventeenth-century English political philosopher [James] Harrington; Madison; the Federalists, including Chief Justice Marshall; and the historian Richard Hildreth. All of these antedated Marx.

In this claim to be the inheritor of the Federalist Party interpretation of American history, Beard was correct. The Federalist view of the struggle over the Constitution was that it represented a class conflict between wealthy commercial capitalist creditors on the one hand and poor agrarian debtors on the other. This Federalist interpretation was carried on and applied throughout early-nineteenth-century American politics to the agitation over paper money, over stay laws for debts, over land policies, over the tariff, etc. It was carried on by Whig historians (National Republicans) such as Hildreth.

The difference between the attitude taken by the Federalists and Whigs to these struggles, as against later twentieth-century socialists, was that the former favored the allegedly "capitalist" side, while the latter favored the allegedly "agrarian" or "anticapitalist" side. But despite the vast political differences, the economic and class interpretations of history were the same by both camps. Both the eighteenth- and nineteenth-century Federalists and Whigs, and the latter-day socialists believed that the poor debtor farmers were anti-tariff, pro–paper money, anti–Central Bank, anti-Constitution, etc.; while the rich capitalist creditors were pro-tariff, anti–paper money, pro–Central Bank, pro-Constitution.

Beard could not bring himself to believe that any of the contenders actually believed in such vague abstractions as states' rights, national unity, general welfare, etc. He believed it much more likely that they were really motivated by their *immediate* economic class interest. Thus, manufacturers would tend to be pro-tariff, farmers opposed, creditors for hard money, debtors for paper money, etc.

In answering the charges of Marxism leveled by Professor T.C. Smith, who dealt with clashes of *ideas* in political history, Beard objects that Smith "does not say how those (ideas) . . . got into American heads" and does not show that they may [not] have been "conditioned if not determined by economic interests and activities." Beard told historians that when we see people advocating or resisting political changes in terms of abstract theories such as states' rights or national power, we should ask the question, what interests are behind them—to whose advantage will changes, or maintenance of status quo, accrue?

Accepting the Federalist-Whig tradition, Beard termed the Constitution the instrument of the propertied class to protect itself from the nonpropertied. In general, government itself is based on the making of rules and the defense of property relations. Beard also cited [Rudolf von] Jhering and [Ferdinand] Lassalle as predecessors in this type of analysis. In sum, he declared that party doctrines and so-called political principles "originate in the sentiments and views which the possession of various kinds of property creates in the minds of the possessors."

Baldly, his class-interest doctrine is sheer nonsense, both methodologically and for American history. There are no homogeneous classes on the market, only individual interests. Indeed, the alleged "classes" on the market are usually the ones in strongest competition with each other. There is no basic conflict of interest between the propertied and the nonpropertied; in the first place, they are not rigid "classes" on the free market; secondly, it is one of the great truths of economics that the nonpropertied as well as, if not even more than, the propertied benefit from the free market economy based on the defense of the rights of private property. On the free market, therefore, there are no clashing class interests.

As Professor Mises has pointed out, the basic difference almost never explained is between "class" and "caste." The class-conflict theorists, from Madison to Beard through Marx, use analysis appropriate only to the latter applied to the former. Where certain groups are specially privileged or specially disabled through the coercive power of the state, they become *castes*, and these castes are definitely in conflict. While on the free market, one man's gain is another man's gain, wherever government intervenes and establishes favored and unfavored castes, one man's or one caste's gain is another caste's loss. Where government intervenes, there is inevitable "caste conflict." Thus, if wool manufacturers ask for a tariff on wool and fail to get it from the State, they remain diverse individuals competing on the market; but if they do get it from the State, they become a privileged caste with a common interest against other castes.

Here it should be pointed out that Professor Richard Hofstadter, a Beard disciple, has applied the class-struggle theories to Calhoun, making Calhoun to appear an ancestor of Marx. On the contrary, Calhoun in essence had the caste theory, although he used the term *class*. Calhoun defined the ruling caste as being the caste that receives more in government subsidy than it pays in taxes, while the ruled caste are the people who pay more in taxes than they receive from the government.

Furthermore, it is nonsense to assert that men will always follow their immediate monetary interest, that all other ideals are pure sham. This is flagrant error. Rather than being motivated by objective monetary interest, in fact, man is motivated by all sorts of ideas, including ideas about his monetary advancement. But even there, the latter are not necessarily controlling. This notion of so-called purely "economic" motivation is not specifically Marxism, which concentrates more on the productive forces, but Marx himself made much use of this technique, which verges closely on polylogism. When abstract ideas are written off and reduced to their alleged "economic" motives, this is a Marxist polylogism, and something I am sure the Federalists never committed. A particularly flagrant use of polylogism by Beard is his dismissal of Bancroft's religious view by calling it "his deference to the susceptibilities of the social class from which he sprung."

Beard's specific class analysis was completely erroneous as well. Thus, as [Joseph] Dorfman and others have shown, in all of the early American controversies cited above, there were capitalists, merchants, manufacturers, farmers, etc. on both sides of each issue. It is obvious theoretically, and illustrated historically, that various "capitalists" will favor, as well as oppose, paper money in any given period. It is absurd to consider debtors as confined to poor, or to farmers. There were, even in those days, a great many wealthy debtors. Furthermore, it is impossible without minute investigation of a man's financial record to say whether or not any given merchant was a "debtor" or "creditor" at any given time. The so-called "class lines" of this favorite class of the historians were almost ludicrously fluid.

Despite these overwhelming defects, Beard did make an important contribution to historiography. If material motives are not the whole story, they are certainly part of it, and in the time that Beard began his work, this area was almost completely neglected by American historians. Furthermore, it is precisely these pecuniary motives that the various figures on the historical stage will be most inclined to conceal. If people hold certain political views from a mixture of motives, they will almost always proclaim their "idealistic" motives and hide their "personal interest" in the matter. Beard performed a great service in impelling historians to devote their attention to uncovering the latter factors.

This is particularly true in the historiography of the Constitution, where an almost ludicrous myth had been created about the Founding Fathers. Beard pointed out that there were excellent caste reasons why holders of government securities, for example, were anxious to create a strong central government with tax powers to greatly increase the value of their bonds, which had been heavily in arrears of interest; why speculators in western lands wished to create a strong government to crush the Indian tribes in the West so that their lands would rise in value; why the politically powerful society of army officers agitated for a central-taxing government both for increase in the value of their old bonds and to spur the creation of a larger army, etc. Certainly it is no more than common sense for the historian to take such motives into account when evaluating the historical role of people, provided of course that this is not taken as eliminating the need for examining the validity of their ideas on their own grounds.

It is probable that Beard deliberately overstated his Marxian position because of the general neglect of the monetary motives. In later works he toned down his position considerably until in the *Open Door at Home* he declared that ideas and interests were equally determining and mutually interacting.

2. Review of Jackson Turner Main, *The Antifederalists*

April 23, 1962

Mr. Kenneth S. Templeton, Jr.
William Volker Fund
Burlingame, California

Dear Ken:

Jackson Turner Main's *The Antifederalists* is a desperate, chaotic rear-guard action on behalf of the Beard-Jensen "class struggle" interpretation of the adoption of the Constitution.[10] The "orthodox" [Charles A.] Beard-[Carl L.] Becker-[Merrill M.] Jensen view has been riddled from all sides in recent years, for the revolutionary and later periods. Main attempts to restate the old shibboleths while still defending them from the "revisionist" attacks.

The result is a tangle of confusion and chaos. Time and time again, Main stubbornly affirms the essentials of the class-struggle view: that the Constitution was an imposition of the "well born" and the "few" against the small farmers and the "many"; of the "creditor class" against the "debtors"; of the urban against the rural, etc. And

---

[10] Jackson Turner Main, *The Antifederalists: Critics of the Constitution, 1781–1788* (Chapel Hill, N.C.: Published for the Institute of Early American History and Culture at Williamsburg, Va., by the University of North Carolina Press, 1961).

yet, in each case he is continually forced to admit grave exceptions and concessions, until the "class struggle" viewpoint becomes a desperate shibboleth rather than a conclusion from the facts. The whole book impresses me as a struggle by Main to maintain his fallacious *a priori* categories in the face of the recalcitrant historical facts.

All the old absurdities are yet revived: e.g., that the anti-Federalists were in favor of paper money (the "debtor classes") even though many of the leaders were against it, etc. And so, if Main grudgingly admits that the anti-Federalist *leaders* were wealthy, well, then, their *followers* were poor, small farmerish, etc. If he admits that the urban masses—the mechanics, artisans, etc.—were pro-Federalist as well as the merchants, well, then, the "class struggle" is modified, so that while the whole struggle is one of poor vs. rich, it turns out that the urban poor were enlisted in the "rich" group, etc. Many states simply do not fit at all.

It is remarkable that Main is able to drag in all of these class-struggle interpretations even though he also admits that they are mutually contradictory: the urban poor among the rich, the *rich* debtors who favored paper money, etc. In his desperate attempt to salvage the class-struggle thesis, Main adds yet *another* "class" and class struggle to this chaotic mélange: the "mercantile community."

The "mercantile community," led by the wicked merchants, includes *all* the urban people (although somehow at least the physicians were anti-Federalist) plus the farmers, big *and* small (although he tries to maintain that in essence they were big), who live in the trade-centered river valleys *vs.* the "self-sufficient" community of subsistence farmers. *Why* the entire "mercantile community" is supposed to form one "class" or economic interest group, is never really explained, nor is it explained why they should all be pro-Constitution. Nor is the "self-sufficient" interest in proposing the Constitution, explained—the shibboleths about "democracy," "aristocracy," etc., which Main tosses around continually, explain nothing here.

Forrest McDonald has shown in his *We the People* that the self-sufficient farmers could be said to have economic interest both for and against the Constitution, depending on the state involved, and that the merchants, much less the catch-all "mercantile community," must be split up into numerous different interest groups if one wants to talk of mercantile interests intelligibly.

Similarly, Main's hobbyhorse "democracy" is another vague, catch-all, ill-defined concept (in fact, never defined by Main) that he sees as the key to the anti-Federalist position, in a struggle against the "few" and "aristocracy." These concepts are peculiarly ill fitting to the times and irrelevant to the main struggle over the Constitution—which is over centralized power vs. states' rights, and not over "democracy" vs. the "few"—as well as slippery and undefined.

Main, typical of his continuing war with the facts, admits that the word "democracy" was used but seldom by the anti-Federalists, but explains it away as a tactic to disarm the opposition. Again, the leaders—or some leaders—are conceded not to be concerned with democracy, but the followers are supposed to be. But the leaders were the ones who articulated the position, which leaves Main's position a rather mystical one. Indeed, if *both* groups were led by wealthy and eminent men—as is true of every broad-based movement in politics—and the followers are poor, what happens to the struggle for "democracy" vs. "aristocracy" or the quasi-Marxian struggle of rich vs. poor?

Main also links egalitarianism in with "democracy," even though there is almost no evidence of egalitarian views either. For "proof" of his contentions, Main is reduced to isolated quotations by one writer or another, denouncing the opposition as being a "rabble" or by someone talking of the "middling interest" or the "well-born."

Naturally, in every country and every age, there are well-born, poor, and people in between. And if one wants to separate them into "classes," one can spend one's time doing so, though fruitlessly. But so are there an infinite number of other "classes" in society: occupational groups, religious groups, chess players and non–chess players, etc. The reason why Jack Main insists on proliferating and imposing his "class" schema on the events is that he insists that these classes are *inherently* in conflict: that the "class interests" of the various groups are innately at loggerheads; that the small property owners are innately in conflict of interest with the large property owners, that the merchants and farmers are inherently at odds, that creditors and debtors form distinct antagonistic "classes," etc.

This is the *a priori* mistake, the methodological fallacy, that sets Jackson Main in quasi-Marxistical and perpetual war with the facts, trying desperately to fit recalcitrant reality into his supposedly conflicting class categories. All of this would be swept away if he realized that these classes—and all other classes, for that matter—are *not* inherently conflicting, that if they have anything to do with each other at all, it is, objectively, a peaceful harmony, a peaceful, productive, voluntary network of trade and exchanges, linking all individuals—and *individuals* are the primary reality, *not* the constructed "classes"—into the mutually advantageous free market.

Also, in Marxist manner, Main, while dealing slightly with the libertarian, anti–central power aspect of anti-Federalism, tends to dismiss it brusquely as a "rationalization" of class interest, and subordinate also to "democracy" and egalitarianism.

Actually, there is a small nub of truth in the class-struggle thesis, and its attempted application to the Revolution-Constitution period by Beard. The nub of truth has been twisted by the Marxists and neo-Marxist historians, indeed by Marx himself. Marx postulated that there are inherently conflicting classes *within* society, within the market, as well as outside it, and that their evolution through conflict was determined by "laws of history." (Beard, the Populist historians, etc. use the class and class-conflict analysis of history without necessarily accepting the "laws of history" prophesying.) But Marx acquired his class theory from Saint-Simon, who, in turn, garbled and twisted it from its *original* thesis, which was, in contrast, highly libertarian.

This thesis—which Mises would call a *caste*-conflict theory—and which anticipated its modern formulation by Albert Jay Nock, was developed by Charles Dunoyer and Charles Comte in the immediate Restoration period in France. This postulated *two* essential "classes" or castes: the *State*, and its subsidized favorites; and the *public*, who are exploited by the State.

This was the original "class" analysis and exploitation analysis; the State, and its subsidizees, *exploited* the *producing* public. The producers included everyone on the free market, from manufacturers to laborers. Saint-Simon, Marx, etc. twisted this around to *add* the "capitalists" to the list of exploiters and to dub the "producers" as only the proletariat. The only remnant of Beardian hypothesis that has interest, therefore, is when he concentrated, e.g., on the class (caste) interest of veteran army officers in federal government pensions or on the interests of government security holders. (Here the *empirical* importance of security holders has turned out to be negligible for the Constitution but at least the *hypothesis* was cogent. However, there appears to be much more foundation for government security-holder interest behind the Hamiltonian debt-assumption program—a much more direct causation, of course, than in considering the Constitution as a whole.)

To do a completely thorough evaluation of the book would require detailed checking of the sources, detailed comparison and contrast of Main and McDonald, more reading on the Main-McDonald controversy, etc. But the whoppers are plentiful enough to say that this book is hopeless as any sort of significant grappling with the problem.

Contrast to this tangle the brilliant and incisive article of Professor Cecilia Kenyon, "Men of Little Faith."[11] Kenyon, not shackled by Marxist categories, sees clearly and demonstrates incisively that the anti-Federalists were essentially *not* "democrats" or egalitarians or wild-eyed rebels, but basically libertarian types, who feared and disliked the increased centralization of State power (via control of commerce, new federal taxes, "general welfare," etc.) manifesting itself in the new Constitution. Here, in the ideological realm, and in the problem of liberty vs. more central power, is the nub of the conflict. And while Kenyon of course defends the central power and chides the anti-Federalists as being "men of little faith" in the new opportunities of bigger government, the reputation of the anti-Federalists is

---

[11] *William and Mary Quarterly* 12 (1955): 3–46.

in better hands with their opponent, Kenyon, than with their ardent supporter, Professor Main.

3. Review of R.W. Van Alstyne, *The Rising American Empire*

March 18, 1962

Mr. Kenneth S. Templeton
William Volker Fund
Burlingame, California

Dear Ken:

R.W. Van Alstyne, *The Rising American Empire* (Oxford University Press, 1960) is a lively work that forms an extreme example, perhaps, of recent "revisionism" in the historiography of American foreign policy—which maintains that the imperialism of 1898 did *not* constitute a new, unusual break in an isolationist American past. The stress on this theme is always used as an argument against the Beard thesis that imperialism and the later internationalism and foreign interventionism were breaking with American traditions. Van Alstyne, indeed, claims that America began its plunge into "empire" even *before* the American Revolution, and continued surging onward from then on, 1898 only constituting its climactic *end*. This "completed" the "structure of the American Empire," and since then American empire building has been "more of a problem of consolidation and rendering secure what has been gained."

Now this guiding thesis I believe to be nonsense; certainly British expansionism before the American Revolution can hardly be attributed to America, despite occasional American support. Nor can the sensible and hardly imperialist attempt of the Revolutionary country to solicit aid from France be called significant. While it is true that America and American agents did many aggressive and imperialistic things throughout the nineteenth century, they can hardly be comparable in extent with the brazen acquisitions of the Spanish-American War.

Further, Van Alstyne is able to make his case by the inadmissible method of lumping expansionist actions into virtually *uninhabited* territory—or even such purchases as Louisiana—with aggressive actions against lands populated by other peoples, and also by lumping economic expansion (such as increased trade in the Pacific) with *governmental* expansion—though, admittedly, the American Navy tended to follow—and sometimes precede—the trade. American expansion throughout the world *since* 1898 can also hardly be called mere consolidation of previously won empire; *it* is the real shift from republic to empire. Thus, Van Alstyne can only make his point through distortion of quantitative judgment and confusion of categories.

Keeping this in mind, however, there is a great deal of fascinating and useful material in Van Alstyne, especially of neglected and little-known instances of American governmental intervention overseas, in Mexico, etc. There is useful material on the machinations of President Polk, of agitation to invade and acquire Canada and Mexico, of the aggressive designs of Theodore Roosevelt, etc.

It is also good to see Van Alstyne not falling for the lure of recent "revisionism" whitewashing Polk, Madison in the War of 1812, etc., and also to see the Monroe Doctrine considered an *anti*-British, rather than pro-British, policy. There is no "Britain the naval bulwark and partner" myth making in Van Alstyne; indeed, there is a refreshing cynicism toward much cant, such as the Open Door, U.S. missionary activities in China and Hawaii, etc. There is a great deal of interesting material on imperialist drives toward the Caribbean, on New England connivance at the atrocity in Acadia, etc.

Van Alstyne's guiding principle is hostility to moral principle or moral crusading in foreign policy; as a result, the *material* that he presents would ordinarily be taken as damaging to American imperialism. But Van Alstyne, divorcing himself from morality and concerned only and rather cynically with *realpolitik*, is evidently enamored of American imperialism, of Theodore Roosevelt, etc. Not isolationism, not the crusading of Wilson or FDR, but the blunt imperialism of T.R. ("[t]he American Bismarck, without the arrogance and the aloofness") seems to be Van Alstyne's foreign policy ideal.

4. Review of Robert V. Remini, *Martin Van Buren and the Making of the Democratic Party*

March 8, 1961

Mr. Kenneth S. Templeton
William Volker Fund

Dear Ken:

Martin Van Buren, one of the best presidents the United States ever had, is also one of the most underrated by historians, who generally have dismissed Van as being weak and wily, a mere trickster. Robert V. Remini, in his *Martin Van Buren and the Making of the Democratic Party* (Columbia University Press, 1959) sets out to right the historiographic balance for a critical period in Van's life and does a good job of it.

Remini's book deals not with Van Buren the president but Van Buren the chief architect of the Democratic Party, which emerged out of the era of the 1820s. In this well-written and well-researched book, Remini revises the usual view of historians of Van Buren as a mere political trickster and organizer, who brought about Jackson's victory in 1823 for purely personal reasons of party intrigue.

Not only does Remini correct the errors of these and other historians in refuting various allegations of trickery (such as the accepted myth that Van Buren introduced the Tariff of Abominations in 1828 *intending* to defeat it); Remini also shows, in excellent fashion, that Van Buren's main aim, at which he succeeded brilliantly, was *ideological*—that he was out to forge an ideologically-based party, and chose General Jackson as the proper vehicle, not *vice versa*. In this book, Remini shows us some of the true stature of Martin Van Buren.

Historians have generally misleadingly called the era of Monroe the "Era of Good Feelings," as if everything were quiet and content politically. Remini knows that this was very far from the case. Actually, President Monroe had strong leanings in the direction of the old Federalist cause, and, with the disappearance of the Federalist Party during the War of 1812, Federalists began drifting into the Republican ranks. Monroe began to use the one-party result to bring about "unity," i.e., to make more and more appointments that were quasi-Federalist and to move, though very cautiously, in Federalist-étatist directions at home and abroad. Though a Virginian, Monroe was never trusted by the great Virginia libertarians, and the problem grew as he began to maneuver to deny the nomination to his "natural" heir, the "Old Republican" William H. Crawford.

The principles of the "Old Republican" cause, the famous "principles of '98," were the principles of American liberty: individual liberty, minimal government, rigid economy, states' rights, strict construction, opposition to "internal improvements" or to government intervention, "isolationism" and "neutralism" in foreign affairs. What had happened to the great principles of '98? After four excellent years under the Jefferson administration, Jefferson and Madison began to desert their old cause in a drive toward war with England, and in that war came the Bank of the United States, internal taxation, high tariffs, larger government, etc. Through these war years, only such patriots as John Randolph of Roanoke and the Quaker George Logan stood fast to the old principles.

Martin Van Buren was never a great theoretician—certainly not in these years. But he sensed the important problem of the early 1820s—the slow, steady withering away of Old Republican principles, what with affairs being conducted by Monroe and Chief Justice Marshall, and Federalists drifting into office. A man who thought brilliantly in terms of parties and politics rather than in theoretical issues, Van Buren saw (1) that the Old Republican principles were dissolving, and (2)—and *here* was his great contribution—that it was necessary to reconstitute the Republican Party to make it, once again, an ideological vehicle for what were essentially libertarian views.

In the critical 1824 struggle, he therefore joined with his fellow "radicals," such as the great leader of the Richmond Junto, Thomas Ritchie, to support Crawford, and he was loyal to Crawford to the very end. Particularly important—and Remini captures the drama of this moment very well—was Van Buren's personal meeting with his idol, Jefferson; this meeting sharpened Van Buren's Jeffersonian ideology, especially when he realized that Jefferson's view of the Monroe administration was essentially the same as his own.

After the election, as John Quincy Adams began to unfold the essence of his Federalist plan to aggrandize the national government at home and abroad, Van Buren's views sharpened as he lashed out at Adams for infringing on individual and states' rights at home and abroad. Finally, Van Buren set himself the task of building a new party out of this now-dead Republican Party, a party, as he put it, composed of "Old Republican" loyalties carried forward by the magic of the hero, Andrew Jackson.

With brilliant organization, allying himself with "Old Republican" forces, such as Ritchie, in other states, Van Buren succeeded in forging the new party, converting the purely personal Jacksonian movement of 1824 into a libertarian-ideological Jackson party of 1828. In short, realizing that Jackson's ideological views were barely formed, Van Buren *pushed* Jackson into the Old Republican camp by presenting him with a fully structured Jacksonian party along those ideological lines.

Thus was the great Democratic Party born, and so well was it forged that it was to continue along a similar ideological path for the rest of the century. (It was one of the ironic quirks of history that Van Buren's tragic shift into the anti-Southern camp, causing him to oppose the admission of Texas in 1844, broke up the Democratic Party on the slavery issue, an issue that was to cripple the party for generations.)

This, of course, is not to imply that Van Buren was a pure, or notable, libertarian theorist; he always trimmed, for example, on the tariff question, undoubtedly due to pro-tariff sentiment in New York and the North. But his services as a political organizer were first-rate, and, in Remini's account, he at last receives his due.

Remini's work, as I've said, is well written and well researched—and worth reading for any student of American political history. There are numerous indications of unfortunate bias on the part of Professor Remini, however, which should be noted:

(1) How properly Remini understands the "Old Republican" principles is open to question, especially as, at the conclusion, he speaks in terms of the Democratic "people," the "many" versus the Federalist "few," the Democrats as the party of the "common man," etc. This is mainly rubbish and reflects orthodox historiography. Actually, as Remini himself shows, Van Buren did yeoman work for the caucus system of nominations, in loyalty to Jeffersonian principles, and also, for quite a while—and in face of fierce local opposition—opposed democratizing the electoral laws in New York. Also, Remini, in presenting the usual view about extensions of suffrage in this era, ignores the recent research of Robert Brown, Chilton Williamson (which, to be sure, was published after Remini's book), and others, which indicate that the extent of democratizing voting in this period was very small. (A recent study has shown that a significant increase of votes, in proportion to total adult males, only came in the election of *1840,* which confirms what I have long suspected: that the *real* outpouring of "democracy" and mass voting came as a result of demagogic campaigning by the desperate Whigs in 1840, led by the conniver Thurlow Weed.)

(2) Remini, several times, attacks Van Buren's loyal adhesion to states' rights and strict construction, deprecating various constitutional amendments that Van Buren proposed to limit government power still further (e.g., the power to spend on internal improvements). (Van Buren, by the way, wanted to limit *state,* as well as federal, internal improvements.)

(3) Remini attacks Van Buren for his loyal adhesion to the cause of William Crawford in 1824.

(4) Remini several times levels unwarranted and deprecatory personal attacks on various eminent statesmen. Most flagrant is his

dismissal of the great Randolph as "lunatic" and "half-crazed." (It was during this very period, by the way, that Randolph was influential in forming the subsequently libertarian social philosophy of Thomas H. Benton.) Remini further dismisses Rep. George Kremer of Pennsylvania as a "ridiculous" figure, without telling us why. Kremer distinguished himself as being one of the purest libertarian politicians in the history of the United States, voting against almost every appropriation bill, every extension of government, etc. (Once, he voted against the "extravagance" of paving Washington's streets!)

(5) Remini calls the doctrine of nullification "pernicious."

(6) Van Buren's idea of curbing executive appointment and other power, Remini dismisses brusquely as flagrantly partisan.

(7) Remini makes too much of a concession of "greatness" to the designs of John Quincy Adams.

It seems indicated that Remini, while certainly approving of Van Buren, and doing a service by concentrating on Van and rehabilitating his reputation, is himself far from a believer in the Old Republican principles for which Van Buren fought. He seems to be more of a current-type historian, favoring the supposed "democracy" and common-man aspects of Democratic-Republican doctrine. However, I am looking forward to the biography of Van Buren—who has virtually no biographies—on which Remini is apparently working—with great interest.

5. Report on George B. DeHuszar and Thomas Hulbert Stevenson, *A History of the American Republic*, 2 vols.

September 1961

To begin with an "overview" (to use a favorite and perhaps overused term of DeHuszar's), this is, to put it bluntly, a poor book. Any work on American history, even a textbook, has certain tasks that it must perform and standards to which it must cleave. In the first place, the factual material must be rich and not skimpy; the reader must get an idea of the lavish tapestry of American history, and he must get a full and comprehensive picture. Most of the detailed critique below is devoted to protestations about the great amount of important material that DeHuszar has left out of the narrative. Just to pick an isolated instance, I do not think much of a text on American history that does not so much as mention Senator Thomas Hart ("Old Bullion") Benton.

This is an almost extraordinarily skimpy work, a skimpiness that pervades the book but that reaches embarrassing proportions in the treatment of the colonial period and of the late-nineteenth-century period. Sometimes we find that almost the only people mentioned in an era are the presidential candidates. Furthermore, a critical defect is the almost complete absence of any quantitative or numerical data. It is often difficult to find the *dates* at which happenings occur, so vague and imprecise is the narrative. Apart from a few references to population figures, there are virtually no statistics of any kind in the work.

Now, I am an open and long-time condemner of the overuse of statistics, and I deplore as much as anyone the new trend in "scientific" economic history to hurl vast quantities of processed statistics at the reader, and conclude that one has captured the "feel" and essence of the past. But *some* statistics, surely, are necessary; and it becomes annoying to read constant references to "increases" in steel production, or living standards, or whatnot, when not the foggiest quantitative notion is presented to the reader of *how large* these increases and movements are. There is also an almost desperate need to present governmental budget statistics, so that the reader will know how large government in relation to the private economy has been in any given era; but neither in this nor in any other area does DeHuszar give a shred of quantitative data.

The first test of a historical work then, and one that DeHuszar fails, is a richness of factual material. But the historian is more than a chronicler; he must also have a command of the significance of events, he must be able to convey to the reader the meaning and interpretation of the past. If we would be grandiloquent, we might even use Schumpeter's term of "vision"; the historian must have a "vision" of the meaning, of the significance, of the material he is presenting. Lamentable as is the skimpiness of DeHuszar's factual material, it is in this area of *meaning* in which he fails the most; for the largest bulk of the narrative, there is no meaning, no interpretation, no vision presented of the American past: there is just dull, uninspired, unimaginative chronicle.

What good is it to list the provisions of the Compromise of 1850, or of the Kansas-Nebraska Act, if there is not the slightest attempt to explain the causes of the Civil War? There is no need to revert to the "Paul Revere Ride" school of historical writing to realize that the American past is filled with high drama, and it is tragic if this drama is not conveyed to the reader and student. But to convey it, one must realize it is there, and DeHuszar shows no sign of doing so: there is, for example, the high drama of the Republican movement, of the great ideological war between the Jeffersonian Republicans and the Republican idea, and the Federalist-Whig idea. Not understanding the connections, DeHuszar never presents the meaningful conflict.

From DeHuszar's narrative one would never know that Van Buren reconstructed the Republican Party into the Democratic Party because he was inspired by what were fondly referred to for many years as the Principles of '98 (the Jeffersonian movement, the Virginia and Kentucky Resolutions, as against the "despots of '98") and wanted to cast out the Federalist taint; one would never realize the continuity of Jeffersonian and Jacksonian principles, or of Federalism and Whiggery (Federalism's mass-based variant).

Never do we get any insight into the political-philosophic meaning of the Jackson war against the Bank: a drive for the separation of banking and the State, as part of a general libertarian drive for separation of the government and the economy, for highly limited government, etc.

Never do we see the high hopes brought in by the Revolution of 1800, only to find Federalism returning because of the drive for war in the War of 1812. Never do we get a sense of the tragic consequences of the Civil War, or of its permanent fastening of Federalist-Whig étatism on American life and the tragic wreck of the Democratic Party. The reader will not realize that it was the Civil War and its Republican aftermath that fastened upon America excise taxation, high tariffs, heavy public debt, federal governmental banking, the draft, the income tax, government intervention in railroads, etc. Many of these facts are mentioned very briefly, but the meaning of the change is never brought to the fore.

Note what I am *not* asking for here: I am not asking simply that DeHuszar present American history from a libertarian point of view, that he favor liberty and oppose its restriction. I am asking that he present a meaningful picture of the American past, and not simply a World Almanac chronicle of events, which is what most of the book boils down to.

In fact, most of the book reads like some other American history textbook boiled down into its bare outlines; it reads as if the authors have virtually no first-hand familiarity with the material, or with monographic works. Indeed, I found that large portions of the book had such a close similarity to the detailed organization, and even style, of Hicks's famous text *The Federal Union* as to begin to challenge coincidence.

Not understanding the import or meaning of *political* events in the American past is joined, in this work, with an almost absolute failure to point out the *consequences* of various government actions. This is particularly true and particularly unfortunate in DeHuszar's *economic* history. The pitfall that DeHuszar falls into is this: if a history of economic events is simply *chronicled*, as DeHuszar does, it is inevitable that an inner bias is given *in favor* of the event, whatever that event may be—and this is the reason why so much of American historiography simply celebrates the events that happened. In economics, this is particularly true; thus, if the historian records that government subsidized railroads, if just left as is, it seems like a fine thing that more railroads were built. But a historian with sound economic knowledge must point out that such railroads represented "overinvestment" and malinvestment in railroads, which they did. But DeHuszar does not do this, and as a result, his economic narrative, in addition to being chronicle rather than meaningful history, is often unwittingly biased in favor of the government action he records.

This failure in the economic realm is not chance; for throughout the volume, DeHuszar conveys a lamentable failure to understand even elementary economic principles; almost all the economics is garbled, even when well meant, and is generally valueless.

For the great bulk of their text, DeHuszar and Stevenson hack out their narrative of dull, uninspired chronicle, bereft of significance or of sound economics—and with the chronicle extremely skimpy at that. (A *World Almanac* that fails even as an almanac!)

In the last half of the second volume, the book suddenly begins to come to life, and the authors begin to introduce interpretation, etc. One feels that if they are not interested or in tune with the bulk of the American past, they *are* interested in American history since, say, 1929. DeHuszar makes a heroic attempt to present a sound, "revisionist," portrayal of the causes of the 1929 depression, and the Coolidge credit expansion and Hoover New Deal that caused and aggravated it; at some of this they succeed, but the inevitable garbling of economic ideas that pervades the work makes this account spotty, if superior to the rest of the book.

Also, when discussing the domestic measures of the New Deal, the authors rise above their other narrative, and engage in some good criticisms of the economic failure and the political shift of power to the State that the New Deal represents. It is in its discussion of the New Deal that the book takes on some character and value. But even here, poor economic knowledge weighs the authors down. An example of a lost opportunity: there is no better model example of the cumulative errors of government intervention than the American farm program, where one set of controls and interventions created such problems as to lead to still more in a vain attempt at correction. And yet, DeHuszar does not see this, and so lets a fine illustration of economic law and interconnectedness slip by and degenerate again into mere chronicle.

While pretty good on the New Deal, however, DeHuszar and Stevenson slip back into dull insignificance in their discussion of the Truman and Eisenhower eras, and in particular, there is no realization of the significance of the Eisenhower era and its cementing of the New Deal into the bipartisan structure of American political life. By failing to see the significance of Eisenhower as Republican conservator of the New Deal, DeHuszar lapses back into chronicle, and by implication, sometimes even express, implies that while the New Deal was unfortunate, the Eisenhower administration was pretty darn good.

But while the Herbert Hoover and Franklin Roosevelt domestic policies are set forth and explained fairly well, this is more than offset by the extreme bias, error, and evasion of fact that characterize DeHuszar and Stevenson's discussion of foreign affairs in this generation. While inadequate and biased on World War I, the authors adopt and trumpet every bit of propaganda nonsense of American foreign policy for World Wars II and III. Oversimplified absurdities about "German and Japanese aggression" abound, after which we segue awkwardly into similar absurdities about "Soviet aggression." Naturally, as with his historical confreres, there is an awkwardness in the transition from celebrating the great battle against the German enemy into sounding the alarm against the Soviet one. But not an iota of revisionism has been allowed to correct the florid colors of "official" history that the authors ladle into their presentations of American foreign policy. Going further back, the authors welcome the shift of America into imperialism, claim that imperialism showers benefits as it goes, and take the myth-making view of the alleged sanctity of the alleged "Open Door."

Thus, while, in the later decades, DeHuszar and Stevenson inject some interpretation into their previously dull and skimpy chronicle, their interpretation of the Hoover and Roosevelt New Deals is fairly sound though not outstanding, but this is more than offset by the extreme bias in favor of the official historical "line" that the authors lavish on the reader *in re* World Wars II and III.

Of the difficulties of skimpiness that I have mentioned, one needs a little more elaboration here. That is the almost complete absence of *intellectual* history, of the people and the ideas that have been important in America. It is typical, for example, of the intellectual paucity of this work that, while Communism is held up to be a diabolic enemy, it is never even passably defined; the reader only knows that the Communists are a band of people who took over Russia in 1917 and who want to "conquer the world."

As a result, the reader never learns that Communism is simply one consistent wing of *socialism* (DeHuszar persistently refers to Communists and socialists only as "political extremists"—a peculiarly uninformative term), and therefore there is no link between Communists and previous Marxian and other socialists, much less any realization that socialism, in turn, is simply an extreme wing of statism. If DeHuszar had begun to point these things out, as any competent historian should, then the reader *might* get the idea that the reason why Communism may be considered an enemy is precisely that it represents socialism or extreme statism—but this would mean a recasting of the reader's mind into examining ideologies, and domestic ideologies at that, rather than launching yet another crusade against yet another band of foreign devils, who obscurely want to "conquer" people.

DeHuszar's treatment of domestic Communists as simply "agents of Moscow"—ignoring the fact that they are only "agents" because they are ideological allies—perpetuates this misrepresentation.

We can only conclude from this "overview" that a good textbook on American history was almost desperately needed; and, after reading the DeHuszar-Stevenson manuscript, we can only say that it is *still* needed, perhaps even all the more.

And now for a detailed critique of the DeHuszar manuscript:

The Colonial Era

There is virtually *nothing* on the entire American colonial period; surely it is a disgrace to condense the century and a half of the American colonial experience into thirty-odd pages.

- There is nothing, for example, about early Plymouth Rock communism and its failure.

- Page 3 seems to slight American rebelliousness by saying that, after 1763, Americans "felt oppressed" by the British, while before they "accepted" British protection.

- There is insufficient stress on the British increase of measures of intervention and restriction.

- It doesn't explain that overweighting of property owners on the *coast* in the colonial legislatures largely and inevitably due to the fact these are the older areas, and therefore will be overrepresented as populations shift, and apportionment lags.

- "Many" people could vote is too fuzzy and imprecise; there should be more use of recent voting studies (Brown, Williamson, etc.).

- Page 10—In DeHuszar's own terms, the evidence presented for colonial precedent for judicial review is highly dubious. There is no mention of fact that judicial branch was not separate, but was headed by the governor and his council. Neither was the British government's ultimate power at all akin to the later judiciary.

- Frontiersmen also "resented" the poll tax because *any* money tax is a hardship when the bulk of one's "income" is barter, or self-production.

- There is no mention of the different treatment of the Indians by the Quakers, and the different results, in the colonial period. (In fact, Indian affairs are underweighted throughout the book.) The Quakers, who had no guns, treated the Indians fairly and had no need for protection.

- The Episcopal Church "did make some effort" (p. 17) to restrict other faiths. What efforts? More specifics, please!

- There is no mention whatever of Roger Williams!

- Where were the slaves (p. 21)? Only in the South? Primarily? Or everywhere?

- What is the justification for attacking New England farming methods as "poor" (p. 22)? Poor by what standard? Wasn't land so abundant that it wasn't economic to invest in "good" methods, conserving labor instead? Did farmers not know any better, or did others know better?

- On Southern agriculture, there is a similar attack on "waste" (p. 23). By what standards again? Why "crop yield per acre"? What about crop yield per person? Or per dollar invested?

- Throughout the book, there is economic nonsense about "shortage of money"; mercantilist regulations did not compel purchases of British goods with money, so there was no expansion for alleged money shortage. There is not enough explanation of colonial paper-money schemes and their effects.

- Page 30—Was colonial medicine poorer than European medicine? Or just poor everywhere?

- On the John Peter Zenger case, see the important corrective of "Zenger revisionism" in Leonard W. Levy, *The Legacy of Suppression.*

- What *were* the Iroquois demands (p. 38)?

- There should be some more on British brutality against the Acadian French.

- There is, in the treatment of the background of the American Revolution, a distinct undertone of British apologetics. On page 42 and again on pages 47–48, for example, DeHuszar seems to agree with the British argument that the colonists must be forced to pay for British "protection." And who is to protect them from their unwanted "protectors," the British? If the colonists do not wish to pay for this "protection," what right do the British have to quarter troops among them? DeHuszar also defends the British Proclamation Line, which arbitrarily kept settlers out of western territory, and engages in nonsensical statements about the Quebec Act of 1774, saying, e.g., that the British gave the natives little political freedom "to please the people, so as to make it easier to rule them." This should be reworded and explained more clearly.

- The Pontiac War is also treated grossly inadequately; it is not pointed out that Pontiac had a good case, since the British were arbitrarily restricting Indian trade. Also, there is unfortunately no mention of Britain's great "contribution" to the art of *germ warfare*, when the British sent to Pontiac and his men blankets infected with smallpox.

- There is almost no mention of Sam Adams and Patrick Henry, and their contributions to the Revolution; the onset of the Revolution cannot be fully understood without setting forth Sam Adams's role as agitprop leader (see, for example, John C. Miller's *Sam Adams*).

In addition to the above omissions, the following are also grave omissions in the DeHuszar narrative of the colonial and pre-Revolutionary period:

- The Explorations
- The Indians—their way of life, who they were, etc.
- The problem of land tenure: feudalism, head rights, quitrent, etc.
- Puritans, witchcraft, witch-hunting, Cotton and Increase Mather
- Anne Hutchinson
- Lord Baltimore
- The British principle of "salutary neglect"
- The Regulator Rebellion—against governmental tyranny, land monopoly, and taxes
- The intellectual influence of the Enlightenment and rationalism, and John Locke
- Leisler's Rebellion
- Negro insurrections: Cato Conspiracy (1739) and the anti-Negro reign of terror in New York (1741)
- Origins of the post office
- Land grants and land speculation

- Wage and price controls in many areas
- The Rev. Jared Eliot, scientist
- The Rev. Jonathan Mayhew, rationalist
- There is nothing on the Twopenny Act and the Parson's Cause, nothing on the burning of the Gaspee, nothing on Thomas Jefferson and Richard Henry Lee and the Committee of Correspondence of Virginia.
- Discussion of the 1st Continental Congress is very weak and skimpy; there are no details of the Declaration and Resolves, no mention of Joseph Warren and the Suffolk Resolves, etc.
- The Revolutionary War period is, again, treated in a very skimpy manner. Along with the over-romanticizing of George Washington, there is nothing whatever about the pervasive price controls and the shortages they engendered, nothing on the Bank of North America: the origins of banking in America, as part of the finance of the government in war.
- Almost nothing on the connections between the American rebels and the British Whigs
- Nothing on Pelatiah Webster on the continentals
- Very little on the ouster of the Loyalists and the confiscation of their property—one of the great blots on the Revolutionary record
- No mention of Dickinson and the Olive Branch Petition, or Lord North's Conciliation Plan, or of Rockingham and Shelburne in Britain

The Confederation Period

- DeHuszar conventionally regards the federal government under the Articles as being "too weak," including the lack of power to exact taxes!
- The gravest error and bias of DeHuszar in this period is his enthusiasm for the Ordinances of 1785 and 1787, which he considers accomplishments of this period's government, "whatever

may have been its shortcomings in other fields." There is, first, no regret expressed that the states turned over their western lands to the federal government, thus adding huge unearned property to the federal government's unearned "public domain." Second, the Ordinance of 1785 was a dictatorial intrusion into the western region, which set too high a minimum land sale and price, thus restricting settlement, and also enforced rectangular surveying, thus forcing the purchase of submarginal land within an otherwise good "rectangle," instead of conforming, as in the Southern methods of surveying, to the natural topography of the land in question. In colonial days, unowned land was free to all settlers, and this represented a sharp change in the direction of étatist restriction of land settlement and increasing government revenue from land. DeHuszar shows no sign of realizing this significance of the ordinance. Furthermore, the Ordinance of 1785 foisted public schools upon each township in the region, thus taking the first step toward public schools and toward federal dictation over education. None of this seems to impress DeHuszar or dampen his enthusiasm for the ordinance.

- There is no mention of the treaty with Prussia (1785), outlawing privateering; or of the Virginia Ordinance of Religious Freedom, of which Jefferson was proudest. On the Ordinance of 1785, DeHuszar omits the fact that it *almost* provided for setting aside a section of land in each township for an established church of the denomination of the majority of residents.

- On Shays's Rebellion, DeHuszar follows the usual Federalist distortions, ignoring the large role played by hostility to increased state taxes for paying war debts in appreciated money. (Forrest MacDonald, certainly not hostile to the Federalist cause, points out that many of the Shaysite leaders favored the Constitution.) Furthermore, the discussion, again too skimpy, of the Constitution's formation, omits any mention of veterans' pensions, of public securities and government bondholders, etc.

- And yet, insofar as DeHuszar *does* present an interpretive framework for this and the subsequent years, it is watered down and naively Beardian. All sorts of complications are swept away, as we find that inflation is always backed by the "debtor interests," almost always identified with agrarians, and opposed by "creditor interests," presumably urban folk. Never does DeHuszar give any indication that these categories are not only oversimplified but fundamentally wrong (debtors, especially in that era, were not always, or even usually, agrarian). Further, he never gives any indication that the objective observer has any reason for favoring or opposing inflation, if he does not happen to be a debtor or creditor. On these monetary questions, DeHuszar can only offer a simplistic Beardianism.

The Constitution

- DeHuszar is surely impossibly naive when he declares that the reason the Constitution was submitted to special state conventions rather than legislatures was that the framers believed the people to be the source of political power. The reason was obviously because there was no hope of ratification in many of the state legislatures.

- The state battles over ratification are underplayed and neglected to such an extent that they become almost nonexistent.

- DeHuszar gratuitously sets forth a pernicious constitutional doctrine (p. 121) to the effect that, in foreign affairs, the federal government power is necessarily supreme, and not based on any power delegated by the Constitution. Somehow, he considers such power inherent.

- DeHuszar's practice of detailed annotation of the Constitution, inserted right into the text, instead of an appendix, is inherently confusing to the reader, and is more in keeping with a political science text than a history text, where it is decidedly unhistorical. Thus, in one annotation, he notes that the direct tax provision has not been used since the Civil War. What Civil War? This has not yet been established in the text.

- DeHuszar defends the tyrannical provision of Section 5 that a Congress may deny the seat of any member; surely this leaves an instrument of tyranny against an unwanted party or creed; yet DeHuszar praises this "protection for Congress"; what of protection for the individual Congressman?

- In another gratuitous, despotic, and unhistorical annotation (p. 144), DeHuszar defends the obviously unconstitutional practice recently developed of making military appropriations for more than two years' time.

- Again, in annotating Article 2, Section 3, DeHuszar, in unhistorical fashion, acts as if it is a natural law that the president submits a list of legislation ("must legislation") which Congress is then supposed to pass or reject. The original intent was not to make the president the initiator of all legislation.

- Explanation of the "full faith and credit" clause is sloppy; if DeHuszar's account is correct, how come many states do not extradite criminals to other states? This needs some explanation. Why doesn't the clause compel extradition?

- DeHuszar again (as in his jejune foreign affairs-power-to-the-president-theory) presumes to call Article 4, Section 4 "needless," because to say that the federal government is to "defend each state against invasion," ignores the fact that this is implied by any invasion of the United States. But it is obvious that the Founders, in contrast to DeHuszar, did *not* regard an invasion of one state as *automatically* an invasion of all others, because *they* regarded sovereignty as essentially in each state, not in the federal government.

- DeHuszar also justifies a violation of the clause that the state must *apply* for federal troops against domestic violence, to add that, of course, the federal government can call in troops to protect *its* property. This action is *still* unconstitutional.

- DeHuszar is illogical in annotating Article 5. He says that it is unlikely that state legislatures will ever propose constitutional conventions for amendments; why not have Congress propose them? This ignores the prime fact that the original Constitution *itself* was proposed in a convention, not in existing legislatures, and that it was ratified in conventions not legislatures.

- DeHuszar is rather too "revisionist" on the Magna Carta (importance restricted because only rights of barons involved, etc.). DeHuszar should consult the recent swing back to high importance of Magna Carta, trial by jury, etc. in such works as Faith Thompson, R.L. Perry.

- DeHuszar complacently accepts the current state negation of the Second Amendment, in the Sullivan Law, etc. Didn't the Fourteenth Amendment extend the Bill of Rights to the states? Shouldn't there be bills of rights for protection of the individual against the state? Not considered by DeHuszar.

- On the question of "due process of law," DeHuszar seems to accept meekly the current narrow "formal due process" interpretation, without mentioning the great nineteenth-century doctrine of "substantive due process."

- Is DeHuszar complacent about current state-federal evasions of the provision against double jeopardy?

- DeHuszar's interpretation of the much-neglected Ninth Amendment is highly confused. While he admits that it implies the existence of natural rights of the individual, he then weakens the import by saying that the "Ninth Amendment is not designed to protect any rights." On the contrary, if the rights *enumerated* in the rest of the Constitution are not to "deny or disparage others retained by the people," this must *mean* that the other natural rights are equally sacrosanct and are to be defended against government (both federal *and* state), and that these rights are to be discovered by the courts. This Ninth Amendment, unbeknownst to

DeHuszar, or to our jurists, is the great potential charter for libertarian constitutional law.

The Federalist Era

The leading flaw in DeHuszar's discussion of the Federalist era is his general bias in favor of the Hamiltonian étatist program. The Hamiltonian program was adopted to a sufficient extent to fasten Federalist statism on America almost permanently; the Republican program emerged as an almost desperate revolution against the collectivistic aims of the Federalists; against the federal government's special privileging and regulating of banking, leading to inflation; against its foisting of a public debt on the country; against its high tariff program; against its high taxes, internal taxes, and high budget; against its development of a big and standing army and navy, against its correspondingly bellicose foreign policy, against its contempt for free speech, etc.

DeHuszar (1) fails to see any of this, fails to see that with the emergence of Hamilton and the Federalist era, the lines were to be drawn for what were essentially to be the party of statism and the party of liberty; and (2) DeHuszar supports the Hamiltonian program, and defends it with the usual Federalist myths.

Thus, DeHuszar states (p. 190) that the "establishment of financial stability was another major accomplishment" of Hamilton, that the Hamiltonian central bank, the Bank of the United States, "stabilized American finances," and was a "successful business undertaking" (no wonder it was successful! being permitted by the U.S. government to create money and lend it out, with the government a star borrower).

DeHuszar also interprets the Hamilton conflict in oversimplified, "class-conflict" [Charles A.] Beard-[Vernon L.] Parrington terms: *for* Hamilton's system were the "merchants, bankers, and manufacturers"; *con* were the "farmers." It is peculiarly unfortunate that DeHuszar should perpetuate these Beardian class-conflict myths, especially because they have been in the process of being riddled and overturned for fifteen years now ([Joseph] Dorfman, [Bray] Hammond, etc.). Actually, there were plenty of merchants and businessmen who were pro-Jefferson and anti-Hamilton.

Though, in the twentieth century, DeHuszar seems to oppose high tariffs, he backs the Hamilton program as providing "balance," encouraging American industry (but artificially!), etc.

- DeHuszar's treatment of George Washington is jejune and eighth-gradish: Washington is supposed to have gained experience for managing the United States from managing his estate and similar rubbish.

- DeHuszar gives almost no space to, and doesn't realize the significance of, the Whiskey Rebellion. The Whiskey Rebellion was one of the first shots fired (literally and figuratively) in the libertarian Republican movement that began to form in protest against étatist Federalist rule. Albert Gallatin, for example, played a considerable role as a theoretician of the Whiskey rebels, although he did not favor open rebellion. DeHuszar hardly knows of Gallatin's existence.

- The gravest error in DeHuszar's class-conflict view of the Hamiltonians and Jeffersonians is that he actually links up the Jeffersonians to the modern Democratic Party as an alliance of the Southern and Northern "urban workers"!!! In this way, DeHuszar not only adopts oversimplified Beardianism but also Arthur Schlesinger Jr. and the Marxists. It cannot be emphasized too strongly that there virtually *were no* "workers" in the modern sense in that era, but independent self-employed businessmen-artisans. To talk of "urban workers" has been shown to be fanciful and unhistorical for the Jackson era (by Dorfman), much less for the 1790s.

- DeHuszar should not give the impression that George Washington, in 1792, etc. was an Olympian figure, above the political battle. He was much closer to being a tool of Hamilton and the Federalist program.

- With DeHuszar's persistent deficiency in intellectual history, there is no mention whatever of the body of Republican theory that was being developed in this era: of the writings of George Logan, of John Taylor of Caroline, of the absolute free speech views developed by such as Tunis Wortman, etc. None of these people are so much as mentioned by DeHuszar.

- DeHuszar's discussion of the French Revolutionary wars is highly distorted, placing sole blame for the wars on the French. This is certainly untrue, and overlooks the counterrevolutionary monarchical alliances to crush the French Revolution, especially before the Napoleonic era.

- There is no mention of the famous Paine-Burke confrontation.

- I suppose that we should be grateful for the fact that DeHuszar is a moderate Federalist rather than a "High Federalist," and therefore takes the Adams rather than the Hamilton position on war with France; on the other hand, he is pretty complacent about the letters of marque and navy seizures of French ships.

- DeHuszar's position on the Alien and Sedition Acts is poor. They were not just "severe" and "vengeful"; they were unconstitutional aggression against freedom of speech, press, and opposition to the policies of the government. Under cover of a virtual war with France, the Federalists, scenting "subversion" and an international Jacobin conspiracy, moved to suppress dissent at home. DeHuszar greatly underestimates both the quantitative extent of the prosecutions under these acts, as well as the qualitative impact: the pinpointing of the most influential Republican editors, etc. DeHuszar also shows bias in stating that the opposition to Adams was vicious, bitter, and made false statements in the press, thus almost justifying the Alien and Sedition suppression; he neglects to point out that the Republican press was no more vituperative than the gutter Federalist press; vituperation in politics was the style of the day, and there was no "Madison Avenue" politeness to camouflage the different views.

- DeHuszar seems to have no conception of the fact that the Eleventh Amendment was an invasion of individual liberty by protecting a state government against suit by a private citizen of another state.

- DeHuszar, as I've indicated before, has no conception of the great significance of the "Revolution of 1800."

- DeHuszar repeats the old myth, now exploded, of Hamilton being the deciding voice in picking Jefferson and Burr for president. Also, naval war with France began in 1798, *not* in 1796.

In addition to the above omissions, DeHuszar omits the following important matters of this era:

- Hamilton-Republican conflict on federal internal improvements

- The Logan peace mission and the Logan Act (1798) outlawing a private individual's helping to make peace with a foreign country

- The Neutrality Act of 1794; George Washington's tyrannical action (1796) in refusing to let the House see papers relating to Jay's treaty, thus setting the executive above the representatives in Congress

- Fries's Rebellion (1799) against property taxation, and his conviction for "treason"

- The "army of the black cockade" raised to fight France, and its actions

- The espionage interception by the administration of the Monroe-Logan letter (1796) and subsequent recall of Monroe

- The first federal bankruptcy law (1800)

- The federal expansion of the post office and post roads (1794)

- *Who* was selected to be on the Supreme Court

- The critical Supreme Court ruling that the internal direct tax on carriages (1794) was not "direct" but an "excise," and therefore not restricted by the Constitution (*Hylton v. U.S.*—1796);

or the decision restricting the constitutional prohibition on state *ex post facto* laws to criminal, not civil, laws (*Calder v. Bull*—1798)—both highly unfortunate decisions

- The invention of the steamboat, the pioneering textile entrepreneurship of Samuel Slater; the growth of Deism (Elihu Palmer)
- Jefferson's unfortunate plan for a state public school system
- Franklin's *Autobiography*, such libertarian poets as Philip Freneau, or Joel Barlow and the "Hartford Wits"
- The common federalist smears of Jefferson as an opponent of property and religion, as a Jacobin agent, etc.
- Hamilton's further domestic program, as developed toward the end of the 1790s: extended federal judicial bureaucracy; federal improvement of roads; construction of canals; laws to punish sedition; higher taxes; large increase of army and navy; federal institutions for promoting the arts and sciences; reducing the frequency of elections (and hence of checks by the public on the rulers)
- Hamilton's youth, dubious ancestry, etc.

The Revolution of 1800 and Jefferson's First Administration

- Again, DeHuszar indulges in the false and mechanistic interpretation of the Revolution of 1800 and Jeffersonians as being "agrarians," anticommerce, etc.
- Since DeHuszar puts in virtually no personal data about Americans of the past (except for his romanticizing of Washington), it is uncalled for to put in insults about Jefferson being "untidy"; somehow, DeHuszar has the room for this backdoor gossip but omits any mention whatever of Jefferson's historic first inaugural address.
- Also Beardian is DeHuszar's dismissal of the tax-lowering, anti–public debt policies of the first Jefferson administration as simply being "agrarian" favoritism; thus DeHuszar manages to

ignore the sophisticated and consistent *laissez-faire* ideology of the Republican theorists. The burden of taxation, Mr. DeHuszar, was not just on farmers; it was on *all producers*.

- Page 225: What *is* the "Mason-Dixon" line, suddenly referred to? How was it established?

- There is no mention of the ratification of the Convention of 1800 with France, this time with no conditions required.

- There is no mention of democratic step of opening congressional debates to the public.

- On *Marbury v. Madison*, DeHuszar is, strangely, almost apologetic about judicial review and its infringement on the "legislative power" of Congress; surely, judicial review is an essential part of the Court's judicial function.

- DeHuszar is weak and vague in explaining the Yazoo land claims. *Who* were the "anti-Jefferson Republicans?" No mention of John Randolph of Roanoke, who broke off from the Jefferson administration on the Yazoo land subsidies; DeHuszar fails to point out that Randolph realized that the Yazoo payoff was a departure from Old Republican principles (the "Principles of '98") to award $48 million to fraudulent Yazoo claimants.

- DeHuszar doesn't point out the importance, and the unfortunate nature, of *Fletcher v. Peck* (1810), which protected government grant of special privilege as if such a grant were equivalent to a sacrosanct private contract.

- DeHuszar is, unfortunately, happy about the failure to impeach Justice Chase, thus creating precedent for unchecked judicial tyranny or error—unchecked by constitutional provisions for impeachment, now a dead letter. (Chase deserved impeachment if any judge did.)

- *What year* was the Louisiana Purchase? Dates?

- *What year* was the Burr Conspiracy?

- As indicated above, there is no mention of Jefferson's historic first inaugural address, with its emphasis on limited government, states' rights, individual liberty, and "neutralism-isolationism": "peace, commerce, and honest friendship with all nations, entangling alliances with none."

- There is a very skimpy discussion of the highly important financial policy of Jefferson-Gallatin in the first administration, with its great reduction in the national debt, its cut in government expenditures, and its repeal of all internal taxes (e.g., the whiskey tax).

- DeHuszar's treatment of the Burr conspiracy is very skimpy. Burr's challenge to Hamilton of a duel was *not* due primarily to the 1800 election (where Hamilton's role was not very important anyway), but to Hamilton's blocking Burr from becoming governor of New York in 1804. Also, DeHuszar doesn't realize that Burr's was to be a private expedition against the Spanish territories, and therefore not really "treason." DeHuszar is not appreciative enough of John Marshall's very proper strict construction of the "treason" clause in the Burr case.

The Abandonment of Republican Principle, and the Road to War

DeHuszar is totally oblivious to the high drama and tragedy of the Jefferson administration: that while on the high road to the completion of the promise of the Revolution of 1800, toward the abolition of the public debt, the virtual abolition of federal taxes and tariffs, the abolition of the U.S. armed forces, the Republican Revolution was halted and reversed by a drive toward war with England—launched by Jefferson and Madison. This tragic reversal led to the virtual reestablishment of Federalism:

- To a big army and navy, a bellicose foreign policy

- High tariffs and the virtual ending of foreign trade for quite a while

- The governmental promotion of inflation, bank expansion, and fiat paper—thus turning away from the Republican promise of bankless ultrahard money
- Increase in the public debt and government budgets
- The resumption of internal taxation, etc.

Never was there a clearer case of the poisonous influence of power on a statesman as on Jefferson and his fellow Republicans in the second Jefferson administration and under Madison. For a while, during and after the War of 1812, Jefferson even toyed with high tariffs and paper fiat money. Albert Gallatin, on the eve of the war, brought forth a grandiose scheme for federal internal improvements (not even mentioned by DeHuszar). Almost all Republicans went along with the tide, forgetting their Republican principles, or partially forgetting them, in the process, with a few honorable exceptions, such as George Logan and John Randolph of Roanoke—especially the former.

DeHuszar understands very little, not only of the above central political issue of the time, but even about the road to war itself. Thus, his view of the *Chesapeake* affair is almost the reverse of the truth. He claims that "The American people were united in their anger, and wanted to go to war. Jefferson, by contrast, hoped for peace." The facts are almost the reverse: the American people were never united, the Federalists resisting the war because of their pro-British views, and joined by antiwar people like Logan and Randolph.

In contrast, Jefferson here began the descent down the slippery slope to war. Incredibly, there is not even any mention of the Nonimportation Act of 1806–1807. Also no mention of the fiasco of the Monroe-Pinkney Treaty of 1806. The discussion of the *Chesapeake* affair is highly skimpy; we are not even informed that the British not only fired on but also killed and wounded some Americans, which generated the uproar. There is also no mention of the British offer of reparations for the Chesapeake affair, nor of the fact that Jefferson blocked this settlement for years because he continued to order British warships out of U.S. waters. Here again, DeHuszar is terribly skimpy; he says that Jefferson banned British "ships" from American waters; it was only *warships* that were banned.

DeHuszar has no mention of Napoleon's use of the Embargo Act to seize millions of U.S. goods and shipping under the Bayonne Decree (1808); nor is there mention of the strengthening of the American embargo by the Enforcement Act (1809). There is virtually no mention of the growth of a nullification-interposition sentiment in New England, nor of the federal court decree (1808) upholding the constitutionality of the embargo.

DeHuszar doesn't mention that the British had been using impressments and other interferences with shipping for a long while.

DeHuszar doesn't pose or answer the question: did the U.S. government know that Napoleon had not really suspended the Berlin-Milan decrees when it was plunging into war ostensibly to force Britain to revoke its Orders in Council? Neither is it satisfactory to say that the United States went to war without knowing of Castlereagh's surrender on the Orders in Council: what was there to prevent us revoking the declaration of war when this was discovered?

It must be granted that, while DeHuszar's account is too pro-administration, most of the way, he does concede that the neutral rights question was not the real cause of war, but rather such drives as the drive for land expansion in Canada and Florida.

There should have been more stress on Jefferson's power-poisoned vindictiveness in prosecuting Burr for treason, plus his arrogant refusal to bring pertinent papers on the Burr case to Justice Marshall—thus continuing the Washington tradition of holding the executive unaccountable to either the legislative or judicial branches.

DeHuszar doesn't realize the important nature of the election of 1812, which, since the Orders in Council had already been repealed to no avail, was a true test of war vs. peace; nor does he indicate that George Clinton was the peace candidate. DeHuszar indicates some of this, but not clearly enough. Clinton was a peace Republican, an "Old Republican," now supported by the Federalists on the peace question.

DeHuszar does not mention:

- the conflict over renewal of the Bank of the United States and its liquidation in 1811

- Jefferson's taking up the permission of the Constitution, promptly, to outlaw the slave trade after January 1, 1808

- mention of the Jefferson administration making it possible for Congress to make specific appropriations, thus increasing its check of the executive branch, plus annual accountings of executive acts

- that the Republican betrayal of their own principles began, in fact, early in the administration by the failure to repeal the Logan Act, despite Jefferson

- Madison's attempt to prosecute a panel of lawyers under the Logan Act for agreeing with Spain that certain American claims were invalid (1803)

- the beginning of the slavery-in-the-territories problem with Logan's resolution to prohibit the import of slaves into the new Western territories

- Jefferson's general bellicosity in his second administration, as exemplified in his near-generation of war with Spain, aggressions and threats of force in the Gulf and over West Florida and Texas, etc.

- Logan's tragic peace mission to London (1810), after which his old Republican defenders virtually treated him as a pro-British traitor

- the fact that, while the old-line pro-British Federalists opposed the war, such ominous figures as ex-Federalist John Quincy Adams, virtually prowar on principle, joined heartily in the drive to war. Jefferson, Madison, Gallatin, etc. working hand-in-hand with John Quincy Adams began to favor national internal improvements, a national university, etc.

- the disastrous refusal of Jefferson to even consider submitting the Monroe-Pinkney Treaty with Britain to Congress

Also, DeHuszar is wrong in thinking that Jefferson overturned a large number of Federalist officeholders; actually, he partially betrayed Republican principles of democratic selection of public officials and rotation in office by *not* turning out very many Federalists from office!

War and Postwar, 1812–24: the Consolidation of Federalism and the Virtual Liquidation of the Republican Party

This deliberately paradoxical title (superficially, of course, the reverse happened) catches the inner meaning of the events of this era. For, under the retreat from Republicanism into war, in collaboration not only with John Quincy Adams but with other neo-Federalists like Clay and the younger [John C.] Calhoun ("the war hawks"), the upshot of the war was as follows: monetary chaos, bank paper inflation and the reimposition of the Bank of the United States, revival of the public debt, a return to internal taxes, a shutting off of foreign trade leading to hothouse manufactures and a subsequent drive for a permanent protective tariff (successful in 1824), an increased budget and army and navy. In short, while the aims of the war (both on sea and on land) were a complete and utter failure, the "accomplishment" of the war was a liquidation of the Republican principles and a reversion to Federalism, although only the Republican Party label remained.

With the Federalist Party dead, the Monroe administration represented the quiet, bipartisan consolidation of this notable event, with Federalists seeping increasingly into the Republican Party. Monroe, by instituting "bipartisan" appointments to replace the very mild Jeffersonian "spoils system," consolidated *organizationally* this shift of political *principle*. There was, however, a significant difference between what we may call the new Federalists and the old: the old were pro-British and pro-aristocrat; the new were simply bellicose American nationalists, who also threw in their lot with *democracy*, with the mass of the people. In short, the new Federalism (later Whiggery) was the program of Federalism expanded and revitalized on a mass-base support. It should not be overlooked that the aristocratic-like caucus system of nomination was destroyed, in favor of democracy, not by the Old Republicans but by Adams, Clay, and their followers. None of this important saga penetrates to DeHuszar.

Instead, DeHuszar deplores, conventionally, the failure to renew the First Bank of the United States in 1811, thus depriving the war effort of needed resources. He deprecates the unwillingness of state militia to cross the lines of their states during the war. And, while in a previous page, he pointed to the Canada and Florida objectives of the war hawks, he also, and contradictorily, apologizes for the war by calling it, inanely, the "Second War of Independence," a battle for "economic liberty," etc. (pp. 260 ff.). He also thinks that the rise of industry and more self-sufficiency during the war was a *benefit*, his ignorance of economics preventing him from realizing the detriment and distortion of cutting off international trade and the most efficient allocation of resources. It is also absurd for DeHuszar to find as a benefit of the war the machinery for settling disputes emerging from the Treaty of Ghent: the dispute had been settled without the war. The historian must face up to the fact that the War of 1812 was an unmitigated disaster, whether from the point of view of the aims of the war or of its political consequences.

These details are also worth noting:

- DeHuszar, incredibly, makes no mention whatever of the suspension of specie payments by the banks from 1814–1816, or of the function of the new Bank of the United States to appease the banks by joining in their inflation.

- DeHuszar actually goes to the length (p. 280) of defending wildcat banking as leading to increased growth, prosperity, etc., thus unwittingly adopting the most egregious fallacies of the present-day Keynesians, and such Keynesian economic historians as Carter Golembe. "Rag paper" did *not* relieve a "shortage of specie." There is no mention of the very important experiments (all abject failures) with state-owned fiat-paper banks in the West during the Panic of 1819, or of the judicial decisions on their unconstitutionality. There is no mention of the strict constructionist theory (which makes a great deal of juristic sense) that the constitutional prohibition against state "bills of credit" also implies prohibition of state banking.

- On the steamboat, DeHuszar fails to mention the political and judicial disputes that raged around attempts to grant steamboat monopolies by state governments.

- DeHuszar has virtually nothing on the construction of governmental canals and their widespread failures.

- DeHuszar is wrong in simply stating (p. 275) that U.S. foreign trade suffered many difficulties from the European wars; on the contrary, U.S. foreign trade and shipping prospered by neutral selling to both sides, until the Jeffersonian embargoes, etc. and the U.S. entrance into the war.

- Again, on wildcat banks, these were expressions of outright fraud, not just expressions of "boundless optimism."

- DeHuszar defends fractional-reserve banking, without even mentioning the opposition case.

- The Keynesian balance-of-trade-school is again adopted in DeHuszar's fallacious "explanation" of the "shortage of specie" in the West and South: because the West and South bought more from the North and East than *vice versa*. Another expression of DeHuszar's economic ignorance. Everyone would like to "buy more"; the question is the cause of this, which was the excessive inflation in the West and South relative to the East. DeHuszar has the causal sequence reversed.

- It is absurd to give such short space to discussion of banking and industry, sandwiched inside a small chapter, together with religion, the life of the people, etc. Religious Revivalism, says DeHuszar, "contributed much to the development of individual character" (p. 283).

- There is no mention of Thomas Cooper, of Thomas Ritchie, or of John Randolph of Roanoke.

- DeHuszar gives an erroneous impression of the newspapers and magazines of the time and of their influence. It should be emphasized that the cultivated American of the time was widespread, that the leading businessmen and statesmen, etc. were remarkably well read in English reviews, books, Adam Smith and his followers, etc., and that reference to these permeated the American newspapers as well.

- Favoring the Second Bank of the United States, DeHuszar omits mention of the cogent Webster and Randolph opposition and its arguments.

- DeHuszar's account of the causes of the Panic of 1819 is inadequate and garbled; he doesn't understand the consequences of the Bank of the United States's inflation of 1817–1818, and pins most of the blame on land speculation, which was only one consequence of that inflation.

- DeHuszar's discussion of the tariff and the tariff movement is skimpy and erroneous; he doesn't see, first, that the tariff of 1816 was not supposed to be a higher tariff, but, instead, a gradually lower tariff than the prohibitive "tariff" that the War of 1812 and its blockade had imposed. The protectionist movement as a pressure group of the modern type began in 1820, and DeHuszar does not see this at all: there is no mention of the bellwether of this movement, Mathew Carey, of Hezekiah Niles, or of the Pittsburgh center, such as Rep. Henry Baldwin.

- DeHuszar has no mention of the crucial effect that the Panic of 1819 had in the later formation of the Jacksonian movement, by imparting an unforgettable lesson about the evils of inflationary banking to such men as Thomas Hart Benton, Amos Kendall, and Jackson himself, and stimulating hard-money thought among economic writers.

- By gravely citing the arguments of the "American System" without even mentioning the arguments of its opponents,

DeHuszar seems to be biased in favor of that system and its fallacies.

- Further, DeHuszar doesn't seem to realize that, as we pointed out, above, the American System was not so much new, as a reversion to and expansion of Federalism—placed on a new mass base. The New Federalism favored the Bank of the United States, high tariff, governmental internal improvements, etc. To describe this doctrine as "nationalist," as DeHuszar does, omits the crucial element of the theory: its étatism, its collectivistic expansion of government over the life of the individual and of the economy. It is not only the glorification of the nation, but of the nation-state.

- We have already indicated that DeHuszar has no comprehension of the political meaning of the Monroe era; it was hardly an "Era of Good Feelings," to quote the nonsensical title usually given it: this was the era when slavery, the tariff, the central bank, and internal improvements became "hot" political issues. The only "Good Feeling" was the superficial fact that America was living under a one-party system, because of the death of the old Federalist Party. Monroe was *not* handpicked by Madison, contrary to DeHuszar; there was a great deal of enmity there. Furthermore, DeHuszar omits the crucial struggle between Monroe and William H. Crawford for the presidential succession in 1816. Monroe, a former deep-dyed Republican, now a "bipartisan" federalist type, defeated Crawford, the candidate of the "Old Republican" forces. Crawford was *supposed*, then, to succeed Monroe; this was the general agreement. Yet in the Monroe administration, such men as Adams and Clay had prominent roles, and in 1824, Monroe took the crucial (anti-Crawford) step of refusing to name his successor, and refusing even to uphold the old caucus system (where Crawford would have won renomination easily). Thus, Monroe completed his final betrayal of the "Old Cause." None of this penetrates to DeHuszar, who hardly knows of Crawford's existence, much less of the principles and the cause that he represented.

- There is no criticism of *McCulloch v. Maryland*, and no mention of the substantial opposition to the decision by Jefferson, and by Jefferson's legal theorist Judge Spencer Roane of Virginia.

- One of the expressions of Monroe's new-Federalism was his bellicose "Monroe Doctrine," which DeHuszar treats throughout as something akin to Holy Writ; the so-called doctrine had no legal standing, but was just the pronunciamento of one president, a pronunciamento which, indeed, was to launch the career of American imperialism in Latin America. The operative word here is "imperialism," not, as DeHuszar believes, "elder brother" to our sister nations. No mention of Monroe's designs on Cuba. (This foreign affairs bellicosity and imperialism was really a joint policy of Monroe and Adams as his Secretary of State). DeHuszar omits the fact that part of Adams's motivation in rejecting joint British declaration of the "Monroe Doctrine" was the wish to preserve a free hand for potential conquest of Cuba.

- There is no mention of such important Supreme Court decisions as *Cohens v. Virginia, Martin v. Hunter's Lessee,* and *Green v. Biddle* (1823), which, again, treated a contract between states as a private contract.

- There is no mention of the fur-trade monopoly virtually granted to John Jacob Astor by congressional prohibition of aliens from engaging in the fur trade.

The Polarization of American Politics, 1824–28: the Drive toward Federalist Statism, and the Reconstruction of the "Old Cause" in the Democrat Party

The mid-1820s was an era of high drama and great significance for American politics, a drama and significance that totally escape DeHuszar. What happened was that a few libertarian and quasi-libertarian malcontents saw, by 1820, what had happened to Old

Republican principles, and saw that Federalism had crept back to power by the back door. Thomas Jefferson, a libertarian once again and now out of power, chafed at Monroe's neo-Federalism; so did Thomas Ritchie, and the "Richmond Junto"; so did William Duane, the old Jeffersonian warhorse of the Philadelphia *Aurora* (also not mentioned by DeHuszar); so did John Randolph of Roanoke and John Taylor of Caroline, and some others, including the brilliant young New York politician Martin Van Buren.

Martin Van Buren was one of the greatest statesmen in the history of the United States, and his almost heroic accomplishment has gone unrecognized by DeHuszar as well as by most other historians. (See the recently developing biography of Van Buren by Robert Remini.) For Van Buren, a politician rather than a theorist, strongly sensed the desertion of the Old Cause in the Monroe era. Never an ideologist, Van Buren's political sentiments were fused in a momentous meeting he had with the venerable Jefferson, a meeting from which Van Buren emerged to be dedicated lifelong to a reconstitution of the Old Republican Cause. The Crawford candidacy of 1824 was, unbeknownst to DeHuszar, the final attempt of the Old Republicans, resting on the old caucus system, to take back control of the Republican Party, only to lose to the natural combination of neo-Federalism in Adams and Clay.

Facing the heightened drive toward étatism and Big Government by the consistent étatist John Quincy Adams, Martin Van Buren set about, deliberately and using every skill of political organization, to create a new "Republican" party upon the ruins of old; he set out, virtually single handed, to bring back the libertarian principles of the Old Cause by creating a new political party as a vehicle for those principles: the Democratic Party. It is one of the most monumental feats in American history that Van Buren was able, in a few years, to succeed at this task, to weld together such formerly disparate elements as Tammany Hall, Thomas Benton of the West, Thomas Ritchie, etc., into a great new party.

Contrary to what most historians have written, Van Buren did not simply do this for political patronage, nor did the Adams-Clay versus the Jackson parties emerge immediately after the Adams election as a vehicle for Jackson. Van Buren, after seeing the étatist trend of the Adams administration, risked his political life for principle, by breaking with it, and setting out on the enormous task of welding a new political party. His pick of Jackson was deliberate as he was the only man with prestige enough to appeal to the new mass of voters. Jackson, a military man with sound instincts but at this time of scarcely formed ideology, was deliberately presented by Van Buren with a *fait accompli*, with a party, the only party with which Jackson could win, *already* committed to Old Jeffersonian principles. And with this vehicle and this candidate, Van Buren engineered the monumental "Revolution of 1828." All of this escapes DeHuszar completely. (It should also be noted that the other great ideologist-statesman of the new Democracy, Thomas Hart Benton, was converted to the Old Cause as a young Senator by none other than John Randolph of Roanoke: thus Jefferson and Randolph passed on their principles to the younger generation of leaders.)

As I've said, all of this escapes DeHuszar. DeHuszar doesn't mention the wrecking of the caucus system, or the dramatic moment when Stephen Van Rensselaer mystically betrayed the Crawford Cause.

- DeHuszar is totally wrong when he says that the Democratic Party and Jackson "paid little attention to principles"; on the contrary, it was dedicated to limited government, low budgets, strict construction, separation of government from banking, hard money, opposition to internal improvements, states' rights, etc. (Only on the tariff, for sectional reasons, did the party equivocate, although it was essentially for free trade, especially in the South.)

- DeHuszar paints Adams as unfortunate and confused; Adams failed politically, however, not because he was confused but because he was consistent, driving forward beyond what was politically acceptable at the time, toward statism at home and abroad; yet DeHuszar does not even mention Adams as an advocate of the American System.

- DeHuszar again repeats the Schlesingerian fallacy that Van Buren's and Buchanan's machines were backed by "urban workingmen." Neither is there any evidence that the "less prosperous" voted for Jackson and the "more prosperous" for Adams; indeed, there is considerable voting evidence in the big cities to the contrary. (See various journal articles on "Who Voted for Jackson?")

- There is no mention of significance of Adams's first address to Congress: it favored a strong army and navy, federal bankruptcy law, a national university, a national astronomical observatory, federal internal improvements (roads, canals, rivers, and harbors), and a bellicose and interventionist foreign policy in Latin America.

- There is no mention of Adams's Latin American meddling and the Panama Congress, the drive toward a possible war with Spain, and Adams's bellicose desire to close U.S. ports to some British shipping to exact reciprocal concessions—this foreign intervention and bellicosity being important ingredients in inducing Van Buren and the others to form their opposition party.

- There is no mention of the Anti-Masonic Party (opposed, then, to Jackson as a Mason).

Era of the Jacksonian Democracy

- DeHuszar shows no comprehension of the ideological role of the Jacksonian movement, nor of the hard-money economics and *laissez-faire* politics behind the war against the Bank, nor of the important role of the classical hard-money economists such as William M. Gouge or Amos Kendall. There is no mention of the consistent, pure Jacksonian formation: the Loco-Focos, centered in New York, nor of their important ideological organ, the New York *Evening Post*, with its editors William Leggett and William Cullen Bryant.

- Jackson did *not* "introduce," as DeHuszar deprecatingly claims, the "spoils system" of appointments. He was carrying out a philosophical Republican principle—of responsibility of office-holders to the public, of rotation of office, etc.—that Jefferson had previously mildly inaugurated. There are only two alternatives: a rotating "spoils system," responsive to elections, or a permanent perpetuating oligarchical caste of "civil servants" of the bureaucracy; as we shall see further below, one of DeHuszar's major defects is his wholehearted bias in favor of the "civil service" system, without even recognizing the opposing arguments.

- DeHuszar's "overview" here is grossly inadequate, with almost no mention of the slavery question, of the continuity between Federalist and Whig principles, or even of the great significance of the Democrat-Whig conflicts.

- Again, DeHuszar totally misreads the Jacksonian movement by saying that Jackson's significance was the introduction of "personal politics." The truth is almost the reverse: the crucial significance of the Jacksonian movement was the *reestablishment* of political parties in American life as the vehicle for political principles. This was back to the political party system of the 1790s.

- Jackson's Bank War is given absurdly little space: his veto message only receiving one paragraph, and the reasons not fathomed at all. DeHuszar thinks Jackson was simply anti-foreign and against the Bank as "undemocratic"; it was, of course, much more than that.

- The Bank of the United States did not, in general, restrain the state banks; it *stimulated* bank credit expansion.

- It is absurd for DeHuszar to have a chapter entitled "Politics in an Age of Depression: 1837–1843"; first, the depression was not that important, especially after the first years of the Panic; secondly, this melds in the later Jacksonian era with the Whig interlude.

- There is no mention of the significance of Van Buren's independent treasury as the logical extension of the hard-money, separation-of-government-from-banking position of the Jacksonians.

- There is no mention of Van Buren's magnificent insistence upon strict *laissez-faire,* lower budget, and no interference with the economy or governmental relief, in coping with the depression of 1837. (The fact, as will be seen below, that DeHuszar *does* recognize the *laissez-faire* significance of the 1921 recovery a century later, indicates that Benjamin Anderson was, as it were, grafted onto a completely different and inferior remainder of the text.)

- He doesn't mention Jackson's achievement in getting rid of the public debt (or of the failure of Jefferson to carry through the *original* Republican principle of debt repudiation!).

- DeHuszar doesn't realize, again, the significance of the election of 1840, won by mobilizing the mass of voters through the use of modern demagogic techniques, organized by the crafty Thurlow Weed. As recent studies show, it was the election of 1840 that mobilized an outpouring of new voters, more than previous elections.

- There is no mention of Jackson's reversion to a foreign policy of peace, settling shipping problems with Great Britain that Adams had exacerbated to near the point of war, etc.

- There is no mention of the failure of Jackson to ally himself with Benton on the nullification question, etc. No mention of the U.S.–Canada friction of 1837–1838, or of Van Buren's neutrality proclamation.

- There is no mention of the unfortunate and fateful decision of Marshall in *Barron v. Baltimore* (1833), which decided that the Bill of Rights' protections for the individual were *not* binding upon the state governments. No mention of *Briscoe v. Bank of Ky.* (1837) or *Charles River Bridge decision* (1837) or of dissent in the former by Mr. Justice Story. No mention of the unfortunate decision of *New York v. Miln* (1837), upholding the state police power to regulate vessels into New York.

- It is not true, as DeHuszar maintains, that Jackson believed in the "increased power of the national government." The truth is precisely the contrary.

- One grave defect of DeHuszar's treatment of the 1830s is the near-failure to mention, and total failure to emphasize, the rise of antislavery and abolitionist sentiment; William Lloyd Garrison and *The Liberator*; the crucial distinction between the Garrisonian, nonviolent, "no-government" abolition (involving, e.g., a secession *from* the South), and the coercive abolitionists; no mention of the Nat Turner slave revolt (1831); no mention of the fateful rejection by the Virginia convention of 1831–1832 of state emancipation and, instead, the Southern drive toward a tightening of slave restrictions: curbs on slaves, their education, etc., and prohibition of voluntary manumissions. No mention of the rise of "personal liberty" laws in the North. No mention of the Southern reaction of antiabolitionist propaganda laws, and the Jackson acquiescence in postal censorship in the South to this effect. This extreme minimizing of the growth of the slavery issue in the 1830s makes the emergence of slavery as the critical issue in American politics in the mid-1840s seem like a bolt from the blue—which it was not.

The Breakup of the Democratic Party and the Slavery Question: 1844–60

- The Whig victory in 1840 was, or should have been, merely an interlude in the march to victory of Jacksonian principles. The Jacksonian succession was firmly established: it was to be two terms of Van Buren, followed by two terms of Benton, an era in which the Old Republican cause could have triumphed throughout the Union, and with such depth that it could not have been dislodged. The fateful interruption of this seemingly inevitable Democratic era was *not* the Whig interlude of 1840–1844; it was the tragic and fateful split engendered in the Democrat Party by the Texas Question. It was Van Buren's (and Benton's) firm opposition to the admission of Texas into the Union in 1844 that effectively ended the chances for the Van Buren-Benton succession, and thus ended the chances for a sixteen-year reign of ultra hard money, minimal government, and *laissez-faire*.

- The tragedy of the 1844 split, furthermore, is that Van Buren and Benton made a great tactical error in picking the Texas issue for making their stand against the extension of slavery. The aim—opposition to any expansion of slavery into the Western territories—was a noble and sound one; but the tactic was tragically wrong. For, on well-established principles, a territory that desired admission into the Union, even though the Republic of Texas was slave, should have been admitted without fuss, and the free-soilers should have held their fire until the Western territories became a problem. By taking their stand against the overwhelmingly popular move to admit Texas, Van Buren and Benton killed the chances for the Old Cause—a point that the dying Jackson saw with crystal clarity. It is possible, though of course not certain, that if Van Buren had held his fire, as president he—and Benton—would have been able to steer the Democratic Party firmly into free-soil principles, and thus have avoided the Southern secession.

- Again, none of this penetrates to DeHuszar, who doesn't even realize that there *was* a split within the Democracy in 1844. Not that the immediate Jacksonian aims were not achieved; on the contrary (and here again DeHuszar doesn't realize this), President Polk was the last Jacksonian, and his administration advanced the Old Republican ideals of hard money (with the restoration of the independent treasury), and low tariffs approaching free trade. The cog in the machinery, of course, was the war against Mexico, something that would not have been undertaken by Van Buren.

- In the Tyler administration, there is no mention by DeHuszar of the Federal Bankruptcy law (a favorite Federalist device—1841), of the Dorr Rebellion in Rhode Island, or of the slavery problem in the Creole case or the Giddings resolutions; no mention of beginnings of Know-Nothing party (the American Republican Party); no mention of Clay's loss in New York in 1844 due to the new Liberty Party, angered by Clay's weak stand on Texas.

- There is omission of the key links in the story of the annexation of Texas, specifically Secretary of State Upshur's pressing for annexation after Texas had, for the time, lost interest; also of Tyler's sending troops to Texas and the Gulf.

- There is no mention of the Antirent War, and the subsequent end of feudalist remnants in New York (1839–1846).

- On the Mexican War, DeHuszar, unfortunately, by omission of crucial facts, reveals a bias in favor of the United States' aggression. He overlooks the crucial fact that the Adams-Onís Treaty of 1819 had defined the Texas boundary as being at the Nueces River; after the Texas annexation, the United States cavalierly tossed away the treaty, to claim that annexation rendered it obsolete, and then claimed the territory to the Rio Grande (as well as chunks of New Mexico territory). DeHuszar also leaves out the crucial fact that the war was precipitated by Polk's order to General Taylor to march across the Nueces and down to the Rio Grande—a naked act of aggression. Yet, even after this act of aggression, the Mexicans (whom DeHuszar claims "wanted war") did not fight. Polk, in private, was preparing a declaration-of-war message, but of course it was better to maneuver the Mexicans into firing the first shot—this was done by the aggressive blockade of the Mexican town of Matamoras (on the Mexican side of the Rio Grande) by Taylor's troops. When the Mexicans crossed the Rio to try to relieve the blockade, Polk inserted flag-waving rubbish about Mexican attack on American soil, and the war was on. None of this penetrates into DeHuszar's account.

- There is no mention of Calhoun's opposition to the Mexican-American War, and virtually no mention of the widespread American opposition to the war, including Tyler, Benton, the Whigs, etc., or of the Whig gains in the congressional elections of 1847 in reaction against the war. There is no mention of the Frémont affair.

The end of the Mexican war ushers in the critical era of the growing dispute about slavery. The gravest failure of DeHuszar here is his failure to give any sort of interpretation of the causes of the Civil War, and instead to offer skimpy chronicle. My own view is that the road to Civil War must be divided into two parts: the causes of the controversy over slavery leading to secession, and the immediate causes of the war itself. The reason for such split is that secession *need not have led* to Civil War, despite the assumption to the contrary by most historians.

The basic root of the controversy over slavery leading to secession, in my opinion, was the aggressive, expansionist aims of the Southern "slavocracy." Very few Northerners proposed to abolish slavery in the Southern states by aggressive war; the objection—and certainly a proper one—was to the attempt of the Southern slavocracy to extend the slave system to the Western territories. The apologia that the Southerners feared that eventually they might be outnumbered and that federal abolition might ensue is no excuse; it is the age-old alibi for "preventive war." Not only did the expansionist aim of the slavocracy to protect slavery by federal fiat in the territories as "property" aim to foist the immoral system of slavery on Western territories; it even violated the principles of states' rights to which the South was supposedly devoted—and which would logically have led to a "popular sovereignty" doctrine. Actually, with Texas in the Union, there was no hope of gaining substantial support for slavery in any of the territories except Kansas, and this had supposedly been settled by the Missouri Compromise. "Free-Soil" principles for the Western territories could therefore have been easily established without disruption of existing affairs, if not for the continual aggressive push and troublemaking of the South.

If Van Buren had been president, he might have been able to drive through Congress the free-soil principles of the Wilmot Proviso, and that would have been that. As it was, President Taylor's bill would have settled the Western territory problem by simply adopting "popular sovereignty" principles in New Mexico, Utah, Oregon, and California territories—admitting them all eventually as free states. Instead, the unfortunate death of President Taylor and the accession of Fillmore, ended this simple and straightforward solution, and brought forth the pernicious so-called "Compromise" of 1850, which exacerbated rather than reduced interstate tensions by adding to the essential Taylor program provisions for stricter enforcement of the Fugitive Slave Law. Since the Fugitive Slave Law not only forced the Northern people to collaborate in what they considered—correctly—to be moral crime, but also violated Northern state rights, the strict Fugitive Slave Law was a constant irritant to the North.

The shift from free-soil principles in the Democratic Party and toward the Compromise of 1850 wrecked the old Jacksonian Democracy. The open break became apparent in Van Buren and the Free Soil candidacy of 1848; the failure of the Democratic Party to take an antislavery stand pushed the old libertarians into Free Soil or other alliances, even into the new Republican Party eventually: this tragic split in the Democratic Party lost it its libertarian conscience and drive. Pro-southern domination of the Democratic Party in the 1850s, with Pierce and Buchanan, the opening up of the Kansas territory to slave expansion (or potential slave expansion) in 1854, led to the creation of the antislavery Republican Party. One tragedy here is that the surrender of the Democrat and Whig parties to the spirit of the Compromise of 1850 forced the free-soilers into a new party that was not only free-soil, but showed dangerous signs (in Seward and others) of ultimately preparing for an abolitionist war against the South. Thus, Southern troublemaking shifted Northern sentiment into potentially dangerous channels. Not only that: it also welded in the Republican Party a vehicle dedicated, multifold, to old Federalist-Whig principles: to high tariffs, to internal improvements and government subsidies, to paper money and government banking, etc. Libertarian principles were now split between the two parties.

The fantastic Dred Scott decision changed the political scene completely: for in it the Supreme Court had apparently outlawed free-soil principles, even including the Missouri Compromise. There was *now* only one course left to the lovers of freedom short of open rebellion against the Court, or Garrison's secession *by the North* from a Constitution that had indeed become a "compact with Hell"; and that escape hatch was Stephen Douglas's popular sovereignty doctrine, in its "Freeport" corollary: i.e., in quiet, local nullification of the Dred Scott decision.

At this critical juncture, the South continued on its suicidal course by breaking with Douglas, insistent on the full Dred Scott principle, and leading to the victory of their enemy Lincoln. Here again, secession was only "preventive," as Lincoln had given no indication of moving to repress slavery in the South.

It is here that we must split our analysis of the "causes of the Civil War"; for, while this analysis leads, in my view, to a "pro-Northern" position in the slavery-in-the-territories struggles of the 1850s, it leads, paradoxically, to a "pro-Southern" position in the Civil War itself. For secession need not, and should not, have been combated by the North; and so we must pin the blame on the North for aggressive war against the seceding South. The war was launched in the shift from the original Northern position (by Garrison included) to "let our erring sisters depart in peace" to the determination to crush the South to save that mythical abstraction known as the "Union"—and in this shift, we must put a large portion of the blame upon the maneuvering of Lincoln to induce the Southerners to fire the first shot on Fort Sumter—after which point, flag-waving could and did take over.

I apologize for the length of the above discussion; but I think it important to establish a framework of analysis of the complex slavery and Civil War issues before pointing to the DeHuszar errors.

- In the first place, none of this penetrates the DeHuszar narrative; but this is not as grave a defect as the fact that *no* interpretation has penetrated that narrative.

- More specifically, DeHuszar doesn't recognize the significance of Van Buren's break with the party he virtually founded, including his willingness to compromise with Whig principles (tariff, internal improvements, etc.) for alliance on free-soil; DeHuszar is extremely vague on the Free Soil platform—only it, he says, was "affirmative" (meaning?); the Wilmot Proviso problems are skipped over blithely, and there is no mention of the prohibition of slavery in Oregon, or the Clayton Compromise. Nor does DeHuszar grasp the significance of the Taylor proposals.

- DeHuszar's deprecation of "lynch law" in California does not do justice to some of the important successes of "vigilante justice" (cf. Alan Valentine's book).

- DeHuszar again lapses into inflationist error by opining that the Gold Rush "relieved chronic shortage of specie" in America.

- What does DeHuszar *mean* when he says that the small Southern farmers were "economic subjects" of the planters who "fixed prices"? This is economic ignorance again, as is the nonsensical criticism of New York businessmen "who controlled" shipping and merchandising of cotton "and therefore reaped most of the profits." This is utter economic nonsense of the Marxist-populist variety.

- DeHuszar makes many errors in his brief discussion of education and social conditions in the first half of the nineteenth century. He doesn't seem to realize that women had *always* worked; female labor was not introduced in the factories. Neither is it right to say that the factory system "deprived children of schooling"; they had never had schooling before. In fact, the Sunday-school system was invented by a private businessman, Samuel Slater.

- DeHuszar is apparently biased in favor of state laws to impose minimum compulsory schooling.

- It is, again, economic nonsense to talk of the high price of slaves causing a "money shortage" in the South.

- DeHuszar does not seem to see clearly that the main reason for the rise in the price of slaves was the prohibition on their importation.

- What in the world does it *mean* to say that "transcendentalism is particularly adaptable to American life" (p. 380)?

- Again, on page 382, DeHuszar indicates that the cities became more desirable because they provided tax-supported schools.

- What sense is there in saying that "family ties" were "weakening" because women's rights became wider, and divorce easier? Is a "strong family" only to be achieved by treating wives as chattels of husbands, or by prohibiting divorce (compulsory maintenance of marriage)?

- DeHuszar joins most fellow historians in deprecation of Garrison: "too extreme" on the slavery question. Garrison and his confreres presented "distorted" propaganda against slavery and depicted slave owners "in the worst possible light." Surely it should not be difficult for a professed libertarian to understand that the *institution* of slavery is an inherent evil— equally as evil, for the persons victimized—as socialism (which it resembles), and that the issue is not whether slave-masters regarded their slaves benevolently. As Burke once said about government: "The thing! The thing itself is the abuse!" Further, DeHuszar omits the extraordinarily significant solution of Garrison—not war, but secession *from* the South.

- DeHuszar omits the severe tightening of antislave regulations in the South.

- There is no mention of Thoreau's theory of civil disobedience. There is no mention of the goals of the Mann-Barnard educationist movement: public schools, the compulsory molding of the "whole child," etc.

- It is surely illogical to sandwich mention of the abolitionists in a chapter with other obscure reformers, such as temperance advocates, etc.

- DeHuszar misses the significance of the death of Silas Wright (who is never mentioned), who, if he had not died in 1848, would probably have been the candidate of the Democracy, thus possibly saving the Old Republican team.

- There is no mention whatever of the Negro slave revolts.

- There is no mention of the [Preston] Brooks assault on [Charles] Sumner (1856).

- There is no mention of the aggressive Southern Convention at Vicksburg (1859), which called for legalization of foreign slave trade, as well as for a federal territorial slave code.

- No hint of knowledge appears that bank credit expansion caused the Panic of 1857.

- Why must there be the euphemism about Commodore Perry's "persuading" Japan to open its ports to U.S. trade? The operative word here, Mr. DeHuszar, is force, coercion. Once again DeHuszar displays a strong tendency (redoubled later) to be an apologist for American imperialism.

- The exposition of the Ostend Manifesto is very weak. Not giving the date of this bellicose war threat against Spain for the seizure of Cuba, DeHuszar gives the impression that it was issued by Polk; actually it was issued by Buchanan and endorsed by Pierce in 1854.

- Incredibly, DeHuszar completely omits the struggle within the South over secession—the views of the cooperationists, etc.

- There is also much too little on the Northern shift of view from peace to war, and a consequent failure to give sufficient significance to Lincoln's maneuvering of the South to fire the first dramatic shot to make the South look like the aggressor.

- There is no mention of the Crittenden plan, or of such important books of the time as Hinton Helper's *The Impending Crisis.* Nor is there any discussion of the growth of outright pro-slavery-for-all theory, such as that of George Fitzhugh and Henry Hughes, America's first "sociologists." There is no treatment of the important shift of Southern sentiment over the years from an anti- to a proslavery position.

- DeHuszar misses the significance of the whole realignment of parties due to the slavery issue: with the Compromise of 1850, Southern and pro-Southern Democracy was joined, in effect, by the conciliatory Whigs (Clay, Webster), while many Jacksonian free-soil Democrats drifted into the Republican ranks.

The War Against the South and Its Consequences

To say that DeHuszar's treatment of the Civil War is hopelessly inadequate would be a grave understatement. Here is one of the great defects of this book. The Civil War was one of the most momentous events in American history, not only for its inherent drama and destruction, but because of the fateful consequences for America that flowed from it. Yet there is not a hint in DeHuszar of any realization of this great drama or these momentous consequences. Instead, we have a hasty chronological run-through of the Battle of Bull Run, the Emancipation Proclamation, et al.

We have said above that the War of 1812 had devastating consequences for the libertarian movement; indeed, it might be said that it took twenty years of devotion and hard work for the Jacksonian movement to undo the étatist consequences of that utter failure of a war. It is the measure of the statist consequences of the Civil War that America never recovered from it: never again was the libertarian movement to have a party of its own, or as close a chance at success. Hamiltonian neo-Federalism beyond the wildest dreams of even a

John Quincy Adams had either been foisted permanently on America, or had been inaugurated to be later fulfilled.

Let us trace the leading consequences of the War Against the South: there is, first, the enormous toll of death, injury, and destruction. There is the complete setting aside of the civilized "rules of war" that Western civilization had laboriously been erecting for centuries: instead, a total war against the civilian population was launched against the South. The symbol of this barbaric and savage oppression was, of course, Sherman's march through Georgia and the rest of the South, the burning of Atlanta, etc. (For the military significance of this reversion to barbarism, see F.J.P. Veale, *Advance to Barbarism*). Another consequence, of course, was the ending of effective states' rights, and of the perfectly logical and reasonable right of secession—or, for that matter, nullification. From now on, the Union was a strictly compulsory entity.

Further, the Civil War foisted upon the country the elimination of Jacksonian hard money: the greenbacks established government fiat paper, which it took fourteen long years to tame; and the National Bank Act ended the separation of government from banking, effectively quasi-nationalizing and regulating the banking system, and creating an engine of governmentally sponsored inflation.

So ruthlessly did the Lincoln administration overturn the old banking system (including the effective outlawing of state bank notes) that it became almost impossible to achieve a return—impossible that is, without a radical and almost revolutionary will for hard money, which did not exist. On the tariff, the virtual destruction of the Democratic Party led to the foisting of a high, protective tariff to remain for a generation—indeed, permanently, for the old prewar low tariff was never to return. It was behind this wall of tariff-subsidy that the "trusts" were able to form. Further, the administration embarked on a vast program of subsidies to favored businesses: land grants to railroads, etc. The post office was later monopolized and private postal services outlawed. The national debt skyrocketed, the budget increased greatly and permanently, and taxes increased greatly—including the first permanent foisting on America of excise taxation, especially on whiskey and tobacco.

Thus, on every point of the old Federalist-Whig vs. Democrat-Republican controversy, the Civil War and the Lincoln administration achieved a neo-Federalist triumph that was complete, right down the line. And the crushing of the South, the military Reconstruction period, etc., assured that the Democratic Party would not rise again to challenge this settlement for at least a generation. And when it did rise, it would have a much tougher row to hoe than did Van Buren and company in an era much more disposed to *laissez-faire*.

But this was not all. The Civil War saw also the inauguration of despotic and dictatorial methods beyond the dreams of the so-called "despots of '98." Militarism ran rampant, with the arrogant suspension of *habeas corpus*, the crushing and mass arrests in Maryland, Kentucky, etc.; the suppression of civil liberties and opposition against the war—among the propeace "Copperheads," the persecution of Vallandigham, etc.; and the institution of conscription. Also introduced on the American scene at this time was the income tax, reluctantly abandoned later, but to reappear. Federal aid to education began in earnest and permanently with federal land grants for state agricultural colleges. There was no longer any talk, of course, about abolition of the standing army or the navy. Almost everything, in short, that is currently evil on the American political scene, had its roots and its beginnings in the Civil War: but to read DeHuszar, one would never begin to realize this.

I have said above that, because of the slavery controversy of the 1850s, there was no longer a single libertarian party in America, as the Democratic had been. Now the free-soilers had left the Democrat ranks. But, especially after Dred Scott had pushed the Douglas "Freeport Doctrine" to the fore as libertarian policy, there was hope for a reunited Democracy, especially since the Democrat party was still very good on all questions except slavery. But the Civil War wrecked all that, and monolithic Republican rule would impress its neo-Federalist program on America to such an extent as to make it extremely difficult to uproot.

- In addition to not catching any of the above, DeHuszar omits any mention of the interesting provisions of the Confederate Constitution (which repealed the general welfare clause, prohibited as unconstitutional federal subsidies, tariffs, or internal improvements!).

- He almost omits the whole crucial problem of the early desire on the part of many Northerners to let the South depart in peace.

- He calls Stanton "honest."[12]

- He fails to mention the opposition of the majority of Lincoln's cabinet to his provocative decision to reinforce Fort Sumter.

- He fails to mention the rush to clamber on the war bandwagon by such former pro-Southerners or conciliators as Buchanan, Douglas, Everett, Pierce, et al., and even Garrison and the American Peace Society.

- He overlooks the flag-waving reaction in the North at the maneuvered firing on Fort Sumter (compared to the lack of interest in the North to the Southern firing on the ship the *Star of the West* near Sumter only a few months before).

- DeHuszar doesn't mention the huge inflation in the North and the fall in the value of the greenbacks.

- He doesn't mention Jay Cooke's maneuvering to enact a National Bank Act so as to provide a guaranteed bank market for Cooke's government bonds.

- DeHuszar absurdly chides the oppositionist Southern governors for resisting the high taxes, the conscription, and the crushing of states' rights by the Davis administration. To DeHuszar the matter is simple: these things "had to be done" to "carry on the war"; yet the Southern governors logically believed that it was pretty absurd, not to say ironic, to surrender in war those very things in defense of which the

---

12   Editor's note: Edwin M. Stanton (1814–1869) was secretary of war from 1861 to 1868.

war was supposedly being fought. Granted that this kind of attitude is today considered rather quixotic; but an attempt should be made to understand it.

- DeHuszar ignores the move of Fernando Wood for secession of New York City from the Union, in protest against the War Against the South.

- DeHuszar, in keeping with his general bias in favor of American warmongering, seems to favor Seward's threat of war with France, which had "violated the Monroe Doctrine."

- DeHuszar doesn't seem to realize that the Emancipation Proclamation made war to the death inevitable: it was something like the equivalent of the later "unconditional surrender" policy.

- DeHuszar is very vague on the railroad land grants: "some land," "some money": How much? To whom? There is no mention of the Crédit Mobilier scandals, or the failures of the subsidized railroads.

- There is no mention of Vallandigham.

- At one point (p. 439), DeHuszar adopts the fallacious Beardian theme that the support for the Republican economic policies of the Lincoln administration came from "northeastern business-men." This is highly oversimplified (cf. the recent research of Unger, Sharkey, and Cobe); the eastern bankers, for example, remained Democrats, devoted to hard money and to free trade, while the Pittsburgh iron and steel magnates supported inflation and high tariffs (e.g., Thaddeus Stevens, "Pig Iron" Kelley, etc.).

- I do not expect DeHuszar to adopt wholeheartedly the theory of what we may call "Lincoln-assassination revisionism"—that Secretary of War Stanton was responsible for, or at least a member of, the assassination conspiracy, but certainly this hypothesis should be mentioned, especially in view of Stanton's highly mysterious actions after the assassination, the mysterious demise of Booth, and the highly irregular trial of Booth's coconspirators in a military court. The recent finding of a coded note by one of Stanton's key aides implicating Stanton adds fuel to the fire.

- There is no mention of Vice President Stephens, of the Confederacy's great fight against Southern conscription and suspension of *habeas corpus*.

- There is no mention of Charles Sumner!

- There is no mention of the *Trent* affair.

- There is almost no mention of the Union's naval blockade.

- He does not mention the "Confiscation Act" of July 1862, prefacing the later Emancipation Proclamation by freeing the captured slaves of "rebel" masters.

- There is complete omission of important Supreme Court cases arising from the Civil War: *Ex Parte Merryman* (1861), the *Prize Cases* (1863), *Ex Parte Vallandigham* (1864), for example; also no mention of earlier Supreme Court decisions: the *License Cases* (1847), legalizing state restrictions on the sale of liquor; the *Passenger Cases* (1849), prohibiting state taxes on immigrants; *Cooley v. Board of Wardens* (1851), legalizing state police power over pilots in the Philadelphia port; *Ableman v. Booth* (1859), upholding constitutionality of fugitive slave law.

"Overview" of 1865–1896 Period

Here, once more, is one of DeHuszar's gravest and almost inexplicable, failures: the extraordinarily skimpy treatment of the entire 1865–1896 era. This was an era that virtually created modern American life, and yet only a scant 150 pages are devoted to its entire scope.

There is, in particular, no mention *whatever* of the "robber barons," or the whole problem that they represented. There is no discussion in anything like the needed scope of the rise of big business, the methods of the rise, the distinction between *laissez-faire* and artificial subsidy, etc. It is truly astonishing that this most important fact of the era is virtually ignored. There is only one fleeting reference to Rockefeller and one to Morgan; much, much more is needed.

This era, too, saw the rise of the strange gods of socialism and socialistic movements, yet DeHuszar barely mentions Karl Marx once, or the socialistic movements emanating at least in spirit from him. On the labor union movement, DeHuszar, if anything, tends to be favorable; on the antitrust movement, DeHuszar is mixed, but generally approves. Thus, insofar as he takes sides on the crucial issues of the era, DeHuszar meekly takes the wrong ones.

Also, he tends to favor, without being too explicit, the alleged "needs of the farmer," so that there is no really incisive criticism of the Populist and even the later Progressive movements. The great wave of federal regulation beginning with the ICC in the 1880s is greeted pretty much with approval by DeHuszar, who does not realize that this is the beginning of quasi-socialism, which was, in the twentieth century, to go far beyond the étatism of the neo-Federalists.

Neither does DeHuszar understand what was happening to the Democrat Party; not once does he mention the word "Bourbon."[13] Yet the problems facing Bourbon Democracy are the key to understanding the continuity of quasi-libertarian thought that the Democrat Party brought to the United States throughout the nineteenth century.

To understand the problems facing the libertarian as the Civil War ended, let us picture his point of view: the Old Cause, indeed America itself, was in complete shambles. What was to be done? The first and most obvious task to the libertarian—who had become a so-called Bourbon Democrat—was to free the South from its savage burden of military tyranny. This was task number one, finally concluded in 1876. On the money question, the Jacksonian ideal of ultrahard money was so thoroughly left behind by the Lincoln revolution that the Bourbons, unfortunately but understandably, lost sight of the ultimate Jackson-Van Buren goals. It seemed impossible to free banking from federal intrusion; indeed, it was also clear that the first monetary task was to end fiat greenback paper and to restore the gold standard. This task, after much travail also, was accomplished by 1879.

---

[13] Editor's note: The Bourbon Democrats (1876–1904) were classical liberals who supported Grover Cleveland and, later, Alton B. Parker.

Lowering the budget and taxes significantly seemed beyond reach, although the Cleveland administrations later made a try, and the massive internal improvement subsidies to railroads ended after the Panic of 1873. Throughout the states, government roads had replaced private turnpikes (this trend started before the Civil War) but not much seemed to be able to be done about that. What was left, then, as a viable Old Republican issue, was the protective tariff, and this became a dominant political issue after the mid-1870s.

Thus, by the mid-1870s, the Bourbons had helped to accomplish their most pressing tasks, and had restored America at least to some semblance of prewar "normalcy" in the South and in monetary matters. The tragedy of Bourbon Democracy was not only that the Old Republican *laissez-faire* fervor had begun to recede—because in Bourbon ranks it was often notable and strong—but the fact that the Bourbons had to face the new upsurge of quasi-socialism of a proletarian-farmer based drive for (1) breaking up big business, (2) farm subsidies, (3) fiat and silverite inflation, (4) regulation of industry, etc.

The Bourbons did not, like the Jacksonians, have decades with only a neo-Federalist enemy to face; they had to face also the aggressive onslaught of the new quasi-socialist movements. Hence the failure and the ultimate disappearance of Bourbon Democracy—but this is for a later section. Even from the beginning of the postwar era, Bourbons had to face quasi-socialist challenges from within the Democrat Party itself.

Needless to say, all of this escapes DeHuszar.

- In DeHuszar's overview, he absurdly places the major credit for U.S. industrial development on the technological improvements in steelmaking; he asserts ominously that the "activities of some corporate managers led both national and state governments to place limitations on them" (p. 448), thus justifying these interventions; he states rather naively that workers formed unions to "protect themselves"—thus ignoring, as he does throughout, the dominant strain of violence (over the worker as well as the employer) in the labor union movement.

- DeHuszar asserts the utter absurdity that the Granger movement was the "first large-scale, public effort by any economic group to win government power for its own advantage"; what of the protectionist movement or the movement for railroad subsidy? He also ignores the substantial business participation in the Granger movement (cf. Benson).

- He states flatly that there was "no difference between the parties" and "scarcely any issues" from 1877–1896; this ignores the critical differences between Bourbon Democracy and the Republican Party.

The Reconstruction Era: 1865–76

- DeHuszar, while commendably opposed to the Radical Reconstructionists, again misconstrues their composition, in a Beardian manner, by stating that they were pro-tariff; this was not true of many, e.g., Charles Sumner.

- Why the gratuitous and unhistorical assertion (p. 460) that the Fourteenth Amendment "has been used by the federal Supreme Court in ways that its authors probably never imagined"? Why single this amendment out when this is true of most of the Constitution?

- While DeHuszar opposes Radical Reconstruction, he approves, surprisingly, of the socialistic welfare-state measures of the carpetbag-Negro governments of the South: tax-supported schools, welfare aid, etc., which to DeHuszar made these states "more nearly on a par with other sections of the country in welfare measures." Oh?

- Similarly, DeHuszar defends much of the extravagant carpetbag spending: "still, some of these [state] debts were incurred for such purposes as building schools and roads"—this is supposed to make the expenditures *good*?

- Contrary to what DeHuszar writes, recent research shows there were few farmers favoring greenbacks in 1868; most of the inflationist pressure of this period came from iron and steel magnates, etc. (Sharkey, etc.)

- DeHuszar takes the unfortunate step, here as later, of supporting wholeheartedly the movement for "civil service," a terribly antidemocratic principle (a fact now apparently forgotten), and one which foisted upon America a permanent, secure, uncheckable bureaucratic caste. To DeHuszar, this is simply "demonstrated ability" superseding the "spoils system."

- Again, DeHuszar discusses the problems of cheap vs. hard money as simply and naively "debtor interests" vs. "creditor interests"—as if there is nothing that an objective observer can say about the problem, or no general or "public" interest.

- DeHuszar makes no mention whatever of Charles O'Conor and the Straight[-Out] Democratic ticket of 1872, which tried to rebel against the Democrat abandonment of principle to nominate the old archenemy Horace Greeley (pro–high tariff, Fourierite socialism, etc.).[14]

- It is distorted to say that "manufacturers and bankers contributed large sums to the Republican Party"—and to the Democratic Party as well!

- There is no mention of *Ex Parte Milligan* (1866)!

- There is no mention of the Supreme Court decisions permitting Reconstruction, or of other Reconstruction decisions, such as *Ex Parte McCardle* (1868), *Texas v. White* (1869), *Ex Parte Garland* (1867), *Cummings v. Missouri* (1867), *Mississippi v. Johnson* (1867).

- There is no mention of "Black Friday" and the attempt to corner gold.

- There is no mention of the beginning of naval imperialism, with U.S. naval seizure of the Midway Islands (1867).

---

14   Editor's note: The Straight-Out Democrats held a convention in Louisville, Kentucky, in 1872 and nominated Charles O'Conor for president. He did not officially accept the nomination and did poorly in the election.

- He does not mention the Alabama Claims—the various arbitration treaties, etc.

- There is no mention of Grant's imperialist attempt to seize and annex Santo Domingo, rejected by the Senate (1870).

- There is no connecting up of the Depression of 1873 with inflation and credit expansion.

- DeHuszar is wrong in thinking that the impeachment of Johnson would have set a terrible precedent: the impeachment of a president. On the contrary, while Johnson was right in the concrete case, the impeachment precedent would have been magnificent! As it is, the defeat of the Johnson impeachment, like the earlier defeat of the Chase impeachment, almost permanently placed the executive beyond congressional reach.

- DeHuszar's account of the *Slaughterhouse Cases* (1873) so garbled as to be virtually unintelligible (p. 480). What happened was the emasculation by a 5–4 decision of the privileges and immunities clause of the Fourteenth Amendment, for the protection of individual rights against the states.

The Rise of the Industrial Era, 1877–96

- What, DeHuszar, are "monopolistic rates" by railroads? What standards define "monopolistic"?

- There is no mention of the economic consequences of federal railroad intervention and regulation: virtually a model case, down to the current ills of the railroads.

- What was the *date* of *Munn v. Illinois*?

- There is no interpretation or analysis of the consequences of the Sherman, etc., antitrust acts.

- It is nonsense of DeHuszar to say that the major support for such urban machines as the Tweed Ring were the "new immigrants" from southern and eastern Europe. The new immigrants had hardly made a dent: the major support was "old immigrant" Irish.

- The "Russian" immigrants were actually Russian *Jews*—a substantial ethnic difference.

- This chapter includes the economic nonsense that "in bargaining over wages, hours . . . the employee in larger industry was scarcely a match for his employer." Must historians always be economically ignorant?

- It is highly overdrawn to say that the "AFL forthrightly supported capitalism." (I am getting tired of "Gompers worship" among conservatives.)

- There is a completely distorted account of the Haymarket riots because DeHuszar fails to mention that it involved the persecution (almost openly unjust) of *anarchists*; yet DeHuszar doesn't mention anarchists or anarchism once in the book (including the great contribution—and unique contribution—that the "individualist anarchists"—Warren, Tucker, Spooner, etc.—made to American political thought).

- There is no mention of the key political figure of Senator Roscoe Conkling.

- DeHuszar justifies antitrust laws: "When some corporations [made] formal agreements of various sorts that aimed, among other things, at limiting competition and raising prices, many Americans brought pressure . . . to pass laws that would dissolve these agreements and restore the principles and practices of free enterprise *[sic]*."

- He virtually favors land grant subsidies to railroads as hastening development; he doesn't point out that lack of profits were due to the overbuilding and premature building caused by the subsidy process.

- There is almost no discussion of the conservation movement and certainly no mention of economic interests backing it (e.g., raising the price of western lands).

- There is no mention of large-scale state and local government loans and grants to railroads.

- There is no mention of how retailers tried to suppress successive innovations in retailing by law.

- In the list of advantages of the corporation, he doesn't mention limited liability.

- He inserts some Marxian nonsense about the different interests of "finance capitalists" and "industrial capitalists," whose interests are supposed to be clashing—or perhaps Veblenian nonsense. Again, economic ignorance. (p. 508)

- DeHuszar thinks that one group of business buyers or sellers can interfere with the "free market" by "setting the price for all others." Nonsense once more.

- Happily, DeHuszar does concede that monopoly is very difficult to establish on the market, and that the railroads were vigorous competitors.

- Also, he is good on opposing the post-1871 compulsory driving of the Indians onto reservations [that were] made tribal property, and good on favoring the Act of 1887, breaking up Indian land to distribute to individual families.

- There is no economic analysis of the problem of open range vs. fencing, etc.

- He subscribes to the economic nonsense about "excessive" production of cotton caused by the credit system. Did the credit-granting merchants deliberately sustain losses by insisting on cotton as the crop in the South?

- He seems to favor the governmental agricultural experimental stations of the states, and of the federal government—very "effective"?

- DeHuszar is apparently very favorable toward the chronic griping of the farmer: "farm depression," need for "coping," etc.

- He writes as if disparity between rich and poor is somehow unique in the *cities*. Why? (p. 560)

- He doesn't mention that E.L. Godkin—and his *Nation*—was a leading advocate of *laissez-faire* (with the unfortunate exception of civil service reform).

- He is too kind to the often socialistically inclined settlement house.

- He favors modern prison reform and the alleged ideal of "rehabilitation" of prisoners. Justification?

- DeHuszar's treatment of Darwinism is terribly garbled; not just that "man has evolved from some type of animal," but that higher forms all evolved from lower forms.

- He gives much too favorable a view of pragmatism. *Not* that "any idea to be accepted as true" must be tested as "working," but that the true is *only* that which "works"—and "works" for what? By what standard? Pragmatism was not only critical of religion, but also of so-called "formalism" in social and other philosophy, in short, of abstract logic.

- There is no mention of Marxism (virtually); almost nothing on communitarians.

- There is nothing on Sumner, Lester Frank Ward, the clash of the older *laissez-faire* economists (Walker, Perry, Sumner) with the "new" socialistic economists.

- There is a completely garbled account of the social gospel; no mention of previous *laissez-faire* clergymen or the great *laissez-faire* tradition of the "Common Sense" clergymen/moral philosophers of the mid-nineteenth century (Wayland, etc.).

- DeHuszar appears to approve of the public-library movement.

- There is no mention of such important magazines as *North American Review* or *The Forum*.

- He is biased, as I have indicated, in favor of the Pendleton Act of 1883.

- He neglects to mention President Garfield's *laissez-faire* views (unfortunately superseded by the civil-service reformer Arthur).

- To DeHuszar, the new warships built in 1882 signal the end of a "long period of neglect" of the U.S. Navy—more evidence of DeHuszar's promilitary bias.

- DeHuszar, further, fails to appreciate the significance of the new bursts of étatism in the Arthur and Harrison administrations.

- *What* "act of considerable immorality" of Cleveland? If it could be a highlight in a political campaign, it can be mentioned in a text.

- Again, DeHuszar makes the mistake of identifying "business interests" with a pro-tariff stand; only some business interests.

- He seems to favor the pan-American imperialism of Secretary Blaine.

- DeHuszar is definitely biased in favor of Cleveland and Olney's war-mongering intervention in the Venezuela-Britain dispute. Therefore, he does not recognize this as a betrayal of old neutralist principles.

- There is no mention of the close linkages between Mark Hanna, the "Ohio Gang," and the Rockefeller-Standard Oil interests.

- There is no mention of Congress's Anti-Force Act, vetoed by Hayes in 1879.[15]

- There is no mention of the dubious achievement of Secretary of the Navy Whitney's status as founder of the "new navy."

- Not nearly enough space is given to the significant Interstate Commerce Act—under Cleveland, the Democrat—or such previous bills as the Reagan bill or the McCrary bill.

- There is no stress, incredibly, on Cleveland's reversion to an income tax.

---

[15] Editor's note: The reference is to Hayes's May 1879 veto of "An Act to Prohibit Military Interference at Elections," which in general prohibited the presence of federal troops at places of election.

There is no mention of:

- the weakening of the ICC in the Supreme Court decisions of the *Maximum Freight Rate Case* and the *Alabama Midlands Case* (both 1897)
- the repeal of the *Tenure of Office Act* (1887)
- the brouhaha over the Sackville-West letter to "Murchison," which virtually ruined Cleveland in the campaign of 1888
- Coxey's Army
- the conservation question
- the Federal Bankruptcy Act of 1898

There is insufficient mention of U.S. imperialism over Hawaii, but there is no mention of:

- the U.S.-Samoan treaty, for a naval base in Samoa, and its vicissitudes in the Senate in the 1870s
- the United States joining the Madrid Convention (1880)
- the Burlingame Treaty with China on immigration (1868) or its revision in 1880

He is skimpy on Blaine's aggressive meddling in Latin America, e.g., his attempt to abrogate the Clayton-Bulwer Treaty with Britain in order to gain exclusive control over any Isthmian canal. There is no mention of:

- the Frelinghuysen-Zavala treaty of 1884
- Senate approval of the Geneva Convention for prisoners (1882)
- near war with Germans over Samoa and virtual war under Cleveland
- near war with Canada over fishing rights, settled by the Bayard-Chamberlain treaty of 1888
- a tripartite protectorate over Samoa emerging from the Berlin Conference (1889)

- severe friction with Italy (1890–1891) over the lynching of a "Mafiosi" in New Orleans

- Harrison's near war with Chile over a slight (1891)

- the *Springer v. U.S.* decision (1881) upholding the constitutionality of income tax, later reversed by *Pollock v. Farmer Loan and Trust* (1895)

- the crucial adoption of the "substantive due process" doctrine by the Supreme Court in *Santa Clara v. Southern Pacific RR* (1886)

- the "separate but equal" decision of *Plessy v. Ferguson* (1896) until late in the second volume—the present placing is unhistorical

- the decision on the constitutionality of state regulation of insurance rates, under police power, in *Holden v. Hardy* (1898)

- *Smyth v. Ames* (1898) or of *Addyston Pipe and Steel v. U.S.* (1899)

- the split in the religious denominations caused by slavery, of the development of rationalist-individualist Protestantism (Wayland), of Bishop McQuaid's opposition to proposed federal aid to education, or of the founding of Reform Judaism (Isaac Mayer Wise)

- Walter Rauschenbusch or Billy Sunday

- the establishment of Ph.D. degrees and graduate study for the social sciences, based on Germanic models

- the *laissez-faire* jurists such as Cooley and Tiedemann, or of Supreme Court Justices Bradley, Brewer, and Field—or, in contrast, the left-wing views of Justice Harlan

- Hamilton Fish or Stephen Foster or the McGuffey Readers or Booker T. Washington or Frederick Douglass or even, I believe, Thomas A. Edison

- the laws on contract labor

- the Statue of Liberty

- Ignatius Donnelly

- the highly significant development: the imposition of Jim Crow laws on the South *by the Populists* after their overthrow of the Southern Bourbons (cf. Woodward, etc.)
- Horatio Alger novels

There is almost no mention of Senator Edmunds's opposition to the antitrust laws as unconstitutional.

Another indication of DeHuszar's bias in favor of the various government interventions in business in this era:

> Industrial and financial owners and managers had now become aware in many cases that industrial growth had brought harm as well as good, and united with the many other Americans who sought change . . . by means of government action. (p. 598)

There is no mention of the rise of racist thought, Anglo-Saxon supremacy, etc. in this era, nor of later figures such as Lothrop Stoddard and Madison Grant.

And, incredibly, there is no indication at all that DeHuszar grasps the significance of the Bryan candidacy of 1896: that this represented the end, the final defeat, of Bourbon Democracy, and the virtual end of the *laissez-faire* principle as an effective force in American party politics.

From Republic to Empire

In his discussion of the Spanish-American war, and the preceding and subsequent acts of American imperialism, DeHuszar acts throughout as a fallacious apologist for the drive to empire. It is in his treatment of the launching of the American empire that this book shifts gears, so to speak, as it greatly accelerates the degree and extent of its biases and distortions.

On the one hand, DeHuszar is highly naïve: the Americans helped the natives, brought roads, schools, hospitals (all public!), etc. The subject peoples reaped "many benefits." There is virtually no mention, *per contra*, that any American economic interests benefited from the special privileges of American military rule and intervention.

On the other hand, DeHuszar virtually adopts the disastrous neo-Marxian, neo-Leninist argument for imperialism that was set forth by the theoretician of imperialism, Brooks Adams (who goes unmentioned by DeHuszar). Imperialism was justified, opines DeHuszar, because "the industrial capacity and the financial resources of the U.S. had become so great that [they] could be put to use on a wide scale . . . abroad" (p. 598).

As we saw above, DeHuszar's treatment of the beginnings of American imperialism in the naval incursions of the late-nineteenth century (Midway, Samoa, etc.) are very skimpy—if they are treated at all.

Imperialism, vaguely opines DeHuszar, "contributed to satisfying at least some of certain economic, strategic, and emotional needs of the American people at the time." *Whose* needs, DeHuszar? And satisfied at whose expense?

In his discussion of the Hawaiian Revolution against Queen "Lil," DeHuszar omits the most important fact of all: that this revolution was stimulated, and participated in, by U.S. Minister Stevens and by the United States Marines. It was not just vague "Americans" who participated. *This* is the reason for Cleveland's vigorous, and proper, repudiation, and was the conclusion of the Blount Mission, of which there is also no mention.[16]

While there are flashes of good material against the launching of the Spanish-American War and on the opposition of businessmen to war, DeHuszar tends to justify the results of the war and the establishment of empire.

- Cuba, he proclaims, gained from being a U.S. protectorate and the United States' "usual humanitarian [public] works." The United States, he declares, euphemistically, "managed" to have the Cubans accept the Platt Amendment. "Managed"?

---

[16] Editor's note: Cleveland refused to support a treaty of annexation of Hawaii, after his agent, James Henderson Blount, reported American collusion in the revolution.

- There is no mention of such early imperialist acts as the guano island seizures (1856, etc.) and the Tyler-Webster threats against any European conquest of Hawaii (1842). There is no mention of the Senate rejection of Hawaiian annexation in 1897, nor of Secretary of State Gresham's excellent attack on imperialism and entangling alliances (1894).

- There is no mention of the creation of a Naval Advisory Board, in the 1880s, of "kept" civilians to agitate for increased naval appropriations (centering largely, I will wager, in contractors selling to the Navy). There is no mention of the Naval Act of 1890 and the "navy second to none" agitation, developing a huge navy by 1900.

- There is no mention of the Ocean Mails Subsidies Act, giving subsidies to the merchant marine.

- There is no mention of the neo-Leninist imperialism of Senator Albert Beveridge, nor mention of the gallant opposition (followed by resignation) of Speaker Thomas Reed to the war with Spain.

- There is no mention of the absurd—and deliberate—State Department exaggeration of the degree of U.S. property damaged in the Cuban rebellion. The State Department claim was $16 million; a U.S. claims commission later found the total to be a mere $360,000, but that was after the war.

- Why doesn't DeHuszar point out the crucial fact that the United States Army, in its bloody suppression of the Philippine Rebellion (of Aguinaldo, et al.) used precisely the same methods as those of "Butcher" Weyler in Cuba that had stirred American jingoes into attack on Spain? This includes the infamous "concentration camp" policy and execution of prisoners. (How often am I reminded of Isabel Paterson's phrase, "The Humanitarian with the Guillotine"?)

- Why doesn't DeHuszar mention the strong possibility that it was the Cuban rebels who blew up the *Maine*, so that they could engineer precisely the flag-waving hysteria that occurred? Why couldn't this possibility occur to people at the time?

- DeHuszar glosses over the fact that the N.Y. *Journal* stole the de Lôme letter from the post office. Why wasn't this crime prosecuted by the United States?

- On the Philippines again, there is no mention of "Hell-Roaring" Jake Smith, who, in his bringing of humanitarianism to the Philippines, decreed that, in a certain area, every building be burned and every native over ten years of age be killed. Nor does he mention the fact that the suppression of the Philippine fighters for independence cost the United States almost $200 million. Did the U.S. taxpayer benefit?

- DeHuszar falls for the "Open Door" myth, hook, line, and sinker, and treats it as Holy Writ equivalent in standing to the Monroe Doctrine. No mention of its being an instrument of U.S. economic and political imperialism.

- An enormous defect is that there is no mention of Teddy Roosevelt's pro-Japanese policy before the War of 1905 with Russia, and, indeed, his egging on of the Japanese to launch their attack on Russia. If he had included this, this would have spoiled the myth of perpetual Japanese "aggression," which, as we shall see, DeHuszar clings to in his treatment of World War II.

- DeHuszar finds—or rather, adopts—all sorts of excuses for Taft's economic imperialism. He is not conscious of the irony of a cumulative imperialist policy (cumulative as is domestic intervention) where first territory X is conquered, then Y must be conquered to "protect" X (X being much more exposed, by definition, to foreign countries than the home country), and then Z must be conquered to protect Y, and so on virtually *ad infinitum*. Far from analyzing this process inherent in imperialism, DeHuszar falls into the trap.

- DeHuszar seems completely oblivious to the significant change of foreign policy by Taft to be anti-Japanese (after the pro-Japanese policies of T.R.). This is tied in with Willard Straight, the Harriman interests in Manchuria, etc., a story that needs some presentation (cf., for example, the book of Charles Vevier).

- It is absurd—and wildly anti-Japanese—to say that the Twenty-One Demands "practically made China a Japanese colony."

- In defense, once again, of the so-called "Open Door," DeHuszar is biased against the Lansing-Ishii Agreement, which recognized the reality of special Japanese interests in China.

- Throughout, indeed, the current and later chapters, DeHuszar errs grievously in treating China as a noble, dedicated, unified country, when it was never unified (until the conquest by the Communists, as a matter of fact) but was always divided up among numerous war lords. Central-government Chinese rule over Manchuria is just as much "imperialism" as Japanese rule. DeHuszar, as we shall see, cannot permit himself any objective look at pre–World War II China or Japan, because he has to put Chiang Kai-shek into a (retrospectively) heroic and correct mold, to justify a pro-Chiang position today. In this, of course, he enthusiastically follows the line of "official," antirevisionist, U.S. historiography.

- In the Panama Revolution, DeHuszar fails to point out that Teddy Roosevelt and Hay worked hand-in-glove with the revolutionaries.

- While DeHuszar is biased in favor of the numerous bellicose interventions in Latin America as "protecting American investments," he also fails to pursue the matter and point out who these investors were, and what their pressure role was on the American government.

- DeHuszar is biased in favor of the imperialist "Roosevelt Corollary" to the Monroe Doctrine. He also says nothing against Roosevelt's launching of the tyrannical and unconstitutional device of an executive agreement to put into effect the meddling into the Dominican Republic the Senate had already rejected as treaty.[17] But for DeHuszar all was well, for "soon the Dominican Republic was enjoying both financial stability and political quiet."

- DeHuszar is also biased in favor of Taft's "dollar diplomacy" in the Caribbean: this time in "defense of the Panama Canal" (itself the result of imperialism, subterfuge, and socialism— DeHuszar makes no mention of the socialism of the Canal Zone, where the U.S. government owns all), and in Haiti, Honduras, Nicaragua, etc. Wilson pursued a similar policy in the Dominican Republic, Cuba, etc., again with DeHuszar's approval.

- DeHuszar justifies the so-called "purchase" of the Virgin Islands (1917)—a "purchase" effected under a virtual threat of war against Denmark, which is not mentioned by DeHuszar.

- There is no mention of the substantial economic interests backing the various figures in the Mexican Revolution, specifically the "Oil War" between American and British interests (an oil war that influenced much American policy in the 1920s, also unknown to DeHuszar). Francisco Madero (whose *laissez-faire* views are also not mentioned by DeHuszar) was backed by the Standard Oil interests, while General Huerta, who overthrew Madero, was backed by Lord Cowdray and British Royal Dutch Shell Oil. This was the reason for Wilson's otherwise inexplicable war to the death against Huerta, his refusal to recognize Huerta for years, etc. (Wilson vowed, in a letter to Lord Grey, that he would oust Huerta; he did.)

- The essentials of the Panamanian Revolution are omitted: particularly the fact that T.R.'s indignation against Colombia was against requiring the Panama Canal Company to pay some money to Colombia, *not* the U.S. taxpayer. This issue

---

[17] Editor's note: The Senate did not approve a treaty with the Dominican Republic in 1905, under which the United States would collect Dominican custom duties. Roosevelt then issued an executive order that put the plan into effect.

was completely misrepresented in the U.S. press, as was the administration's close tie-in with speculators who "took" the taxpayer for a $40 million ride as result of the revolution (the Canal Company's concession was to expire very shortly, so that none of this $40 million was necessary). There is no mention of T.R.'s disgraceful libel suit against the New York *World* for uncovering the facts or of the Supreme Court decision throwing out the suit. (See the recent work of Earl Harding, *The Untold Story of Panama*.)

- There is no mention of the influence on the Open Door doctrine of American business interests in China, who had formed an expansionist pressure group, the American Asiatic Association. There is no mention either of Hay's not very open-doorish attempt to obtain an American naval base in China at Samsah Bay (1900)—at which point, we might add with amusement, the Japanese reminded its founder, John Hay, of the Open Door.

- There is no mention of the Perdicaris-Raisuli incident (1904).

The Progressive Era and the New Freedom

DeHuszar is weak and ambivalent on the Progressive movement. He sees and criticizes it for strengthening the national government vis-à-vis the public, but he *also* concedes that its legislation "corrected" business practices.

- He is too brief on the Progressive movement's figures, and too skimpy, for example, on Charles Beard, on his stress on realty vs. personalty,[18] and, in particular, on Beard and his fellow Progressive historians and political scientists bringing to the fore economic motives for political actions.

- DeHuszar mentions here the new Progressives; but *who* were the *laissez-faire* people of the previous era against whom they were rebelling? Why are they not mentioned? DeHuszar is

---

[18]   Editor's note: Real estate or land property versus personal possessions or moveable property.

biased in favor of the local and state social welfare legislation of the Progressive Era, or at least seems to be: housing codes, maximum-hour laws, workmen's compensation laws, etc.

- There is no hint of the role played in insurance regulation—as a means of quasi-cartelization—by the insurance companies themselves. The same is true of other government regulation, and DeHuszar makes no mention of it there either.

- DeHuszar seems to be biased in favor of the inheritance tax. He also adopts the Progressive mythos of "special privileges" to local utilities, presumably thus justifying their regulation. Such things as permission to use the streets are hardly special privileges, and much of the bribery that went on was "defensive" rather than "aggressive"—none of this is indicated by DeHuszar.

- Czolgosz, the assassin of McKinley, is called an "extremist," a word that DeHuszar uses from now on as a catchall. What in the world is an "extremist"? Actually, Czolgosz was a self-styled anarchist, though he was not connected with any anarchist movement. Once more, DeHuszar thus overlooks the problem of the anarchist movement, and the flood of repressive anti-anarchist legislation that was passed in the wake of the McKinley assassination, particularly in state sedition laws.

- DeHuszar is openly biased in favor of the Elkins Act of 1903, outlawing railroad rebates; he doesn't realize that the fact that railroads themselves approved the bill indicates the use of government regulation as a compulsory cartelizing device against the maverick or efficient railroads.

- Further, DeHuszar supports the economic nonsense of the "conservation movement," agreeing about the "rapid and wasteful" use of forests, etc. By what standards? At one point, he recognizes that wealth comes only through use, and appears to defend some of the "exploitation," but he ends by justifying the conservation laws: the Forest Reserve Act, the Carey Act, etc. There is no mention whatever of the substantial economic interests behind conservation laws: the landowners subsidized by irrigation, the landowners whose prices are raised by government withholding of land, etc. (See Hays, Peffer.)

- In the monetary sphere, DeHuszar adopts the myth of bank "inflexibility"; the problem was just the reverse.

- There should be more stress on the fact that Judge [Alton B.] Parker's nomination by the Democrats in 1904 was the last gasp of Bourbon Democracy. Parker's overwhelming defeat by T.R. ended the attempted conservative comeback in the Democratic Party, and from then on the Democrat Party was to be a left-wing instrument.

- DeHuszar is wrong when he agrees that the corporation income tax was legitimate because it was an excise tax, since it is "passed on" to consumers in prices. The fact is that it is *not* passed on, so that the corporate income tax should have been unconstitutional as well as the personal.

- There is almost no mention of the Sixteenth Amendment, and the subsequent income-tax law inaugurated by Taft, or of the corporal's guard opposition, or of the [Cordell] Hull promise that tax rates could never get much over one percent!

- In what way, to comment on DeHuszar's adoption of the old bromide, was Taft "ineffective" in his handling of Congress? It seems to me that the problem of the Taft administration was that Taft was much *too* effective.

- There is no mention of George W. Perkins.

- (To backtrack, there is no mention of the fateful decision of the Supreme Court to acquiesce in the federal outlawry of polygamy.)

- DeHuszar fails to point out the great significance of Champ Clark's defeat for the nomination; for if Clark, an "isolationist," had been nominated, the United States would probably never have entered World War I; there would have been no absolute defeat of Germany and Austria, no Hitler, and probably no Bolshevik Revolution. The fateful and dramatic act was Bryan throwing his votes to the "Progressive" Wilson! Yet DeHuszar lets all this go by.

- DeHuszar follows the usual tradition of being biased in favor of the Federal Reserve System (FRS): it made banks "safe," "held reserves," etc., except that DeHuszar's economic explanation of the Federal Reserve is highly garbled. He fails completely to understand the inherently inflationist nature of the establishment and continuance of the FRS. He concedes, further, that the FRS "did well" in World War I: did well, that is, by inflating the money supply to provide the government funds for the war effort—thus following in the tradition of the Civil War and War of 1812.

- DeHuszar also repeats the old economic nonsense about how workers achieved higher wages *because* of Henry Ford's great, creative act of increasing wages for his workers. This is sheer economic absurdity and implicitly depreciates the great achievement of the capitalist, free-market economy.

- There is no mention of the Supreme Court decisions of *Hammer v. Dagenhart* (1918), declaring unconstitutional the Keating-Owen Act of 1916 outlawing shipment of goods made by child labor. Also no mention of the fateful decision of *Muller v. Oregon* (1908), which declared a constitutional maximum-hour law for women—fateful particularly because it was based on a sociological (instead of legal) brief submitted by Louis Brandeis.

- There is no mention of T.R.'s flamboyance on the Negro question: first, dining with Booker T. Washington, scandalizing racists, and then turning around to dishonorably discharge three companies of Negro soldiers simply because a few AWOL Negro soldiers had rioted in Brownsville.

- There is no mention of Taft's setting up the socialistic postal savings system.

- There is no mention of Taft's tyrannical Mann Act (1910).

World War I

DeHuszar no more understands the significance and impact of World War I than he does the previous wars. One of the most important truths about American history is the fateful impact that wars have had in aggrandizing the State and crippling individual liberty, not only during but also as a permanent legacy after the war.

World War I gave the United States an enormous push down the road to socialism, toward the Big State. In the first place, World War I was the first war in which the burgeoning crew of left-wing ideologues and experts (many of whom are still around) were called in to "plan" and mobilize the economy for war. No previous wars required "mobilization" of the economy; but in this war the whole crew of economists, industrial planners, sociologists, etc. were ready: price control, labor control, priorities, production planning, etc.—all had their baptism of fire in World War I.

DeHuszar understands none of the significance. From then on, World War I became the great model and inspiration for the later generations of socialists and planners: "if we can do it for war." . . .

Further, World War I saw an enormous increase in the government budget and tax rates, especially income-tax rates. DeHuszar's hailing of Mellon's cutting of income-tax rates in the 1920s obscures the whole significance, because he does not inform us that these were highly piddling cuts compared to the enormous tax rate increase in World War I—left to America as a permanent legacy.

If there was conscription in the Civil War, World War I was the first war where Americans were drafted to fight in "foreign wars"—an act that many constitutional lawyers (see John W. Burgess) insisted was unconstitutional.

As in previous wars, there was an *effectively* higher "tariff" which was cemented by a high tariff right after the war. The Army and Navy budgets greatly increased. World War I also led to enormous suppression of civil liberties, including the passage of state and federal antisedition laws, and anti-alien laws. Monetarily, the United States went effectively off the gold standard for the duration, thus going on fiat paper, and multiplying inflation.

And, moreover, World War I was the first era in which the federal government acted to sponsor, favor, and even create labor unions. It was also the initiator of federal public housing.

None of this significance is really grasped by DeHuszar.

- In discussing European militarism, DeHuszar fails to point out that Great Britain began far ahead of Germany in the size of its navy, etc. Germany was the last of the colonial powers, the others already having grabbed their share—there is no recognition of this.

- The account by DeHuszar of the onset of World War I is completely garbled, almost completely tied to the "official" Allied history, and completely ignorant of revisionist scholarship. Germany is presented as virtually forcing war upon everyone. It is not true, for example, that Great Britain went to war because of Belgium; one would have thought it common knowledge by now that this was the official British line later acknowledged to be myth. Britain was committed to go to war by secret alliance, and Belgium was seized on as a cynical excuse (Belgium had been pushed by Britain and France into violating its neutrality anyway. See [Alexander] Fuehr, *The Neutrality of Belgium* [1915]). There is no mention whatever of the roles played by [Sergei] Sazonov, [Alexander] Izvolski, Raymond Poincaré, etc. (Cf. innumerable works, e.g., [H.E.] Barnes, [*Genesis of the World War*], [Sidney B.] Fay, [*Origins of the World War*].)

- Further, DeHuszar neglects to mention that Serbia mobilized before Austria did, and before Serbia rejected the Austrian ultimatum.

- Also, there is no mention of German attempts to restrain Austria.

- There is no mention of Russia's long-term Pan-Slav ambition.

- There is an overblown account of German espionage in the United States, no mention of British espionage, and inadequate mention of the British propaganda machine.

- The explanation is inadequate on the correctness of the German submarine position in international law, especially as compared to the British blockade position. (See, for example, [Edwin M.] Borchard and [William P.] Lage, *Neutrality for the United States* [1937].)

- He overlooks the critical role of the "munitions makers" in fomenting "preparedness" and the big arms budget. It is disingenuous in extreme, for example, for DeHuszar to say that the National Security League "consisted mainly of private citizens wanting to strengthen the armed forces of the United States." Yes, indeed, but *which* private citizens? The munitions makers, who reaped contracts from big arms budgets. (See the famous speech in Congress by Representative Clyde Tavenner, 1915, on the economic interests represented in the "Navy League.")

- DeHuszar neglects Wilson's secret war plans for economic mobilization. (See, for example, Margaret Coit, *Mr. Baruch.* DeHuszar, by the way, makes no mention of the key role in American politics that Baruch played from World War I on, *whichever* the political party in power—in fact, he makes no mention of the rather mysterious growth of a whole group of people, not civil servants but high policy officials and advisers, who seem to be equally "beloved" by both parties—Baruch being the first. Other, current examples: Sidney Weinberg, C. Douglas Dillon, General Clay, etc.)

- There is no mention of the stirring opposition to the war by LaFollette, et al.

- DeHuszar proclaims that the World War I effort "required" economic mobilization. Why? Thus, DeHuszar concedes the arguments of the "war socialists."

- DeHuszar even goes so far as to justify the government's seizure of the railroads—a terrific precedent for socialism—as a measure simply to "coordinate their operation more quickly." Is government a more efficient coordinator than private enterprise, Mr. DeHuszar?

- DeHuszar seems to justify, also, the War Labor Board, which originated the tradition of compulsory arbitration, government favoritism to unions, etc.

- DeHuszar seems to be totally unaware of the significance of the Treaty of Brest-Litovsk, which was a notable recognition of reality by Russia, as well as a treaty of ethnic self-determination for the nationalities of the Ukraine and White Ruthenia ("White Russia").

- There is no mention of the fact that the Allies continued their starvation blockade of Germany after the armistice, and until the peace treaty was signed.

- There is no mention of the Polish reign of terror amongst the Germans in Silesia before the plebiscite.

- He does not mention the Allied promise to Germany that *they* would disarm if Germany accepted the Versailles *diktat*—after which, of course, the Allies never did.

- DeHuszar is vague and uninformative about the actual effects of the Versailles and other *diktats* in Eastern and Central Europe, though he does concede their excessive severity. No mention, therefore, of the dismemberment of Hungary, the creation of a truncated and economically unviable Austria (especially with tariff barriers everywhere, etc.), the creation of a Czech despotism over the Slovaks, the Ukrainians, the Sudeten Germans, and the Hungarians in the "country" of Czechoslovakia, the creation of a Serb tyranny over the Croats, etc. of Yugoslavia.

- DeHuszar is definitely biased on behalf of the League of Nations, and endorses the mythological nonsense that it was the "greatest tragedy that the U.S. failed to join the League"

(p. 725). Again, he asserts that the United States' failure to join the League, "thereby lessen[ed] whatever chance the other nations of the world might have had to guarantee peace . . . " (p. 787). Thus, DeHuszar utterly fails to recognize the role of the league as the attempted enforcer of the territorial *status quo* imposed by the Versailles *diktat*, preventing revision by the victimized nations—all under the camouflage of "collective security."

One of the gravest failures of this book now appears: the absolute inadequacy of DeHuszar's definition of Communism. This is *all* he says of the nature of the Communist movement: the Communists, he says, were "a band of professional revolutionaries," who "started making it [the Soviet Union] the base for a campaign of world conquest." I can think of no more absurd and inadequate treatment of the Communist movement. What has happened is that the Communists are *defined* as simply a band of people who decided that they want to conquer the world. This type of "Fu Manchu" treatment ignores the crucial fact of what Communism *is:* Communism is militant Marxism—it is the attempt to carry through Marxist revolution, to establish a thoroughgoing, 100 percent, proletarian-led, socialism. Communism, then, is socialism militant.

How can it be that DeHuszar introduces the subject of Communism while giving no indication that its meaning and goal is Marxian socialism? Because to do so would mean that (a) Communism is simply a wing, a variant, of socialism; and (b) that socialism, in turn, is statism rampant, statism pushed to a logical conclusion. In short, DeHuszar's version of "Communism" permits him to lead the reader into a simplistic World War III (so far in the form of a "cold war") against a mysterious gangster enemy, a set of foreign devils who simply want to "conquer the world" (i.e., like Fu Manchu). Were the reader to find out that Communism is a variant of socialism, and socialism is, in turn, statism writ large, then he is likely to turn his attention from prosecuting a war against a set of foreign devils called "Communists" (along with their so-called "agents" at home) to the larger and more domestic problem of socialism and statism. The reader might begin to believe that the "enemy" is ideological and domestic, rather than personalized and foreign—but in that case, of course, the DeHuszar "official history" case for World War III (the Cold War) goes by the board.

The Nineteen Twenties

The 1920s launches DeHuszar into the most distorted and biased sections of the book: his bias in favor of the "official line," the "court history" of World Wars II and III. No hint of revisionism or even of doubt is allowed to mar the façade; the previous pedestrian chronicle, almost disinterested in the topic, now changes, and meaning, passion, and bias infuse the account—unfortunately almost completely in an erroneous direction.

We begin with DeHuszar's deploring U.S. postwar isolationism: "The great difficulty was that the American people wanted peace, but the majority of them would not allow the U.S. government to use its enormous political, economic, and military power to prevent the aggressive acts of other countries" (p. 790).

During the 1920s, declares DeHuszar, the Soviet Union "was waging the war against all non-Communist nations that it had declared in 1917." This is myth and absurdity, and rests on a semantic equivocation on the term "war"; "war" should have a precise meaning (as should any important term), and to the ordinary reader it conveys that meaning: of military battle across boundaries, etc. Standing on this precision, the absurdity of this statement is clear: Soviet Russia was waging war against nobody in the 1920s; it was all too happy to be left alone. The Allied powers had just concluded their lengthy intervention with troops in the Russian civil war (a fact which DeHuszar hardly mentions); the Soviets had re-lost much of their western borders to Poland; it was the reverse of bellicose in foreign affairs.

If the term "war" is used in the *ideological* sense, this is superficially more plausible, but actually this is completely equivocal and distorted semantics. Furthermore, ideologically, conflict between socialists, quasi-socialists, libertarians, etc. was waged within various countries before the Russian Revolution and after. If Soviet Russia and other countries with Communist rulers were suddenly wiped out tomorrow, "domestic" Communists and, more important, other wings of domestic socialists and statists, would still remain. So let us abandon this dangerous and mischievous equivocation on the term "war," this pernicious confusion of the military and the ideological, the foreign (inter-State) and the domestic (intra-State).

- DeHuszar says that "a group" opposed to the Versailles Treaty gained control of Italy. Why say "a group"? Why not name it: the Fascists. Furthermore, Italy was not exactly anti-Versailles.

- DeHuszar says, rather ominously, that Russia "regained" areas lost by the Treaty of Brest-Litovsk. But how? It regained them because the Allies (favorites of DeHuszar) insisted at Versailles that Germany must renounce the Brest-Litovsk treaty. Ergo . . .

- DeHuszar fails to mention Lenin's New Economic Policy, which was a significant retreat back to capitalism after the utter economic failure of Lenin's "War Communism." None of this is mentioned by DeHuszar, who doesn't even indicate the relationship between Communism and socialism.

- DeHuszar is biased against the Washington Conference and the London Naval Treaty, which he denounces as "pro-Japanese."

- DeHuszar utterly fails to see the significance of the collective-security, war-inducing nature of the Kellogg-Briand Pact.

- DeHuszar's view of the basic nature of the 1920s domestically is highly erroneous. He thinks it saw a dismantling by the Republicans of the Wilsonian apparatus of State intervention. Except for the specific "war socialism" that Wilson himself dismantled, very little of the increased statism was dismantled: taxes and the budget were still very high. Indeed, the Republicans sharply raised the tariff, and imposed a Federal Reserve System that was more interventionist and inflationist than ever. The virtual prohibition on immigration, ending the "melting pot" policy traditional of America, completes a corrected picture of an *increase* of statism in many crucial areas of American life. The fact that the Republicans were "friendly to business" means little; "business" can be statist (the mercantilists, Hamiltonian-Whigs, etc.), and even collectivist too (see later fascistic experiments in the National Recovery Administration, etc.).

- DeHuszar is ambivalent on farm price supports and subsidies, often seeming to favor them: at last, a "paying attention to problems" of the farmer, etc.

- He also seems to favor veterans' pensions "to provide care for veterans."

- He does not mention Hoover's imposition of federal radio-channel socialism and the owning of channels by the federal government, a truly tragic retreat from a developing private radio-channel system under the common law.

- DeHuszar's only vague reference to the Palmer raids was that they were restrictions on "political extremists." Huh? Why not mention: pacifists, socialists, etc.?

- There is no mention of the political use of the Red Cross during and after World War I.

- DeHuszar neglects the racist nature of the immigration restrictions, and the racist basis for fixing the quota system.

- There is no mention of the Rockefeller-Sinclair rivalry underlying much of the Teapot Dome affair.

- DeHuszar, unfortunately, justifies the quasi-fascist, quasi-cartelist attempts of Hoover in the 1920s to encourage "fair business practice" codes in industry.

- DeHuszar is biased in favor of government intervention and regulation of meat packers and stockyards: an "effort to protect farmers from possibly unfair treatment" (?) [in original].

- He offers more garbled economics: the McNary-Haugen bills were not designed, as DeHuszar states, to "get farmers the

American price" for their crops; they already had the American price. The object was to *raise* that price above the world price.

- There is no mention of the economic interests of the founders of McNary-Haugen (Peek and Johnson) in the farm price supports (as sellers of farm machinery).

- There is no mention of the relation of Benjamin Strong, kingpin of the Federal Reserve, to the Morgans; in fact, no mention of Strong at all.

- There is no mention of inflation and credit expansion as a cause of the 1920–1921 depression.

Here I may mention one of the good aspects of the book: DeHuszar has obviously read Benjamin Anderson and included some Andersonian revisionism about the 1929 depression—and the 1921 depression. He points out, for example, that the federal government let the economy recover by itself in 1921, in contrast to 1929. This is broadly true and welcome, but there should be mention of the attempts of Hoover to upset this policy, and intervene in the economy (as he did in 1929).

- DeHuszar also includes Andersonian revisionism about Federal Reserve credit expansion being a cause of the Depression in 1929. This is also good, but some of the case is bungled, as DeHuszar believes that *speculative*, stock-market credit was somehow inherently worse than other types of credit. Also, he favors the government lending money to banks in need. (For DeHuszar's treatment of the Hoover New Deal, see below.)

- It is also pleasant to note DeHuszar's criticism of the high Fordney-McCumber Tariff, followed by his criticism of the Hawley-Smoot Tariff and its depression-worsening effects. Mildly pro-protection or neutral in early years, DeHuszar comes to recognize the unfortunate effects of protection with the high tariffs of the 1920s.

There is no mention of the fateful incident when the federal government intervened in a pro-union manner in a labor dispute for the first time in peacetime: the Hoover-Harding intervention in the steel strike's aftermath and the call for a ten-hour day.

- There should also be mention here of the crucial role played by the burgeoning left-wing social-gospel control of "social-action" groups, etc. in the various church denominations. Also, the tie-in with socialist and Communist groups should be mentioned (the leader of the steel strike was W.Z. Foster, for example).

- DeHuszar is overly critical of installment credit, as not "increasing real wealth." Installment credit is an excellent and productive institution; the trouble is overly and artificially cheap credit throughout the economy, as in the 1920s.

- There is *no* proof of increased concentration in American industry, though DeHuszar asserts this as a fact.

- DeHuszar is surely excessive in thinking there is a simple, direct connection between "progressive education" and the Progressive movement.

- There is no mention whatever, in DeHuszar, of the following important events:
  - the institution of the AMA medical quasi-monopoly with state laws following the Flexner report on medical education and the compulsory closing of many medical schools;
  - the Sacco-Vanzetti case
  - the Scopes trial and the whole problem of evolution vs. fundamentalism
  - the Holmes-Brandeis dissents and legal philosophy
  - the Railway Labor Act—the pro-union, interventionist legislation in peacetime
  - such Supreme Court decisions as *Adkins v. Children's Hospital* (1923), *Bailey v. Drexel Furniture* (1922)

- o the Sheppard-Towner Act (1921)

- o welfare aid to states

- o and the founding of the FBI

- He gives an unfair description of Mencken, who did not simply ridicule values Americans held dear; he was a battler for liberty and for individual excellence, and against frauds and unwise reforms of all sorts, and he exerted a liberating effect on the youth of the day.

The Hoover Administration

- Adding more Andersonian revisionism, DeHuszar correctly points out that the effect of Hoover's White House conferences was to prolong the Depression and unemployment by keeping wage rates up. I would like to see some more details on this.

- However, DeHuszar is not nearly as sound on the remainder of the "Hoover New Deal" program. He doesn't clearly indicate that the Farm Board program led to increased surpluses. While he has a good criticism of pump-priming public works, he favors the RFC, which "prevented people from losing bank deposits" and "followed principles of private banking"—an absurd claim. He fails to mention Hoover's inflation program or the Glass-Steagall Act of 1932. He also fails to mention Hoover's fateful tax-raising action (especially income tax) in 1932. There is no mention, curiously, of the important Norris-LaGuardia Act, with its significant consequences for granting special privileges for violence to labor unions.

- On the causes of the Depression, DeHuszar again displays his lack of economic knowledge. He attributes it to three things: overexpansion of credit (good, except he places special emphasis on speculative credit); overproduction; and the preceding farm depression, with its lesser real purchasing power for the farmers. The latter two are wholly fallacious, and the last clause reflects again the adoption of the egregious "purchasing-power" fallacy where the farmers are particularly concerned.

- DeHuszar's depiction of the Japanese war in Manchuria is straight from the official mythology. In 1931, DeHuszar thunders, the Japanese "opened the first of a series of aggressive campaigns against China," and the road to World War II. This is supposed to have occurred just as Chiang was about to unite China. Overlooked is the fact that China consisted of numerous warlords, that Chinese warlords were destroying Japanese investments in Manchuria (which places Japanese invasion of Manchuria *at least* on a moral par with aggressions against Latin American countries to protect U.S. investments—which DeHuszar supports). Also overlooked as a motive for the expansion, is Japan's fear of Soviet Russia on its northern border. Also overlooked is the problem of the Chinese Communists, who do not exist for DeHuszar until after World War II, when there is no longer any necessity to be retrospectively pro-Chinese. (see [Charles C.] Tansill, *[Back Door to War]*, [William L.] Neumann, *[America Encounters Japan]*).

- In discussing the League of Nations and Japan, DeHuszar doesn't mention the fact that the league report was quite sympathetic with the Japanese position and recommended that Japan's special interest in Manchuria be accepted.

- There is no mention of the spread of collectivist ideas in the business world during 1932, symbolized in the widespread business support for the fascistic Swope Plan, ancestor of the NRA. There is also no mention of the rise of socialistic thought in that year, with books by [George] Soule, Stuart Chase, etc. calling for a "New Deal" and a planned economy.

The New Deal

The discussion of the New Deal is generally good, though not outstanding, since there is not adequate analysis of the economic consequences of the various New Deal measures. DeHuszar sees that this was a radical shift in the direction of State power, and also that it failed to cure the Depression, for which that shift supposedly occurred.

Yet, DeHuszar maintains that the New Deal "did bring valuable safeguards into industry, banking and trade" (p. 876).

- There should be more of a realization of the significance of the union-privileging Section 7a of the NIRA.

- DeHuszar is very poor on the Wagner Act: he persists with its apologists in seeing the Wagner Act as guaranteeing "the right to join unions," which workers had had for a century. He does not see that the essence of the Wagner Act was compulsory unionization (in the sense of collective bargaining) of an arbitrarily defined production unit if a majority of workers approve, and the outlawing of an employer's firing someone for being a union organizer or adherent.

- Also, there is no mention of the substantial Communist (both Stalinist and Trotskyist) influence in the newly formed CIO, and its sit-down strikes.

- There is no analysis of the economic consequences of the Fair Labor Standards Act. DeHuszar also writes favorably of federal housing subsidies. He is good, however, in criticizing the TVA.

- His account of the famous *Literary Digest* poll is garbled: the point is that the *failure* of the poll stimulated more scientific polling techniques.

- There is no mention of the increase in Federal Reserve requirements as a precipitant of the Depression of 1937–1938.

- DeHuszar is biased in favor of ICC regulation of trucks and buses.

- The "debunking" school of historians is unfairly attacked, and their merits not recognized. Further, DeHuszar does not realize that they began in the 1920s, not the 1930s.

- He mentions the Neutrality Acts of 1930s without explaining them or stating what they are (p. 968).

- It is *John Maynard*, not "Alfred" Keynes (p. 968).

- There is no mention of the Sugar Act, with its vast sugar cartel.

- He shows ignorance of the reality of "Good Neighbor" imperialism in Cuba (cf. R. Smith).

World War II

As was indicated above, DeHuszar here offers a *simpliste* and totally uncritical version of the official line: German, Japanese, and Soviet aggressors push forward, finally to be met by the resistance of noble Allies. Predictably, as with all official historians, there is great difficulty figuring out the sudden transition between all-out war against the German and Japanese aggressors, to cold war against the Soviet aggressor. There is always the danger of the reader beginning to wonder exactly *when* the Soviets launched their aggression and stopped being a defender against German aggression, whether perhaps German and Japanese aggression were justified against Soviet aggression, or maybe vice versa.

- DeHuszar states that for the Soviet Union, World War II was "one more phase in the drive to overthrow non-Communist governments." Since the Soviet Union was attacked by Hitler and almost beaten, it is difficult to make sense out of this statement.

- At one point, DeHuszar states flatly that the Soviet Union "began the Cold War," and at another that it launched the Cold War "in 1944," but that the United States only realized this in 1947. All this makes little sense. *What* did the Soviet Union do in 1944 to launch the Cold War?

- On Italy's "aggression" against Ethiopia, nothing is said of the Walwal incident, or of Ethiopian slavery.

- What year did the Spanish Civil War end? Date? There should also be more on the war, in addition to its large emotional impact on the United States, the Abraham Lincoln Brigade, etc. There is virtually no mention of it.

- There is no mention whatever of Vichy France.

- If Soviet diplomats functioned as spies, so do most diplomatic organizations maintain spies.

- DeHuszar has the usual official line on the Munich Pact: the "inability to stand up to Hitler," and all the rest, as well as references to Hitler's "unlimited ambitions," etc. (Taylor's *The Origins of the Second World War* needed here, along with Tansill, Barnes, and Burton Klein.)

- DeHuszar is totally wrong about "desperate efforts by Polish leaders" to avoid war. The truth is just the opposite: Poland broke off negotiations and refused to resume them, even when Hitler's offer on the corridor was so "weak" that the Weimar Republic would have scorned it as a sell-out of German interests. Britain urged Poland to maintain this intransigent stand.

- DeHuszar says that "German planes repeatedly bombed Polish cities," thus implying that Germany launched the bombing of civilians. He doesn't realize that the bombed Polish cities were right behind the lines, and therefore came within the laws of war permitting bombing of "garrison" cities. On the other hand, there is no mention whatever of the fact that it was *Britain* who launched the obliteration bombing of civilians in cities way behind the lines; Germany didn't want to do this (it had virtually no strategic bombers) and was forced to take up the British on it. (See Veale, *Advance to Barbarism*.)

- It is naïve to say that the Poles "never received the aid promised them by Britain and France." How in the world *could* they? Doesn't this indicate that the promise should never have been made? Or that the moral was the folly of a "tough" policy with Hitler, and not the presumed folly of appeasement?

- DeHuszar neglects the Russian offer with the Finns to exchange territory for the Karelian Isthmus, and that Karelia was strategically considered a "dagger pointed at Leningrad," especially in German or pro-German hands? There is no mention that

Germany only invaded Norway after it had discovered Britain was imminently going to invade Norway itself, and after Britain had mined Norwegian waters.

- Again, DeHuszar directly states that Germany opened air-raid campaigns against British cities, when the reverse is true. Further, he says that Britain bombed German "air bases," when Britain, and later the United States, concentrated on obliteration bombing of crowded working-class districts. There is no mention, furthermore, of the atrocity of the American bombing of Dresden, when it was no military target whatever, but crowded with many thousands of refugees.

- There is nonsense about the German-Italian-Japanese alliance "apparently directed against the U.S." Why apparently? It would be more logical that it was directed against the Soviet Union. Contrary to what DeHuszar writes, the Germans did not deliberately attack U.S. destroyers before Pearl Harbor. The Germans always sought to avoid naval action with the United States, but the United States persisted in seeking it.

- There is no mention whatever of the numerous Allied atrocities committed against the German people—and in the discussion of Potsdam, not a word about the agreement to ship back behind the Iron Curtain many thousands of German refugees (cf. [F.J.P.] Veale, [Freda] Utley, [Montgomery] Belgion, [Austin J.] App).

- There is no mention of the reign of terror committed by Communist partisans in France and in Italy right after the war, against alleged collaborators (see Huddleston, for France; Villari, for Italy; Veale, *War Crimes Discreetly Veiled*).

- He takes the "Atlantic Charter" seriously! (See Flynn, Crocker.)

- A typical chapter title reads, "Firm U.S. Resistance to Japanese Expansion."

- There is no mention of the November 27, 1941 Hull ultimatum to Japan to get out of China.

- The book is very weak on Pearl Harbor. There is no mention of FDR and Stimson's "maneuvering the Japanese into firing the first shot," or of FDR's knowledge of the Pearl attack a few days in advance, and his deliberate failure to warn Pearl Harbor in case the Japanese should find out and call off the attack. (Cf. Theobald, Kimmel, Barnes, Morgenstern, etc.)[19]

- To say that "[a]s a result of the Soviet viewpoint, there is still no settlement with Germany" is rather an odd statement, in view of Russia's continual pleading that a peace treaty be signed with Germany, and our persistent refusal to do so.

- There is no mention of the pernicious consequences of the wartime OPA, nor of the unionizing and compulsory arbitration engaged in by the War Labor Board, nor of the vast governmental inflation, joined with the maintenance of very low interest rates. There is no mention of the savings-bond drives, and its result in inflationary expropriation of the holders.

- There is a terribly distorted discussion of our treatment of the Nisei. He does not mention the fact that, despite no evidence whatever of Nisei disloyalty through the whole war, the Nisei were herded into concentration camps for the duration of the war. Surely it is the height of euphemism to call this "moving . . . to places" removed from the coast.

- There is no mention of the mass-sedition trial, or of the use of the Smith Act to jail Trotskyite opponents of the war.

- What *were* Henry Wallace's political views? Be specific.

- There is no mention whatever of the leading role that U.S. Communist advisers played in getting the United States into the Pacific war; the Communist espionage agent Lauchlin Currie

---

[19]   Richard Theobald, *The Final Secret of Pearl Harbor* (New York: Devin-Adair, 1954); Husband Kimmel, *Admiral Kimmel's Story* (Chicago: Henry Regnery, 1955); Harry Elmer Barnes, ed., *Perpetual War for Perpetual Peace* (Caldwell, Idaho: Caxton Printers, 1953); George Morgenstern, *Pearl Harbor* (New York: Devin-Adair, 1947).

was our adviser to Chiang, and in that role, persuaded Chiang to keep fighting the Japanese, and not to conclude any peaceful agreement. To admit this would be to destroy the recent image of the noble Chiang. There is also no mention of the fact that Stalin and the Communists were ardently pro-Chiang until the middle of World War II.

- Contrary to DeHuszar, the Axis powers had not been "readying themselves for aggressive war." Hitler, for example, was terribly unready, especially for a war of any length. (See Burton Klein [*Germany's Economic Preparations for War*].)

- Most of the lend-lease aid and its impact came *after* Stalingrad rather than before.

- There is no mention of General Vlasov's surrender to the Germans, or of the Ukrainians and White Ruthenians first welcoming the Germans as liberators, until they began to oppress the peoples in turn.

- There is no mention of the persistent record of U.S. aggression against (Vichy) France: Guadalupe, Martinique, North Africa, etc.

- There is no mention of the whole "Second Front" controversy, or of Churchill's desire to invade the Balkans.

- There is no mention of U.S. refusal to recognize the rebels against Hitler—the German underground.

- There is no mention of the U.S. occupation and torture of SS prisoners at Malmedy.

- There is no mention of the Eastern European expulsion of millions of Germans, mass slaughter, etc.

- DeHuszar's account of Hiroshima is almost incredible for its distortions. DeHuszar says that the Japanese, after Hiroshima, at last surrendered unconditionally *except* that they were allowed to keep the emperor. But this was *precisely* the only condition that they had insisted on for surrender months before. So

Hiroshima and Nagasaki butchery accomplished precisely nothing. Yet DeHuszar implies the reverse!

- Astonishingly, all mention of the important Teheran Conference is omitted. The Quebec Conference is also omitted.

- DeHuszar neglects to point out that the Russian acquisition of "Eastern Poland" was based on the old British Curzon Line, which demarcated an area that was not and is not Polish, but rather Ukrainian, White Ruthenian, and Lithuanian.

- There is no mention of the Communist-inspired Morgenthau Plan for the pastoralization,[20] and therefore barbarization of Germany, nor of its partial going into effect before 1948, nor of the socialistic planning, price controls, etc. that this entailed.

- DeHuszar evades mention of the *reason* why Russian troops were withdrawn from Austria, and a peace treaty signed by all: Austria was agreed to be permanently neutral and relatively disarmed.

- There is no mention of the socialistic policies foisted on Japan by our occupation troops.

- There is no mention of U.S. permanent seizure of Japanese territory after World War II; the Ryukyus (Okinawa), Guam, etc.

- There is no mention of the *ex post facto* nature, the illegality of Nuremberg Trials, the failure to maintain proper rules of court procedure, etc.

- There is no mention of UNRRA failure to help *German* refugees. There is a sloppy description of the operation of the Security Council: any of the Big 5 can veto proposal for action, not just action "against itself."

- There is no mention of *which* German or Japanese leaders were tried: Göring, Hess, Yamashita, etc. There is no mention of the

---

[20] Editor's note: The Morgenthau Plan memorandum signed by Roosevelt and Churchill concluded with "is looking forward to converting Germany into a country primarily agricultural and pastoral in its character."

WAC or WAVES, or the Eleanor Roosevelt proposal of a labor draft, during the war.

- There is no mention of the problems of the conscientious objector in World War II (see Sibley and Jacob).

To backtrack a bit, there was also no mention of the following, covering both the 1930s and 1940s: the Jehovah's Witnesses decisions of the Supreme Court; General Hugh Johnson or Professor Warren's gold buying plan; Father Charles Coughlin; the FDIC; the Nye Committee; General "Vinegar Joe" Stilwell, Chiang, and the Burma Road; the "Hundred Days" of FDR; the Silver Purchase Act; the National Resources Planning Board; the Walsh-Healey Act, for minimum wages in government contracts; the Smith Act; the Ludlow Resolution for a referendum on any war; the Gold Clause Cases of 1935.

The Postwar Era

Let's pause and take an overview of DeHuszar's treatment of the postwar era.

While good on the original New Deal, DeHuszar doesn't seem to realize that this New Deal has been fastened on the country, and that World War II only served to vastly expand the State; greatly increase the size of the government budget, the public debt, and the arms budget; foisted apparently permanent conscription in peace or war; established a tradition of government meddling everywhere, and increasingly so. But somehow DeHuszar doesn't realize this, so that he generally praises the Eisenhower administration for reducing the scope of government. It *increased* the scope; but the main point is that the Eisenhower administration made no move to roll back the New Deal revolution, and therefore the administration performed the function of consolidating the New Deal-Fair Deal system. In short, the first Republican administration in a generation placed its stamp of approval on the New Deal, and thus made sure it would be a permanent, irreversible part of American life. This was its major "achievement," and yet DeHuszar doesn't seem to recognize this at all.

Further, the organization of this last part of the book is very poor: the Truman administration; the Eisenhower administration; economic and social affairs; and then, at the last, the United States in world politics—thus with the latter material illogically split from the first chapters, the organization doesn't hang together at all.

- In treatment of Truman, there is no mention whatever of his emergence from the notorious Pendergast machine.

- There is a very skimpy account of the Truman-Wallace break. Cause?

- *Why* were Marshall and Acheson "memorable"? (They are hardly mentioned on any other page.)

- There is an absurdly idyllic picture of government using its war surplus sales to promote "free enterprise"—these were almost always subsidies.

- There is not enough stress on shortages as *consequences* of OPA price control.

- DeHuszar greatly underestimates the importance of the CEA, and overlooks its creature and ally in Congress, the Joint Committee on the Economic Report.

- DeHuszar is biased in favor of the government control of atomic energy.

- There is no mention of the Pearl Harbor Inquiry.

- There is no mention of the important crisis on the Left, when the Eleanor Roosevelt–Reuther-CIO-Hillman forces deserted Henry Wallace after first backing him (1946–1947), and formed in the process the ADA. A key here was Reuther's victory in the United Automobile Workers over the Communist-conservative (?) [in original] coalition backing Thomas.

- There is no mention of the non-Communist oath provision of the Taft-Hartley Act—nor of the 1947 shift of NAM from backing repeal of the Wagner Act to a Taft-Hartley-like proposal. This backdown, and also the backdown by Taft, eliminated the fervor of the anti-union forces who thought, mistakenly, that Taft-Hartley was effective. This is *not* pointed out by DeHuszar.

- Most Republicans, not only Truman, were and still are in favor of high farm price supports.

- DeHuszar seems to be biased against the Twenty-second Amendment (no-third-term amendment).

- There is no mention of public housing, Title I, etc.

- There is no mention of Truman's seizure of the steel industry, nor of the Supreme Court decision that it was unconstitutional [see Decision of Mr. Justice Black: *Sawyer v. Youngston Sheet and Tube* (1952)].

- There is no mention of the juristic controversy over civil liberties between Black, Douglas *vs.* Frankfurter, Clark, et al.

- There is no mention of the McCarran Act being a bill of attainder or of it violating Fifth Amendment provisions.

- There is no mention of the bill of attainder aspect of the attorney-general list.

- Perhaps the Russian atomic bomb was advanced by its espionage activities in the United States, as DeHuszar states, but there is no mention of the fact that Russia acquired the H-bomb before us.

- Contrary to the impression of DeHuszar, the Jews did *not* accept the UN partition boundaries for Israel. The Arabs, furthermore, did *not* invade Israel. How could they, when admittedly *all* the fighting took place on Arab soil? The Arabs went into Arab Palestine territory to help their unarmed Palestinian brethren against attack. There is no mention of the continual Jewish guerrilla warfare against Britain, or of the Israeli aggression against Arab Palestine—symbolized by the fact that its current boundaries are far beyond what was grabbed for Israel by the UN partition. There is also no mention of the one million Arab refugees driven out of their homes, their properties confiscated, or of Israel's refusal to readmit them!

- Neither was the UN action in the Congo in 1960 a "success." DeHuszar should have been able to see this even at the time of writing, for the entire principle of the UN action was the centralization of the so-called "Congolese nation" (which has only existed as a figment of Belgian imperialist boundary carving), and the crushing of such independent and viable countries as Katanga.

- There is no mention of the fact that Russia's reoccupation of Hungary was only done *under cover* of the much more "aggressive"—by international law—British-French-Israeli invasion of Egypt, which the allied forces launched while the Hungarian crisis was going on.

- There is no mention of the highly left-wing propaganda systematically spread by UNESCO—not just interested in international "cooperation."

- Further, while the IMF, according to DeHuszar, was "designed to help countries avoid inflating their money," the truth is precisely the opposite: the IMF is designed to help countries keep inflating when they don't want to stop!

- DeHuszar, in general, has much too favorable a view of the various allied international agencies of the UN.

- There is no mention of the huge increase in the arms budget that resulted from the Korean War, or of the restoration of the excess-profits tax.

- That DeHuszar seems to be highly complacent about the post-war institutionalization of the New Deal-Fair Deal and its expansion may be seen in this comment: "Government authorities at all levels found it necessary" to have high taxes and budgets. "Found it necessary"?

- *What*, specifically *what*, "reduction" of government power was effected by the Eisenhower administration, as DeHuszar claims? Where? On the contrary, note the size of the budget, other indications, etc., and it will readily be seen that the extent of government power over the individual was much greater at the end of the Eisenhower era than at the beginning.

- There is no mention of the concentration camps provided—and built—by the Communist Control Act of 1954.

- The recent Supreme Court decisions did not *only* hamper governmental fighting of Communists; they *also* protected civil liberties of the individual. DeHuszar does not seem to consider this at all.

- Also, DeHuszar doesn't seem to realize that Ike's many "pro-business" appointments did not necessarily (here, did not at all) reduce the power wielded by the appointed offices. The same mistake is made here as in analyzing the 1920s. "Pro-business" does not necessarily mean "pro–genuine free enterprise."

- There is no mention of Ike's firing of conservative Clarence Manion (1956) as head of the Intergovernmental Relations commission, and of his replacement by "modern Republican" Meyer Kestenbaum.

- There is no mention of the failure of Republicans to return to the gold standard.

- In the Dixon-Yates affair, it was not just one officer of the Bureau of the Budget who was linked with the banking firm that financed the project; the officer was the one *who wrote the contract* (Adolphe Wenzell).

- This is a truly incredible blunder: there is no mention of the Democratic recapture of Congress in 1954!

- There is no mention of the substantial conservative third party entering the campaign of 1956: the Andrews-Werdel ticket, mainly on the repeal of the income tax.

- *Why* are such things as increased social security, grants for medical care, college scholarships by government, etc.—all extensions of New Deal-Fair Deal welfare state measures under Ike—considered by DeHuszar to be "notable accomplishments"? (p. 1096)

- Why would a rapid reduction in taxes, in the 1958 recession, have meant that the government had not allowed the economy to recover by itself? Surely a tax reduction connotes less government repression and interference with the economy.

- There is no mention of the important Treasury-Federal Reserve "Accord" of 1951, which freed the Fed from the obligation of supporting the prices of government bonds.

- There is no mention of the McClellan Committee investigation of union racketeering, or of the Landrum-Griffin law.

- There is no mention of the peacetime draft, nor of the jailing of Lucille Miller for opposing the draft.

- There is no mention of the hotly debated issue of fluoridating water, or of the problem of the possible poisonous or cancerogenic properties of many food, hormone, etc., additives that have permeated American agriculture since the war.

- There is no mention of the inquisitorial Buchanan Committee, or of the Rumely case decided by the Supreme Court.

- There is no mention of the detention and final release of Ezra Pound.

- DeHuszar does not seem to realize the significance of the fact that Eastern Europe was occupied by Soviet Russia in the inevitable wake of the conquest of Germany and its Eastern European "puppet" allies. Nor does he realize that much of Communist expansion after the war was also due to the fact that the main body of guerilla troops against Germany and Japan were Communists.

- He gives a distorted account of Ike's invasion of Lebanon (1958), which gives the impression that the invasion succeeded in averting a threat of Communist rebellion. Actually, the facts are the reverse: the troops were called in to aid President Chamoun, who was soon overthrown and replaced by a neutralist rebel (not pro-Communist), after which U.S. troops sheepishly withdrew in failure.

- Also, DeHuszar is wrong in stating that the CIA is simply an information-gathering (espionage?) agency; it is also operational, engaging in guerrilla warfare and sponsored revolution without benefit of congressional constitutional declaration of war (and is therefore unconstitutional): note its operations in Iran, Guatemala, Laos, Algeria (maybe), and Cuba.

- There is no mention of the various critical military and strategic principles of these years: "containment" and George Kennan; "liberation"; "massive retaliation" and "brinkmanship" and Foster Dulles; the theories of "counterforce" and "preemptive war."

- There is no mention of the new "science" of strategy, the Air Force's intellectuals of the RAND Corporation, Herman Kahn, etc.

- There is no mention of the recent growth of the Right: Goldwater, Birch Society, etc.

- There is no mention of Acheson's "dust will settle" speech on Korea; or of constant American trouble with Syngman Rhee.

- There is no mention that the repeated Chinese warnings that it would attack if MacArthur approached the Yalu had been ignored by all (see the book of Allen S. Whiting).

- There is no mention of Hoover–Joseph Kennedy "Fortress America" position.

- Incredibly, there is no mention of the Berlin-German problems, of Quemoy-Matsu problems, of Laos-Indochina problems, etc.

- There is no mention of the Khrushchev-Stalin differences.

- No stress is put on Khrushchev-China differences, on inevitability of war vs. peaceful coexistence.

- The Communist political influence in West Germany is "small" for one simple, unmentioned reason: the Communist Party is outlawed there.

- Iraq and the United Arab Republic are not "Soviet-influenced," but neutralist.

- Why is small Soviet foreign aid to underdeveloped countries an "economic offensive," while huge U.S. foreign aid is not?

- There is no mention of the "dollar-shortage" reasons given for the original Marshall Plan.

- DeHuszar gives a highly colored account of the U-2 incident: Khrushchev "uttered such insults," etc., as to break up the conference. All Khrushchev asked for was that Ike express "regrets" for the spy flights—admittedly illegal under international law and provocative—a custom which every state has followed when caught in espionage. Instead, Ike proclaimed the righteousness of his stand and refused to express regrets.

- It is not accurate that the Soviet Union is "threatening" West Berlin. The Soviet Union wants to liquidate World War II and regularize existing reality: returning permanent Western access guarantees for West Berlin, in exchange for Western recognition-of-reality of the East German government and the Oder-Neisse line. At this point, it looks as if such reasonable negotiations may well succeed. The situation is far more complex, therefore, than DeHuszar's simplistic and haphazard treatment.

- There is no mention of Trygve Lie, or of Dag Hammerskjöld.

- There is no mention of the life terms for Puerto Rican nationalist agitation by Pedro Albizu Campos and others, or of the attempted assassination of Truman and congressmen by Puerto Rican independence fighters.

- There is no mention of the SANE Nuclear Policy Committee.

- There is no mention of postwar revulsion against progressive education and of such leaders of this revulsion as Bestor, Albert Lynd, Mortimer Smith, or the Council for Basic Education.

- There is no mention of the China admission-to-UN problem.

- There is no mention of such leading postwar economists as A.F. Burns, the National Bureau [of Economic Research], Paul Samuelson, and J.K. Galbraith.

- There is no mention of the Southern "massive resistance" policy to compulsory integration and no mention of Prince Edward County, Virginia's abandonment of its public schools and Virginia's repeal of compulsory attendance law.

- There is no mention of the fact that big business is no more concentrated now than in 1900 (Adelman, Nutter, etc.).

- There is no mention of the recent antitrust cases: the breakup of DuPont-General Motors, etc.; and no mention of Lowell Mason's lone fight against antibusiness trust-busting in the FTC.

- There is nothing about the current plight of the railroads.

- There is nothing about the deterioration of the post office service.

- There is nothing about the problems of urban blight, traffic jams, Negro and Puerto Rican frictions in cities, and immigration.

- There is no mention of increasing conservation and national parks, and government recreation.

- DeHuszar seems to be biased in favor of special laws protecting women in industry.

There is the grave flaw of not mentioning one of the great sociological problems of the 1950s: the "Age of Apathy," as generally remarked. Ike's "extreme moderation" and his immunity to opposition until the final year of his term eliminated political strife from public life, and led to the apathetic belief on the part of the public that there *were* no issues anymore. The college youth were the "silent generation" who went, searching for security, into the easiest corporation job with the most attractive pension scheme. DeHuszar has no mention of the phenomenon of the "Organization Man," pointed out in the seminal book of [William H.] Whyte and a host of followers: the man with no ideas of his own, who only adjusts to the "team" and what he thinks are the ideas of others. This profoundly "collectivist" spirit of mind was also embodied in the new type of architecture: the suburban developments with their picture windows and their united hatred of privacy and solitude, etc. In sociology, this was expressed in the interesting and popular categories of David Riesman: there seemed to be general agreement that Americans had largely become "other directed," rather than the self-reliant, Protestant-ethic–guided, "inner-directed" American of the nineteenth century. The dominance of others, of society, was also reflected in the neo-Freudian theories of [Karen] Horney, [Harry Stack] Sullivan etc. None of this penetrates to DeHuszar.

- There is no mention of the shackling of productivity by the featherbedding and other work rules of unions.

- DeHuszar engages in some leftist-type deploring of the alleged plight of the migrant workers, who are paid less than factory workers. Why in the world shouldn't they be paid less? Must everyone be paid as much as a factory worker, regardless of his occupation? Again, this is economic ignorance displayed by the author.

- There is, further, no mention of the governmental prohibition of "wetback" labor—a supposedly "humanitarian" step engineered by leftists, and resulting in prohibition of the wetbacks being able to come to the United States to improve their lot, as they desperately wish (hence the "wet backs").

- There is no mention by DeHuszar of the inflation and ease of credit in the current boom being reminiscent of the 1920s—heralding perhaps another 1929?

- There is no mention of the fact that contemporary religious revival, or much of it, is purely social, part of the current cult of "togetherness" and "other direction," as witnessed in the continual watering down of religious dogma.

- He favors the consolidations of small, local school districts in name of efficiency: but this will lead to a stronger and more centralized educationist bureaucracy.

- There should be a *critique* of the "crash program" idea in scientific research (cf. [John] Jewkes, [D.] Sawers, [R.] Stillerman

[*The Sources of Invention* (1958)]; also J.R. Baker [*Science and the Planned State*, (1945)]).

- He surely gives an exaggerated praise for the Salk vaccine, which has not yet cured polio, and, current reports indicate, might be itself responsible for hepatitis or cancer in some.

- Why is there no mention of the FCC's outlawry of "pay TV"? Surely pay TV will improve the quality of the programs.

- There is no mention of the recent success in the magazine field of *Playboy* and its imitators for adolescent "sophisticates."

- There is no mention whatever of the most famous literary movement and cultural movement since World War II: the "beatniks"—Kerouac, Ginsburg, Zen Buddhism, etc.

- There is no mention of the odd state of modern art (abstractionism), modern music (no melody, or harmony for that matter), and modern sculpture (abstract).

- There is no mention of the rise of Jazz, and its transformation from the exuberant neoclassical polyphony of New Orleans, to the Schoenberg-influenced "bop" and "modern jazz."

- There is no mention of the prevailing influences of Freudianism, and Freudian and pseudo-Freudian categories in modern culture.

Finally, DeHuszar completely omits mention of perhaps the most significant fact of the American economy—and even American society—as we reach the present day. This was the point alluded to by Eisenhower in his highly significant farewell address: the growth of an arms-dominated economy, of a "military-industrial complex" functioning, as C. Wright Mills termed it, as a "power elite."

More and more, the energies of private enterprise are directed not toward the consumer but toward feeding the unproductive maw of the military machine, toward influence purchasing to acquire contracts, etc. The interpenetration of military and industry is embodied in the common practice of retired generals getting posts in the arms industries: obviously not for their business ability but for their influence at the Pentagon. And, increasingly, there is the danger of the society becoming a "garrison state," with discouragement of expression of fundamental dissent, etc.

It is one of the measures of the fundamental failure of DeHuszar's work that none of these problems are so much as mentioned, let alone discussed soundly. DeHuszar is content with pointing to the material boom of America at midcentury, to the "bathtubs" (as we may generically refer to them), which is fine—but he also ignores the problems of America: the threat of a garrison state and a military-industrial complex, the spiritual blight of "other direction," and the "organization man" replacing individualism, etc. And, as I have stated, in ignoring the political function that the Eisenhower administration performed, he somehow manages to forget the menace of the expanding State, and the advancing "Deals" or "Frontiers" at mid-century.

On the 1960 presidential campaign, DeHuszar fails to mention the rather important candidacy of Adlai Stevenson, the deferential, "me-too" campaigning of Dick Nixon, and the Norman Vincent Peale anti-Catholic blunder, as well as Kennedy's impressive showing on the Catholic question in his address before the ministers at Houston.

6. Review of Douglass C. North, *The Economic Growth of the United States, 1790–1860*

May 1, 1961

Dr. Ivan R. Bierly
William Volker Fund

Dear Ivan:

Douglass C. North's *The Economic Growth of the United States, 1790–1860* is an almost totally unfortunate work.[21] It combines all the worst

---

[21] Douglass C. North, *The Economic Growth of the United States, 1790–1860* (Englewood Cliffs, N.J.: Prentice-Hall, 1961).

aspects of the currently fashionable "science" of economic history, as contrasted to the older and sounder disciplines of sound economic theory applied to the fabric of history.

In short, North takes as his "analytic framework" a series of absurd and erroneous hypotheses, all of which are incorrect or, at best, highly one-sided. Some of these hypotheses are "laws" of history, one or two similar historical observations elevated without justification to the status of a scientific law of history. Others are based on highly faulty economic theorizing. Filling in this analytic framework is a book that consists almost completely of a mass of absurdly overstressed and ill-digested statistics. The statistics are hurled at the reader with little or no attempt to explain their significance. The statistics are often irrelevant to the "analytic framework," and almost always irrelevant to any coherent principles of selection.

Furthermore, there is almost no qualitative analysis in the book, no sense of any economic growth processes or legislative effects not incorporated in some chart or table. But actually, such non-strictly-quantifiable material is vitally important in such an economic history. This is especially true in this earlier period of American life, where the statistics, no matter what diligence went into them, were highly inadequate and fragmentary.

Many of the statistics are processed with "moving averages" and other refinements that remove them one more plane from the reality they are striving to describe. Furthermore, despite the vast array of statistics that reduces the actual text to negligible size, there is grave deficiency of even statistical—let alone "literary"—discussion of crucial economic concerns such as wage rates and unemployment. Undoubtedly, the reason is that wage rates and unemployment series are too fragmentary to be organized in large tables and detailed graphs. But they are, nevertheless, too important to be so overlooked.

And so, all the trappings of the scientistic economic historian are there: the faulty theoretical hypotheses; the enormous overweighting of statistics and underweighting of the qualitative, the searching for "laws of history," etc. Obviously heavily concerned with keeping up with the last-minute scholarly fashion, North goes overboard in trying to confine his references largely to 1960 material. As a result, his references are incomplete and weighted far too much on the side of the most recent material. In his discussion of the 1819 Panic, for example, North relies heavily on Schur's 1960 journal article, and also on Folz's earlier, unpublished dissertation, both of which are very poor sources. Actually, North rises above this material, but the fact remains that this is the material that he is apt to confine his footnotes to.

In addition to ignoring wage rates and unemployment, North also virtually overlooks the important field of money and banking, and presents no statistics in this vital field either—probably, again, because they cannot be presented in an imposing table. Thus whatever cannot be quantified at length does not, for North, exist.

Having indicated the poor and completely unsatisfactory quality of North's history, let us turn to his equally poor, if not worse, theoretic framework, which he uses as a Procrustean bed for the history. North has seen the obvious fact that, generally, the most advanced industry, especially in an "undeveloped" country, is a leading *export* industry. But he concludes from this that there is something uniquely powerful and spurring to development of an export industry *per se*. In short, instead of realizing that an industry that is particularly efficient and advanced *will then become* a leading export industry, he tends to reverse the proper causation and attribute almost mystic powers of initiating development, etc., to export industries *per se*. From this he leaps to far more erroneous conclusions and *non sequiturs*. He claims, for example, that an export industry, the receipts of which are then used largely for imports, leaks away and hinders development of the country; whereas, export industries where the spending "stays at home" build up the country, because they retain within the country the "multiplier-accelerator" effect of such spending. This is Keynesian nonsense applied even beyond where Keynes would apply it—i.e., to all situations and not just depressions.

Critical ideas for North are such statements as, "Regions or nations which remain tied to a single export commodity almost inevitably fail to achieve sustained expansion." Now this is nonsense on many levels. First, this is merely a historical generalization elevated into a "law." Second, the causation is once again placed backwards by North: historically, obviously a country that develops only one leading export industry is usually a reflection of a limited development. But North implies that the export industries are the causal *keys* to the problem of development, and therefore all that would be needed to ignite development would be another couple of export industries. Third, even historically, North is incorrect. Australia, for example, was able to prosper and develop with essentially one leading export industry: wool. Fourth, if we pursue the statement fully we see what utter absurdity it is; for North (who realizes that regions are as important an economic unit as the political, artificial "nation") talks of "regions" tied to one export. And yet how big or how small is a "region"? "Region" is an economically meaningless term, as we can make the "region" small enough so that it could never have more than one export commodity. And yet this does not make such a region poor or undeveloped.

The logic of North's position, which apparently he does not carry through, is basically protectionist; industry is weighted more highly than other goods, exports more highly than other industries, etc. North does pursue his logic, however, to proclaim his bias for egalitarianism. Unequal distribution of income he associates with a "plantation" economy, where the planters have the ill grace to spend their money on imported luxuries; this is contrasted to the noble, more egalitarian economy where more people develop home industry and home activities.

Once again, North's position is compounded of both historical and economic errors; the fact that, historically, some plantation systems had unequal incomes does not mean that either the plantation system or the inequality inhibited economic development. Certainly neither did. So protectionist minded is North that he actually says that an export commodity that requires more investment in capital facilities, etc. is better and more conducive to growth than one requiring less, because there will be more spending on home-port facilities, etc. This again is protectionistic nonsense (i.e., the thinking of protectionism—I do not know whether North actually advocates high tariffs) for it claims that a less efficient and less productive industry is better than a more efficient and more productive one because more money is spent by the former on costs, resources, etc. Isn't the money that is saved ever used? Once again, the important desideratum is freedom of the market; a country or region will often best develop, depending on conditions of resources or the market, by concentrating on one or two items and then exchanging them for other items produced elsewhere. If this comes in a free market, it is far more productive and economic than forcing a hothouse steel or textile mill in the name of "economic growth."

Furthermore, Professor North takes the occasion to propagandize, throughout the book, on behalf of the public school system. The noble North and West, since it benefited the people, "invested in human beings" via a free public school system; the plantation-ridden South declined to do so until much later.

North, like all scientistic-minded economic historians, has, at bottom, a highly mechanical and deterministic view of economic growth. There are resources, there are export industries (which he overstresses greatly—thus he virtually makes cotton, in this period, to be the only industry worth discussing, since it was the leading export); and there are various "multiplier-accelerator" models of impact of these various export industries. The role of individuals acting, of entrepreneurs and innovators, North deliberately and frankly deprecates; the role of capital investment—so crucial to development—receives similar slighting treatment (here, too, there are no detailed statistics of capital for this period, so presumably this topic is not worth discussing).

The role of money and banking is also slighted, except that North indicates adoption of the erroneous Leon Schur thesis that the Bank of the United States was an excellent institution not to be blamed for the inflation of 1817–18, which is the reverse of the fact.

In addition, North revives the hoary myth of "long cycles" of economic activity, which he thinks prevailed during this period and are comparable to the well-known, shorter, business cycle. Actually, there is no such "cycle"; if there are long swings in wholesale prices or in particular industries, this has nothing to do with the business cycle as we know it; the important point is that there is no such cycle in *production* or business activity, i.e., production does not fall for twenty or thirty years, etc. (The fact that rates of increase change is *not* the same thing, and is only a "cycle" produced by statistical refinement, not in the real world.) His explanation for these so-called long cycles is lengthy "periods of gestation" of investments; this is the erroneous Schumpeter explanation.

Finally, there is another vast omission: there is virtually nothing on government policies and their positive or negative impact on America's economic development during this era.

To set off against this long and important roster of flaws and failures, I can think of no particular merit in the North book—except for the reflection of recent National Bureau findings that the United States began developing rapidly before the Civil War and that this development was interrupted by the Civil War, in contrast to previous views that the Civil War sparked American development. But this hardly begins to compensate for the defects and fallacies in the book. Needless to say, I would recommend strongly against any National Book Foundation distribution of this unfortunate book.[22]

7. Review of William Appleman Williams, *The Tragedy of American Diplomacy*

August 29, 1962

Dr. Ivan R. Bierly
William Volker Fund

Dear Ivan:

William Appleman Williams's, *The Tragedy of American Diplomacy* is an essay on the history of twentieth-century American foreign

[22]   Editor's note: The National Book Foundation was a subsidiary of the Volker Fund that distributed copies of books favorable to classical liberalism to libraries and individuals, based on the recommendations of Rothbard and other reviewers.

policy, filled with penetrating and suggestive insights.[23] Williams is one of the foremost young socialist historians in the country; in contrast to the bulk of "Establishment historians," Williams is refreshingly frank in his dedication to the socialist perspective. This frankness places him outside of the "Establishment" and thereby permits him to levy penetrating criticisms at what has been going on. There is sufficient to criticize, and Williams is particularly concerned with the rise and maintenance of American imperialism. Williams's central thesis is that the policy of the "Open Door"—generally dismissed by historians as vaguely moralistic and of only ephemeral importance—holds the key to virtually the entire foreign policy of America in the twentieth century, which he refers to as "open-door empire."

The gist of "open-door imperialism" is the shrewdness to refrain from imperial conquest of backward nations, in the style of Western Europe, and instead to exercise such control indirectly and quasi-covertly, masked by an elaborate camouflage of moralizing, Wilsonian idealism to remake the globe, etc. This covert American imperialism—backed up by coercive diplomatic pressures—includes economic pressure (for markets, monopolistic concessions to favored American firms, control of resources, etc.) and the manipulation of foreign governments and political parties. The upshot of all this, as Williams indicates, is that residents of foreign countries are not fooled for very long by the moralizing, but that the American people *are*—with the accelerating result that the foreign natives and the American people find it almost impossible to understand each other's positions: "What does he *mean*, 'American imperialism'?"

There is no need to look very hard for defects in the Williams book. They abound. In the first place, this is in no sense a definitive or highly scholarly work. Presumably, Williams himself would not claim this. There are no footnotes, even to direct quotations,

---

[23]   William Appleman Williams, *The Tragedy of American Diplomacy* (Cleveland, Ohio: World Publishing Company, 1959).

and the material is centered on fruitful insights rather than on detailed scholarship. Furthermore, the insights are often the reverse of fruitful. Williams doesn't seem to understand the period *before* the turn of the twentieth century at all; in particular, he grievously confuses territorial American *expansion* over unused land areas on the American continent with American imperialism in the rest of the world. Here he fails to learn from his mentor Charles Beard and "continentalism" (or rather, the mentor of his own mentor, Merrill Jensen).

He also makes egregious mistakes, such as trying to force William Graham Sumner into the mold of "expansionist"—presumably to fit Williams's preconceived notion that, to be "saved," American capitalism required imperialism to acquire foreign markets, even though he *admits* that Sumner was strongly opposed to the imperialist advent of the Spanish-American War. Also, Williams makes little mistakes showing poor proofreading, such as that Samuel Gompers was a "corporate leader." (Although, Williams might well classify the AFL as part of the *corporativist* structure.) And, his research being skimpy, Williams is content to take a few scattered statements by senators and the like at face value, and also fails to track down the specific economic interests underlying foreign policy, in addition to the person's general economic views.

It is, indeed, in the economic area that Williams, ridden by socialist ignorance, makes the greatest blunders. He persists in confusing legitimate private foreign investment as equally "imperialist" as subsidized or coerced foreign investment by government. He believes that both are equally injurious to the backward countries. He believes with Marx—and, as he shows, with all the Marxist-in-reverse advocates of American imperialism such as Brooks Adams, Theodore Roosevelt, etc.—that the vast productive machine of American capitalism requires foreign investment and foreign markets for survival, due to the falling rates of profit at home.

This fallacy, however, has one especial advantage: that Williams is alive to the numerous people who have held this fallacy; one of his important contributions is to show that not only Brooks Adams used this argument for the Spanish-American War, but such supposedly "enlightened" folk from various shades of the political spectrum, such as Dean Acheson, Marquis Childs, and William Henry Chamberlin, have used the exact same arguments to justify the Cold War, foreign aid, the Marshall Plan, etc.—the latter two even quoting Brooks Adams himself!

Despite the above defects, the Williams book abounds in penetrating insights and leads for further research. He has a searching critique, for example, of Wilson and his "imperialist idealism"; of William Jennings Bryan's phony "anti-imperialism"; a brilliant refutation of the common "legend" that the Republican administration of the 1920s was "isolationist"; and a detailed showing of how it was the reverse; an illuminating discussion of the nature and origins of the Cold War with the Soviet Union: from the Allied intervention in the civil war, through the nonrecognition policy of the 1920s, to World War II and after.

Of particular interest here is Professor Williams's contention that Franklin D. Roosevelt's administration was not notably less anti-imperialist, nor even much less anti-Soviet, than the other administrations. Williams maintains the nonsensical view that Roosevelt's New Deal "saved capitalism" from socialism; but he makes out a stronger case for Roosevelt's "Good Neighbor Policy" being (1) not much different from Hoover's, and (2) a milder but persistent continuation of "open-door imperialism." In addition, Williams takes issue with the standard "left-wing" view of the Cold War and FDR by contending that Franklin Roosevelt, too, pursued a Cold War policy as early as 1942, and he points out quite a few interesting instances.

As in the case of other views of Williams's, these cannot simply be taken whole; they require much more thorough investigations of the historical record. Certainly, the Williams book would not be suitable, for example, for National Book Foundation distribution. But it is books with truly independent points of view that do a great deal for the furthering of historical knowledge.

8. Review of Edgar Eugene Robinson, *The Hoover Leadership*

August 19, 1961

Mr. Kenneth S. Templeton
William Volker Fund

Dear Ken:

Edgar Eugene Robinson's *The Hoover Leadership* (unpublished ms.) is yet another exercise in Hoover hagiography. It is, therefore, doubly worthless; for not only is it a simple apologia for all the works of Hoover as president—and is therefore on the wrong side of almost every issue it takes up—but also it follows in the well-worn paths of the previous Hoover hagiographers.

Robinson adds nothing new to his predecessors, who have set "the Hoover line": William Starr Meyers and Walter H. Newton, *The Hoover Administration*; Ray Lyman Wilbur and Arthur M. Hyde, *The Hoover Policies*; Hoover's own *Memoirs*; the *State Papers* of Hoover, edited by Meyers; and a few subsidiary works, such as Wilbur's recent *Memoirs* (edited by Robinson), Eugene Lyons's biography, etc.

Even as a hagiographer, Robinson contributes astonishingly little. For supposedly he had access to the unpublished Hoover papers, which contain the bulk of the record of his term, and yet almost every reference in Robinson's book is to the published accounts in Meyers and Newton, the *State Papers*, etc. In fact, the book is far inferior to the previous accounts: incomplete, sparse, and evidently totally lacking in understanding of the issues involved in the economic crisis, much less a sound view of the correct policies.

Once again, the hagiologic image of Hoover emerges out of the legendary mist: Hoover, possessor of every conceivable Christian and human virtue, "savior" of his people, engineer, humanitarian, whose statist and interventionist and inflationist policies to combat the Depression were not only right and proper and truly American but which *worked*; yes, they worked, except that circumstances beyond the

Great Hero's control (foreign intrigue and foreign financial troubles; a public propensity toward hoarding; and obstruction by Republican politicians and Democratic politicians) somehow perpetuated and deepened the Depression.

There are many gross inaccuracies here. Thus, Robinson persistently points to the obstructions placed in Hoover's path by the Republican Senate, and yet I can find no important measure proposed by Hoover that the Congress did not pass. Hoover had his way, and no amount of juggling of the issues can obscure his patent failure.

Committed to the view that Hoover was always right, Robinson does some of his own fancy evading in trying to present Hoover's evasive and self-contradictory views on Prohibition as being really the best position obtainable. Robinson's assertion that, without the annoying prohibition issue, Hoover would have won reelection on his outstanding economic record seems pretty farfetched.

Every one of Hoover's socialistic innovations is hailed by Robinson without criticism: the White House conferences, the Farm Board program (which, to Robinson, of course, "succeeded"), the Reconstruction Finance Corporation, the refusal to recognize Russia or Japan's conquest of Manchuria, the public works program, the higher taxes, et al., each is praised in turn. Not only that, but, even within this biased ideological framework, the factual discussion is hopelessly inadequate: there is virtually no mention of Hoover's inflation program, no mention of the rise of business collectivist opinion (Swope Plan, etc.), no follow-through on the consequences of, or even details on the nature of, Hoover's economic program, etc.

Here are some passages typifying Robinson's hagiography and ideological bias:

- Hoover was a "scholar, statesman, prophet . . . savior."
- Hoover believed in "private enterprise—fostered, aided and at all times regulated by a powerful government."
- Hoover's sponsoring of federal radio, merchant marine, and aviation regulation "brought cooperation" between government and business.

- Hoover's "New Day" brought a "new epoch in conservation."
- Hoover was a "strong executive."
- Hoover believed in big government as an "indirect agent of economic arbitration and economic stimulation."
- Hoover's White House conferences (which disastrously kept up wage rates for several years) "promoted cooperation" for the "welfare . . . of the whole people."
- Hoover, champion of all mankind, believed in "strengthening the economic structure of all nations."
- There is also the usual Hooverite complaining at FDR's lack of "cooperation" in the interregnum, and blaming the remainder of the Depression on that; actually, it is rarely pointed out that the "cooperation" would have meant cooperation in New Deal inflationist measures.

Throughout the book, Robinson, as in the case of his fellow hagiographers, virtually ignores any alternatives or criticism of the Hoover policies, except the extreme New Deal or socialist one. The fact that there were numerous and trenchant *laissez-faire* or quasi-*laissez-faire* critics of the Hoover position is almost totally ignored. In this way, Robinson and the others are permitted to obscure the fact that, in virtually every sense, Hoover, not FDR, was the true founder of the New Deal; FDR, of course, took the New Deal much further down the collectivist road, but Hoover laid all of the groundwork.

There are, in sum, no discernible merits to this manuscript whatever; neither in ideological position, nor in new factual material. An inadequate rehash of the Myers-Newton-Wilbur-Hoover line is hardly needed. It is an unfortunate commentary on this work that, while I read it eagerly looking for additional notes for my 1929 work[24] (since Robinson presumably had access to the Hoover papers), I found almost nothing to note.

---

[24] Editor's note: What Rothbard refers to as "my 1929 work" was later published as *America's Great Depression* (New York: D. Van Nostrand, 1963).

9. Review of Paul W. Schroeder, *The Axis Alliance and Japanese-American Relations, 1941*

April 6, 1959

Mr. Kenneth S. Templeton
William Volker Fund

Dear Ken:

Paul W. Schroeder's *The Axis Alliance and Japanese-American Relations, 1941* is remarkable as a measure of the extent to which the American Historical Association—which gave its official imprimatur to this work—has traveled in the tolerance for revisionism since the end of World War II.[25] A decade ago, this book would undoubtedly have been branded as "profascist" and a "follower of the Goebbels line" by the same people who are endorsing it today.

Schroeder's is a highly interesting, scholarly, well-written essay on American-Japanese negotiations during 1941, with the particular reference to the Tripartite Pact. It is a highly useful contribution to revisionist literature, all the more remarkable, as I have said, for bearing an official seal, as it were. Schroeder tells the facts of the case, showing that Japan, far from being an irrational, hell-bent aggressor, was actually pushed into war by the United States, which insisted on forcibly cutting off Japanese access to oil and other important goods, freezing Japanese assets in America, while delivering insufferable, virtual ultimatums to Japan to get out of China, which it had been occupying for several years.

The sincere desire for peace on the part of all Japanese—*including* the "war party"—the almost minuscule tie-up with the Nazis in the Tripartite Pact, the making of concession after concession by the Japanese to the United States only to find the U.S. always increasing

---

[25] Paul W. Schroeder, *The Axis Alliance and Japanese-American Relations, 1941* (Ithaca, N.Y.: Published for the American Historical Association by Cornell University Press, 1958).

its demands are depicted very well in this book. Schroeder is particularly bitter, and deservedly so, about the extremist unrealism and fanatical aggressiveness of Cordell Hull and such advisers as Stanley Hornbeck. It is also refreshing to see Schroeder couple his attacks on Hull's moralizing with the recognition that a propeace policy toward Japan in 1941 would not only have been the wisest and only realistic course, but would also have been a more *moral* one.

The chief weakness of the Schroeder volume is that the author shrinks from the clear interpretations of the excellent data that he has organized and presented. For example, he shows that the United States, before mid-1941, took an anti-Japanese posture, to be sure, but one that was essentially "defensive"—really aggressive, as far as I am concerned, but more a policy of "containment" than "liberation," to use fashionably current phrases. Then, suddenly, in July 1941, just as the Japanese became significantly more conciliatory and anxious for peace, the Americans suddenly increased their belligerence to almost fanatical lengths, practically calling for war. Why the change? Schroeder has no answer; he mentions the overwhelming anti-Japanese state of public opinion in the United States, and has a very good, if brief, section on the fanatical anti-Japanese opinion molding of American liberals, but he still does not explain the shift, except in terms of sudden irrationality.

There are two important strands of interpretation that are spurned by Schroeder, one in direct attack, another by sheer omission. For one basic explanation of the shift was that earlier, the main emphasis was to keep Japan from further aggression and to concentrate on fighting Nazi Germany. But by summer of 1941, it became clear to FDR and his advisors that Germany would *not* fight the Americans, despite the extreme provocations in the Atlantic, so the United States turned to the aggressive provocation of Japan as the "back door to war." Schroeder simply scoffs at this Tansill-Morgenstern *ur*-revisionist thesis as being absurd, looking for bogeys, etc., and simply claims honest mistakes or irrationalities. And yet this thesis is the only one that explains the shift, on other grounds so absurd. Schroeder only scoffs at the thesis without refuting it; indeed his data tend to lend support, as I have said, to the theory.

The second point, which Schroeder unaccountably omits altogether, is the influence of domestic Communists on U.S. foreign policy, as well as of the [Richard] Sorge spy ring on Japanese foreign policy. My contention is that much of the almost fantastic devotion to China was due not only to missionary sentimentality but to Communist policy advisors who wished to see the United States kill off Japan—Russia's and Communist China's great foe in the Far East. Communist policy was therefore to embroil the United States in a war with Japan—although not of course Russia, which would move in at the end of the war for the spoils. Schroeder does not even *mention* the fact that Germany attacked Russia in July 1941, and that *this* accounts for the sudden increase in American belligerency after that date. For, with Russia endangered, it became imperative to divert Japan from any possible foray into Russia by going southward and bringing the United States in at the "back door" to war—a double objective.

This thesis of Communist influence in America is also the only one that accounts for a fact that Schroeder puzzles over but cannot explain: after months of bellowing about how fighting for China was practically the highest absolute value an American could achieve, when we finally were in a war in Asia, America promptly forgot about China, and gave it much lower priority than the German conflict. Again, once the United States was in the war, the Communists were interested primarily in killing off Germany—the prime threat to Soviet Russia.

It is probably that Schroeder understands this, for in his citations from liberal anti-Japanese fanaticism in 1941, he quotes liberally from [Thomas A.] Bisson, [Nathaniel] Peffer, and other leftist writers in *Amerasia* and mentions the advice of Owen Lattimore and even Alger Hiss at one point (all anti-Japanese) without pointing out to the reader that *Amerasia* was a center for Soviet party-line and even espionage. (All the articles he cites from *Amerasia* and similar sources were *after* July 1941.)

All this is to say that Schroeder has not written the definitive book on this period and has not been bold enough in his conclusions. And yet, with that caveat, this is an important addition to revisionist literature. Japan is considered sympathetically; Hull is put in his true perspective; and the author ends with a good, hard-hitting attack on the Tokyo "war crimes" trials of the Japanese leaders.

10. Review of J. Fred Rippy, *Globe and Hemisphere*

February 21, 1959

Mr. Kenneth S. Templeton
William Volker Fund

Dear Ken:

J. Fred Rippy's *Globe and Hemisphere*[26] is not only a superb book, it is "doubly" superb on many levels; for above and beyond its subject matter, it indirectly raises questions about historiography that are vital to all of us.

After a slow start—where Rippy wanders around among lengthy hortatory quotations about Hemispheric solidarity, and then shifts to statistics of American investment in Latin America—he builds up his story in an excellent and controlled manner, ending in a hard-hitting crescendo. Building up his case carefully out of highly illuminating and well-researched examples, Rippy leads up to his general principles, which are clearly and very strongly opposed to economic foreign aid (indeed, all except clear military-security aid).

Rippy attacks the support of foreign socialist governments (e.g., Bolivia) via foreign aid, the wastes and boondoggling in government "investments" (extremely enlightening chapters on the Inter-American Highway, on the Rama Road boondoggle in Nicaragua, and on the Rubber fiasco—and here, as elsewhere, Rippy displays high courage

---

[26] Chicago: Henry Regnery, 1958

in exposing the phony alibis of "national defense" and military secrecy—the highway robbery of Latin American governments in exacting tribute from, and regulating, our tuna-fishing fleets, etc.) all at the expense of the long-suffering American taxpayer. Rippy continually shows his complete awareness of the plight of the American taxpayer and ridicules the idea that compulsory "charity" can fulfill the ideals of benevolence implied by voluntary charity.

Rippy also explodes the myth, and beautifully so, that Latin America has in some way been shortchanged by American aid—actually, it has been proportionally perhaps more heavily aided. Rippy bitterly exposes—in a fine combination of scholarship and a willingness to call a spade a spade—the mooching attitude of the Latin American countries out to milk the American taxpayer for every cent they can get.

He also shows, in a thoughtful chapter on the Galindez-Trujillo case, that foreign aid in itself is interventionist and, therefore, clashes with the ideal of nonintervention in Latin America. For if an American government gives aid to a Latin dictator, it is really propping him up, whereas if it shifts aid from him to a "democratic" country, it is intervening on the other side. Thus, and in other ways (as when he deals with pressure groups demanding foreign aid), Rippy shows how the intervention of the State creates insoluble conflicts between different groups, each of which wants to replace the other on the gravy train. His excellent chapter on U.S. sugar policy is good evidence of this, with various groups warring over sugar quotas. On sugar, and implicitly other tariff questions, Rippy indicates his sympathy with the American consumer, and therefore his opposition to these special-privilege schemes.

Again and again, Rippy defends free enterprise and opposes the growth of statism and governmental subsidy and aid, and presents specific cases where these apply. And he ends by reminding us that opposition to socialism is just as important as anti-Communism, and that foreign aid will really have the effect of promoting rather than hampering Communism, increasing as it does the role and importance of government in the economic life of the aided countries.

Further, Rippy advocates pulling out of expensive overseas bases where countries can blackmail us for further aid, and retiring to a continental missile defense at home; and he opposes policies of inflation, farm price support, etc.

There are jewels on almost every page and even in the footnotes. A few examples: the shocking spectacle of American politicians applauding the Marxist-Trotskyite confiscation of the Patino and other tin mines in Bolivia, with Senator Humphrey constantly calling for "jail" for the Patinos. There is the deflating of the pretenses of the "Voice of America," the mendacious propaganda of bureaucrats calling for "just a little more" aid from Congress year after year, the attack on our aid to the Marxist Bolivian government, the exposure of the Somoza "holdup" of American aid, etc., etc.

If this were all, this would still be a fine book, an excellent example of history as sound principle illustrated in a group of important, neglected, illuminating concrete cases. But there is more; for there is one reason why I regard J. Fred Rippy as one of the best of present-day historians, and this raises a basic problem in current thought. For some reason, almost all other "right-wing" historians, economists, or observers of the current scene have considered it somehow "Marxist" or anticapitalist or perhaps just plain impolite and bad mannered, to point out the probable true motivations for government actions and for the pressures for those actions. Now this, I have maintained for a long time, abdicates the responsibility of the historian to weigh and estimate, as best he can, the motivations for different actions. But because of this abdication, the field for this realistic investigation has been left to the distortions of the "muckrakers" and the far greater distortions of the Marxists. As a result, the common charge against sound, free-enterprise economists that they are "apologists for business interests" is invested with a good deal of truth.

Here is what I mean: let us take the case, for example, of an import quota on zinc. The historian who simply records the fact that the government put a quota on zinc, and who gives only the reason enunciated in the canned press releases of the government, would be abdicating his responsibility to the truth and distorting the true picture of what occurred. He is required to add that the pressure for this measure came from the zinc manufacturers. Now in the case of tariffs, this is universally recognized. But, for some reason, other historians and especially "right-wingers" stop there, and refuse to pursue the more indirect and subtle, if just as important, forms of subsidy.

For example, take the Marshall Plan (or foreign aid in general). In addition to the humanitarian and Marxist influences for the plan, there was also the economic interest of export firms who benefit from such government aid. In fact, foreign aid is, in good part, a subsidy extracted from American taxpayers and handed over to favored, selected export firms. Yet, how many historians have mentioned, for example, that the chief author of the Marshall Plan was Undersecretary of State Will Clayton, whose cotton broker firm of Anderson, Clayton and Co. received the lion's share of the cotton orders from the Marshall Plan after it was adopted? Now, perhaps such uncovering of economic interests is impolite, but it is necessary if the reader is to be told the truth of what really happened.

The great thing about J. Fred Rippy—and one that sets him, as far as I know, above all other current historians—is that he is not afraid to dig for the camouflaged economic motive. No other historian has pinpointed this so exactly. Thus, Rippy shows in this book how foreign aid has been promoted by the export industries, under the guise of altruism, national interest, etc., thus to mulct the American taxpayer.

In short, Rippy *really* believes in free enterprise, enterprise that is free, and not aided or subsidized by government—and he is willing and courageous enough to dig for the subsidy and to name the men who are engaged in it. Thus, he shows the economic interests behind the American propaganda drive for the boondoggling Inter-American Highway, promoted in large part by American automobile manufacturers, and by American construction companies, all of which stand to benefit by this subsidy. And, furthermore, Rippy recognizes that the *bureaucracy* itself (which he clearly despises in large part) has its own economic and power interests to promote, and that joined in this bureaucratic interest is the interest of the kept intellectuals who work and propagandize for the various programs. Rippy thus shows that joined with these auto and construction interests were the bureaucrats of the Public Road Department, etc.

Rippy also has the high courage to investigate who the bureaucrats actually are, and to see if they have any personal ties with the economic interests that they are engaged in subsidizing. This is another very important phase of historical inquiry that is completely neglected by almost all historians (Will Clayton is an example.)

Thus, Rippy cites the case of Henry Holland, Assistant Secretary of State, who led the government in urging aid to the Marxist government of Bolivia. Recently, this government has mysteriously veered from its socialist course to the extent of giving concessions to oil companies, and Rippy adds that Holland is an attorney for oil interests and that he might be investigated by Congress for improper influence. These are the things that historians must ferret out, and particularly right-wingers, if they would prove their devotion to their own professed cause.

After all, the sound, free-enterprise economist is not simply in favor of business, or big business; he only favors them insofar as their actions are made *on the free market.* Insofar as they lobby for subsidies (direct and indirect) for themselves at the expense of raids on the taxpayer and crippling of their competitors, the sound economist must oppose them, and the sound historian exposes them.

Other examples of Rippy's magnificent and courageous tough-mindedness: his explanation of much pro-Trujillo sentiment by Catholic congressmen as motivated by common Catholicism; of Rep. Multer's pro-Trujillo views as motivated by approval of Trujillo's pro-Jewish, pro-Zionist policy; of the lead taken in favoring special foreign aid to Latin America by Florida's Senators Holland and Smathers as motivated by the large number of votes of Latin American naturalized citizens in Florida; of Senator Saltonstall's eagerness for foreign aid to Latin America as reflecting the heavy investments in these countries by Boston bankers.

One point should be cleared up: it is wrong to think that such historiography is demeaning because it imputes "low" motives to human actors. In the first place, the "high" motives are trumpeted far and wide by the actors themselves; the "low" motives are precisely the ones that need to be uncovered. Furthermore, the historian cannot penetrate into the mind and heart of every single individual; no one can. It is *possible* that the zinc manufacturer urging a quota has really no interest in the quota as a subsidy, that he is only concerned for the "public welfare"; it is *possible* that Will Clayton had no idea that Marshall Plan funds would be funneled into his own company, and had no interest if he did know. Possible, but highly improbable.

If we assume that people are rational, in any degree, we must assume that they will not be ignorant of their economic interest; if we assume that religion is important in men's lives, then we will entertain the hypothesis that mutual Catholicism or Judaism will affect political actions. At least we will *look further* on these hypotheses, and uncover evidence, as Rippy does.

It is because of Rippy's tough-mindedness, his realism and courageous devotion to truth, his failure to be intimidated by the rarity of his realism among free-enterprisers, that this book reaches an especially high rank and is such a great achievement.

11. Review of the Veritas Foundation, *Keynes at Harvard*

April 6, 1961

Dr. Ivan R. Bierly
William Volker Fund

Dear Ivan:

The Veritas Foundation's *Keynes at Harvard*[27] is an absolute, unmitigated, and unbounded disgrace, an affront to the principles of scholarship or research, and deserving of the severest condemnation. It is also an unfortunate symptom, a symptom of what has been hap-

---

[27] New York: Veritas Foundation, 1960

pening to a large element of "right-wing" and conservative opinion in recent years.

Increasingly, the "Right" has tended to substitute for discussion of the merits or demerits of the issues, attacks on the *people* who sponsor or advocate these issues. Increasingly, the syllogism being adopted is this: the Communists approve (or disapprove) of Policy X; Mr. Jones approves (or disapproves) of Policy X; therefore, Mr. Jones is a Communist, a "dedicated and conscious agent of the Communist conspiracy," and/or a "Communist dupe."

The result of this mischievous logic is not only to make wild and absurd charges of Communism, but also to decide issues solely on the ground of whether or not the Communists approve or disapprove: in short, to abandon one's own thought in favor of the Communists' (in reverse). "Anti-Communism" then seems to require taking a position diametrically opposed to that of the Communists at all times, anyone not doing so then becoming a "Communist dupe," etc. Then, if the Communists are opposed to nuclear war, or war between the United States and Russia, or opposed to protective tariffs, then "anti–Communists" are duty bound to favor nuclear war, support protective tariffs, etc.

Buttressing this view is the wildest forms of "guilt by association"; thus, if Mr. X wrote a book favorably noticed in a Fabian magazine, then X is a Fabian, anyone connected with X is a Fabian, etc.

Keynes at Harvard is an exemplar of the worst of this tendency, with the addition of a special absurdity coined in recent years by Sister Margaret Patricia McCarran, in her fantastic, fortunately "suppressed" manuscript, "Fabianism in America" (a striking contrast to the sober, judicious *Fabianism in the Political Life of Britain*). This addition is what we may call "Fabian-baiting," which applies the same anti-Communist logic and guilt by association to Fabians, adding these "Fabians" in as a separate link to the Communists in what the Veritas people, who offer a condensed version of Sister McCarran's manuscript, like to refer to as the "Communist-Fabian-Keynesist political underworld." The operating principle is that, since Keynes was a member of the Fabian Society at one time, every Keynesian becomes a "Fabian"; since the Webbs were pro-Soviet, every Fabian (or "Fabian" by extension) becomes pro-Soviet; since the Fabians set up the London School of Economics, anyone teaching there becomes a Fabian, therefore a pro-Communist, etc., in virtually endless ramifications.

Using the McCarran-Veritas logic, it is possible to construct a view, for example, making you or me members of the "Communist-Fabian" underworld, and this can be done very readily. (Note: this is not a caricature, since it exemplifies precisely the methods used by these authors.) For example: F.A. Hayek taught for many years at the Fabian-founded London School of Economics. Therefore Hayek is a Fabian. The William Volker Fund gives scholarships for students of Hayek at Chicago; therefore the Volker Fund is part of the Fabian "transmission belt." Ivan R. Bierly works for the Volker Fund, etc.

(As far as I know, the modern founder of this sort of approach was Mrs. Elizabeth Dilling, whose book *The Red Network* proved, in similar ways, that Henry Hazlitt and H.L. Mencken were part of the "Red network." Adding "Fabianism" to the stew, of course, permits the inclusion of virtually everyone.)

The major difference between Sister McCarran and the Veritas authors is that, while the plan and purport of her work are absurd, her factual details are generally accurate. But the Veritas authors are overwhelmingly ignorant and slipshod about even the details of their own material.[28]

Let us turn now to some details of *Keynes at Harvard*. The authors purport to be undertaking a study of "Keynesism" in the Harvard economics department.[29] Yet the most striking fact about this "study" is that there is almost nothing here about the Harvard economics department. Instead, nine-tenths of the booklet is devoted to a Sister McCarran–style "history" of the Fabian movement and its alleged American wing, with emphasis heavily laid on the Harvard connections of Felix Frankfurter, the Harvard alumni status of Walter

---

[28]   Editor's note: Zygmund Dobbs was the author of *Keynes at Harvard*, a fact of which Rothbard apparently was unaware at the time of this report.
[29]   Editor's note: The pamphlet alternates between "Keynesism" and "Keynesianism" throughout, even in its chapter titles.

Lippman, etc., all of which are of course irrelevant to the Harvard economics department.

There is, furthermore, no discussion of Keynesian thought whatsoever—the authors loftily refusing to discuss it. The authors, not knowing anything of Keynesian theory, therefore persist in attributing "Keynesist" views to Keynes all of his life. Politically, of course, Keynes was always an interventionist, and with socialistic tendencies, but this hardly makes him always a "Keynesian" in the proper sense. As a result, there are numerous ludicrous references to someone, in 1914, say, spreading "Keynesist" ideas at Harvard or in the United States, when of course there was *no* Keynesianism in existence until the *General Theory* was published in 1936.

There are only very scant references to the Harvard economics department. Harris and Hansen are mentioned as leading Keynesians, but they are treated only cursorily, the authors preferring lengthy quotations from "Fabians" (i.e., socialists) like George Soule and Stuart Chase, who the authors like to believe are leading Keynesian thinkers. Of course they are not, but they are much easier targets for demolition than Hansen and Harris.

Galbraith is barely mentioned at all, simply being referred to one or two times as a "leading Keynesian economist"—which he most certainly is not. (Leading economist yes, and Keynesian yes, but he is not *known* for his Keynesianism and has made no contributions at all to Keynesian thinking.)

The only other Harvard economist mentioned, and *he* is dealt with in some detail, is Joseph Schumpeter, who is incredibly designated many times as "lifelong old socialist," "leading neo-Marxist socialist," etc. This is a ludicrous desecration of Schumpeter's views and stature. Schumpeter, insofar as he had definite political views, was procapitalist and conservative, aristocratic and skeptical. Far from being a top Keynesian, Fabian, et al., Schumpeter was a distinguished anti-Keynesian, and, for all his eccentricities, a truly distinguished economist. Veritas's mudslinging at Schumpeter is truly disgraceful. One reason that Veritas treats Schumpeter as a "leading socialist" is because, in the Schumpeter memorial volume, all of his Harvard colleagues joined in essays in his honor. Granted that many of these men were left-wingers. But the Veritas authors are clearly incapable of believing that friends and admirers of differing political persuasions might want to get together to honor someone whom they believed to be a great man.

Another fantastic point is the Veritas's treatment of Alfred Marshall as a well-known Fabian socialist. This Marshall was most emphatically not, even though he was hardly a partisan of *laissez-faire*. To bolster their absurd claim (even Sister McCarran did not claim that Marshall was a Fabian member), they cite a passage in Sister McCarran's book, which they completely misinterpret in their typically ignorant fashion. The passage refers to the Fabians, in their economics, using Marshall as the economist whose theories they followed. But this was simply the Fabians adopting the economic theory that was regnant at the time; they never cared about economic theory as such.

For some reason, the Veritas authors miss the story about Shaw being converted from Marxism to Austrian-Jevonsism by Wicksteed. If they had known this, they undoubtedly would have accused Menger and Böhm-Bawerk as being "well-known Fabians," and of course Mises as their disciple. . . . Their other "proof" on Marshall is the citation of the fact that Marshall didn't believe in *laissez-faire*. I am hardly the one to criticize *laissez-faire*, but it is ludicrous to call anyone who doesn't believe in *laissez-faire* a "Fabian socialist." (A methodology similar to calling a non-*laissez-faire* person a "Communist.") It is indeed no wonder that the Veritas authors see virtually everyone as part of the Communist-Fabian-Keynesist political underworld. (Query: if virtually everyone is a part of this network, how can it be called an "underworld"? It would be more accurate, if impolite, to call the Veritas-McCarran group the "underworld.")

But now for some details, to convey some of the flavor of this incredible performance. Perhaps the essence of the Veritas thesis encapsulated on page 39, as follows:

> Hansen, Harris and Galbraith, besides being Fabian
> type socialists, are considered the leaders of American

Keynesism. The pattern is the same although the names and labels keep shifting. Fabian socialism uses Keynesism as a political weapon. The Kremlin followers use the Fabian organizations as a cover for their operations. Keynesism is used to snare the unwary and bring them by degrees into a socialistic turn of mind. The communists then work hard to propel such socialistic converts along the road to Soviet socialism.

Some further statements:

- "You find clerics like Reinhold Niebuhr supporting the worst of the communists." (A gross distortion, of course.)

- "That is why you will find Hitler, Mussolini, and Stalin all enthusiastically embracing the Keynes system of economics." (Stalin was of course, fervently anti-Keynesian.)

- Seymour Harris's simple and correct statement that detailed economic problems are "intricate and cannot be fully understood even by the intelligent minority," is taken, *by itself*, as a call for rule by a totalitarian elite.

- "Keynesism is not an economic theory. It is a weapon of political conspiracy." (It is about time that the whole "conspiracy" terminology be dropped. If you and I agree on something, or on some objective, it is sound and proper agreement. If someone whom we dislike and his friend agree on something, then this is defined as a "conspiracy.")

- "Taussig took Joseph Schumpeter, an old time socialist of the Austro-German socialist school, into his own home and used his influence to build up Schumpeter as an international authority in the field of economics." (Since Schumpeter was a far greater economist than Taussig, this was not difficult to do.)

- "Harry F. Ward acquired his socialism in Harvard before 1898. There were many such instances of individual indoctrination . . ." (But from *whom*, since the first discussion of socialist activity at Harvard, by any faculty, refers to considerably after 1900?)

- Theodore Roosevelt's hotheaded letter to Felix Frankfurter linking the latter with the "Bolsheviki" is taken by the authors as authoritative evidence of the correctness of the charge.

- "Thus forty years ago Harvard spawned left-wing bureaucrats, socialist-Marxists and socialist-Fabians (Keynesians) who acted as 'transmission belts' for communist penetration of the nation."

- Havelock Ellis, famous sexologist, is mentioned as having achieved "notoriety" in a book "frequently banned on charges of obscenity."

- "The Labor Party policies have since been continuously determined by the Fabian Society." (Absurd exaggeration.)

- "Lange, with his background as graduate of the London School of Economics, had no difficulty in passing himself off as a Fabian socialist. The London School of Economics was founded by Sidney Webb, head of the Fabian Society."

- Aid toward conscientious objectors in World War I is called "extremist," "Fabian," etc.

- Keynes's fine work, *The Economic Consequences of the Peace*, is considered a product of the Fabian conspiracy, to preserve "German socialism" from reparations.

- "The New School for Social Research, which operates as an accredited educational institution," (as do all schools) "has been sold to the general public as an independent and politically neutral institution. Actually the New School was established by men who belong to the ranks of near-Bolshevik Intelligentsia." Here the authors quote from the Lusk Committee Report. They then add, slyly, "Keynes lectured there." (So did Alfred Schutz, late sociologist and friend of Mises, and A. Wilfred May of the *Commercial and Financial Chronicle*.)

- The League for Industrial Democracy is termed "the parent movement connecting the various Fabian 'fronts' in America to this day," which seems to me a lot of nonsense; no evidence is offered.

- Galbraith "aids communism."

- "In Britain the Keynesian theories . . . became a standby of Fabianism throughout the world as early as 1919." (They originated in 1936.)

This covers the more egregious statements in the first half of the book. There is no need to pursue the matter further.

12. Review of Alexander Gray, *The Socialist Tradition*

August 24, 1961

Dr. Ivan R. Bierly
William Volker Fund

Dear Ivan:

The besetting problem among all historians is that they tend, inherently and naturally, to favor the institutions or people whom they choose to study—or, rather, that they choose to study that which they favor. This law has applied fully to histories of socialist thought. The unique merit of Alexander Gray's, *The Socialist Tradition*[30] is that it is the one book in the field that is written from an anti-socialist, rather than a pro-socialist, perspective, and thus provides a healthy and even indispensable offset to the works of [Max] Beer, [G.D.H.] Cole, [Carl] Landauer, et al. Furthermore, many of Gray's criticisms are trenchant and cogent, and his distinct lack of awe for these socialist thinkers—exhibited by almost all the other writers in the field—is refreshing and proper, because many of the socialist arguments deserve caustic ridicule rather than sober and earnest respect.

Having said this, I must also note disquieting features of the book. While Gray is a good critic, he is hardly a great or very profound

---

[30] London: Longmans, Green, 1947

one, and he misses many of the important criticisms or aspects of these criticisms. Thus, in writing of the inefficiency of government in business, he unfortunately limits his discussion to the problem of ministerial responsibility or keeping the nationalized industry "out of politics"; there is no mention of the far more important problems of the impossibility of calculation, the loss of profit-and-loss incentive or calculability, etc. Devoting a lot of space to the anarchists, Gray never grasps the vital distinction between the individualist and the collectivist anarchists, and their contrasting attitudes on property, and thus, his discussion, while valuable in many ways, is in an impossible muddle.

But the most unfortunate aspect of Gray's work is his use of personal ridicule against the socialist and anarchist thinkers discussed. Ridicule against a nonsensical argument is one thing; ridicule against the person, then intertwined with criticism of the argument, is much different and most unfortunate. The personal sneers, to which Gray—a man of obvious wit—is addicted detract, in a scholarly audience, more from the author than the recipient, and properly so.

One glaring example: Karl Marx, a man whom Gray openly dislikes, is savagely attacked for living off Engels all of his life, and, as Gray reiterates, thereby using Engels as his pipeline to reality. Gray berates Marx unmercifully for this "for Reality is precisely the thing that none of us can see through the eyes of another. Marx spent much of his life chewing his intellectual cud, with his back firmly planted towards the window."

After this unfortunate vulgarity, Gray goes on to attack Marx's British intellectual followers with the same taint: "In this country at least, Marx has tended to become in the main the cult of a somewhat anaemic intelligentsia, who, like Marx himself, prefer to see reality through the eyes of another."

If this means anything beyond vulgar bombast, it is dangerously close to the caricature of the conservative American businessman who dismisses all intellectuals or their ideas as people who "have never met a payroll." In addition to this, the argument is totally irrelevant: for, on Gray's terms, if Marx hid from reality, *Engels* most emphatically did not, in fact quite the contrary. (Engels even met a payroll!) So if Marx is to be condemned, then Engels is, in proportion, to be praised; and yet, Engels and Marx had identical views on all questions. The "reality" argument, then, in addition to being *ad hominem*, is self-contradictory, since it cannot be used against the joint Marx-Engels theory.

This sort of personal assault is by no means the whole of Gray, and, as I have indicated, there is much cogent stuff in the book, and the book is important reading as the only work of its kind in the field. And yet this is a grave limitation on the book. Gray does similar injustice to poor Godwin, whose troubled personal life is held up as an example of the deficiency of rationalism and the life of reason, after which Godwin's own rationalistic and altruistic anarchism is used, improperly, to describe anarchist theory as a whole. (Contrary to Gray, most anarchists have been irrationalist rather than rationalist in orientation.) Later on, Gray attacks the syndicalists for being *ir*rationalists.

Gray's own ideological position, which is indicated here and there, in part accounts for the deficiencies of the book. It may be described as very moderately liberal (in the old-fashioned sense), so that at times one wonders whether he dislikes his socialist authors more for their socialism or for their "extreme" devotion to principles. His final paragraphs reveal him gently critical of the British "Road to Serfdom," but more inclined to try to modify its excesses than to oppose it root and branch.

He also, and peculiarly, seems to believe that the British population is entering upon a decline in number, and that this for some reason calls for rigid statism and central planning. Says Gray: "If we are to get through the years of shrinkage, we shall need a State professing an obligation to exercise a guiding and controlling influence in every sphere of the national life, and prepared to act accordingly."

When all the deficiencies have been noted, however, it still remains that Gray's book is the only scholarly history (though it does not claim to be a comprehensive history) of socialist thought from a critical point of view, and this places the book in an important niche for those interested in social philosophy—at least until it is replaced someday by a better book.

13. Review of T.S. Ashton, *An Economic History of England: The Eighteenth Century*

May 31, 1959

Mr. Kenneth Templeton

Dear Ken:

Economic history is almost worthless unless the historian has a knowledge of sound economics as well as of his historical period, and until recently, such knowledge was rare indeed. T.S. Ashton's, *An Economic History of England: The Eighteenth Century*[31] becomes a doubly gratifying work because of its rarity, in addition to its own excellent intrinsic qualities.

Ashton's book is a superb example of what can be done in an economic history volume: combining intimate knowledge of the latest historical research with sound economics enables Ashton to give a sound interpretation of the historical events. As a result, all the processes of the free market are soundly interpreted, as well as all the unfortunate consequences of government regulations and privileges. This fine work is eminently worthy of a National Book Foundation award, or anything else that would widen its scholarly distribution.

The following are some of the gems of insight provided by this work:

- The movement of workers over England as stimulated by wage differentials

- The absence of State and guild restrictions and regulations in the newer industrial areas, stimulating the movement and growth of industry

- The importance of graded inequalities of wealth in stimulating economic development and encouraging worker mobility

- The excellence of the network of *private* turnpikes, *private* canals, *private* river development, and *private* harbor development, in

---

[31] New York: Barnes and Noble, 1955

developing the British transport system in the eighteenth century after governmental bodies had made a botch of these fields

- The role of usury laws and government borrowing in greatly restricting economic progress and the development of capitalist industry

- The fact that war and inflation were generally a *baleful* rather than a beneficial influence on the English economy, refutation of the Hamilton-Keynes thesis that inflation and forced saving were responsible for the Industrial Revolution (On the contrary, there was little inflation in the eighteenth century—until the wars at the end, and then it was largely *agricultural* prices that rose.)

Ashton also settles the enclosure question at last, demonstrating that:

a. The enclosures were often by voluntary agreement and by voluntary purchase of rights

b. The parliamentary enclosures were largely of common land, commonly owned, thus implying that these acts were *not* robbery but the beneficial transforming of communal into individual property

c. That the result was a vast increase in agricultural productivity, due to the larger farms, the end of the vicious open-field system, and the fact that the land was owned by an *individual* leading to its conserving rather than to overgrazing, as in the past (the same point made by Scott for conservation of natural resources)

d. The enclosed forests were conserved properly by the private landlords (again the same point)

As a result, the agricultural population grew instead of diminished—in many cases, small as well as large farms expanded in number. Those farmers who did leave for the cities left in a stream typical of civilization, in response to higher wages and greater job opportunities; they were *not* "driven" off the land, as earlier historians thought.

Further: there is a refutation of the idea that luxury demand was responsible for the growth of capitalism or that war demand was responsible; there is an excellent discussion of banking matters showing that the inefficiencies of government minting, the absurdities of bimetallic ratios enforced by government, etc. led to nationwide shortages of small change and coins, thus hampering daily economic transactions. But Ashton shows that private businesses rushed in to remedy the gap very well, putting forth private coins.

He also distinguishes in superb fashion between note-issue banks, which were inflationary and subject to panics, and the type of banking that grew up particularly in the progressive area of Lancashire, where banks loaned bills of exchange or discounted them for cash, and these were not subject to panic. He fails to point out that the *latter* is the proper, hard-money type of noninflationary banking, and it is heartwarming that this type of banking flourished in precisely the fastest-growing, industrializing areas, thus refuting the orthodox claims that business would be stifled without bank credit inflation.

Ashton also shows the great economic value of smuggling, praising it for expanding trade despite high tariffs and other regulations.

Unions, too, are shown as organizations that could only raise their own wages at the expense of unemployment, restrictions on labor entry (such as apprentice regulations), and lower wages elsewhere; and they are shown as organizations living by violence, rioting, destruction of employer property, etc.

Ashton shows also that the industrial revolution raised wages of labor, provided for growing population and for poverty-stricken immigrants, competed for labor not so much with skilled craftsmen (as in the old mythos) but with miserable, underemployed paupers and squatters, who now became fully employed for the first time.

There is also a masterful description and analysis of the growth of the enterprise economy in manufactures, trade, shipping, agriculture, etc.

Ashton also shows the absurdity of the complaint that the factory system "depersonalized" the workers, by demonstrating that the old "domestic" system was far *less* personal than the factory.

One interesting tidbit: Ashton shows that the English traders did *not*, in the main, carry on actual slave-hunting in Africa (it is the *hunting* of slaves that tends to yield the great profits), but that the original hunting was done by the Africans themselves in tribal war or the slaves were sold by the African chiefs to the English.

And one heartwarming note: so much did private insurance flourish, that Lloyd's and other companies even insured *enemy ships* from English assault during wartimes! Some of the professional patriots grumbled at this, but it went on; can you imagine anything like that today?

Once in a while Ashton nods, as when he excessively defends counterfeiting (thinking that inflation is all right during times of unemployment) or when he defends the tyrannical acts that deprived the English poor of their great solace: cheap gin. However, these slips are hardly noticeable in the superb tapestry of economic history that Professor Ashton has woven in this book.

P.S. Another not-to-be-neglected merit of the Ashton work is that he scorns the excessive use of statistics and knows their limitations; his is a fine blend of qualitative and quantitative history.

IV. Economics

1. Spotlight on Keynesian Economics

October 20, 1947

Its Significance

Fifty years ago, an exuberant American people knew little and cared less about economics. They understood, however, the virtues of economic freedom, and this understanding was shared by the economists, who supplemented common sense with sharper tools of analysis.

At present, economics seems to be the number one American and world problem. The newspapers are filled with complex discussions of the budget, wages and prices, foreign loans, and production. Present-day economists greatly add to the confusion of the public. The eminent Professor X says that his plan is the only cure for world economic evils; the equally eminent Professor Y claims that this is nonsense—so whirls the merry-go-round.

However, one school of thought—the Keynesian—has succeeded in capturing the great majority of economists. Keynesian economics—proudly proclaiming itself as "modern," though with its roots deep in medieval and mercantilist thought—offers itself to the world as the panacea for our economic troubles. Keynesians claim, with supreme confidence, that they have "discovered" what determines the volume of employment at any given time. They assert that unemployment can be readily cured through governmental deficit spending, and that inflation can be checked by means of government tax surpluses.

With great intellectual arrogance, Keynesians brush aside all opposition as being "reactionary," "old-fashioned," etc. They are extremely boastful of having gained the allegiance of all the young economists—a claim that has, unfortunately, a good deal of truth. Keynesian thinking has flourished in the New Deal, in the statements of President Truman, his Council of Economic Advisers, Henry Wallace, labor unions, most of the press, all foreign governments and United Nations committees, and, to a surprising extent, among "enlightened businessmen" of the Committee for Economic Development variety.

Against this onslaught, many sincere liberal-minded citizens have been swayed by the Keynesians—particularly by their argument that the wide governmental intervention they advocate will "solve the problem of unemployment." The most dismaying aspect of the situation is that the Keynesian arguments have not been countered effectively by the liberal economists, who have generally been helpless in the tidal wave. Liberal economists have confined their attacks to the political program of the Keynesians—they have not dealt adequately with the economic theory on which this program is based. As a result, the Keynesians' claim that their program will ensure full employment has largely gone unchallenged.

The reason for this weakness on the part of liberal economists is understandable. They were brought up on "neoclassical economics," which is grounded on careful analysis of economic realities and based on the actions of individual units in the economic system. The Keynesian theory is based on a *model* of the economic system—a model that drastically oversimplifies reality and yet is extremely complex because of its abstract and mathematical nature. For this reason, liberal economists found themselves confused and bewildered by this "new" economics. Since Keynesians were the only economists equipped to discuss their system, they were easily able to convince the younger economists and students of its superiority.

To launch a successful counterattack against the Keynesian invasion, therefore, requires more than righteous indignation toward the proposals for government action in the Keynesian program. It requires a well-informed citizenry who thoroughly understand the Keynesian theory itself, with its numerous fallacies, unrealistic assumptions, and faulty concepts. For this reason it will be necessary to tread a difficult path through a complex maze of technical jargon in order to examine the Keynesian model in some detail.

Another difficulty in the task of examining Keynesianism is the sharp difference of opinion between various branches of the movement. All shades of Keynesians, however, agree in sharing a common attitude towards the function of the State, and all accept the Keynesian model as a basis for analyzing the economic situation.

All Keynesians conceive of the State as a great potential reservoir of benefits, ready to be tapped. The prime concern for the Keynesian is to decide on economic policy—what should be the economic ends of the State and what means should the State adopt to achieve them? The State is, of course, always synonymous with "we": What should "we" do to insure full employment? is a favorite query. (Whether the "we" refers to the "people" or to the Keynesians themselves is never quite made clear.)

In medieval and early modern times, the ancestors of the Keynesians who advocated similar policies also proclaimed that the State could do no wrong. At that time, the king and his nobles were the rulers of the State. Now we have the dubious privilege of periodically choosing our rulers from two sets of power-thirsty aspirants. That makes it a "democracy."[32] So, the rulers of the State, being "democratically elected" and therefore representing the "people," are allegedly entitled to control the economic system and coerce, cajole, "influence," and redistribute the wealth of their reluctant subjects.

A recent important illustration of Keynesian political thinking was the Truman message vetoing income tax reduction. The main reason for the veto was that high taxes are necessary to "check inflation,"

---

[32] This does not imply that democracy is evil. It means that democracy should be considered as a desirable technique for choosing rulers competitively, so long as the power of these rulers is strictly limited.

since a "boom" period calls for a budget surplus to "drain off excess purchasing power."

Superficially, this argument seems convincing, and it is supported by almost all economists, including many non-Keynesian conservatives. They are all very proud of the fact that they are opposing the "politically easy" route of reducing taxes in the interests of scientific truth, national welfare, and the "fight against inflation."

It is necessary, however, to analyze the problem more closely. What is the essence of inflation? It consists of rising prices—some prices rising more rapidly than others.[33] What is a *price*? It is a sum of money (general purchasing power) paid *voluntarily* by one individual to another in *exchange* for a definite *service* rendered by the second individual to the first. This service may be in the form of a tangible commodity or an intangible benefit.

On the other hand, what is a *tax*? A tax is the coercive expropriation of the property of an individual by the rulers of the State. The rulers use this property for whatever purposes they desire—usually the rulers will distribute it in such a manner as to ensure their continuance in office, i.e., by subsidizing favored groups. In addition, the rulers decide which individuals will pay the taxes—the decision consisting of expropriating the property of groups disliked by the rulers.

A *price*, therefore, is a free act of voluntary exchange between two individuals, both of whom benefit by the exchange (else the exchange would not be made!). A *tax* is a compulsory act of expropriation, with no benefit accruing to the individual (unless he happens to be on the receiving end of property expropriated by the State from someone else).

In the light of this distinction, advocating high taxes to prevent high prices is similar to a highway robber assuring the victim that his robbery is checking inflation, since the robber doesn't intend on spending the money for quite some time or that the robber might use it to repay his own debts. When will the American people wake

---

[33] The cause of rising prices is generally an abundance of fiat money created by past or present government deficits.

up to the realization that robbery only benefits the robber, and that the edict "thou shalt not steal" applies to rulers (and Keynesians) as well as to anybody else?

The Model Explained

The Keynesian theory (or model) highly oversimplifies the real world by dealing with a few large *aggregates,* lumping together the activity of all individuals in a nation.

The basic concept used is *aggregate national income,* which is defined as equal to the money value of the national output of goods and services during a given time period. It is also equal to the aggregate of income received by individuals during the period (including undistributed corporate profits).

Now, the fundamental equation of the Keynesian system is *aggregate income = aggregate expenditures.* The only way any individual can receive any money income is for some other individual to *spend* an equal sum. Conversely, every act of expenditure by an individual results in an equivalent money *income* for someone else. This is obviously, and always, true. Mr. Smith spends one dollar in Mr. Jones's grocery—this act results in one dollar of income for Mr. Jones. Mr. Smith receives his annual income as a result of an act of expenditure by the XYZ Company; the XYZ Company receives its annual income as a result of expenditures made by all its customers, etc. In every case, expenditures, and only expenditures, can create money income.

Aggregate expenditures are classified into two basic types: (1) final expenditure for goods and services that have been produced during the period equals *consumption,* and (2) expenditure on the means of production of these goods equals *investment.* Thus, money income is created by decisions to spend, consisting of consumption decisions and investment decisions.

Now, an individual, upon receiving his income, divides it between consumption and saving. Saving, in the Keynesian system, is defined simply as not spending on consumption. A fundamental Keynesian tenet is that, for any particular level of aggregate income, there is a certain definite, predictable amount that will be consumed and a definite amount that will be saved. This relationship between aggregate income and consumption is considered to be *stable*, fixed by the habits of consumers. In the mathematical Keynesian jargon, aggregate consumption (and therefore aggregate savings) is a stable, passive function of income (the famous *consumption function*). For example, we shall use the consumption function: *consumption = 90 percent of income*. (This is a highly simplified function, but it serves to illustrate the basic principles of the Keynesian model.) In this case, the savings function would be *savings = 10 percent of income*.

Consumption expenditures are, therefore, *passively* determined by the level of national income. Investment expenditures, however, are, according to the Keynesians, effected *independently* of the national income. At this stage, what determines investment is not important—the crucial point is that it is determined independently of the income level.

We have left out two factors that also determine the level of expenditures. If exports are greater than imports, the total amount of expenditures in a country is increased, hence national income increases. Also, a government budget deficit increases aggregate expenditures and income (provided that other types of expenditure can be assumed to be constant). Setting aside the foreign trade problem, it is obvious that government deficits or surpluses are, like investment, decided independently of the level of national income.

Thus, *income = independent expenditures*[34] *+ passive consumption expenditures*. Using our illustrative consumption function, *income = independent expenditures + 90 percent of income*. Now, by simple arithmetic, income equals ten times independent expenditures. For every increase in independent expenditures, there will be a ten-fold increase in income. Similarly, a decrease in independent expenditures will lead to a ten-fold drop in income. This "multiplier" effect on income will be achieved by any type of independent expenditure—whether private investment or government deficit. Thus, in the Keynesian

---

[34] Independent expenditures = private investment + government deficit.

model, government deficits and private investment have the same economic effect.

Let us now examine in detail the process whereby an *equilibrium* income is determined in the Keynesian model. The equilibrium level is the level at which national income tends to settle.

Let us assume that aggregate income = 100, consumption = 90, savings = 10, and investment = 10. Also assume that there is no government deficit or surplus. For the Keynesians, this situation is a position of equilibrium—income tends to remain at 100. A position of equilibrium is reached because both main groups in the economy— business firms and consumers—are satisfied. Business firms, in the *aggregate*, pay out 100. Of this 100, 10 is invested in capital and 90 is paid out while producing consumers' goods. Aggregate business firms expect this 90 to be returned to them through the sale of consumers' goods. The consumers fulfill the expectations of business firms by dividing the income of 100 into consuming 90 and saving 10. Thus, aggregate business firms are just satisfied with the situation, and aggregate consumers are satisfied because they are consuming 90 percent of their income and saving 10 percent.

Now, let independent expenditures increase to 20, either because of an increase in private investment or because of a government deficit. Now, income payments to consumers are 90 + 20 = 110. Consumers, receiving 110, will wish to consume 90 percent of it, or 99, and save 11. Now, business firms, who had expected a consumption of 90, are pleasantly surprised to see consumers bidding up prices and reducing merchants' stocks in an effort to consume 99. As a result, business firms expand their output of consumer goods to 99 and pay out 99 + 20 = 119, expecting a return of 99 in consumption sales. But again they are pleasantly surprised, since consumers will wish to spend 90 percent of 119, or 107. This process of expansion continues until income is again equal to ten times investment—when consumption is again equal to 90 percent of income. The point will be reached when income = 200, investment = 20, consumption = 180, and saving = 20.

It is important to notice that equilibrium was reached in both cases when aggregate *investment* = aggregate *saving*. The above equilibrium process can be described in terms of saving and investment: When investment is greater than saving, the economy expands and national income rises until aggregate saving equals aggregate investment. Similarly, the economy contracts if investment is less than saving, until they are again equal.

Note that two very important things must remain constant in order that equilibrium be reached. The consumption function (and therefore the savings function) is assumed to be constant throughout while the level of investment is constant at least until equilibrium is reached. The question now arises: what is so important about aggregate money income that it should be the continual focus of attention? Before this question can be answered, it is necessary to make certain assumptions.

Assume that the following things be considered as *given* (or constant): the existing state of all techniques, the existing efficiency, quantity, and distribution of all labor, the existing quantity and quality of all equipment, the existing distribution of national income, the existing structure of relative prices, the existing money wage rates(!), and the existing structure of consumer tastes, natural resources, and economic and political institutions.

Then, given these assumptions, for every level of national money income, there corresponds a unique, definite volume of employment. The higher the national income, the greater will be the volume of employment, until a state of "full employment" is reached. (We can define full employment as simply a very low level of unemployment.) After the full-employment level is reached, a higher money income will represent only a rise in prices, with no rise in physical output (real income) and employment.

Summing up the above model, known as the Keynesian theory of underemployment equilibrium: To each level of national income there corresponds a unique level of employment. There is, therefore, a certain level of income to which corresponds a state of full employment, without a great rise in prices. An income below this "full-employment" income will signify large-scale unemployment; an income above will mean large price inflation.

The level of income, in a private enterprise system, is determined by the level of independent investment expenditures and consumption expenditures that are a passive function of the income level. The resulting level of income will tend to settle at the point where aggregate investment equals aggregate saving.

Now (and here is the grand Keynesian climax), there is no reason whatsoever to assume that this equilibrium level of income determined in the free market will coincide with the "full-employment" income level—it may be more or less.

This is the model of the private economy accepted by all Keynesians. The State, assert the Keynesians, has the responsibility of keeping the economic system at the "full-employment" income level, since "we" cannot depend on the private economy to do so.

The Keynesian model furnishes the means by which the State can fulfill this task. Since government deficits have the same effects on income as does private investment, all that the State must do is to estimate the expected equilibrium income level of the private economy. If it is below the "full-employment" level, the State can engage in deficit spending until the desired income level is reached. Similarly, if it is above the desired level, the State can engage in budget surpluses through high taxes. The State, if it so desires, can also stimulate or discourage private investment or consumption via taxes and subsidies, or impose tariffs if it desires to create an export surplus. The favorite Keynesian prescription for stimulating consumption is progressive income taxation, since the "rich" do most of the saving. The favorite method of "encouraging private investment" is to subsidize "progressive" and "enlightened" industrialists as against "Tory big business."

The Model Criticized

We remember that for the Keynesian model to be valid, the two basic determinants of income, namely, the consumption function and independent investment, must remain constant long enough for the equilibrium of income to be reached and maintained. At the very least, it must be *possible* for these two variables to remain constant, even if they are not generally constant in actuality. The core of the basic fallacy of the Keynesian system is, however, that it is impossible for these variables to remain constant for the required length of time.

We recall that when income = 100, consumption = 90, savings = 10, and investment = 10, the system is supposed to be in equilibrium, because the aggregate expectations of business firms and the public are fulfilled. In the aggregate, both groups are just satisfied with the situation, so that there is allegedly no tendency for the income level to change. But *aggregates* are meaningful only in the world of arithmetic, not in the real world. Business firms may receive in the aggregate just what they had expected; but this does not mean that any single firm is necessarily in an equilibrium position. Business firms do not make earnings in the aggregate. Some firms may be making windfall profits, while others may be making unexpected losses. Regardless of the fact that, in the aggregate, these profits and losses may cancel each other, each firm will have to make its own adjustments to its own particular experience. This adjustment will vary widely from firm to firm and industry to industry. In this situation, the level of investment cannot remain at 10, and the consumption function will not remain fixed, so that the level of income must change. Nothing in the Keynesian system, however, can tell us *how far* or *in what direction* any of these variables will move.

Similarly, in the Keynesian theory of the adjustment process toward the level of equilibrium, if aggregate investment is greater than aggregate saving, the economy is supposed to expand toward the level of income where aggregate saving equals aggregate investment. In the very process of expansion, however, the consumption (and savings) function *cannot* remain constant. Windfall profits will be distributed unevenly (and in an unknown fashion) among the numerous business firms, thus leading to varying types of adjustments. These adjustments may lead to an unknown increase in the volume of investment. Also, under the impetus of expansion, new firms will enter the economic system, thus changing the level of investment.

In addition, as income expands, the distribution of income among individuals in the economic system necessarily changes. It is an important fact, usually overlooked, that the Keynesian assumption of a rigid consumption function assumes a *given* distribution of income. Therefore, the change in the distribution of income will cause change of unknown direction and magnitude in the consumption function. Furthermore, the undoubted emergence of capital gains will change the consumption function.

Thus, since the basic Keynesian determinants of income—the consumption function and the level of investment—cannot remain constant, they cannot determine any equilibrium level of income, even approximately. There is no point toward which income will move or at which it will tend to remain. All we can say is that there will be a complex movement in the variables of an unknown direction and degree.

This failure of the Keynesian model is a direct result of misleading aggregative concepts. Consumption is not just a function of income; it depends, in a complex fashion, on the level of past income, expected future income, the phase of the business cycle, the length of the time period under discussion, on prices of commodities, on capital gains or losses, and on the cash balances of consumers.

Furthermore, the breakdown of the economic system into a few aggregates assumes that these aggregates are independent of each other, that they are determined independently and can change independently. This overlooks the great amount of interdependence and interaction among the aggregates. Thus, saving is not independent of investment; most of it, particularly business saving, is made in anticipation of future investment. Therefore, a change in the prospects for profitable investment will have a great influence on the savings function, and hence on the consumption function. Similarly, investment is influenced by the level of income, by the expected course of future income, by anticipated consumption, and by the flow of savings. For example, a fall in savings will mean a cut in the funds available for investment, thus restricting investment.

A further illustration of the fallacy of aggregates is the Keynesian assumption that the State can simply add or subtract its expenditures from that of the private economy. This assumes that private investment decisions remain constant, unaffected by government deficits or surpluses. There is no basis whatsoever for this assumption. In addition, progressive income taxation, which is designed to encourage consumption, is assumed to have no effect on private investment. This cannot be true, since, as we have already noted, a restriction of savings will reduce investment.

Thus, aggregative economics is a drastic misrepresentation of reality. The aggregates are merely an arithmetic cloak over the real world, where multitudes of firms and individuals react and interact in a highly complex manner. The alleged "basic determinants" of the Keynesian system are themselves determined by complex interactions within and between these aggregates.

Our analysis is confirmed by the fact that the Keynesians have been completely unsuccessful in their attempts to establish an actual, stable consumption function. Statistics bear out the fact that the consumption function shifts considerably with the month of the year, the phase of the business cycle, and over the long run. Consumer habits have definitely changed over the years. In the short run, a change in family income will only lead to a change in consumption after a lag of a certain period of time. In other cases, changes in consumption may be induced by expected changes in income (e.g., consumer credit). This instability of the consumption function eliminates the possibility of any validity of the Keynesian model.

Still another fundamental fallacy in the Keynesian system is the assumed unique relation between income and employment. This relation depends, as we have noted above, upon the assumption that techniques, the quantity and quality of equipment, and the efficiency and wage rate of labor are fixed. This assumption leaves out factors of basic importance in economic life and can only be true over an extremely short period. Keynesians, however, attempt to use this relation over long periods as a basis for predicting the volume of employment. One direct result was the Keynesian fiasco of predicting eight million unemployed after the end of the war.

The most important device that insures the unique relation between income and employment is the assumption of constant money wage rates. This means that in the Keynesian model, an increase in expenditures can only increase employment if money wage rates do not rise. In other words, employment can only increase if *real* wage rates fall (wage rates relative to prices and to profits). Also, there cannot be an equilibrium level of large-scale unemployment in the Keynesian model unless money wage rates are rigid and are not free to fall.

This result is extremely interesting, since classical economists have always maintained that employment will only increase if real wage rates fall, and that large-scale unemployment can only persist if wage rates are prevented from falling by monopolistic interference in the labor market. Both Keynesians and liberal economists recognize that money wage rates, particularly since the advent of the New Deal, are no longer free to fall, due to monopolistic governmental and trade-union control of the labor market.

Keynesians would remedy this situation by deceiving unions into accepting lower real wage rates, while prices and profits rise via government deficit spending. They propose to accomplish this feat by relying on trade-union ignorance, coupled with frequent appeals to a "sense of responsibility by the labor leadership." In these days when unions emit cries of anguish and threaten to strike at every sign of higher prices or larger profits, such an attitude is incredibly naive. Far from having a sense of responsibility, the aim of most unions seems to be wage rates that increase rapidly and continuously, lower prices, and nonexistent profits.

It is evident that the liberal solution of reestablishing a freely competitive labor market through the elimination of union monopolies and governmental interference is an essential requisite for the rapid disappearance of unemployment as it arises in the economic system.

Keynesians, particularly those who are rabid partisans of the "liberal-labor movement," attempt to refute this solution by contending that cuts in money wage rates would not lead to a reduction of unemployment. They claim that wage incomes would be reduced, thereby reducing consumer demand, and lowering prices, leaving real wage rates at their previous level.

This argument rests on a confusion between wage rates and wage incomes. A reduction in money wage rates, particularly in industries where wage rates have been most rigid, will lead immediately to an increase in hours worked and the number of men employed. (Of course, the amount of the increase will vary from industry to industry.) In this way, the total payroll is increased, thus increasing wage incomes and consumer demand. A fall in money wage rates will have an especially favorable employment effect in the construction and capital-goods industries. It is just these industries that now have the strongest unions.

Furthermore, if wage incomes are reduced, then the incomes of entrepreneurs and others will be increased and total "purchasing power" in the community will not decline.

The "Mature Economy"

It is important to recall that Keynesianism was born and was able to capture its widespread following under the impetus of the Great Depression of the thirties, a depression unique in its length and severity, and, especially, in the persistence of large-scale unemployment. It was its attempt to furnish an explanation for the events of the thirties that gained Keynesianism its popular following. Using a model with assumptions that restrict its application to a very short period of time, and completely fallacious in its dependence on simple aggregates, all Keynesians confidently ordered government deficits as the cure.

In interpreting the significance of the Depression, however, Keynesians part company. "Moderates" maintain that it was simply a severe depression in the familiar round of business cycles. "Radical" Keynesians, headed by Professor Hansen of Harvard, assert that the thirties ushered in an era in the United States of "secular (long-run) stagnation." They claim that the American economy is now mature, that opportunities for investment and expansion are largely ended, so that the level of investment expenditures can be expected to remain at a permanently low level, at a level too low to ever provide full employment. The cure for this situation, according to the Keynes-Hansenites, is a permanent government program of deficit expenditures on long-range projects, and heavy progressive income taxation to permanently increase consumption and discourage savings.

Where the Hansen stagnation thesis goes beyond the Keynesian model is in its attempt to explain the determinants of the level of investment. Investment is supposed to be determined by the "extent of investment opportunities" that are, in turn, determined by (1) technological improvement, (2) the rate of population growth, and (3) the opening of new territory. The Hansenites go on to draw a gloomy picture of private investment opportunities in the modern world.

The decade of the thirties was the first in American history with a decline in population growth, and there is no new territory to develop—the "frontier" is closed. Consequently, we can rely only on technological progress to provide investment opportunities, opportunities that have to be much greater than in the past to "make up" for the unfavorable changes in the other two factors. As for technological progress, that too is slowing down. After all, the railroads have already been built and the automobile industry has reached maturity. Whatever minor improvements there might be will probably be withheld by "reactionary monopolists," etc.

Let us examine each of Hansen's alleged determinants of investment. The gloom concerning the lack of new lands to develop—the vanishing of the "frontier"—can be dispelled quickly. The frontier disappeared in 1890 without appreciably affecting the rapid progress and prosperity of America; obviously it can be no source of trouble now. This is borne out by the fact that, since 1890, investment per head in the older sections of America has been greater than in the recent frontier sections.

It is difficult to see how a decline in population growth can adversely affect investment. Population growth does not provide an independent source of investment opportunity. A fall in the rate of population growth can only affect investment adversely if:

(1) All the wants of existing consumers are completely satisfied. In that case, population growth would be the only

additional source of consumer demand. This situation clearly does not exist; there are an infinite number of unsatisfied wants.

(2) The decline would lead to reduced consumer demand. There is no reason why this should be the case. Will not families use the money that they otherwise would have spent on their children for other types of expenditures?

In particular, Hansen claims that the catastrophic drop in construction in the thirties was caused by the decline in population growth, which reduced the demand for new housing. The relevant factor in this connection, however, is the rate of growth in the number of families; this did not decline in the thirties. Furthermore, Manhattan has had a declining total population (not merely the rate of growth) since 1911, yet in the 1920s Manhattan had the biggest residential building boom in its history.

Finally, if our malady is underpopulation, why has no one suggested subsidizing immigration to cure unemployment? This would have the same effect as a rise in the rate of growth of population. The fact that not even Hansen has suggested this solution is a final demonstration of the absurdity of the "population growth" argument.

The third factor, technological progress, is certainly an important one; it is one of the main dynamic features of a free economy. Technological progress, however, is a decidedly favorable factor. It is proceeding now at a faster rate than ever before, with industries spending unprecedented sums on research and development of new techniques. New industries loom on the horizon. Certainly there is every reason to be exuberant rather than gloomy about the possibilities of technological progress.

So much for the threat of the mature economy. We have seen that of the three alleged determinants of investment, only one is relevant, and its prospects are very favorable. The Hansen mature economy thesis is at least as worthless an explanation of economic reality as the rest of the Keynesian apparatus.

So ends our lengthy analysis of the most successful and pernicious hoax in the history of economic thought—Keynesianism. All of Keynesian thinking is a tissue of distortions, fallacies, and drastically unrealistic assumptions. The vicious political effects of the Keynesian program have only been briefly considered. They are only too obvious: the rulers of the State engaging in direct robbery through "progressive" taxation, creating and spending new money in competition with individuals, directing investment, "influencing" consumption—the State all-powerful, the individual helpless and throttled under the yoke. All this is in the name of "saving free enterprise." (Rare is the Keynesian who admits to being a socialist.) This is the price we are asked to pay in order to put a completely fallacious theory into effect!

The problem of the explanation of the Great Depression, however, still remains. It is a problem that needs thorough and careful investigation; in this context we can only indicate briefly what appear to be promising lines of inquiry. Here are some of the facts: during the decade of the thirties, new investment fell sharply (particularly in construction); consumer expenditures rose; tariffs were at a record high; unemployment remained at an abnormally high level throughout the decade; commodity prices fell; *wage rates rose* (particularly in construction); income taxes rose greatly and became much more sharply progressive; strikes and trade-union membership increased greatly, especially in the capital-goods industries. There was also a huge growth of federal bureaucracy, burdensome "social legislation," and the extremely hostile antibusiness attitude of the New Deal government.

These facts indicate that the Depression was not the result of an economy that had suddenly become "mature," but of the policies of the New Deal. A free economy cannot successfully function under the constant attacks of a coercive police power. Investment is not decided according to some mystical "opportunity." It is determined by the prospects for profit and the prospects of keeping that profit. Prospects for profit depend on costs being low in relation to expected prices, and the prospects for retaining the profit depend on the lowest possible level of taxation. The effect of the New Deal was to drastically increase costs through building up a monopoly union movement, which led directly to increasing wage rates (even when prices were low and falling) and to lowered efficiency via "make-work," slowdowns, strikes, seniority rules, etc. Security of property was jeopardized by the continual onslaughts of the New Deal government, especially by the confiscatory taxation that dried up the needed flow of savings and left no incentive to invest productively the savings that remained. These savings, instead, found their way into purchasing government bonds to finance all types of boondoggling projects.

Economic well-being, therefore, as well as the basic principles of morality and justice, lead to the same necessary political goal: the reestablishment of the security of private property from all forms of coercion, without which there can be no individual freedom and no lasting economic prosperity and progress.

2. Fisher's Equation of Exchange: A Critique

October 1952

I

Fisher describes the chief purpose of his work[35] as "the causes determining the purchasing power of money." Money is a generally acceptable medium of exchange, and purchasing power is rightly defined as the "quantity of other goods which a given quantity of goods will buy." He explains that the lower the prices of goods, the larger will be the quantities that can be bought by a given amount of money, and therefore the larger the purchasing power of money. Vice versa if the prices of goods rise. This is correct; but then comes this flagrant *non sequitur*: "In short, the purchasing power of money

---

[35] Irving Fisher, *The Purchasing Power of Money* (New York: Macmillan, 1913), esp. pp. 13ff.

is the reciprocal of the level of prices; so that the study of the purchasing power of money is identical with the study of price levels."

From then on, Fisher proceeds to investigate the causes of the "price level." Thus, by a simple "in short," Fisher has leaped from the real world of an array of individual prices for an innumerable list of concrete goods, into the misleading fiction of a "price level," without discussing the grave difficulties that any such concept faces. The fallacy of the "price level" concept will be treated further below.

The "price level" is allegedly caused by three aggregative concepts: the quantity of money in circulation, its velocity of circulation (the average number of times in a period that money is exchanged for goods), and the total volume of goods bought for money. These are related by the famous equation of exchange: $MV = PT$. This equation of exchange is built up by Fisher in the following way: first, suppose an individual exchange transaction. Smith buys 10 pounds of sugar for 7 cents a pound. An exchange has been made, Smith giving up 70 cents to Jones, and Jones transferring 10 pounds of sugar to Smith.

From this fact, Fisher somehow deduces that "10 pounds of sugar have been regarded as *equal* to 70 cents, and this fact may be expressed thus: 70 cents = 10 pounds of sugar multiplied by 7 cents a pound." This offhand assumption of equality is not self-evident, as Fisher apparently assumes, but a tangle of fallacy and irrelevance. Thus, *who* has regarded the 10 pounds of sugar as *equal* to the 70 cents? Certainly not Smith, the buyer of the sugar. He bought the sugar precisely because he considered the two quantities as *unequal*; to him the value of the sugar was greater than the value of the 70 cents and that is why he made the exchange. On the other hand, Jones, the seller of the sugar, made the exchange precisely because the values of the two goods were *unequal in the opposite direction*, i.e., he valued the cents more than he did the sugar. There is thus never any equality of values in an exchange; on the contrary, there is a reverse double inequality of values on the part of the two participants.

The assumption that an exchange presumes some sort of equality has been the bugaboo of economic theory since Aristotle and it is surprising that Fisher, an exponent of the subjective theory of value in many respects, falls into the ancient trap. Thus, there is certainly no equality of values between the two goods, or, in this case, between the money and the good. Is there an equality in anything else, and can Fisher be redeemed by finding such an equality? Obviously not; there is no equality in weight, length, or any other magnitude. But to Fisher, the equation represents an equality in value between the "money side" and the "goods side"; thus Fisher states,

> The total money paid is equal in value to the total value of the goods bought. The equation thus has a money side and a goods side. The money side is the total money paid. . . . The goods side is made up of the products of the quantities of goods exchanged multiplied by their respective prices.

We have seen, however, that even for the individual exchange, and setting aside the holistic problem of referring to "total exchanges," there is no such equality that tells us anything about the facts of economic life. There is no "value of money" side equaling a "value of goods" side. The equal sign is an illegitimate one in Fisher's equation.

How then do we account for the general acceptance of the equal sign and the equation? The answer is that, mathematically, the equation is of course an obvious truism:

$$70 \text{ cents} = 10 \text{ pounds of sugar} \times 7 \text{ cents per pound of sugar}$$

In other words, 70 cents = 70 cents. But this truism conveys to us no knowledge of economic fact whatsoever. Indeed, it is possible to discover an endless number of such equations, on which esoteric articles could be published. Thus:

$$70 \text{ cents} = 100 \text{ grains of sand} \times \frac{\text{number of students in a class}}{100 \text{ grains of sand}}$$

$$+ 70 \text{ cents} - \text{number of students in a class.}$$

Then, we could say that the causal factors determining the quantity or money are: the number of grains of sand, the number of students per grain of sand, and the quantity of money. Thus, what we have in Fisher's equation is two money sides, one identical with the other. To say that such an equation is not very enlightening is self-evident. All that his equation tells us about economic life is that the total money received in a transaction is equal to the total money given up in a transaction—surely an uninteresting truism.

Let us reconsider on the basis of the determinants of price, since that is the center of interest. Fisher's equation of exchange for an individual transaction can be rearranged as follows:

$$\frac{7 \text{ cents}}{1 \text{ pound of sugar}} = \frac{70 \text{ cents}}{10 \text{ pounds of sugar}}$$

Fisher considers that this equation yields the significant information that the price is *determined* by the total money spent divided by the total supply of goods sold. Actually, of course, the equation, as an equation, tells us nothing about the determinants of price; thus, we could set up an equally truistic equation:

$$\frac{7 \text{ cents}}{1 \text{ pound of sugar}} = \frac{70 \text{ cents}}{100 \text{ bushels of wheat}} \times \frac{100 \text{ bushels of wheat}}{10 \text{ pounds of sugar}}$$

This equation is just as mathematically true as the other, and, on Fisher's own mathematical grounds, we could argue cogently that Fisher has "left out the important wheat price in the equation." We could easily add innumerable equations with an infinite number of complex factors to "determine" price.

The only knowledge we have of the determinants of price is the knowledge deduced logically from the axioms of praxeology. This will give us our theory of the determinants of price; *reliance on mathematics can at best only translate our previous knowledge into a relatively unintelligible form*—or, at worst, *it misleads the reader*, as in the present case. The price of the sugar transaction may be made to equal any number of truistic equations; but it is determined by the supply and demand of the participants, in turn governed by the utility of the two quantities of goods on the value scales of the participants in the exchange. *This* is the fruitful approach in economic theory, not the sterile mathematical one.

If we consider the equation of exchange as revealing the determinants of price, we find that Fisher must be implying that the determinants are the "70 cents" and the "10 pounds of sugar." It should be clear that, if we are interested in causal determinants, *things* cannot determine prices. *Things*, whether pieces of money or pieces of sugar or pieces of anything else, can never act—they cannot set prices or supply-and-demand schedules. All this can only be done by *human action*—only individual actors can decide whether or not to buy, only their value scales determine prices. It is this profound mistake that is at the root of the fallacies of the Fisherine equation of exchange—that human action is abstracted out of the picture, and things are assumed to be in control of economic life. Thus, either the equation of exchange is a trivial truism—in which case it is no better than a million other such truistic equations and holds no place in science, which rests on simplicity and economy of methods—or else it is supposed to convey some important truths about economics and determination of prices.

In this case, it makes the profound error of substituting for correct logical analysis of causes based on human action misleading assumptions based on an absence of human action and action by things instead. At best, the Fisher equation is superfluous and trivial; at worst, it is wrong and misleading. Fisher himself thought it conveyed important causal truths and proved this by use of the trivial truisms.

II

Thus, Fisher's equation of exchange is seen to be a pernicious one even for the individual transaction. How much more so when he extends it to the "economy as a whole"? For Fisher, as in the other parts of his theory, this is also a simple step. "The equation of exchange is simply the sum of the equations involved in all individual exchanges" in a time period. Let us now, for the sake of argument, assume that there is nothing wrong with Fisher's individual equations, and consider his "summing up" to bring about the total equation for the economy as a whole. Let us also abstract from the statistical difficulties in discovering the magnitudes for any given historical situation. Let us look at several individual transactions that Fisher tries to build into a total equation of exchange:

    A. exchanges 70 cents for 10 pounds of sugar.

    B. exchanges 10 dollars for 1 hat.

    C. exchanges 60 cents for 1 pound of butter.

    D. exchanges 500 dollars for 1 television set.

What is the "equation of exchange" for the community of four? Obviously there is no problem in summing up the total amount of money spent: $511.30. But what about the other side of the equation? Of course, if we wish to be meaninglessly truistic, we could simply write $511.30 on the other side of the equation, without any laborious building up at all. But if we merely do this, there seems to be no point in the whole procedure. Furthermore, Fisher wants to get at the determination of prices, or "the price level," so that he cannot rest content at this trivial stage. Yet, he continues on the truistic level:

$$\$511.30 = \frac{7 \text{ cents}}{1 \text{ pound of sugar}} \times 10 \text{ pounds of sugar}$$

$$+ \frac{10 \text{ dollars}}{1 \text{ hat}} \times 1 \text{ hat} + \frac{60 \text{ cents}}{1 \text{ pound of butter}}$$

$$\times 1 \text{ pound of butter} + \frac{500 \text{ dollars}}{1 \text{ TV set}} \times 1 \text{ TV set}$$

This is what Fisher does, and this is still the same trivial truism that total money spent equals total money spent. This triviality is not redeemed by referring to the quantities in the parentheses as $p \times Q$, $p' \times Q'$, etc., with each p referring to a price and each Q referring to the quantity of a good, so that:

E = Total money spent = $pQ + p'Q' + p''Q''$, etc. Writing the equation in this symbolic form does not add to its value.

Fisher, attempting to find the causes of the determination of the price level, has to proceed further to try to discover the determinants by means of this equation. We have already seen that, even for the individual transaction, the equation $p = E/Q$ (price equals total money spent divided by quantity of good sold—the price of sugar equation in Fisherine symbolic form) is only a trivial truism and is erroneous when one tries to use it to analyze the *determinants* of price.

How much worse is Fisher's attempt to arrive at such an equation for the whole community and to use this to arrive at the *determinants* of a mythical "price level"? For simplicity's sake, let us take simply the two transactions of A and B, for the sugar and the hat. Total money spent, E, clearly equals \$10.70, which of course equals total money received, $pQ + p'Q'$. But Fisher is looking for an equation to explain the price level; therefore he uses the concept of an "average price level," P, and a total quantity of goods sold, T, such that E is supposed to equal PT. But the transition from the trivial truism $E = \Sigma\, pQ + p'Q' \ldots$ to the equation $E = PT$ cannot be made as blithely as Fisher believes. Indeed, if we are interested in the explanation of economic life, it cannot be made at all.

For example, for the two transactions (or for the four), what is T? How can 10 pounds of sugar be added to 1 hat or to 1 pound of butter to arrive at T? Obviously, no such addition can be performed, and therefore Fisher's holistic T, total physical quantity of goods exchanged, is a meaningless concept and cannot be used in scientific analysis. If T is a meaningless concept, then P must be also, since the two presumably vary inversely if E remains constant. And what, indeed, is P? Here, we have a whole array of prices, 7 cents a pound, \$10 a hat, etc. What is the price level? Clearly, there is no price level here; there are only individual prices of specific goods.

But, here, error is likely to persist. Cannot prices in some way be "averaged" to give us a working definition of a price level? This is Fisher's solution. Prices of the various goods are in some way averaged to arrive at P, then $P = E/T$ and all that remains is the difficult "statistical" task of arriving at T. The concept of an average for prices is a common fallacy. It is easy to demonstrate that *prices can never be averaged* for different commodities; we shall use a simple average for our example, but it will be seen that the same conclusion applies to any sort of "weighted average" such as recommended by Fisher or by anyone else.

What is an average? Reflection will show that for several things to be averaged together, they must first be totaled. In order to be thus added together, the things must have some unit in common, and it must be this unit that is being added. Only similar units can be added together. Thus, if one object is 10 yards long, a second is 15 yards long, and a third 20 yards long, we may obtain an average length of 15 yards. Now, money prices are in terms of ratios of units: cents per sugar, cents per hat, cents per butter, etc. Suppose we take the first two prices:

$$\frac{7 \text{ cents}}{1 \text{ pound sugar}} \quad \text{and} \quad \frac{1{,}000 \text{ cents}}{1 \text{ hat}}$$

Can these two prices be averaged in any way? Can we add 1,000 and 7 together, get 1,007 cents, and divide by something to get a price level? Obviously not. Simple algebra demonstrates that the only way to add the ratios in terms of cents (certainly there is no other unit available) is as follows:

$$\frac{(7 \text{ hats and } 1{,}000 \text{ pounds of sugar}) \text{ cents}}{(\text{hats}) (\text{pounds of sugar})}$$

Obviously, neither the numerator nor the denominator makes sense; the units are incommensurable.

Fisher's more complicated concept of a weighted average, with the prices weighted by the quantities of goods sold, solves the problem of units in the numerator but not in the denominator:

$$P = \frac{pQ + p'Q' + p''Q''}{Q + Q' + Q''}$$

Thus, any form of averaged price-level concept involves the adding or multiplying of the quantities of completely different units of goods, such as butter, hats, sugar, etc., and is therefore meaningless and illegitimate. Even pounds of sugar and pounds of butter cannot be added together, in this equation, because they are two different goods and their valuation is completely different. And if one is tempted to use poundage as the common unit of quantity, what is the weight in pounds of a concert, or a medical or legal service?

It is evident that PT, in the total equation of exchange, is a completely fallacious concept. Whereas the equation $E = pQ$ for an individual transaction is at least a trivial truism, although not very enlightening on causation, the equation $E = PT$ for the whole society is a false one. Neither P nor T can be defined meaningfully, which would be necessary to giving any validity to this equation. We are left only with $E = pQ + p'Q'$, etc., which only gives us the useless truism, $E = E$.

Since the P concept is completely fallacious, it is obvious that Fisher's use of the equation to reveal the determinants of prices is fallacious. He states that if E doubles, and T remains the same, P (the price level) must double. On the holistic level, this is not even a truism; it is false, false because neither P nor T can be meaningfully defined. All we can say is that when E doubles, E doubles. For the individual transaction, the equation is at least meaningful; if a man spends $1.40 on 10 pounds of sugar, it is obvious that the price has doubled from 7 cents to 14 cents a pound. Still, this is only a mathematical truism, which tells us little of the causal forces at work. But Fisher never attempted to use his equation to explain the determinants of individual prices; he recognized that the logical analysis of supply and demand is far superior here. He used only the holistic equation, which he felt explained the determinants of the price level, and was uniquely adapted to such an explanation.

Yet the holistic equation is false, and the price level remains pure myth, an undefinable concept.[36]

3. Note on the Infant-Industry Argument

(date unknown)

The "infant industry" argument has been considered as the only justifiable ground for a protective tariff by many "neoclassical" economists. The substance of the argument was clearly stated by one of its most noted exponents, Professor F.W. Taussig:

> The argument is that while the price of the protected article is temporarily raised by the duty, eventually it is lowered. Competition sets in . . . and brings a lower price in the end. . . . [T]his reduction in domestic price comes only with the lapse of time. At the outset the domestic producer has difficulties, and cannot meet foreign competition. In the end he learns how to produce to best advantage, and then can bring the article to market as cheaply as the foreigner, even more cheaply.[37]

---

[36] Editor's note: The page ends with this (incomplete) paragraph:

We have been charitable in not analyzing in detail Fisher's money side of the equation $E = MV$, the average quantity of money in circulation in the period times the average velocity of circulation. V is an absurd concept. Even Fisher, in the case of the other magnitudes, recognized the necessity of building up the total from the individual exchanges. He was not successful in building up T out of the individual Q's, P out of the individual p's, etc., but at least he attempted to do so. In the case of V, *what is the velocity of an individual transaction?* Velocity is not an independently defined variable, as its place in the equation would indicate. Fisher can only derive V as equal to . . .

The rest of this report is missing.

[37] F.W. Taussig, *Principles of Economics*, 2nd ed. rev. (New York: Macmillan 1916), p. 527. Taussig went on to assert that "the theoretical validity of this argument has been admitted by almost all economists," and that the difficulties lay in the *practical application* of the policy.

Thus, older competitors are alleged to have historically acquired skill and capital that enable them to outcompete any new "infant" rivals. Wise protection of the government for the new firms will, in the long run, promote, rather than hinder, competition.

The troublesome question arises; if long-run prospects in the new industry are so promising, why does private enterprise, ever on the lookout for profitable investment opportunities, persistently fail to enter the new field? Such unwillingness to invest signifies that such investment would be uneconomic, i.e., would waste capital and labor that might otherwise be invested in satisfying more urgent wants of consumers.

An infant industry will be established if the superiority of the new location outweighs the economic disadvantages of abandoning already-existing, nontransferable capital goods in the older plants. If that is the case, then the new industry will compete successfully with the old without benefit of special governmental protection. If the superiorities do not balance the disadvantages, then government protection constitutes a subsidy causing a wastage of scarce factors of production. Labor and capital (including land) is wastefully expended in building new plants, when an existing plant could have been used more economically. Consumers are forced to pay a subsidy for a wastage of goods needed to serve their wants. This does not imply that if, at one time, an infant industry is unprofitable on the free market, and hence uneconomic, that such will always be the case. In many instances, the new location becomes superior after a portion of the existing capital goods in the old plants has been allowed to wear away.

Protectionist economic historians are under pains to assert that no important infant industry can be established without substantial tariff protection against entrenched foreign competition. The high degree of tariff protection in the greater part of the history of the United States, has made this preeminent industrial country a favorite "proof" of the infant-industry argument.

Ironically, it is the United States that provides the most striking illustrations of the fallaciousness of the infant-industry doctrine.

Within its vast borders, the United States offers an example of one of the world's largest free-trade areas. The frequent regional shifts in American industries provide numerous examples of birth and growth of infant industries, and decline of old, established industries. One of the most striking examples is that of the cotton textile industry.

One of America's important industries, cotton textiles were manufactured almost exclusively in New England from 1812 to 1880. During that period, there were practically no textile plants in the cotton-growing areas of the South. In 1880, the cotton textile industry began to grow rapidly in the South, rising at a far greater rate than the industry in the "entrenched" New England area, despite absence of special protection. By 1925, half of the country's cotton textile production occurred in the South. In the early 1920s, moreover, cotton textile production in New England began a sharp *absolute* decline as well, so that, at present, the South produces approximately three-fourths of the country's cotton textiles, and the New England area less than one-fourth.[38]

Another striking example of a regional shift is the clothing industry, which was highly concentrated in New York City and Chicago (close to the retail markets) until the 1921 depression. At that time, under the pressure of union-maintained wage rates and work rules in the face of falling prices, the clothing industry moved with great rapidity to disperse in rural areas. Other important shifts have been the relative dispersal of steelmaking from the Pittsburgh area, the

---

[38]   Cf. Jules Backman and Martin Gainsbrugh, *Economics of the Cotton Textile Industry* (New York: National Industrial Conference Board, 1946). Some of the reasons for the shift in capital from North to South were (1) lower wage rates for comparable labor in the South—about half in 1900; (2) development of power in the South; (3) more rapid unionization in the North, and hence, shorter hours, and great work restrictions, raising the unit labor cost; (4) earlier wage and hour legislation in the North; (5) higher taxes in the North. These factors took on greater importance after World War I, when immigration restrictions sharply reduced the supply of mill labor in the North, while the labor supply of the poor Ozark Southerners continued to be plentiful, and when unions and social legislation became more powerful.

growth of coal mining in West Virginia, airplane manufacturing in California, etc.

Logically, the "infant industry" argument must apply to interlocal and regional as well as national trade, and failure to apply it to those areas is one of the reasons for the persistence of this point of view. Logically extended, the argument would imply that it is difficult or impossible for any firm to exist and grow against the competition of existing firms in the industry, wherever located. Illustrations of this growth, and of decay of old firms, however, are innumerable, particularly in the United States. That, in many instances, a firm with almost no capital can successfully outcompete a firm with existing "entrenched" capital need only be demonstrated by the case of the lowly peddler, who is legally banned or restricted at the instance of his rivals throughout the world.

Historical Appendix

It is ironic that the American cotton textile industry provides a major example of the growth of an unprotected infant industry, for the infant-industry argument first came into prominence precisely in connection with this industry. Although the infant-industry argument has been traced back to mid-seventeenth-century England,[39] it was first widely used after the War of 1812 in America. During the war, when foreign trade had practically ceased, American capital turned to investment in domestic manufactures, particularly cotton textiles in New England and the Mid-Atlantic states. After 1815, these new firms had to compete with established English and East Indian competition. The protectionists first appeared in force upon the American scene, urging that the new industry must be protected in its infant stages. Mathew Carey, Philadelphia printer, brought the argument into prominence, and he exerted great influence on

---

[39] Cf. Jacob Viner, *Studies in the Theory of International Trade* (New York: Harper and Brothers, 1937), pp. 71–72.

young Friedrich List, who was later to become the infant-industry argument's best-known advocate.[40]

4. Report on Ronald Coase Lectures

July 16, 1957

Mr. Kenneth S. Templeton

Dear Ken:

The lectures by Professor Ronald H. Coase on *Radio, Television, and the Press* are an excellent piece of work, which I would recommend most heartily.

Lecture 1, on the general principles of freedom of the press, is a superb piece of work—crackling with wit, keen insight, and libertarian doctrine—which I would advise everyone to read *in toto*. Note Coase's points:

(1) That under planning, government, if it cannot force labor directly, must use exhortation and condemn any public criticism as subversive

(2) That experts in an industry threatened with nationalization must keep silent or lose their jobs once they are nationalized—so that more and more the only criticism of the socialist program is by the remote and ill-informed

(3) His keen discussions of the bureaucrat

The tyranny of the U.S. Post Office is exquisitely set forth.

One thing, I must confess, gave me particularly keen pleasure: the unfrocking of Professor Jules Backman of NYU as a "right-winger."

---

[40] Cf. Carey, *Essays in Political Economy* (Philadelphia: H.C. Carey & I. Lea, 1822); Joseph Dorfman, *Economic Mind in American Civilization*, vols. 1 and 2 (New York: Viking Press, 1946).

Backman is deftly exposed for what he is: a kept economist who has no firm principles at all.

Coase's point about government housing and its inevitable results is excellent—he shows its effect on free speech and freedom generally. He notes the de Jouvenel–Director position that intellectuals are pro–free speech and anti–free enterprise because of their vested interests.

Finally, after showing that a loss of free enterprise will also eliminate free speech, he says, "If we had to sacrifice either economic freedom or political freedom . . . it is in the general interest that political freedom should be abandoned rather than economic freedom. For most people it is more important to preserve the market than to preserve democracy."

Lecture 2 is also excellent—and comes out magnificently for private property in air frequencies. Coase shows that the problems of "unrestricted competition" that are supposed to result from *laissez-faire* were actually the result of not granting private property rights in air channels. Unfortunately, Coase hedges a bit at the end, but this detracts little from his bold statement of basic libertarian principle. There is a hint that Coase may favor antitrust laws, but this again detracts very little from his overall position here. Once again, the wit sparkles, and leftist arguments are skewered with aplomb and dispatch.

Lecture 3 carries on Coase's fine work with an argument for subscription TV. Coase is too harsh on the present commercial TV system when he claims that it injures consumer satisfaction. But certainly he shows conclusively the damage involved in the FCC's prevention of freedom for subscription TV. The socialistic arguments against permitting subscription TV are skewered neatly. (If commercial TV is distortive at present, it is undoubtedly due to the suppression of subscription TV.)

Lectures 4 and 5 apply his previously developed principles to the British scene. Lecture 4 reveals the development and the philosophy of the BBC, and the personality of the guiding genius of the BBC is deftly pointed up as the prototype of the arrogant bureaucrat. The dictatorial philosophy of the BBC is very neatly demonstrated. Lecture 5 is the story of competition at last emerging in British television. A high standard of wit and insight is retained throughout. Thus, there was the anti–commercial TV argument of Miss Margery Fry, who "suggests that competition, apparently in any field, is undesirable. Miss Fry pointed out that when several ladies are competing for the attentions of a gentleman, 'they are not likely to compete with the noblest sides of their nature'." And we are left with the optimistic note that the new commercial TV seems to be succeeding and out-drawing the BBC.

In sum, Coase's lectures are a splendid affair, and I am looking forward with enthusiasm to his final research on the matter. I hope that the final publication will not water down the "radical" spirit of these lectures too much.

The Ronald Coase Lectures

Professor Coase's lectures are excellent. Essentially he repeats his previous set of lectures on the post office, radio, and television, and is squarely for private enterprise and freedom in each of these fields. He shows that the post office originated in government thought control attempts and that the government still continues to censor and suppress communications it does not like.

He shows how both the high-cost and the low-cost consumers of postal service suffer from the uniform rate, which functions as a subsidy to the high-cost areas. Coase realizes that government control and censorship of radio and TV is as indefensible as government control of the press. The fallacy behind the argument that government must allocate limited radio wave frequencies is exploded. And Coase is particularly fine in making clear that private individuals should be able to own wave-frequencies in the same absolute sense as they can own land.

He defends the informative and even creative functions of advertising, and attacks any government regulation in this field, ending this section with a caustic statement that political propaganda is far worse, and consistently so, than any business propaganda in advertising.

Coase has a keen analysis of why subscription TV would be preferable ideally to present-day TV, but the real proof would have to be in the marketability: if the present setup is more economical, then it is the most preferable. Coase, unfortunately, fails to see this adequately. Coase has good defenses of subscription TV against the leftists who complain that TV viewing would no longer be free.

Coase's other errors: he concedes that advertising by business can be "wasteful," if not informative or in error on estimating profits; he overstresses the problems involved in allocating owned frequencies to broadcasters; he worries about the international problems, without considering that, since frequencies are regional and waves lose their power after a certain range, there is no reason why absolute ownership over frequencies cannot be granted over their possible range of broadcast, or, rather over the range at which the first user is actually making the broadcast.

There are a lot of merits in the summary of Coase's first, general lecture on government and the economy: the dangers to liberty of government planning, as well as to economic freedom; the inevitable moral corruption and self-righteousness of government officials—and of left-wing intellectuals.

Yet despite all this, at the beginning of his lectures Coase reveals grave collectivist deviations in his thinking. He admits frankly that "he was not opposed to State intervention in the economic "system." A modern free-enterprise system, Coase believes, requires a highly developed legal system to settle contracts and disputes. Fine, if he defines it properly, but he then goes further: to call a corporation a "creature of law," which it is not *de facto*, and to say, wrongly, that "individuals, left to themselves, would act without proper regard for the effects of their actions on others," and this includes not only violence, but "a wide variety of harmful acts" which the government must punish, "including those that have the effect of making the economic system less competitive." But since the State can and has defined almost any act as reducing competition, this opens the gates for tyranny, or, as Coase admits, "a very considerable regulation of business by the State."

5. Review of Lawrence Abbott, *Quality and Competition* and Anthony Scott, *Natural Resources: The Economics of Conservation*

July 21, 1958

Mr. Kenneth S. Templeton
William Volker Fund

Dear Ken:

Lawrence Abbott's *Quality and Competition*[41] and Anthony Scott's *Natural Resources: The Economics of Conservation*[42] are two of the best economics works I have read in many a year. They are both delightful, and it will be a great day if every book you sent me were of comparable quality.

Abbott's book is a masterpiece and displays fine theoretical acumen coupled with ability to get down to essentials and avoid all the mathematical mumbo-jumbo—a rarity these days. Abbott attacks neoclassical competition theory in such a way as to bring him very close to the Austrian position without knowing it. Abbott shows that quality competition is not only *not* a poor substitute for price competition, as modern theorists proclaim, but an essential to what he calls "complete competition," which combines price and quality competition, so that it is really a deficiency when quality competition is absent. He also follows Hayek and J.M. Clark in stressing competition as a dynamic process and not as a set of static equilibrium conditions. Further, he takes the extremely good step of stressing that the only real block to competition is *restraint* of the market, rather than "too few firms," "too large a share of the market," etc.

He stresses the value for competition of brand names, advertising (to satisfy consumer wants more fully and give them more information), diversity of product. In short, his emphasis is not on some arbitrary concept of "pure" or "perfect" competition, as in the

---

[41]   New York: Columbia University Press, 1955
[42]   Toronto: University of Toronto Press, 1955

case of most modern theorists (and where diversity, advertising, etc. are considered "monopolistic"), but on *free* competition, on the freedom of entry into a field or industry and the absence of institutional restraints. Unfortunately, Abbott considers voluntary cartels restraints along with government monopolization and interference, but his attitude is so infinitely better than almost all of his colleagues in the field that there is no point of caviling here.

There are many gems scattered throughout the book. Completely original is Abbott's ingenious definition of quality competition. Before this, economists, including myself, have thought that *theory* need not account specially for quality because a different quality good for the same price is equivalent to a different price for the same good. A different quality would, further, be simply treated as a different good for most purposes, as the same good for others. Up till now, no one has been able to distinguish theoretically between a different quality and a different good. Abbott furnishes an excellent distinction based upon the thesis that the same good satisfies the same *want*, so that there can be quality variations within the same want. This is consonant with the Austrian tradition and is an innovation within it. Further, as Abbott points out, using this stress on class of wants, he can show (in the Austrian tradition) that a greater variety of goods or an increasing standard of living fulfills more wants, or fulfills them with greater precision and accuracy than before. He also distinguishes usefully between "horizontal," "vertical," and "innovatory" differences in quality (a "vertical" difference is one that would be agreed upon by everyone—a soap that cleans better, etc.—and a "horizontal" caters to different tastes: different colored ties, etc.)

I am not prepared to say how fruitful Abbott's distinction will turn out to be, particularly in the development of economic theory, where my hunch is that current Austrianism will do well enough without tacking on Abbott's "quality models" to the price models of current theory. But this is no matter; the important parts of the book are not the attempt to build up a new equilibrium theory, but in his excellent insights into the nature of competition, his new approach to quality, and his approach to Austrianism in the course of his attack on current fallacies. His attacks on monopolistic and pure competition theory are excellent. His discussion of innovation theory is better than Schumpeter's. All in all, this is a fine book, and the author is definitely worth pursuing.

Anthony Scott's book also deserves the warmest praise. Here is a great book on conservation, theoretical and yet covering the crucial factual details for each important country and natural resource. Here is a definitive blast, at long last, at the conservation hokum. Scott shows that there need be no worries, on the free market, about excess depletion, because any resource will be preserved so that its capital value will be taken into consideration, and this will be the capitalized value of expected future returns. Nobody ravages a forest if he also owns that forest and is interested in its capital value. The key then, as Scott sees, is that private ownership should rule in natural resources, for if the resource is unowned, then surely it will be ravaged.

Scott also sees that many current cases of "ravaging" are due to the fact that there is no "unitization" of the resource; i.e., the resource should be owned as a technological unit. This implies first-user ownership, say, of a whole-unit oil pool or fishery. Numerous anticonservation arguments are included. Scott shows that forests should be privately owned; wildlife should be converted into private property, etc.

In practical politics, Scott hints that he would go very slowly, etc., but the whole brunt of his argument really cuts in our favor, even though the volume has all the wariness of conclusion (and the bad writing) of a PhD thesis.

Scott, as the outstanding anticonservationist that I know of, is definitely worth investigating.

6. On the Definition of Money

April 1959

The recent excellent articles by Gordon W. McKinley and Donald Shelby highlight the importance of a still unresolved problem: the proper definition of money.[43] When McKinley likened the argument that savings deposits (in contrast to demand deposits) are only money "substitutes" to the old doctrine that demand deposits are themselves substitutes rather than true money, he touched briefly on a highly important point in the elusive problem of defining "money." Nowadays, it is simply and casually accepted by all economists that demand deposits are part—and the largest part—of the money supply. Yet the reasons for this acceptance have been forgotten and, in the process, important insights into money have been foregone.

For it should not be forgotten that demand deposits are only money so long as the bank is considered safe; let the bank be thought in imminent danger of failure, and a bank run develop, and then its demand deposits will no longer be readily accepted at par, and will no longer function as part of the money supply. This truth is obscured nowadays because of the public faith that the FDIC will protect any bank from runs; but it was well known before 1933, when bank runs were often heavy and even endemic. Furthermore, in the pre–Civil War days when all banks printed their own notes, the notes often circulated at great discounts. This was especially true beyond the home areas, where people did not have full confidence in the bank's ability to redeem.

This dependence of the *moneyness* of demand deposits on public confidence is not a function of the gold standard; it is true today as well (or would be in the absence of the FDIC). The point is that whether the ultimate standard—the ultimate money—is gold or paper, demand deposits of commercial banks are *not* that standard; they are only redeemable in standard cash. In the strict and narrow sense, only the ultimate money, that which is not redeemable in something else, is truly money.

To confine the term "money" thus to legal tender would be a cogent definition, but not a very useful one. It would not be useful because

---

[43] Gordon W. McKinley, "The Federal Home Loan Bank System and the Control of Credit," *The Journal of Finance* 12 (1957): 319–32; McKinley, "Reply," *The Journal of Finance* 13 (1958): 545–46; and Donald Shelby, "Some Implications of the Growth of Financial Intermediaries," *The Journal of Finance* 12 (1958): 527–41.

such money-substitutes as demand deposits play the role of money in the economic system: they act as would an increase in money in their effects on the economy. They do so precisely because people believe that they *do* stand for money, that they are redeemable in cash. As long as people continue to believe this, they are willing to exchange demand deposits, or to hold them in their cash balances, as absolutely equivalent to money. Both are equivalent "dollars." Thus, demand deposits may be considered, so long as they are thus equivalent, as part of "money" in the broader sense.

But what of such assets as savings deposits? Those who would confine money-in-the-broader-sense to demand deposits assert that the two are uniquely different: that the latter are used as media of exchange while savings deposits are not. But this difference, while important in many respects, is not at all decisive here. For here we have only a difference in the form in which money is kept. Suppose, for example, that through some cultural quirk, everyone in the country decided that they would not use their five-dollar bills in exchange. They would only use their ten- and one-dollar bills, and keep their cash balances in fives. As a result, the five-dollar bills would tend to circulate far more slowly than the other bills. Now suppose that, when a man wants to reduce his cash balance, he may not spend his five-dollar bill directly; he goes to a bank and exchanges it for five one-dollar bills, which he proceeds to trade. In this hypothetical situation, the status of the five-dollar bill would be exactly the same as the savings deposit today. The five-dollar bill—like the savings deposit—would never be used as a direct medium of exchange; and, again like the savings deposit, it could only be used as a medium at one remove: the holder must go to a bank and exchange it for that type of money which will serve as a medium. Yet would anyone say that the five-dollar bill is not part of the money supply? But if it is, we must also say that the savings deposit is likewise part of any broader definition of money that includes demand deposits.

In short, a savings deposit is money of a different form than demand deposits. It circulates more slowly, and more of people's long-term cash balances are held in this form; and yet, whenever the holder wishes to use it as a medium, he simply goes to his bank and obtains the demand deposit. Or, indeed, he may just as readily obtain cash directly, as he could with a demand deposit.

Those who stress the use of demand deposits as direct media forget *why* they are media in the first place: because they are generally regarded as redeemable at par for cash—the *original* medium. But then are not *any* assets, likewise redeemable at par, also part of the money supply? If so, then savings deposits, both in commercial and savings banks, must be considered as part of the money supply because they are redeemable at par. And, furthermore, so must we consider savings-and-loan shares, which the savings-and-loan association promises to redeem at par.[44] But McKinley and other writers who have argued persuasively for the inclusion of savings deposits and savings-and-loan shares in money have neglected other assets: notably, government savings bonds and the cash-surrender values of life insurance. Government savings bonds, with their fixed guarantee of redeemability in cash, certainly are just as much money as savings deposits. To be precise, of the nonmarketable Treasury liabilities, savings bonds, savings notes, and Series A investment bonds (redeemable in cash whereas Series B bonds are not), must be treated as part of the money supply.[45] Marketable securities, like all other assets, are exchangeable for money, but only at varying and nonfixed rates, and are therefore not money but "goods." And this is true even for short-term government bonds, which are highly liquid and can function as "near-money" substitutes for part of a person's cash balance; for they are only exchangeable for money at the market risk. There is no fixed, guaranteed relationship, and therefore they cannot be perfect substitutes for money, i.e., money itself.

It is also a radical step to include cash surrender values of life insurance policies as part of the money supply. And yet, they too

---

[44] Credit union shares, redeemable at par, as well as savings deposits in credit unions, must then also be included in the money supply.

[45] See Helen J. Cooke, "Cash Borrowing of the United States Treasury: Nonmarketable Issues," in *The Treasury and the Money Market* (New York: Federal Reserve Bank of New York, 1954), pp. 17–21.

are balances that may be redeemed at any time, by promise of the life insurance company, that the policyholder cancels his policy. Like savings deposits, savings and loan shares, and savings bonds, they are considered by individuals as cash, and are valued as assets firmly at their cash value.[46] If savings deposits are accepted as part of the money supply, even though not directly used as media, then there is no cogent criterion for keeping out savings bonds and cash surrender values.[47] Yet those many economists who include savings deposits in the money supply have not yet pushed their logic to its final conclusion.[48]

Much has been made of the legal permission to require notice for redeeming savings deposits and the other assets mentioned above. Yet everyone recognizes the economic fact that this provision is merely a dead letter; if notices were ever enforced, the bank would

---

[46] On the other hand, the face value of accident or fire insurance policies, or of term life insurance, may not at all be considered money because they are not redeemable at the will of the policyholder. They can only be cashed if the disaster—presumably unforeseen—occurs. If it *is* "foreseen," then we have a case for the criminal courts.

Furthermore, pension funds, not being redeemable, are not part of the money supply. And, contrary to McKinley, neither are shares in "open-end" mutual funds, which are only redeemable at market value and not at par, and are therefore no more money than any other stock.

McKinley surely errs also in saying that "every extension of debt . . . involves the creation of money," since, on his own grounds, not all liabilities are "generally and usually considered as money," nor are credit transactions (involving the issue of claims to money at a specific future date) the same as issuing claims to money on virtual demand. The latter, being redeemable at par in money, are themselves effectively money. See McKinley, "Federal Home Loan Bank System," pp. 325–26.

[47] In one sense, savings deposits have a greater claim to inclusion—and a claim clearly as great as demand deposits. For in some cases, time deposits are used directly to make payments, with individuals using cashier's checks on them directly as money. See, for example, *Business Week* (November 16, 1957): 85.

[48] But see the hint on life insurance policies in Arthur F. Burns, *Prosperity Without Inflation* (Buffalo, N.Y.: Smith, Keynes, and Marshall, 1958), p. 50.

For a summary of many economists who have, and have not, included time deposits in their definition of money, see Richard T. Selden, "Monetary Velocity in the United States," in *Studies in the Quantity Theory of Money*, Milton Friedman, ed. (Chicago: University of Chicago Press, 1956), pp. 184–85, 237–44. Selden is certainly correct in including Treasury cash, and Treasury demand deposits at the Federal Reserve Banks, in the money supply.

soon fail, as the enforcement would be considered by all as a sign of impending insolvency.[49] And the permitted notice requirements for the other assets are much shorter than the legal thirty days for savings deposits: life insurance surrender values and Series E savings bonds being practically immediate.

Neither is it permissible to distinguish between demand deposits and the other assets on the grounds that demand deposits do not pay interest. In the first place, commercial banks did pay interest on demand deposits until 1933, when the practice was outlawed.[50] And secondly, life insurance policies also do not obtain interest on the cash surrender values for the policyholder.

Thus, economists have a choice: they may either adopt the coherent but inexpedient definition of "money" as the narrow supply of legal tender; or, if they broaden their definition to include perfect money-substitutes, they should proceed onward to include *all* such assets, as outlined above.

Even if we adopt the latter course, however, we must still recognize the particularly strategic role of demand deposits as the direct medium. Here the analyses by McKinley and Shelby of the inverted money pyramids come into play. While savings banks, life insurance companies, etc. add to the money supply, they also keep the great bulk of their reserves in *demand deposits* rather than in cash, precisely because demand deposits are in such preponderant use as a direct medium. When we add up the total money supply outstanding in the hands of the public, then, we must not only deduct the cash reserves of the commercial banks, we must also deduct the demand-deposit

---

[49]   Many heavy bank runs in 1931–33 took place in *time* deposits, which were recognized as effectively deposits on demand by bankers and Federal Reserve officials alike. See Senate Banking and Currency Committee, *Hearings On Operation of National and Federal Reserve Banking Systems, Part I* (Washington, 1931), pp. 36, 321–22, and the excellent, neglected article by Lin Lin, "Are Time Deposits Money?" *American Economic Review* (March 1937): 76–86.

[50]   See Lin Lin, "Professor Graham on Reserve Money and the 100% Proposal," *American Economic Review* (March 1937): 112–13.

reserves of these other *money creators*.[51] And because these institutions keep their reserves in demand deposits, the Federal Reserve System, as the above authors have pointed out, exerts much greater control over them than purely legal considerations would lead us to believe.

7. Review of John Chamberlain, *The Roots of Capitalism*

July 5, 1959

Dr. Ivan R. Bierly
William Volker Fund

Dear Ivan:

John Chamberlain's *The Roots of Capitalism*[52] is divisible into two parts: the prologue and chapters 1–3, which deal with political philosophy and its history, and the remainder (chapters 4–12 and the epilogue), which deal with economics. When I had finished reading the first three chapters, I thought that this was going to be one of the best introductions to libertarianism and capitalism—to the whole complex of history, political philosophy, and economics that makes up the libertarian picture—that had ever been published. When I finished reading the entire book, I realized that this book essentially fails. Since the excellent political chapters constitute only one-fourth of the book, they cannot offset the thundering failure of John's economic chapters, which are the meat of the book.[53]

---

[51] *Money creators* is a far better term than the currently fashionable "financial intermediaries," which implies that both commercial banks and the other financial institutions are not really money creators but simply credit intermediaries between savers and investors. There is no space here to re-argue the old currency school–banking school controversy, as would be necessary for a full critique of this attempt to revive the banking-school doctrines.

[52] Princeton, N.J.: D. Van Nostrand, 1959

[53] Editor's note: John Chamberlain was a frequent book reviewer for *National Review* and the *Freeman*, and Rothbard knew him as a colleague.

First, as to the beginning chapters, they are an excellent guide to the historical and political backgrounds of libertarianism and capitalism. One particularly fine thing about them is that they approach history in a truly libertarian manner: it is anti–George III, pro-Leveller, pro-Locke, pro-smuggling in England, etc. This is particularly welcome because this sort of historiographic attitude has been unfortunately passé on the Right for quite some time—especially ever since Russell Kirk has befogged the political philosophy of our time. The current fashion has been to be pro-Metternich, pro-Tory, anti-Leveller, and pro-Stuart, etc., and the prevalence of this fashion makes John's approach all the more refreshing.

Another excellent quality is John's grounding himself on natural rights of the individual, on natural and common law, on property right, and on the preeminent importance of man's freedom of choice. And John rejects the current fashionable deprecation of the Magna Carta, and rightly defends John Locke's libertarian credentials against the interpretations of Bertrand de Jouvenel and Willmoore Kendall.

Some of the other good points in these first chapters: they show the planning propensities of George III, the fact that the road network built in eighteenth-century England was privately owned, the libertarian implications of the Ten Commandments, and a brief slap at the Sixteenth Amendment.

In these first chapters, there are just two important errors made by Chamberlain. One is in overly excusing the statist restrictions and dictations of the feudal system on the ground that they were somehow necessary because the "Christian Order" was in a "state of siege" against the heathens without: this is the old fallacy of using a vague foreign threat as an excuse for all manner of domestic tyranny. The second is Chamberlain's gratuitous and jejune use of Locke to try to justify a policy of outlawing the Communist Party. Not only is this a vulgar use of history, it is also a whopping *non sequitur*: for if Locke's constitution did not grant any group the "liberty of attempting to coerce others to its beliefs," this does not simply mean outlawing Communists, but, presumably, any socialist group, even if "democratic."

But now for the bulk of the book. What, precisely, is the failure of Chamberlain's economics? I think, basically and profoundly, it is a failure to understand economics and economic theory. And since the bulk of this book deals with economics and economic theory, this failure is disastrous for the impact of the book as a whole.

Before getting to the content of these chapters, a word should be said about the organization. Chamberlain is, of course, a superb stylist, and this is true in everything he writes. But the *organization* of a book reflects one's understanding of the subject matter and is not a question of style; and here, already, Chamberlain is poor.

The organization of the economic chapters is slipshod. After discussing contract, Chamberlain suddenly talks of unionism, and then he goes back to Ricardo and Malthus. Next, suddenly, Chamberlain devotes a whole chapter of his book to the rather unimportant Robert Owen, and then another whole chapter to the also unimportant Francis Amasa Walker. Suddenly, we find ourselves dealing with Henry Ford, and then we are up discussing the modern question of monopolistic competition (in the only really good economic chapter, by the way), then back to unions and on to Keynesianism. And that's it!

The allocation of space is inchoate and peculiar. There is not one word, for example, about the great flowering of American capitalism in the late nineteenth century, about the whole problem of the robber barons. *Not one word*, while a couple of chapters are devoted to Robert Owen and Francis Amasa Walker. There is almost no mention of Karl Marx, which is almost as incredible, and none of Veblen until the epilogue, when Veblen suddenly pops up, as if by afterthought.

This extremely poor organization reflects Chamberlain's lack of understanding of economics, as we shall now see. The basic problem, I believe, is this: Chamberlain absolutely fails to understand the nature and the importance of economic law. To Chamberlain, *all* economic science—and not just the Ricardians whom Chamberlain criticizes at excessive length—is "static," "gloomy," repressive. Chamberlain somehow thinks of all economics as gloomy and European, and thinks of the achievement of American capitalism as "refuting these gloomy laws by the dynamic technological breakthroughs of our practical men." Now this is absolute nonsense, and yet again and again Chamberlain returns to the theme of scoffing at the "iron" laws of economists, and of the saga of how American technology and mass production was supposed to have shown the world how to conquer these laws. Actually, the two are unrelated; economic laws are not "refuted" by technological improvement or capitalist development.

It is because of this flouting of economics that Chamberlain devotes so much time to Owen and Henry Ford; to Chamberlain, they somehow founded modern capitalism because they showed that what employers should do is to give their employees high wages; this will increase their efficiency, or as with Robert Owen, give them welfare programs and do the same. Now, this, as a general principle, is nonsense; the payment of wages is *not* up to the employers, who are guided by market laws and pay market wages. Any welfare payment of the Owen variety simply comes out of the wage the employer would have paid; which means the worker gets less money and more "medical benefits" from his employer. And to go further and to imply, as Chamberlain does, that the reason European capitalism never developed is because the other employers were not as humanitarian and farsighted as Owen, is pure mythology. For the same reason, Chamberlain overvalues and distorts Henry Ford's achievement; Henry Ford was *not* the founder of American capitalism or of some great new economic principle.

Chamberlain's paeans to Robert Owen as manufacturer are sheer romantic absurdity and display profound ignorance of economics: Owen, he said, gave "tangible proof that money could be made . . . without grinding the faces of the poor"—obviously implying that all the other manufacturers of the day *were* so grinding; Owen "went into the coal business to keep his employees from being gouged on fuel" (gouged by whom?); "he offered medical attention to all"; Owen knew—again in contrast to other manufacturers—"that there was no long-term profit in the sheer exploitation of one's help." Owen's good gray father-in-law was one of the first industrialists who "chose to flout . . . the 'iron law of wages.'" Owen anticipated "modern 'consumer capitalism'"—whatever that is supposed to mean: when *didn't* a market economy rest on consumer demands?

One of the great "iron" bogeys of Chamberlain, which he deals with almost continually in this book, is the terrible bleak "wages-fund theory." Hence, his enthusiasm, expressed at length, for Henry Ford, who like Owen "walked boldly up to the ghost [the wages-fund theory] and proved its insubstantiality."

"It was Henry Ford's decision to pay $5 a day without raising the price of his car that proved the wage fund and the other preconceptions of British economics had little to do with industrial realities in a dynamic world." Chamberlain doesn't seem to realize that a businessman's actions of this sort cannot refute an economic theory like the wages-fund theory; they are two orders of discourse.

Chamberlain fails utterly to realize that the whole point of economics rests on an analysis of *scarcity*: the fact that means are scarce (and always will be), in relation to human ends. In his bog of fallacy, Chamberlain says this: "Always, before Eli Whitney and Frederick Taylor and Henry Ford, the world struggled with scarcity. And when economics ceased to be wholly a matter of the deployment of scarce means . . . " it is now, because of Whitney and Taylor and Ford, based on "contrived fecundity" rather than "contrived scarcity." Rarely have more critical fallacies been packed into so short a space: economics has, still does, and will continue to be wholly concerned with "scarcity," and so will the world, notwithstanding Whitney, Taylor, Ford, or whatever other heroes Chamberlain dredges up. Here again, we see Chamberlain's fatal lack of understanding of what economic science is all about, and his naïve belief that economic principles can somehow be refuted by some dynamic new manufacturer.

Another example of Chamberlain's failure at economics is his discussion of rent theory as if it were somehow up to the landlord how much rent he will charge, and that rents depend solely on the landlord's humanitarian or miserly traits. That there is a *market* and *market prices* for rents, and therefore that there are economic principles determining these prices, is completely overlooked.

It will be noted, incidentally, that while Chamberlain is of course severe on Robert Owen's later communal utopias, he says nothing of his hero Henry Ford's persistent penchant for cranky funny-money.

For quite a while I was puzzled about the problem of why Chamberlain singles out, among all the economists, only the rather obscure and not too important Francis Amasa Walker for praise—indeed, for rhapsodic eulogy. He mentions a few times the Austrians J.B. Clark and Ludwig von Mises, but only very perfunctorily and ritualistically. Almost his entire enthusiasm for economists is poured out for Walker. But, in the context of the book as a whole, the reason seems clear: Walker was the first *American* to be critical of the wages-fund theory. He was also the first to stress entrepreneurship, but it is clear that the paeans are referred mainly to his attack on the wages-fund theory.

And the grandiloquent title to this chapter, "Prometheus Unbound," is to be explained as part of Chamberlain's eternal war against "iron" economic laws, for Walker was supposed to have destroyed the hated (by Chamberlain) wages-fund theory. Actually, the singling out of Francis Amasa Walker of all the economists for lengthy eulogizing is impermissible. Walker's theory of entrepreneurship and profit was interesting, but hardly deserves mention when the author omits the equally important, or better, theories of Böhm-Bawerk, J.B. Clark, Frank Knight, and Ludwig von Mises, or, for that matter, of the German von Mangoldt.

We come now to Chamberlain's *bête noire*, the wages-fund theory. It would come as an enormous shock to John, I'm afraid, but actually the wages theory was substantially correct, despite its crudities. Walker and Chamberlain to the contrary, it is *not* refuted by the productivity theory of wages—again, the two explain different things. The wages-fund theory explains the aggregate amount of money wages at any given time. It is correct that, at any given time, there is a certain fixed capital fund, determined by saving and investment, from which employers can pay wages, and the old classical "iron" law that union pressure for wage increase can only reduce the amount of wages paid to workers elsewhere in the economy, is also substantially correct.

The productivity theory of wages explains, in the first place, each individual's wage, rather than the wage level in general; and, second, it explains his real wage, how much output the worker will receive for his wages. The wages-fund theory explains the *money* wage received by the average worker. Actually, the wages-fund theory is a crude one, it should be called a wage-and-rent fund, etc., but the essence of it is correct, as Böhm-Bawerk and Wicksell point out. Needless to say, Böhm-Bawerk is hardly mentioned in this volume, and Wicksell not at all.

Furthermore, Walker's statement of wage theory was a highly crude one; he did not really have a good statement of marginal productivity theory; that was left, in America, to J.B. Clark.

And finally, one would never know from Chamberlain's rhapsodic discussion that Walker, while quite conservative, was a bitter opponent of *laissez-faire*.

In the light of all this, it seems to me sheer presumption for Chamberlain to criticize textbooks in the history of economic thought for underrating Francis Amasa Walker. Such a charge is hardly viable coming from someone with Chamberlain's lack of economic knowledge.

Chamberlain's other leading error in economic theory is his critique of Keynesianism, which occupies the last chapter of the work. This is a very weak, fumbling critique, giving away a large part of the case, making hardly any dent in the Keynesian structure. Chamberlain concedes a good bit of the Keynesian case: that inflation is really just as good as a cut in wages, economically, which is not true; that liquidity preference and hoarding really may be a generator of depression, which is untrue; and that a failure of consumer demand may be a cause of depression, also untrue.

Chamberlain also has the colossal effrontery to try to modify a Mises critique of Keynes, saying that when Mises says that Keynes is dead wrong, this is true—but only for the long run. But, Chamberlain warns, Keynes may be right for the short run, and the long run may even be Keynes's by a series of *cumulative* short-run troubles. Here again, Chamberlain is wrong, period, and it seems to me effrontery for someone with as little grasp of economic theory as Chamberlain has to presume to correct an economist like Mises.

At the end, Chamberlain simply throws up his hands and admits that he doesn't know whether Keynes is right or wrong economically, but he is certainly wrong politically, because the government will never check inflation in a boom enough to make "cyclical compensatory spending" work.

Thus, Chamberlain: "an honest commentator must admit that there are analytical phases of the *General Theory* that are hard to laugh off. Given enough cumulative short-term failures of Say's Law," etc. And: "The whole of Keynes [*sic*] *General Theory* remains in the realm of logical deduction from premises that may or may not be true." And: "From the standpoint of pure economics his analyses of the failure of demand in a depression era . . . do have a general correspondence with the 'feel' of the facts."

Enough of Chamberlain's utter failure as an economist. We now turn to several grave politico-economic errors and biases displayed by Chamberlain in this book. The worst and most persistent is on trade unions. Again and again, Chamberlain identifies the only aspect of trade unions that he deems "coercive" as the closed shop. The closed shop, he maintains, interferes with a worker's "freedom of choice."

Actually, while we may abhor the closed shop, it does *not* interfere with a worker's freedom of choice, unless we assume, as Chamberlain tacitly does, that any loss of a job is "coercion," or "interference with freedom." Actually, the important question is the *employer's* freedom of choice, for he is the fellow who is paying out his money for certain tasks, and therefore he should have the right to set whatever terms of employment he wishes; he should, therefore, have the right to insist on workers belonging to a closed shop if he should be perhaps foolish enough to want to.

The critical problems about unions are (a) their habitual use of violence, (b) their nature as parasitic organizations, and (c) their monopoly privileging through the Wagner Act. Yet, oddly enough, Chamberlain not once mentions union penchants for violence and not once mentions such grants to unions of monopoly privileges as the Wagner Act.

Furthermore, he attacks the old-style management opposition to all unionism. This opposition was actually cogent and proper, because unions can only be trouble-making, production-lowering organizations. But instead, Chamberlain bitterly criticizes the "old habit of union baiting," which Chamberlain wrongly considers "interference with workers' freedom of contract." He criticizes employers calling federal troops to break strikes, without once considering why such troops were even considered necessary: no troops *ever forced* any strikers to work! So what did they do? Obviously, their only function was to protect employer property and personnel, to protect strikebreakers from the characteristic goon-squad violence of organized labor. The troops were, then, perfectly called for. Yet Chamberlain's reference to violence in labor disputes is to attack management!

Because British labor unions have never stressed the closed shop, Chamberlain's exclusive emphasis on the closed shop as the only union evil actually leads him to praise the British unions, the mainstay of the British Labour Party, as being somehow conservative and devoted to collective bargaining contracts. (Actually, Chamberlain also does not see that collective bargaining "contracts" are not true contracts in the libertarian-law sense, for (1) they do not specifically agree to transfer property—just to set a certain wage or terms should any property *be* transferred; and (2) the workers' end of the "contract" is invalid, anyway, because workers cannot be forced to keep working against their will.) Chamberlain's weakness for labor unions also leads him to say that Philip Murray was tending away from left-wing unionism.

Thus, Chamberlain's outrageously weak attitude toward unionism leads him to make such statements as the following:

> the English union man has always returned to his
> Ernie Bevin . . . the English worker has lived in the
> tradition of John Locke. . . . Possibly the willingness
> to compromise that has characterized English and

Swedish big ownership has enabled labor in the two
enlightened North European countries to have faith
in the possibilities of the contractual way.

This in two countries that have gone the farthest down the road
to welfare socialism and Labour Party activity! And the comparison
between Ernie Bevin and John Locke is peculiarly inapt, to say the least.

Chamberlain also wrongly stigmatizes the "yellow dog" contract as "coercion," and equivalent to a closed shop. But perhaps
Chamberlain's worst and most outrageous statement on the union
question is the following:

> If management should return to the old habit of
> union baiting, which amounts to an attempted inter-
> ference with a worker's freedom of contract, or if it
> refuses to bargain with open unions on an above-board
> basis, then we shall get the universal closed shop or a
> condition of chaos and industrial slavery. . . .
>
> In either case the state must walk in. . . . In the case
> of chaos and industrial slavery the state must inter-
> vene to guarantee social security to the underdog. (It
> must go far beyond such things as minimum wage
> laws and forced unemployment payments, which are
> themselves minor and absorbable infringements of
> free contract.)

Aside from the fact that minimum wage laws and unemployment
insurance are *not* simply minor and absorbable, Chamberlain has
gone to the length of pure leftist demagogy here by characterizing
a system where employers determinedly refuse to have anything to
do with unions as "chaos and industrial slavery," requiring massive
state intervention and guarantees. This sort of statement in any book
would be cause for chastisement—but in a book by a purported
libertarian?

There are other important political aberrations and biases in
the book. Chamberlain comes out flatly in favor of the SEC; he also

declares that railroad rebates to oil companies, etc., were political. He says that there must be a minimum amount of interference of political power with social power and uses as his bolstering argument the hoary old fallacy about the necessity for traffic regulations, which Mises so brilliantly exploded in *Human Action* (anyone who *owns* the roads must regulate them, so if private enterprise owned the roads, etc.).

He also looks too benignly toward consumer cooperatives, at one point saying that they may be called for "to protect living standards." This is nonsense; a consumer cooperative (1) is an inefficient form of business enterprise; and (2) the actual movement has boasted of trying to replace capitalist enterprise. None of these salient points are mentioned by Chamberlain.

Chamberlain's discussion of the problem of monopoly, competition, and "monopolistic competition" in chapters 9 and also 10 are the only really valuable parts of the economic sections of the book. There is much excellent material here. And yet, while Chamberlain says that "in the days of the classical economists 'monopoly' had a clear and simple reference: it was what happened when the state gave an individual or a trading company the sole right to exploit a given market. Monopoly was a grant of privilege by government," he inconsistently, in several places, praises the Sherman Act as a combater of monopoly. He also misconceives the common law, by repeating the old error that the Sherman Act "elevated the common-law tradition to federal dignity"—a myth exploded five years ago by William Letwin. And this flowery rapture: "the Sherman Antitrust Act continues to work its overall watchdog magic." Magic, indeed!

Turning to the concrete political problems of our day, what does Chamberlain approve? He overly praises the West German recovery and its neoliberalism, for while giving the West Germans their just due, he also says that the "government has still been able . . . to behave in a generally humane way." Also, these resurgent "true liberals" of Western Europe are hardly "true" but much diluted.

Finally, in his proposal as to what to do next in America, Chamberlain actually comes out and says that a gradual dismantling of the welfare state would be better than none at all. It is perhaps true that a gradual dismantling would be better than no dismantling at all, but to say that it is better than *rapid* dismantling is to give away a good part of the case against the welfare state, and to concede short-run practicality to the collectivists as he halfway conceded it to Keynes. In actual fact, libertarianism, *laissez-faire*, is more practical in the short as well as in the long run. And yet, Chamberlain concludes by first praising the Committee for Economic Development plan for the federal government to compensate marginal farmers out of tax funds while they are learning new trades, and goes on: "Some of them [methods of returning to voluntary action] would require the temporary continuation of government aid"; otherwise, as he indicated in another place, rapid removal is "brutal." (Contrast this attitude with an excellent leaflet once written by Leonard E. Read: *I'd Push the Button.*)

I think I have demonstrated why John Chamberlain's book must be set down as a flat failure, despite the good intentions of the author, and despite some valuable material. (If it be perhaps objected that not every writer can be expected to be a knowledgeable economist, the answer of course is that nobody forces him to write about economic problems.) It is a token of the intellectual failure of our time that the failure of this book will not be made known in any of our "right-wing" journals of opinion, for apparently it is felt that if an author is a certified right-winger and member of the club, then his book receives an automatic rave review by some other club member—in many cases, a reviewer who hardly needs to read the book before grinding out his formula review. (Left-wing reviewers will not assess the book properly either, if they discuss it at all, for they will simply attack it as too procapitalist.)

While this situation is, I suppose, understandable among a Right that considers itself in perpetual battle and therefore never to criticize one of "their own" in public, this is a most unfortunate situation. For not only does it betray the truth, which is the ultimate value for which the Right is supposed to be battling, but it is not even "practical" in the long run. A knowledgeable and open-minded economist who reads, let us say, a typical rave review of the Chamberlain book in some right-wing journal, or by some rightist, and then proceeds to read the book and discover its true lack of worth, will, after that, have little respect for either the reviewer or the magazine.

8. Letter on Henry Hazlitt and Keynes

July 18, 1959

Dr. Ivan R. Bierly
William Volker Fund

Dear Ivan:

In a forthcoming review of Henry Hazlitt's *The Failure of the "New Economics"* in *National Review*, I write that this is the best book on economics to be published since Mises's *Human Action*, ten years ago. I do not think this an exaggeration. Exempting reprinted books, such as Mises's *Theory of Money and Credit* or the Böhm-Bawerk volumes, what book can compete with this one? (Mises's *Theory and History* and Hayek's *Counter-Revolution of Science* are more philosophical or epistemological than straight economics.) Abbott's *Quality and Competition*, Bauer's two books on underdeveloped countries (that does *not* include Bauer and Yamey's book) all are impressive, but they cannot come close to Hazlitt for the accolade.

Frankly, I didn't realize that Henry had it in him. I always knew that he was an excellent journalist, and that he faithfully applied Misesian principles to his journalistic work, a difficult task in itself. And I knew that his *Great Idea* [*Time Will Run Back*] was a highly underrated work, and because cast in novel form, didn't get the recognition that its acute discussion of economic principles deserved. Still, I did not realize that Henry would be so fine on the highest scholarly levels, as he has here shown himself to be. This is, in short, an excellent work, at long last providing us with a minute, bit-by-bit, and yet also overall critique and demolition of the Keynesian heresy. There is no hesitation here, no namby-pamby ritualism about how "Keynes, despite his many errors, really contributed a great deal, etc." Keynes contributed only mischief, fallacy, and obfuscation, and Hazlitt is courageous enough to call a spade a spade.

This was a grueling but vitally important job, this cleansing of the Augean stables, and Hazlitt deserves the highest commendation for the job he has done. There are few other economists who really could have done it, for to do it requires thorough grounding and thorough knowledge in Misesian principles, and this Hazlitt has and uses. No Chicago economist, for example, could have done this job adequately, sharing, as the Chicagoans do, many of the Keynesian errors and lacking the "Austrian" insights.

I went through this book with great and particular care, with the *General Theory* at my elbow, looking for flaws, but could find none. Oh, there were various places where I would have preferred further elaborations or differences in emphases, but this is true of any reader about any book. Hazlitt differs from the Misesian pure time-preference theory of interest to some extent, although by the end of his discussion he has ingeniously worked around to agreeing pretty much with Mises there, and he tends to dilute Austrianism with Walrasian concepts, but these were so inconsequential in this book that we can definitely say that there are no important errors in the work. In contrast, there are a great many virtues overall, and also minute critiques of the various aspects of the Keynesian system and of its political implications, a dissection of the fallacies of mathematical economics, etc.

Some may say (and I understand that Buchanan said something like this in his review) that an analysis of Keynesianism is not important nowadays. It is true that Keynesianism is not seemingly a hot issue today, although even here Hazlitt shows how Keynesianism is at the root of the current national income and "economics of growth" analyses. But, on the other hand, the real reason why Keynesianism is not a hot issue is because it has been so thoroughly *accepted*, especially by the so-called "conservative" side in the political debate. It is unquestioned by any prominent conservative or business magazine: let the first sign of depression appear on the horizon, and the sure way to cure it is to have government deficit spending and inflation. Nobody believes in a balanced budget during depressed times anymore. This is the measure of the mass and intellectual acceptance of Keynesianism. And, as a matter of fact, the Chicago economists like Buchanan have the very neo-Keynesian virus in them. So let it never be said that Henry's book is not important or timely. It should be read by every economist or everyone interested in fundamental economic problems. It is worthy of National Book Foundation or any other form of distribution.

I worked 20 hours on this book—a rather long time relative to others, but, as I say, I wanted to exercise particular care with this one.

All the best.

9. Business Advocacy of Government Intervention

November 1959

To: Robbie
From: Murray

The NRA, with its proposal for a virtual national compulsory cartelization of American industry, was perhaps the most ambitious plan in American history—certainly the most ambitious in peacetime—to end the competitive system and to substitute for it a giant system of regulated and enforced monopolies or cartels, somewhat similar to fascism. It had its inception in September of 1931, when Gerard Swope, head of General Electric, unveiled his Swope Plan in a speech before the National Electrical Manufacturers Association. Every industry would be mobilized into trade associations, under federal control, which would regulate and stabilize prices and production, and prescribe codes of trade practices. Overall, these associations and the federal government, aided by a joint administration of management and employees representing the nation's industry, would "coordinate production and consumption." Swope had first unveiled his plan, six months before, to his colleague and fellow "enlightened" businessman, Owen D. Young, chairman of General Electric, who had heartily approved. The fellow industrialists, softened up by Swope and Young beforehand, heartily approved the plan, which became front-page news all over the country.

One of the most enthusiastic supporters of the Swope Plan was Henry I. Harriman, head of the New England Power Company, and at this time president of the U.S. Chamber of Commerce. In his report on the Swope and similar plans, as head of the chamber's Committee on the Continuity of Business and Employment, Harriman wrote, "We have left the period of extreme individualism. . . . Business prosperity and employment will be best maintained by an intelligently planned business structure."

With business organized through trade associations and headed overall by a National Economic Council, any dissenting businessmen will "be treated like any maverick. . . . They'll be roped, and branded, and made to run with the herd." Under Harriman's sponsorship, the U.S. Chamber of Commerce, in its December 1931 meeting, endorsed the Swope Plan by a large majority.

President Nicholas Murray Butler of Columbia University hailed the plan as an "example of constructive leadership." Wallace B. Donham, dean of the Harvard School of Business and influential in business circles, cited the success of the Soviet Union as demonstrating the value and necessity of a "general plan for American business." (Nicholas Murray Butler also considered Soviet Russia to have the "vast advantage of a plan.") Paul Mazur, of Lehman Brothers, referred to the "tragic lack of planning" in the capitalist system. Rudolph Spreckels, president of the Sugar Institute, urged governmental allocation to each company of its proper share of market demand. Ralph E. Flanders, then head of the Jones and Lamson Machine Company, called for fulfillment of the great "vision" of a new stage of government planning of the nation's economy.

One of the Swope Plan's leading boosters was J. George Frederick, who helped Swope publish and edit *Gerard Swope, The Swope Plan*[54] and then followed it up with a lengthy praise of planning in general and the Swope Plan in particular, along with business comments upon it, in J. George Frederick, *Readings in Economic Planning*.[55] Frederick called for compulsory business membership in, and obedience to, the rules of their trade associations, and believed that such trade-association government, with its return to a guild system, would eliminate the wasteful and destructive competition of irresponsible cranks. "A broader social control over economics is inevitable," he declared. Similar plans were concocted by another "enlightened" business-man, Henry S. Dennison, president of the Dennison Manufacturing Company, who had his own "five-year plan" for the American economy, with industry to be fully brought under trade-association rule by the second year. Benjamin A. Javits had also had a plan similar to the Swope Plan as early as 1930. Commenting favorably on the Swope Plan was Charles F. Abbott, director of the American Institute of Steel Construction. Abbott declared,

> The Swope Plan can be called a measure of pub-
> lic safety. . . . We cannot have in this country much
> longer irresponsible, ill-informed, stubborn and non-
> cooperating individualism. . . . The Swope Plan, seen
> in its ultimate simplicity is not one whit different in
> principle from the traffic cop . . . an industrial traffic
> officer. . . . "Constitutional" liberty to do as you please
> is "violated" by the traffic regulations but . . . they
> become binding even upon the blustering individual
> who claims his right to do as he pleases.

A.W. Robertson, chairman of the board of Westinghouse Electric, supported the plan, but more moderately, saying that the "spirit of cooperation" the plan called for would undoubtedly benefit the

---

[54] New York: The Business Bourse, 1931
[55] New York: The Business Bourse, 1932

economy. The president of the National Association of Manufacturers not only supported the Swope Plan, but wanted to go further in forcing all firms to join the regulated trade associations, including those employing below fifty people (which the Swope Plan had excluded). Magnus W. Alexander, president of the National Industrial Conference Board, backed the plan. And H.S. Person, managing director of the Taylor Society, snorted, "we expect the greatest enterprise of all, industry as a whole, to get along without a definite plan."

Specific industries also had their individual plans within the overall framework. The Associated General Contractors of America, in 1931, called for a governmental licensing of contractors. And C.E. Bockus, president of the National Coal Association, in an article called *"The Cost of Overproduction in the Bituminous Mining Industry,"* declared that the "precise need of the [coal] industry is the right to secure, by cooperative action, the continuous adjustment of the production of bituminous coal to the existing demand for it, thereby discouraging wasteful methods of production and consumption. . . . The European method of meeting this situation is through the establishment of cartels."[56]

One of the most important supporters of the compulsory cartelization idea was Bernard M. Baruch, Wall Street financier and perennial "elder statesman." As early as 1925, Baruch, inspired by his experience as chief economic mobilizer in World War I, had conceived of a great economy of trusts, regulated and run by a federal commission. In the spring of 1930, Baruch proposed to the Boston Chamber of Commerce a "Supreme Court of Industry."[57] It might also be pointed out that Swope's younger brother, Herbert Bayard Swope, was Baruch's closest confidant.

Herbert Hoover had been leaning in this direction ever since his stint as secretary of commerce in the 1920s, and liked to pepper his

---

[56] C.E. Bockus, "The Cost of Overproduction in the Bituminous Mining Industry," in *The Menace of Overproduction: Its Cause, Extent, and Cure,* edited by Scoville Hamlin (New York: J. Wiley and Sons, 1930. Reprint, Freeport, N.Y.: Books for Libraries Press, 1969), pp. 14 and 13. Page references are to the 1969 edition.

[57] K.R. Kingsbury, president of the Standard Oil Company of California, declared that "the government . . . should encourage and sanction agreements to promote economy in production and distribution."

speeches with vague but disquieting talk about interindustry "coop-eration" and "elimination of waste." To his eternal credit, however, Hoover was horrified at this scheme, and, despite the concerted business pressure upon him, turned it down cold. In a note, sending the Swope Plan to his attorney general for comment, and published much later in his memoirs, Hoover wrote about the plan:

> The plan provides for the mobilization of each vari-ety of industry and business into trade associations, to be legalized by the government and authorized to "stabilize prices and control distribution." There is no stabilization of prices without price fixing and control of distribution. This feature at once becomes the organization of gigantic trusts such as have never been dreamed of in the history of the world. This is the creation of a series of complete monopolies over the American people . . . if such a thing were ever done, it means the decay of American industry from the day this scheme is born, because one cannot stabilize prices without restricting production and protecting obsolete plants and inferior management. It is the most gigantic proposal of monopoly ever made in this country.

And the pressures on Hoover were severe indeed. Hoover relates that Henry I. Harriman warned him that if he persisted in oppos-ing the Swope Plan, the business world would support Franklin D. Roosevelt for president, because Roosevelt had agreed to adopt the plan! (And adopt it he did!) Truly, Virgil Jordan, economist for the National Industrial Conference Board, was right when he wrote at the time (with approval) that the world of business was ready for an "economic Mussolini"—and they could hardly have picked a better candidate than FDR.

The whole Swope-Harriman movement was summed up well by one of the most radical and socialistic of the brain trusters, Rexford Guy Tugwell, who has recently written of Swope, Harriman, and the rest that they believed that more organization was needed in American industry, more planning, more attempt to estimate needs and set production goals. From this they argued that . . . investment to secure the needed investment could be encouraged. They did not stress the reverse, that other investments ought to be prohibited, but that was inherent in the argument. All this was, so far, in accord with the thought of the collectivists in Franklin's brain trust [e.g., Tugwell] who tended to think of the economy in organic terms.[58]

When the New Deal arrived, Gerard Swope was called the only industrialist among the FDR brain trusters. Swope helped write the final draft of the National Industrial Recovery Act, and then stayed in Washington to help run the NRA. As a member of the industrial advisory board of the NRA, Swope took part in a famous joint meeting of the industrial and labor advisory boards in June 1933, which hammered out an agreement, setting a minimum wage and a maximum work week for all of industry. Swope was also one of the three industry representatives on the early National Labor Board.

In the meanwhile, Henry I. Harriman turned up as a leader in the agricultural brain trust that put over the AAA and also helped write the NRA. Chosen head of the NRA was General Hugh S. Johnson, a friend of Swope's and an old disciple of Bernard Baruch. When Johnson was removed from his post, Baruch himself was offered the job of head of the NRA, but turned it down. And Johnson's old colleague George Peek, another Baruch disciple, was named head of the AAA. Baruch, it might be pointed out, paid part of Johnson's salary while the latter was in office.

With the draft of the NRA still in the works, President Roosevelt hinted on April 12 about a forthcoming plan to secure "the regulation of production, or, to put it better, the prevention of foolish overproduction." When the U.S. Chamber of Commerce met in Washington

---

[58] Rexford Guy Tugwell, *The Democratic Roosevelt: A Biography of Franklin D. Roosevelt* (New York: Doubleday, 1957), p. 283.

in early May, FDR called on business to work with government "to prevent over-production, to prevent unfair wages, to eliminate improper working conditions." The businessmen were highly enthusiastic; twenty-seven out of the forty-nine speakers urged more government direction of industry. Paul W. Litchfield of Goodyear Tire and Rubber said, "we must make substantial concessions to what we have in the past classified as the more radical school of thought." In his second fireside chat, on May 7, FDR heralded a "partnership in planning" between government and business. When the NRA bill passed on June 13, FDR said that the bill "is a challenge to industry which has long insisted that, given the right to act in unison, it could do much for the general good which has hitherto been unlawful. From today it has that right."

General Johnson assured industry that he was not planning to control them; "It is industrial *self-government* that I am interested in. The function of this act is not to run out and control an industry, but for that industry to come to this table and offer its ideas as to what it thinks should be done."

Johnson used all possible propaganda devices to induce employers and firms to sign the NRA codes and receive the Blue Eagle, symbol of cooperation. Donald Richberg trumpeted to business:

> There is no choice presented to American business between intelligently planned and controlled industrial operations and a return to the gold-plated anarchy that masqueraded as "rugged individualism." . . . Unless industry is sufficiently socialized by its private owners and managers so that great essential industries are operated under public obligation appropriate to the public interest in them, the advance of political control over private industry is inevitable.

In adhering to the NRA, business was forced to accept collective bargaining and wage and labor codes, but expected to raise prices and restrict production in the time-honored manner of cartels. Thus, the National Association of Manufacturers drew up a model industry code that called for the assignment of production quotas to firms by the code authorities; and the trade associations wanted outright price-fixing powers for their industry.

On June 23, business had forced Johnson to agree that industrial codes could include agreements not to sell below the costs of production.

Because of business pressure, many industrial codes included techniques for industrial price control: various forms of minimum-price injunctions, as well as production quotas and other industrial self-controls over production. In the latter class were maximum hours of machine operation, imposed restrictions on the amount of new plant or equipment, refusal of entry of a new firm where the industry decided that "overcapacity" existed, or the maintenance of maximum ratios of output to inventory. The business community, despite these extensive cartelizations, clamored for more.

Ralph Flanders declared that the legislators and administrators could not really be blamed for the price fixing and production quotas of the NRA. "It was our businessmen who were most thoroughly sold on the idea that recovery and prosperity depended on the restraint of competition."

Harold Ickes has noted that "such price-fixing and production control regulations as found their way into the codes, got there almost exclusively at the demand of businessmen themselves."

The NRA itself said that "none of the more restrictive provisions approved remotely approached the stringency of proposals which were offered, demanded and battled for by a large number of industrial groups of fully representative character."

The code authorities, in each industry, were fully bossed by industry. They represented the trade association and had no labor or public members. The NRA delegated its powers over prices and production to these trade associations.

By the fall and winter of 1933 disillusion with the NRA was beginning to set in. William Randolph Hearst called it "absolute state socialism," and Walter Lippmann denounced its "bureaucratic control" and "excessive centralization." There were widespread evasions of the codes and breakdowns of the code system. Yet, business, generally, was simply angry at the pro–labor union codes and wanted the cartelizing turned over completely from government to organized business—but with government, of course, to provide the enforcing arm. By November, Gerard Swope now proposed that the NRA be replaced by a National Chamber of Commerce and Industry, headed by the U.S. Chamber of Commerce, which would replace the NRA as the superorganizer and overseer of trade associations.

Prices, under the spur of the NRA, as well as inflation, rose steadily, but before there was any true recovery or much reduction of unemployment. Criticism for monopoly began to mount against the NRA and its price-fixing, price-raising policies. In vain, the NRA held hearings on its price policy in January 1934, headed by Arthur D. Whiteside of Dun and Bradstreet, one of the outstanding champions of NRA price fixing.

The most persistent and knowledgeable attacker on the national scene was Senator Gerald P. Nye. To meet his criticisms, the president set up a National Recovery Review Board in March 1934, with most of the members nominated by Nye, to survey the NRA's possible tendency toward monopoly. The staff was headed by Lowell B. Mason, recently a member of the Federal Trade Commission, and then as now an opponent of both monopoly and government intervention. Under Mason's guidance, the board delivered a scathing report in May, attacking the NRA as a promoter of monopoly. Donald Richberg, of the NRA, angrily accused the board members of being "philosophic anarchists." John L. Lewis, of the NRA's Labor Advisory Board, blasted the board for getting its information from "irresponsible malcontents, sweatshop employers and business interests which had lost special privileges." But Gerald Nye continued to press his attack in the Senate, and George Terborgh's report for the Brookings Institution in March, *Price Control Devices in NRA Codes*, shook some confidence in the NRA.

After the end of the Johnson regime, in the fall of 1934, the NRA began to move to relaxing the codes and the price-fixing provisions. On this struggle, Arthur M. Schlesinger, Jr. observes with some justice,

For it was the businessmen who wished to turn their backs on the free market and set up a system of price and production control; and it was the New Dealers who opposed them at every turn and tried to move toward a functioning price system and a free market. If the business image of NRA had prevailed, the result would very likely have been in time to put the private economic collectivism thus created under detailed public regulation and thereby bring into existence the very bureaucratic regimentation which business accused the New Deal of seeking for itself.[59]

As late as January 1935, the NRA held a series of price hearings, and 90 percent of the two thousand businessmen that testified insisted on monopolistic price control by the NRA. George A. Sloan of the Cotton Textile Institute said bitterly that if the NRA were to end price fixing, it "might as well turn us back to 1932 and go home."

Despite the mounting criticisms of the NRA, the public cooling of ardor, and troubles of evasion by small-business concerns, organized business, as well as organized labor, enthusiastically supported renewal of the NRA when time for renewal came in mid-1935. To William Green, of the American Federation of Labor, "it is unthinkable on the part of labor that we should go back, after having taken such a forward step in economic planning." The United States Chamber of Commerce voted for continuing the NRA by a four-to-one margin; and the influential Business Advisory Council of the Department of Commerce was nearly unanimous for the NRA.[60]

---

[59] Arthur M. Schlesinger, Jr., *The Coming of the New Deal* (Boston: Houghton Mifflin, 1958), p. 160. See chapters 6 through 10 for a history of the NRA.

[60] In addition to the Swope, Frederick, and Schlesinger books already mentioned, see Arthur M. Schlesinger, Jr., *The Crisis of the Old Order, 1919–1933* (Boston: Houghton Mifflin, 1957); David Loth, *Swope of GE* (New York: Simon and Schuster, 1958); Margaret Colt, *Mr. Baruch* (Boston: Houghton Mifflin, 1957); Wallace B. Donham, *Business Adrift* (New York: Whittlesey House, McGraw-Hill, 1931).

10. Review of Lionel Robbins, *The Great Depression*

November 14, 1959

Dr. Ivan R. Bierly
William Volker Fund

Dear Ivan:

Lionel Robbins's *The Great Depression* is one of the great economic works of our time.[61] Its greatness lies not so much in originality of economic thought, as in the application of the best economic thought to the explanation of the cataclysmic phenomena of the Great Depression. This is unquestionably the best work published on the Great Depression.

At the time that Robbins wrote this work, he was perhaps the second most eminent follower of Ludwig von Mises (Hayek being the first). To his work, Robbins brought a clarity and polish of style that I believe to be unequalled among any economists, past or present. Robbins is the premier economic stylist.

In this brief, clear, but extremely meaty book, Robbins sets forth first the Misesian theory of business cycles and then applies it to the events of the 1920s and 1930s. We see how bank credit expansion in the United States, Great Britain, and other countries drove the civilized world into a great depression.[62]

Then Robbins shows how the various nations took measures to counteract and cushion the depression that could only make it worse: propping up unsound, shaky business positions; inflating credit; expanding public works; keeping up wage rates (e.g., Hoover and his

---

[61] Lionel Robbins, *The Great Depression* (London: Macmillan, 1934).
[62] In Britain the expansion was generated because of the rigid wage structure caused by unions and the unemployment insurance system, as well as a return to the gold standard at too high a par; and in the United States it was generated by a desire to inflate in order to help Britain, as well as an absurd devotion to the ideal of a stable price level.

White House conferences)—all things that prolonged the necessary depression adjustments and profoundly aggravated the catastrophe. Robbins is particularly bitter about the wave of tariffs, exchange controls, quotas, etc. that prolonged crises, set nation against nation, and fragmented the international division of labor.

And this is not all. Robbins also sets the European scene in the context of the disruptions of the largely free market brought about by World War I; the statization, unionization, and cartelization of the economy that the war brought about; the dislocation of industrial investment and agricultural overproduction brought about by war demand, etc. And above all, the gold standard of pre–World War I, that truly international money, was disrupted and never really brought back again. Robbins shows the tragedy of this, and defends the gold standard vigorously against charges that it "broke down" in 1929. He shows that the U.S. inflation in 1927 and 1928 when it was *losing* gold, and Britain's cavalierly going off gold when its bank discount rate was as low as 4½ percent, was in flagrant violation of the "rules" of the gold standard (as was Britain's persistent inflationism in the 1920s).

Robbins also has excellent sections demonstrating the Misesian point that one intervention leads inexorably to another intervention or else repeal of the original policy. He also has a critique of the idea of central planning *and* a fine summation of the Misesian demonstration that socialist economies cannot calculate. Almost every important relevant point is touched upon and handled in unexceptionable fashion. Thus, Robbins, touching on the monopoly question, shows that the only really important monopolies are those created and fostered by governments. He has not the time for a rigorous demonstration of this, but his *apercus* are important, stimulating, and sound. Robbins sums up his book in this superb passage:

> It has been the object . . . to show that if recovery
> is to be maintained and future progress assured,
> there must be a more or less complete reversal of con-
> temporary tendencies of governmental regulation of

enterprise. The aim of governmental policy in regard to industry must be to create a field in which the forces of enterprise and the disposal of resources are once more allowed to be governed by the market.

But what is this but the restoration of capitalism? And is not the restoration of capitalism the restoration of the causes of depression?

If the analysis of this essay is correct, the answer is unequivocal. The conditions of recovery which have been stated do indeed involve the restoration of what has been called capitalism. But the slump was not due to these conditions. On the contrary, it was due to their negation. It was due to monetary mismanagement and State intervention operating in a milieu in which the essential strength of capitalism had already been sapped by war and by policy. Ever since the outbreak of war in 1914, the whole tendency of policy has been away from that system, which in spite of the persistence of feudal obstacles and the unprecedented multiplication of the people, produced that enormous increase of wealth per head. . . . Whether that increase will be resumed, or whether, after perhaps some recovery, we shall be plunged anew into depression and the chaos of planning and restrictionism—that is the issue which depends on our willingness to reverse this tendency.

The Great Depression, in short, is a brilliant work that should be read by every economist. It is not at all outdated. It deserves the widest possible distribution, and would be indeed a fitting companion to Hazlitt's *The Fallacies of the New Economics,* that refutation of the other great explanation of the Depression—the Keynesian.

11. Review of Lionel Robbins, *Robert Torrens and the Evolution of Classical Economics*

October 14, 1960

Dr. Ivan R. Bierly
William Volker Fund

Dear Ivan:

There is no questioning the considerable merit in Lionel Robbins's *Robert Torrens and the Evolution of Classical Economics.*[63] The scholarship is first rate and very thorough; the style is, as usual with Robbins, excellent; and Robert Torrens is resuscitated as a classical economist of considerably more merit and originality than was generally known. Robbins notes Torrens's various improvements on Ricardian theorems and with approval; notable is Torrens's pioneering in the insight that value cannot, in the nature of the case, be measured, and also in the rejection of the labor theory of value.

The most notable chapter in the book is Robbins's exposition of Torrens's great contributions to the development of the currency principle and critique of Banking School doctrines, including the development of the 100 percent gold doctrine, and the hints of anticipation of Wicksell-Mises views on money and interest. Also, Robbins shows that Torrens, of all the currency theorists, was alive to the essential identity of bank deposits with bank notes as money—although he unfortunately did not carry this insight over into policy recommendations. Here, while Robbins generally approves Torrens's position, he makes two mistakes: (1) in criticizing Torrens for overlooking the important functions of the Bank of England in being a "lender of last resort" to bail out banks in trouble; and (2) in attributing originality to Torrens's recognition of bank deposits as being money. Here, Robbins suffers from British insularity, since he overlooks the many Americans who arrived at a correct position over twenty years before Torrens.

---

[63] London: Macmillan, 1958

To some extent in the general theory chapter, and certainly in the money and banking chapter, then, this book is of considerable interest and merit. On the other hand, the two latter chapters—"The Theory of Colonization" and "The Theory of Commercial Policy"—are very disappointing, not only because Robbins joins Torrens in the errors and fallacies that dominated his discussion of these issues, but also because Robbins gives such a commanding position and emphasis to Torrens's views in these particular areas. *Here*, in these two fields, Robbins says repeatedly, Torrens made his most important contribution to economics.

Torrens's—and Robbins's—position in these last two chapters is, essentially, a repudiation of the position of nineteenth-century liberalism, and of the insight that individual and social interests are always harmonized by the free-market processes. In the colonizing chapter, Robbins hails Torrens's conversion to the fallacies and statist views of E.G. Wakefield, which (a) reversed the older liberal scorn at governmental colonization and enthusiastically favored colonization, imperial preference, etc., and (b) advocated—in the name of the common laborer, note—the artificial restriction of free land in the colonies.

It is one thing to fall into the Turner error and attribute to the *existence* of free land all the glories "colonial" civilization (the United States, Australia, etc.); it is, however, an equal error to go to the other extreme (as did Wakefield, Torrens, and even, to some extent, Robbins) and denounce the existence of the boon of free land as evil and oppressive of the worker, because it delays the processes of concentration of population and of industrialization.[64] But this is to fall into the very error that the "underdeveloped countries" are making now: of putting industrialization of their particular area as the prime desideratum for prosperity.

Overall industrialization is fine and important for prosperity; but this hardly means that *every* area of the globe—or, therefore, *every*

---

[64] Editor's note: Rothbard's reference to the "Turner error" is to Frederick Jackson Turner's famous "frontier thesis," first advanced in his 1893 paper "The Significance of the Frontier in American History," which ascribed the American character to the constant presence of the frontier.

country—must be industrialized. On the contrary, it was and is better for, say, Australia to concentrate its resources on its abundant land and agriculture, and then to exchange these agricultural products for imported manufactures, than to try to industrialize itself. Only the market can decide which resources do what; and to put artificial burdens on superior land, to make it artificially expensive, is a cruel penalty on the average worker. Robbins has an easy time—too easy—in disposing of Marx's bitter strictures against Wakefield (who also partially defended slavery, by the way, and is almost defended here by Robbins), but while Marx is clearly wrong in his detailed analysis, I must say that I find his moral indignation at Wakefield's proposals sounder than Robbins's sophisticated defense.

Furthermore, Robbins seems to believe that Torrens's repudiation of Say's Law and adoption of the "Keynesian" or "Hansenian" view that depressions are caused by oversaving—by saving that can't find profitable outlets—is a great contribution to economic thought. Robbins apparently refuses to realize that this is a fallacy through and through.

Furthermore, while he recognizes that Torrens's commercial ventures in colonization in S. Australia colored his pamphlets and made them more propagandistic, Robbins fails to see how much and how thoroughly Torrens's economic interests weakened his analytic capacities in economic theory. It is obvious that this theory of oversaving and "economic glut"—this repudiation of his own previous adherence to Say's Law—was caused by Torrens's desire to find a good argument for encouraging colonization and foreign investment of capital: he found it in the supposedly depressant falling rate of profit at home, which leads to a search for foreign outlets abroad. This fallacious argument led eventually to many pernicious results: specifically, to the Brooks Adams type of championing of American imperialism in the late nineteenth century, and, conversely, to Lenin's explanation of the causes of this imperialism. Thus, both sides were to feed on the same mischievous fallacy.

Finally, in the commercial policy chapter, Robbins devotes himself, at length, to hailing Torrens's desertion of the cause of unilateral free trade and his adoption of the principle of reciprocity—all because of his discovery of the "terms of trade" argument for tariffs, which Robbins takes so seriously as to make up virtually the entire chapter. Yet this is surely a fallacious argument; the tariff is essentially a "negative railroad"—an artificial imposition of transport costs—and, if we take the methodological-individualist point of view, it is clear that a tariff can only benefit a few "monopolists" at the expense of the bulk of the consumers in the area.

We thus see that, despite the numerous merits of the volume, a great deal of it is used to demonstrate—supposedly—the weaknesses and failings of the free market in harmonizing individual and social interests, and therefore where government action must "correct" the free market: specifically, in the areas of colonization (governmental), of imposing an artificial scarcity on land, and of protective tariffs—and there is also a strong implication that Keynesian measures would be required in a depression, since Torrens is hailed for his pre-Keynesian doctrine. I would have to say, therefore, that overall, Robbins's book is not sound enough for National Book Foundation distribution.

12. Untitled Letter Critical of Chicago School Economics

February 3, 1960

Dr. Ivan R. Bierly
William Volker Fund

Dear Ivan:

I must say that the more I read the general, all-around works of the "Chicago School" of economics, the less I am impressed.

A good example of the approach of this school is Clark Lee Allen, James M. Buchanan, and Marshall R. Colberg, *Prices, Income, and Public Policy*.[65] As you will see, I was impressed neither by the technical economic analysis nor by the more politico-economic sections.

---

[65]   2nd ed., McGraw-Hill, 1959

Let us take the broader or more "political" sections first. First it must be said that on the two great foci of attack on the free-market economy by left-wingers—the Keynesian problem of "cyclical instability" and unemployment, and the alleged problems of "monopoly,"—Allen, Buchanan, and Colberg take up the hue and cry against the market with the rest of the "pack." Oh, very gently and very moderately, compared to most other textbooks, it is true; but still the essence of the charges is there, and the case has been given away.

In the "national income" field, the authors enlist themselves wholeheartedly as what we may call "moderate Keynesians." The crucial thing here is that they accept the fundamental Keynesian point and accept it blithely as above discussion: that the free market, left to itself, has no mechanism for keeping its aggregate self in balance, for avoiding business cycles, depressions, unemployment, etc. Government, then, must step in to regulate the system: to keep the price level stable, to pump in money in depressions in order to cure unemployment, to tighten up money in booms. Government is considered the natural and indispensable regulator. The free market has no way of keeping national income high enough or savings and investment in balance. Thus, the fundamental Keynesian point has been conceded.

It is true that surrounding this hard core, the authors put in "conservative" modifiers: they prefer the government to use monetary policy in its contracyclical efforts rather than fiscal policy, and they even hint the latest Friedman line that they might prefer automatic monetary rules to managed, discretionary monetary policy. But while an improvement over most textbooks, this is not good enough. The authors, in the usual Chicago tradition, show themselves completely ignorant of the Misesian theory of the business cycle, and loftily dismiss the gold standard as hardly worthy of note—never even considering that they might find the monetary automaticity they are seeking in the gold-coin standard. But the most important flaw is their conceding the fundamental Keynesian point.

The authors worry a lot, also, about monopoly. Of course, they think that monopoly can abound on the free market—we cannot expect any economist to take the revolutionary step of denying *that* proposition. But they can be condemned for not even getting as realistic about the market as Chamberlin or, from another direction, Lawrence Abbott, whose seminal book is ignored by these authors as well as everyone else. In fact, the authors cling to the absurd and dangerous Chicago model of "perfect" or "pure" competition, which they persist in considering the normative ideal.

Of course, empirically, they overlaid this terrible flaw with some good remarks: indicating that they believe that the most important empirical instances of monopoly power are caused by government intervention, attacking the fair-trade laws, etc. But these good qualifiers are hardly enough to save the day. On the contrary, what the authors do is to say: *Well yes, we admit that the whole market is interlarded with "monopoly power," and this is unfortunate but really unimportant, except that*. . . . And here, the authors feel free to engage in sudden hit-and-run attacks on cases which *they*, for some reason, feel are important instances of monopoly power that should be busted or regulated by government. Thus, the authors are strong for the antitrust laws, and want to see them strengthened further and enforced more stringently. They have the gall to call the decision outlawing basing-point pricing a great "victory for society," and they endorse the FTC's desire to get the power to enjoin any mergers in advance. Using the "perfect competition" model, the authors also show great hostility toward the alleged great "wastes" of advertising.

The authors are pretty good in criticizing the "monopoly power" of unions, but here again their case is greatly weakened by their conceding validity to the absurd and fallacious "problem of monopsony," which somehow makes out employers to be as inherently monopolistic as unions. They also concede that "natural monopolies," such as public utilities, have to be regulated by government, even though they point out, very well, many of the pitfalls and inconsistencies inherent in public utility regulation. But the force of the latter are, once again, vitiated by their concession to the opponents of freedom of their fundamental point: that public utilities simply *have* to be regulated by government.

The authors also endorse all the fallacious arguments for government action such as the "collective good" argument and the free-rider, or external-benefits, argument. Thus, they endorse public education because of the alleged long-run benefits to everyone, which people are too shortsighted to pay for voluntarily. On the theory of exchange rates, they are good as far as they go in pointing to the functions of the free exchange market and the perils of exchange control, but they seem to be completely ignorant of the purchasing-power-parity explanation of the determinants, on the free market, of what makes the exchange rates what they are.

On foreign aid and underdeveloped countries, they are surprisingly poor and weak, their section on underdeveloped countries saying very little and including none of the Bauer insights, and actually endorsing both the economics and politics of foreign aid to these countries.

Rather than multiply examples of flaws further, I think it important to emphasize that this book brings home as few have done to me how much can go wrong if one's philosophical approach—one's epistemology—is all wrong. At the root of almost all the troubles of the book lies the weak, confused, and inconsistent *positivism*: the willingness to use false assumptions if their "predictive value" seems to be of some use. It is this crippling positivist willingness to let anything slip by, to *not* be rigorous about one's theory because "the assumptions don't have to be true or realistic anyway," that permeates and ruins this book.

For example, the authors are keen enough, in the monopoly sections, to sense that there in something very wrong with the whole current theory of monopoly, that it is even impossible to *define* monopoly cogently, or define monopoly of a commodity. But while they see these things, they never do anything about it, or start from there to construct an economics that will stand up—because they are thoroughly misled by their positivist attitude of "well, this might be a useful tool for some purposes." Hence their clinging to the absurd "ideal" of perfect competition, etc.—and in many other ways.

This same grave philosophical confusion permits them to suddenly slip their own ethical judgments into the book, undefended and practically unannounced. Suddenly, they say that the outlawing of basing-point pricing was a great "social victory"—I said that this was *gall* because they had never bothered to construct or present a cogent ethical system on which to make such a remark. Similarly, they feel free, while cloaking themselves in the robes of scientists, to say suddenly that of course there has to be compulsory egalitarianism, with the government enforcing some equality through taxes and subsidies. Why? Simply because it seems evident to them that a little more equality would be better, and that we can't let the weak be "liquidated."

And they have even the further colossal gall to denounce "price discrimination" (e.g., doctors charging more to the rich than to the poor) because it is, for some reason, terribly unethical for private people to engage in their own strictly voluntary redistribution of wealth. Apparently, and they say so explicitly, it is *only* legitimate for the government to effect this redistribution by coercion. This ethical nonsense they don't feel they have to defend; it appears self-evident to them. It is this kind of slipshod, unphilosophic, sophomoric "ethics" that is again typical of the Chicago School in action.

The pervading positivist epistemology pervades the technical economic analysis as well. The usual fashionable jargon of the "short-run" cost curves of the firm, etc. are used, despite the recognition by the authors that it is all rather arbitrary; this they brush aside with the retort that it can have some "predictive value." The term that I think best describes the shoddiness and eclecticism induced by this philosophic approach is "irresponsibility." For if a theory or analysis doesn't have to be strictly true or coherently united to other theory, then almost anything goes—all to be justified with "predictive value" or some other such excuse.

Happily, I can illustrate what I mean in a little exchange of letters that I had last week with Jim Buchanan about one minor piece of technical analysis in this book. I was appalled by the construction of a so-called "fixed demand" curve, which was clearly thrown in so as to have something geometrically symmetric with the standard, and perfectly proper, fixed-supply curve for the immediate market. The authors said that a fixed, vertical demand curve is illustrated by the government's demand for soldiers, and that if not enough people volunteer, the government will draft the rest. Now this is pure nonsense, since drafting cannot be illustrated by a demand curve. But what struck me is that even on the authors' own terms, the analysis is nonsense, since, if say the government wants 100,000 men in the army and its "demand curve" is therefore vertical at this amount, but if so many people are 4-F or exempt that only 60,000 can possibly be hired or drafted, we then have a vertical supply and vertical demand curve which never intersect. On the authors' own premises, then, *no one* would be in the army, which is clearly absurd.

So I wrote to Jim Buchanan asking him to clear up this point, and saying that maybe I was overlooking the happy and obvious solution. What interests us here, as revelatory of Buchanan's philosophical irresponsibility, was his reply. The reply *conceded* my point in full. Yes, his model *does* lead to absurd conclusions. Here is Buchanan's justification:

> Your letter points up the limitations of applying too literally many of our analytical tools. You are quite right in saying that the solution . . . under your assumptions is absurd. But this is really the same in all of those cases in which we make rather extreme assumptions. . . . At best, the fixed demand and fixed supply models are useful in that they isolate certain forces, and in few cases, the models themselves are useful for predictive purposes.

He goes on to say that he tried to find a case of fixed demand as a counterpart to the usual fixed supply case, and could only think of the draft example as remotely suitable.

Now, it seems to me that this kind of philosophy, this positivistic approach to economic theory, corrupts it, if I may use so strong a term, at the very core, and that no theory of lasting merit can emerge from this sort of cauldron. And this book of Allen, Buchanan, and Colberg is a particularly clear example of how this positivistic "corruption" ruins almost every key section of the book.

13. Review of Benjamin Anderson, *The Value of Money*

January 20, 1960

Dr. Ivan R. Bierly
William Volker Fund

Dear Ivan:

While there are many interesting points and facets in Benjamin M. Anderson's *The Value of Money*, I would emphatically advise against adopting it for National Book Foundation distribution.[66] The trouble is that, in relation to the two central themes of the book, the marginal utility theory of value and the quantity theory of money, Anderson comes down squarely and emphatically on the wrong side. He is determinedly opposed to the Austrian utility theory and attempts to replace it with a vague "social value" theory—and with flagrant lack of success. And the bulk of this large work is devoted to a bitter, detailed attack on the quantity theory of money, which, while incomplete in itself, is the groundwork for any correct theory of money.

In his value theory, Anderson hopelessly aligns himself with such social deterministic sociologists as Charles H. Cooley and with John Dewey. In his critique of the quantity theory, Anderson makes much shrewd headway against the mechanical, mathematical type of quantity theory, or "equation of exchange," expounded by Irving Fisher, but these valuable passages are marred, overall, by Anderson's hostility to the quantity theory itself. He therefore, after stoutly and erroneously maintaining that "money is capital," concludes that the quantity theorists are wrong in thinking that, in the long run at

---

[66] Benjamin M. Anderson, *The Value of Money* (New York: Macmillan, 1917).

least, it doesn't matter for business activity how much or how little money there is in society; in attacking this truth, Anderson has to align himself with the inflationists, in maintaining that the American gold discoveries stimulated the growth of capitalism, that inflation can stimulate trade, etc.

It is certainly impossible therefore, to recommend a work whose central themes are emphatically on the wrong side of the issues, regardless of what useful points are made against the Fisher version of monetary theory during the discussion. And certainly his contentions that prices can be "active" in determining the other factors in the equation of exchange, instead of passively determined by them, are simply absurd. All in all, I must conclude that Anderson was simply not a very good or insightful economic theorist, especially when he went beyond technical banking matters and delved into general economic theory.

14. Review of Colin Clark, *Growthmanship*

April 4, 1961

Dr. Ivan Bierly
William Volker Fund

Dear Ivan:

To make a proper evaluation of Colin Clark's *Growthmanship*,[67] it is first necessary to go into a little background on the central theme of Clark's pamphlet: the role of capital investment in economic development. Ludwig Mises has always maintained that the one important item in raising the living standards of the undeveloped countries— the crucial item—is an increase in the quantity of per-capita capital invested, and he has attacked interventionist schemes of many sorts for interfering with the possibility of an increase in capital. In recent years, however, "right-wing" economists (e.g., Peter Bauer, and now

---

[67] Institute of Economic Affairs, 1961

especially Colin Clark) have pooh-poohed the role of capital investment in development, and have increasingly emphasized the point
that other factors (e.g., the labor force, the laws of the country, cultural
factors, and technological improvement) are more important. The
reason for this change in "conservative" economic doctrine is this:
within the last twenty years, socialist and interventionist economists
have, themselves, adopted the idea that capital investment is *the* crucial desideratum for the "underdeveloped countries."

What has happened is this: the leftist economists, in appropriating
the Misesian-classical emphasis on increase of capital, have *absorbed
into* the concept of "capital" government "investment" expenditures!
The syllogism on the Left has now become something like this:

(1) Yes, we agree that the reason Ruritania has not been "growing" faster is that it has not saved and invested enough;

(2) Therefore, since we want more rapid growth, government
must tax people and *itself* make the investments, thus forcing
a more rapid pace of development (e.g., as in Soviet Russia).

Hence, the reaction among "conservative" economists to deprecate
the roles of capital investment.

Mises, in short, left a gap, permitting an "end-run" by his opposition. The point is that Mises never dealt with the problem of government "investment," probably because he pooh-poohs the whole
idea. But this omission has left an important gap in the Misesian
armor. For when Mises says "capital," he obviously means private
capital. *Private* capital does not neglect such "other factors" as
entrepreneurial spirit, laws of the country (security of property, for
example), etc.; for private capital investment *is the resultant* of conditions brought about by the favorable conjunction of such cultural
factors. But since Mises never thought of capital as being anything
but private, he put the crucial development factor as "investment"
without mentioning the other points. The Left was therefore able
to appropriate his and other economists' emphasis on "investment"

by applying it to government "investment," thereby omitting these other implicit factors.

The proper reaction to this would have been to point out (a) that government expenditure is not properly "investment" at all, (b) that it is misallocation of funds that consumers and savers would have spent elsewhere, (c) that investment is only investment if it leads to its proper goal: consumption goods. Since the forced saving of socialist countries leads only to glorification of the rulers via what Clark well terms "conspicuous production" or "conspicuous investment," this is not really investment at all; and (d) that government investment is misallocation because investment (as Lachmann pointed out in his *Capital and Its Structure*) is *not* a mere aggregate quantity, but a subtle, interrelated, fitted network of finely meshed parts. In a free market, governed by the price system, we can take, as a shorthand, the total quantity of investment, because the market sees to it that the various parts are finely meshed and harmonized. But when government "invests," there is no such mechanism to insure harmony, and the result is gigantic malinvestments, and failure of the parts to mesh.

In short, the proper counterattack against the Left should have been to point out that government expenditure is not really "capital," but is actually—via taxes, controls, misallocations, etc.—destructive of the potential capital of a country. But, unfortunately, the current conservatives, while pointing out some of the above factors to a limited extent, have "overreacted" by deprecating the very role of capital itself. For while it is true that entrepreneurial spirit, correct laws, etc. are vital to economic development, they exercise their influence *through* capital investment and not instead of, or apart from, such investment. They are ultimate factors lying behind the degree of saving and productive capital investment that is made in a country. The unfortunate error of the current conservative economists is to fail to realize this and to think of these other factors as competing with capital in importance.

Colin Clark's pamphlet, to return to the main theme, is particularly unfortunate example of this error. For virtually the entire last half of his pamphlet is taken up with such depredation of capital. This error is considerably compounded by Clark's unfortunate penchant for statistical measurement and econometric methods. While he has many interesting and useful things to say in the course of presenting his sheaf of statistical estimates (e.g., his deprecation of the uses made by the Left of capital-output ratios and his discussion of governmentally induced malinvestment in British electricity, coal, railroads, and agriculture), Clark's tabulations are fundamentally either questionable or erroneous.

For example, his attempts at general, aggregate measures of "capital-output ratios" are heroically oversimplified; furthermore, and more grave, he presents statistical estimates of *how much* increased output was "caused by" capital and how much by other factors, such as skill, enterprise, etc. There is, of course, no way to separate these factors conceptually, let alone statistically. This grievous error, which underlies his statistical presentation, is compounded by his evident view that "capital" has a "marginal product" which he can estimate. Actually, as Fetter and Mises have shown, "capital" has no marginal-value product—only capital goods. The acme of the absurdity in Clark's approach is seen in his favorable report of the Norwegian Dr. Aukrust:

> With no additions to capital at all . . . "human factors," i.e., better knowledge, organization, skill, effort, education, enterprise, etc., sufficed to raise productivity at the rate of 1.8 percent per year. A one percent addition to the labor force, all other things being equal, would only raise national product by ¾ percent; and a one percent addition to capital stock by only 0.2 percent.[68]

Now this arrant nonsense has only emerged because, for Clark as for many other econometricians, statistics and mathematics (in this case, multiple correlation and variance analysis) has replaced economics.

The reason why Clark's error here must loom so large in an analysis of his paper is that it plays so large a role there. This, as I've said,

---

[68] Clark, *Growthmanship*, p. 34

is his central theme, and his statistics take up a good portion of the work. Some of the other points against government investment are mentioned, and they are good ones, but many of them are simply quotes from Bauer's booklet on India, and the interested reader can read Bauer's American Enterprise Association pamphlet on India without the need of specially importing and distributing Clark's pamphlet into this country.

A second grave flaw in the pamphlet is its poor organization. A brief pamphlet should be systematic, and above all clear; this one is turgid, disorganized, unsystematic, and wanders all over the lot—not only with little order, but also wandering into various digressions and crotchets of Clark's. In a larger work, such digressions would be charming and perhaps informative; in the very narrow space of this pamphlet, it simply throws the balance of the work askew. Thus, Clark wastes precious space in a detailed statistical account of the prospects for nuclear electrical power in Britain, even though it is completely irrelevant to his discussion. And while Clark has many interesting and keen criticisms to make of the "growth theorists," it is essentially and overall weak.

Clark, for example, omits most of the really important criticisms he might have made of Walt Rostow's theory. He isn't really sharp on the "capital-output ratio," for, after all, he uses it himself. And he fails to level the most important criticisms he might have made of the neo-Keynesian "growthmen" because, after all, Clark too is a Keynesian, as he makes clear—though of the "moderate" variety. He believes that Keynes was perfectly correct *for the 1930s*—though not for now. But the problem here is *not only* that Clark is wrong on depression and unemployment problems, but that, being Keynesian himself, he doesn't have the proper understanding of Keynesian errors to permit him to make a truly outstanding critique of the very "growthmen" that he opposes. Contrast his weak discussion, for example, with the really fundamental theoretical critique of these same "growth models" by Leland Yeager, in his "Some Questions on Growth Economics," *American Economic Review* (1954), an article about which Clark makes no mention.

It is because of these important errors and flaws in the Clark pamphlet that I would, despite the numerous valid insights and points he makes, recommend against any widespread distribution by the fund of *Growthmanship* in this country.

15. Competition and the Economists

May 1961

To: Robbie
From: Murray

To Adam Smith and to his successors, "competition" was not a term defined with mathematical precision; it meant, generally, "free competition," i.e., competition unhampered by governmental grants of exclusive privilege. And "monopoly" tended to mean such grants of governmental privilege.

To Adam Smith, for example, "competition" was used in the common-sense way that businessmen use it: to mean rivalry between two or more independent persons or firms. "Free competition" meant absence of grants of exclusive privilege, freedom of trade and freedom of entry into occupations; "monopolies" meant grants of exclusive privilege.

When Smith used the term "competition," for example, he used it to describe the competition among buyers, which bids prices up when demand exceeds supply, or the competition of sellers, which bids prices down when supply is greater than demand.[69]

When Smith referred to the evils of restraining competition, he referred to "the exclusive privileges of corporations . . . [and] an incorporated trade." Smith was describing the guild and licensing regulations of European towns.[70] That by "monopoly" Smith meant governmental grants of exclusive privilege may be seen in the following passage:

---

[69] Smith, *Wealth of Nations,* Modern Library, pp. 56–57
[70] Smith, *ibid.,* pp. 118 ff.

A monopoly granted either to an individual or to a trading company has the same effect as a secret. . . . The monopolists, by keeping the market constantly under-stocked . . . sell their commodities much above the natural price . . . the price of free competition. . . .

The exclusive privilege of corporations, statutes of and apprenticeship, and all those laws which restrain, in particular employments, the competition to a smaller number than might go into them, have the same tendency, though in a less degree. They are a sort of enlarged monopolies, and may frequently . . . in whole classes of employments keep up the market price of particular commodities above the natural price. . . . Such enhancements of the market price may last as long as the regulations of police which give occasion to them.[71]

Smith's one important—and unfortunate—deviation from this view is his tendency to view land as a "monopoly" because the total supply of land in the society is more or less fixed.

Ricardo had virtually nothing to add to Smith's treatment. He said nothing at all explicitly about competition; and his reference to monopoly was only in two or three places, and there closely followed the Smith position. There are several pages of attack on the British colonial monopolies—grants of exclusive privilege such as the British East India Company, which Smith had attacked vigorously;[72] he also continued, and unfortunately sharpened, the other tendency of Smith to dub as "monopoly" a fixed supply, also indicating land: "Commodities are only at a monopoly price when by no possible device their quantity can be augmented . . ."[73]

Of the role of free competition among the classical economists, Gide and Rist write,

---

[71] Smith, *ibid.*, pp. 61–62
[72] Ricardo, *Principles*, Everyman ed., pp. 229 ff.
[73] Ricardo, *ibid.*, p. 165

their program includes liberty to choose one's employment, free competition, free trade beyond as well as within the frontiers of a single country, free banks, and a competitive rate of interest; and on the negative side it implies resistance to all State intervention wherever the necessity for it cannot be clearly demonstrated. . . . In the opinion of Classical writers, free competition was the sovereign natural law. . . . It secured cheapness for the consumer, and stimulated progress generally because of the rivalry it aroused among producers. Justice was assured for all, and equality attained, for the constant pursuit of profits merely resulted in reducing them to the level of cost of production. *The Dictionnaire d'Economie Politique* of 1852, which may perhaps be considered the code of Classic political economy, expressed the opinion that competition is to the industrial world what the sun is to the physical.[74]

John Stuart Mill continued in the same tradition. To him, too, "monopoly"—the opposite of competition—was artificial grants of exclusive privilege:

The usual instrument for producing artificial dearness [by government] is monopoly. To confer a monopoly upon a producer or dealer, or upon a set of producers or dealers not too numerous to combine, is to give them the power of levying any amount of taxation on the public, for their individual benefit, which will not make the public forgo the use of the commodity. When the sharers in the monopoly are so numerous and so widely scattered that they are prevented from combining, the evil is considerably less: but even then

[74] Charles Gide and Charles Rist, *A History of Economic Doctrines From the Time of the Physiocrats to the Present Day*, Heath, 1930, pp. 357–58

the competition is not so active among a limited as among an unlimited number. . . . The mere exclusion of foreigners, from a branch of industry open to the free competition of every native, has been known, even in England, to render that branch a conspicuous exception to the general industrial energy of the country. . . . In addition to the tax levied for the profit, real or imaginary, of the monopolists, the consumer thus pays an additional tax for their laziness and incapacity.[75]

Mill, however, extended the discussion of monopoly beyond such "artificial" monopoly, to what he called "natural monopoly," which consisted of two categories: the familiar "land monopoly" caused by the fixed supply of land; and the "natural monopoly" of especially unique ability or skill of a laborer. In both cases, the "monopoly" gave rise to a "rent" income.

Amidst this general posture of classical economics, two classical economists deviated—in unfortunate ways—from this tradition, broadening the view of the pervasiveness of monopoly in the economic system. One was Nassau W. Senior. Senior anticipated the much later "monopolistic competition" theorists by seeing monopoly and monopoly elements everywhere. To Senior, if a commodity was not produced under strictly "equal conditions," monopoly, or elements of monopoly, appeared. Senior recognized that such "equal conditions" appeared vary rarely. Senior was particularly ardent in pressing for the idea of a "land monopoly"; not only was land a monopoly, but every product into which land entered as a factor of production partook of a "monopoly" element—and this, of course, meant virtually every product.

Nassau Senior divided his concepts of monopolies into four classes: where one product is more efficient than another, and can thus produce at lower costs and sell at lower prices; fixed natural products (rare wines); patents and copyrights; and the "great monopoly of land."

Haney comments on Senior's theory:

---

[75] John Stuart Mill, *Principles of Political Economy*, Appleton, 1901, II, p. 547

The weakness of defining monopoly in negative terms, as being the absence of equal competition, is apparent. Perfectly equal competition is rare, and elements of differential advantage abound on all hands, so that such a definition would make monopoly the rule. The essential error of Senior's position, however, lies in the confusion of differential advantage with control over supply. The one is price-determined; the other price-determining.[76]

The other classical economist who widened the definition of monopoly was the last of the classicists: John E. Cairnes. In the first place, while the other classicists tended to define free competition as the system that, in the long run, leads to prices being equal to the costs of production, Cairnes defined the *result*—prices equaling costs of production—as free competition. Hence, Cairnes began the fatal modern propensity for defining the ideal of competition, not as the *process* that, in the long run, tends toward a certain equilibrium position, but as the *equilibrium condition* itself. Since the equilibrium position is never really reached, then a position such as Cairnes's, regarding all deviations from that equilibrium position as having elements of "monopoly," tends to brand the whole market economy as having elements of monopoly, as falling short of the ideal, etc.

The other unfortunate widening by Cairnes of the monopoly concept, was to expand on Mill's hint about monopoly of ability; extra skill and extra training of laborers, according to Cairnes, gave them a "monopoly," and therefore gave to higher-wage laborers a "monopoly return." (Classical economists always grouped productive factors: such as "labor," "land," etc. together, and tried to arrive at theories of pricing and distribution on this aggregate basis. Therefore the classicists had no real means of handling the pricing of *individual* labor or land or capital services of specific goods, or the "distribution" of income accruing to them. Cairnes's theory was an attempt praiseworthy in this sense, to break down this lumped mass factor "labor" into more

---

[76] Lewis H. Haney, *History of Economic Thought*, Macmillan, 1949, pp. 347–48

realistic components. But, unfortunately, he termed the differentials in skills "monopoly.") Cairnes also dubbed the different groups of skills among laborers, "non-competing groups," i.e., that laborers only competed among themselves within each group, and not between groups.

It is important to realize that the various wings of socialists, during the nineteenth century, never accused the free-market capitalist system of being "monopolist" or "monopolistic." Instead, they agreed with the classical economists that the market economy was competitive; their strictures and attacks were directed elsewhere. In fact, they often attacked competition itself, as being wicked: Sismondi, the utopians, the Fabians, etc. Karl Marx not only agreed that capitalism was competitive, but the Marxian iron laws of labor, of labor theory of value, of equalization of profit rates, etc. built upon classical foundations, all assumed the workings of competition. It was only much later, at the turn of the twentieth century, that Lenin and other later Marxists coined the doctrines of "monopoly capitalism," of monopoly capitalism leading to imperialism, etc.

Meanwhile, unheralded and unrecognized at the time, the French mathematician Augustin Cournot, founded not only mathematical economics but also modern monopoly and perfect-competition theories, in his *Principes* in 1838. To make things easy for using the calculus in dealing with profits, revenues, and costs of a business firm, Cournot defined competition as that situation where price does not vary with the quantity of the good produced: i.e., where the demand curve for the firm is horizontal, or "perfectly elastic." Not only did Cournot thus found the basic axiom of perfect competition theory, he also believed that such a condition only obtains where the number of firms is large, and that when firms are fewer, "oligopoly" ensues. Cournot worked out a theory of "duopoly."

Thus, with Cournot, the seeds of modern perfect-competition and monopolistic-competition theories were already set, as well as modern mathematical economics: "competition" only occurs when the demand curve for the firm is horizontal; this takes place only when the number of firms in the industry is very large; a smaller number leads to "monopolistic" situations of "oligopoly," etc. Of course, a single firm in an industry, where the demand curve is of course falling, Cournot defined as a "monopoly."

The year 1871 marked the publication of three independent works which were to overthrow the classical era and inaugurate the neo-classical. One, by the founder of modern mathematical economics, was the *Elements* of the Swiss economist, Léon Walras. While Walras brought back Cournot, and Cournot's definition of monopoly as a single seller of a good, with price higher than cost of production, the emphasis in Walras was completely different.

As Walras put it, "Cournot . . . makes the transition from the case of a single monopolist to that of two monopolists, and, finally, from monopoly to unlimited competition. I have preferred, for my part, to start with unlimited competition as the general case, and then to work towards monopoly as a special case."[77]

Walras, in short, saw "free competition" as the ruling case, and monopoly as isolated, special cases of single sellers. Furthermore, Walras, while politically something of a Henry Georgist in favor of land nationalization, in economic theory deplored the idea of the classicists that land is a "monopoly," simply because it had a fixed or limited quantity. As Walras noted, "all productive services are limited in quantity . . . . When the meaning of the term monopoly is broadened to this extent, so that it includes everything, it means nothing."[78]

Carl Menger, the second neoclassical pioneer, founder of the Austrian School, regarded competition and monopoly in much the same way. The economy in general was characterized by competition; "monopoly," in contrast, referred to cases of single sellers. Not being a believer in mathematical economies, Menger was even less tempted than Walras to succumb to the Cournot propositions. While Menger was imprecise in defining "single sellers," the examples he used were those of grants of exclusive privilege by government: the British East India Company, the medieval guilds. Menger's great disciple, Eugen

---

[77] Léon Walras, *Elements of Pure Economics*, Irwin, 1954, p. 440
[78] Walras, *ibid.*, p. 436

von Böhm-Bawerk, didn't discuss problems of monopoly, and in so doing, implied that the economic system was generally competitive.

Of the neoclassicists, it was the Englishman, William Stanley Jevons, *Theory of Political Economy*, who propelled economic thought in the direction of "perfect competition," as compared to the plain classical and neoclassical view of "competition" or "free competition." For Jevons, "perfectly free competition" implied not only absence of price discrimination (which Walras also discussed), but also a large number of buyers and sellers in each industry.

Approaching the view of perfect competition (Jevons was also a mathematical economist, by the way), Jevons defined such a case as "a single trader . . . must buy and sell at the current prices, which he cannot in an appreciable degree affect." To Jevons, also, a "perfect market" implied "perfect knowledge of the conditions of supply and demand, and the consequent ratio of exchange" on the part of "all traders."[79] However, Jevons, while carrying on this Cournot tradition and giving it the name of "perfect," did not carry it through consistently. For he realized, in the preface to his second edition, that since all goods are, in a sense, unique, that (in this sense) "[p]roperty is only another name for monopoly." Therefore, Jevons saw that in the overall market economy "*monopoly* [as he defined it] *is limited by competition*, and no owner, whether of labour, land, or capital, can, theoretically speaking, obtain a larger share of produce for it than what other owners of exactly the same kind of property are willing to accept."[80]

Jevons, however, had been the first to give a rigorous definition of "perfect competition." Continuing in this path was the English mathematical economist, Francis Y. Edgeworth, *Mathematical Psychics* (1881). Edgeworth pressed on to more rigorous definitions, anticipating the modern position: perfect competition involved, Edgeworth maintained, an indefinitely large number of firms and complete divisibility of the product. The enormous influence of mathematics on Edgeworth's definition can be indicated from this passage:

---

79 William Stanley Jevons, *Theory of Political Economy*, Macmillan, 3rd. ed., p. 87
80 Jevons, *ibid.*, pp. xlv–xlvi

A *perfect* field of competition professes in addition
certain properties peculiarly favourable to mathematical calculation; namely, a certain indefinite *multiplic-
ity* and *dividedness*, analogous to that *infinity* and
infinitesimality which facilitate so large a portion of
Mathematical Physics (consider the theory of Atoms,
and all applications of the Differential Calculus).[81]

Alfred Marshall, on this as in on so many other issues, was an
eclectic tangle of confusions and inconsistencies, varying in his
editions of his *Principles* (1st ed., 1890). There were two basic and
conflicting strains in Marshall here. On the one hand, he had a position close to the classicists: considering free competition as a broad
relationship holding throughout the market, and not feeling the need
to make the definition of competition narrow and rigorous. In fact,
he expressly attacked the doctrine of "perfect competition" in his
eighth edition, and said that a negatively sloping demand curve to
a firm was compatible with competition. The term "monopoly" was
used but not precisely defined, but presumably referred to a single
seller of a commodity.

On the "perfect knowledge" assumption in perfect competition,
Marshall was properly caustic:

> we do not assume that competition is perfect.
> Perfect competition requires a perfect knowledge of
> the state of the market. . . . [I]t would be an altogether
> unreasonable assumption to make. . . . The older
> economists, in constant contact as they were with
> the actual facts of business life, must have known
> this well enough; but, partly because the term "free
> competition" had become almost a catchword . . .
> they often seemed to imply that they did assume this
> perfect knowledge.[82]

---

[81] Edgeworth, *ibid.*, p. 18.
[82] Alfred Marshall, *Principles of Economics*, Macmillan, 1938, 8th ed., p. 540

On the other hand, Marshall, too, was influenced by mathematical economists to some degree, and therefore by Cournot. In the third edition of his *Principles*, he introduced the Cournot idea that the horizontal demand curve for the firm was the *ruling* fact in the economy, and that the falling demand curve was the exception. Here was the disastrous concession that perfect competition, or pure competition (the horizontal demand curve), while perhaps not necessary to the whole economy or even ideal, *was* the ruling case in the economy. This position appeared particularly in Marshall's famous Mathematical Appendix, which was heavily influenced by Cournot.[83] Also, Marshall made other concessions about various alleged deviations from the optimum in the free market, due to such things as "external economies" and "external diseconomies."

In 1899, the preeminent American neoclassical economist, John Bates Clark, published his *Distribution of Wealth*. Clark added more restrictions and unrealities to the Edgeworth definition of perfect competition. To the other requirements he added that labor and capital must be *absolutely mobile*; "perfect mobility" of factors had now become another requisite of "perfect competition." The Jevons-Edgeworth tradition of "perfect competition" *as* competition was further developed by the mathematical economist (American) Henry Ludwell Moore, who in a journal article in 1905–06, asserted that the influence of any one producer on price must be negligible, and also declared that no competitor must have to take into account the actions of any other competitor—another condition of perfect competition.

While John Bates Clark added to the development of the model of "perfect competition," he was the reverse of an advocate of using perfect competition as a measure and yardstick for the real economy. For Clark postulated, in the tradition of the classical economists, perfect competition as the *final equilibrium* point of the "static state"; he did not make the mistake of believing that perfect competition is, or should be, ruling in the actual, "dynamic" economic world. In his view of the real world, in fact, Clark was squarely in the classical-neoclassical tradition: he saw monopoly as only a single seller, and

---

83   Marshall, *ibid.*, pp. 849–50

therefore he saw "competition" as the predominant fact of our economic system. Clark worked out his position on these "dynamic" problems, in his *The Control of Trusts*,[84] and his *Essentials of Economic Theory*.[85] Professor Shorey Peterson notes that

> Clark wrote prior to that unfortunate usage by which all that is not pure competition is labeled monopoly. By monopoly he meant unified control of a market, and by competition, in this context, "healthful rivalry in serving the public."[86]

Clark saw the advantages that could come from mergers and large firms:

> A vast corporation that is not a true monopoly may be eminently progressive. If it still has to fear rivals, actual or potential, it is under the same kind of pressure that acts upon the independent producer—pressure to economize labor. It may be able to make even greater progress than a smaller corporation could make.... Consolidation without monopoly is favorable to progress.[87]

Even if an industry consists of a single company, Clark, while considering the situation dangerous, could also see definite advantages of rule by the market. For here Clark saw the enormous importance of *potential competition*:

> The price may conceivably be a normal one. It may stand not much above the cost of production to the monopoly itself. If it does so, it is because a higher price would invite competition. The great company prefers to sell all the goods that are required at a moderate

---

[84] New York, Macmillan, 1901
[85] New York, Macmillan, 1907
[86] Shorey Peterson, "Antitrust and the Classic Model" (1957), reprinted in *Readings in Industrial Organization and Public Policy* (Homewood Ill.: Irwin (for the American Economic Association, 1958), p. 323.
[87] Clark, *Essentials*, p. 534

price rather than to invite rivals into its territory. This
is monopoly in form but not in fact, for it is shorn of its
injurious power; and the thing that holds it firmly in
check is *potential competition. . . .* Since the first trusts
were formed the efficiency of potential competition has
been so constantly displayed that there is no danger
that this regulator of prices will ever be disregarded.[88]

We see that Clark, building on the classical-neoclassical traditions,
can be considered a founder of the modern doctrine of "workable
competition," brought forth by his son John Maurice Clark in 1940,
and highly influential since World War II.

Neither did Clark worry about the so-called problem of "oligopoly."
He believed that "competition usually would, in fact, survive and be
extremely effective" among just a few competitors, until or unless
they formed a union with each other.[89]

Alfred Marshall, in his almost totally neglected applied economics
work, *Industry and Trade* (London, 1919) virtually anticipated all the
significant developments since, by (a) first agreeing with the perfect
competition people that "competition" can be defined as perfect; but then
(b) saying that the real economic world is shot through with "monopoly"
elements—but that this is a good thing (thus anticipating the final position of E.H. Chamberlin over thirty years later). This imprecise form
of competition Marshall saw as perfectly proper. As for monopolies:

Absolute monopolies are of little importance in
modern business as compared with those which are
"conditional," or "provisional" . . . [and the latter keep
their position only if] they do not put prices much
above the levels necessary to cover their outlays with
normal profits.

Marshall also stressed the importance of potential competition,
as well as the interindustry competition of substitutes: "a man of

---

[88] Ibid., pp. 380–81
[89] Ibid., pp. 201–02

sound judgment . . . will keep a watchful eye on sources of possible competition, direct and indirect."[90]

In the meanwhile, while Clark and Marshall were contributing to the classical-neoclassical "workable competition"/"free competition" tradition, as well as giving some concessions to the perfect competition group, the perfect competition doctrine was moving ahead. Alfred Marshall's most famous pupil, Arthur C. Pigou, insisted on perfect mobility and divisibility as part of the "perfect competition" ideal, and attacked the real world for its immobility and indivisibility.[91] Pigou also elaborated greatly on a few hints of Marshall's to coin elaborate doctrines of the failures of the free market in meeting "marginal social costs"—but this is a different field of inquiry. However, even Pigou did not believe that perfect—or what he called "simple"—competition, was technically feasible and therefore really ideal.[92]

We come finally to the culprit who drew all the elements together of what had previously been described as "perfect competition" and welded these elements into a fully analyzed whole. He also extended many of the most important of these elements and set forth a full-fledged theory of competition solely as "perfect competition." This culprit was Frank H. Knight, in his famous first book, *Risk, Uncertainty, and Profit*.[93] The whole of *Risk, Uncertainty, and Profit* is analyzed in terms of perfect competition, and perfect competition most rigorously defined. And, particularly important, whereas J.B. Clark had believed the concept of "perfect competition" applicable only to the static world of equilibrium and did not therefore think it a gauge for the real world, Frank Knight believed that the model *was* applicable as a gauge for the real world—that this was the only sense in which economists could use, analyze, and justify the very concept of "competition." Knight's competition involved complete foresight, perfect mobility, costless change, all elements—products and factors—continuously variable,

[90]   Marshall, *Industry and Trade*, pp. 395–98, 405–09
[91]   Arthur C. Pigou, *Wealth and Welfare*, 1912
[92]   Also see Pigou, *Economics of Welfare*, 4th ed., 1950. Pigou was virtually the creator of "welfare economics."
[93]   Houghton Mifflin, 1921

and infinitely divisible. Demand curves were given and known to all, and exchange instantaneous and costless. Numbers were large, with demand curves to each firm horizontal.

It was this Frank Knight–type of theory—this use of the perfect competition model to describe the real world of the American economy—that Chamberlin reacted against in 1933. Chamberlin said, in effect, Right, "competition" *means* perfect (or rather pure competition—all the above conditions without "perfect knowledge"). But, in that case, Chamberlin declared, it is absurd to keep using this model—as Knight and the others were doing—to describe the real world of business, which emphatically does *not* operate in anything like this way. *Therefore*, we must realize that the economy is *not* competitive, that it is shot through with elements of monopoly. The left-wing Chamberlinians (which partially included Chamberlin himself) used this as a beautiful handle to combine with the Marxists and other critics of business to denounce the whole capitalist system as "monopolistic," and therefore no longer explainable by economic theory. Henry Simons and the other students of Frank Knight during the 1930s advocated breaking up big business *into* atomized units that would be more nearly "perfect."

Finally, as I have indicated, the forgotten tradition of the neoclassical, roughly workable, free-entry concept of "competition" was revived by J.M. Clark and others after World War II. The Chicago School, while considerably mellowed since the 1930s, still uses the "perfect competition" model as the ideal and as the explanatory theory, and therefore still hankers, in many of its members, for rigorous trust busting. Chamberlin himself, realizing that perfect or pure competition is the ideal, is fighting his way toward a theory of "workable competition," but has to do so in the trap of his own terminology. As J.M. Clark once chided Chamberlin, Why *call* this good, workable market economy "monopolistic," when it should better—and more palatably—be called "competitive"?[94]

---

[94] In addition to the references listed above, see George J. Stigler, "Perfect Competition, Historically Contemplated," *Journal of Political Economy* (Feb. 1957): pp. 1–17.

V. Foreign Policy

1. For a New Isolationism

April 1959

It is with a heavy heart that I enter the lists against the overwhelming majority of my friends and compatriots on the Right; also with a sense of futility in trying to combat that tough anti-Soviet foreign policy to which the Right is perhaps even more dedicated than it is to antisocialism. But I must try, if only for the reason that no one else has done so (if, indeed, there are any outright isolationists left anymore).

To begin with, I wish to put my argument purely on the grounds of American national interest. I take it for granted that there are few, if any, world savers on the Right of the Wilson-FDR stamp who believe in the moral obligation of the American government to enforce "collective security" all over the world and to make sure that global Ruritania has no government that we do not like. I assume that the reason that the Right favors a "tough" foreign policy against the Soviet bloc, is that it believes that only such a policy will secure and promote American national interests. And this is the argument that, I maintain, is open to serious challenge.

There is, in the first place, an obviously serious omission in the arguments of the partisans of a policy of "liberation" who constantly denounce the doctrine of mere "containment" to which the administrations, both Democratic and Republican, have been roughly committed for over a decade. In opposition, the Right talks grandiosely but very vaguely about "ultimatums" on Quemoy, Berlin, or any other issue that comes up; but precisely what it really has to offer as a positive program is never mentioned. In all the reams of material written by the Right in the last decade, there is never any precise spelling out of what a policy of ultrafirmness or toughness really entails.

Let us then fill in this gap by considering what I am sure we would all agree is the toughest possible policy: an immediate American ultimatum to Khrushchev and company to resign and disband the whole Communist regime; otherwise we drop the H-bomb on the Kremlin. What about this policy of maximum toughness? It would certainly accomplish one thing: it would bring about a quick show-down between East and West.

What is wrong with this policy? Simply that it would quickly precipitate an H-bomb, bacteriological, chemical, global war, which would destroy the United States as well as Russia. Now, it is true that perhaps this would not happen. Indeed, if we accept the favorite right-wing credo that the Soviet leaders will *always* back down before any of our ultimatums, and will never fight if we are only tough enough, then maybe it is true that the Communist leaders will quickly sur-render, perhaps on the promise of asylum on some remote Elba. But are you, Mr. Right-winger, willing to take this risk? It seems to me that this is the only logical conclusion of the vague talk of toughness that we have adopted for so long.

As for me, it seems clear that, since it is almost certain that the destruction of the United States would follow such an ultimatum, we must strongly oppose such a policy. The fact that Russia would also be destroyed in the holocaust would be cold comfort to someone who holds the national interest of the United States uppermost.

But if we concede that this ultimate and decisive ultimatum must be rejected, then, I contend, we must revise our views on foreign policy as a whole. Perhaps we should think twice about sending ulti-matums about Berlin, Quemoy, or the countless other trouble spots that are bound to erupt in an unending series of crises, so long as we continue the policy of the Cold War. If we are not prepared to go the whole way in a program of liberation, then it makes little sense and creates great risks to keep inching forward part of the way, each time proclaiming our supposed certainty that Russia will not fight.

What, then, of the old policy of containment, which is the only logical alternative to the all-out liberation that has been offered? We have so far been more or less "containing" for over ten years, seemingly doomed forever to huge and crippling armament budgets, an unending chase-your-tail arms race with periodic cries of alarm about the "crisis year" coming up when Russia will be ahead of us in something or other, and an eternal series of hot-spot crises, each of which may touch off a global holocaust. In short, we are sitting on top of an ever-more menacing powder keg. We have all tended to forget the basic rationale of containment as expounded by George Kennan when he was "Mr. X." That is, that time will bring either a revolution inside Russia or a "mellowing" of Soviet power—at any rate, that with a little time, the Soviet menace to the United States would dissolve.

As for the "mellowing," some of us had high hopes after the famous Khrushchev speech of 1956. For here, for the first time, the Communists were denouncing their own hallowed leader, Stalin. Yet, it is certainly clear by now that no mellowing is in the offing; that the Communist parties, far from shaken, have absorbed this shift in line as they have absorbed so many others, and that the so-called "liberal" Communism of the Gomulka stripe is just the same old totalitarianism in another guise. The failure of the Communist regime to crumble after the anti-Stalin shift should be a lesson to all of us proving that people in power never voluntarily give it up; that they must be blasted loose. In short, the Marxists are right when they say that the "ruling class" (in this case, the Communists in Russia) will never relinquish power voluntarily.

The only way for the Communist regime to crumble from within, therefore, is by internal revolution. Now I know that Mr. Eugene Lyons has been valiantly predicting for many years now an imminent revolution inside the Soviet Union. I fervently hope that he is right. But to base a foreign policy on expectation of revolution seems to me foolhardy. The Soviet regime has been in power, after all, for some forty-two years, and unfortunately there are still no signs of revolution on the horizon. Don't misunderstand me: we must all hope and pray for such a revolution, but we cannot count on its arrival. The present regime seems more stable than any since Stalin's death.

If neither liberation nor containment is sensible, what is the alternative? Simply a genuine policy of peace, or, what is the same thing, a return to the ancient and traditional American policy of isolationism and neutrality. This is a policy I think the Right should understand, in view of the Right's gallant fight against the disastrous Roosevelt maneuvering of the United States into World War II. This means total disengagement in Europe and Asia, "bringing the boys back home," and all the other aspects of that policy of sturdy neutrality that used to be America's pride.

But, I will hear from every side, everyone knows that isolationism is obsolete and dead, in this age of H-bombs, guided missiles, etc.

But is it really? It is my contention that our national interest calls for the following policy: *a program of world disarmament up to the point where isolationism again becomes militarily practical.* Specifically, America is threatened now in a way in which it was not threatened a generation ago: by those weapons, H-bomb missiles, disease germs, chemical gases, which can span the old blessed protection of the Atlantic and Pacific Oceans. We are not threatened by Russian tanks or machine guns or infantry. It is therefore the principal task of an American foreign policy truly devoted to American interests, to bring about a universal scuttling of the new weapons. If we all returned to no more than the old "conventional" weapons, and preferably even to the muskets of yore, then America would no longer be endangered. This does not mean, of course, that America should unilaterally disarm. But it *does* mean that America should try its best to effect a disarmament agreement with Soviet Russia, whereby all the nuclear weapons, etc. that could injure us would be dismantled. Khrushchev's speech at the United Nations should not be arrogantly ignored.

I have no fears that a workable inspection agreement cannot be hammered out, if our leaders only have the will that they have so far lacked. In fact, the quite obvious fears of right-wingers that Russia will consent to a viable disarmament program, shows that they agree with me that the Russians are truly sincere in wanting nuclear disarmament. They are sincere, of course, not because the Communist leaders are altruists or humanitarians, but simply because it is also in their best interests to adopt nuclear disarmament.

Here, the right-winger will stop short and say, "Aha, how can a policy be both to the Communists' interests and to ours?" Simply because neither side should want to be destroyed, and, therefore, each side will gain by the mutual disarming of the only weapons (nuclear, etc.) by which each can be mortally hurt. Secondly, mutual nuclear disarmament will certainly leave the Soviet Union in a military advantage *vis-à-vis* its neighbors: since it will have the preponderance of conventional arms. Here, the right-winger thinks he really has me. Isn't the fact that Russia will gain a great arms advantage by nuclear disarmament a clear proof that this policy is unwise?

In the first place, I do not think it at all obvious that Russia will immediately attack the other nations. Believing as it does in eventual internal Communist triumph and fearing an American return to a Cold War policy, it will most likely refrain from any military attack. And, secondly, we can relieve ourselves of even more of the crippling and wasteful economic burden of armaments, as well as take the unilateral propaganda play for peace away from the Russians for a change, by suggesting to them further disarmament of even conventional weapons, perhaps eventually stripping down completely to bows and arrows. But let us assume the worst and suppose that the Russians will really proceed to attack their neighbors with conventional arms once nuclear disarmament has been attained. What then?

I maintain that the only answer we can give to this hypothetical problem is the inelegant "so what?"

Let us not forget our initial axiom: that we first and foremost pursue American national interests. In that case, while we would personally deplore a Communist takeover of foreign countries, we would also adhere to the old isolationist principle of doing nothing about it, because it would not be of official national concern. Deprived of nuclear arms, etc., Russia might be a military menace to Europe or the Middle East, but it would no longer be a menace to the United States, our primary concern. The Russian and Chinese hordes will not be able to swim the oceans to attack us.

At this point, my opponents are sure to trot out that old saw that was used so effectively by interventionists who sobbed about the terrible world that would ensue if Hitler won the war in Europe: perhaps we would not be militarily in danger, the slogan runs, but then America would be an island, forced to a heavy arms budget, and not able to trade with the hostile. In the first place, this argument, never very sensible, is absurd today when we are groaning under the fantastic budgets imposed by our nuclear arms race. Certainly, our arms budget will be less than it is now, especially since it would take far less to protect us from military attack. And we could, as I have said, propose further and progressive disarmament.

We are left with the argument about trade. This strikes one of the oddest notes of all, coming as it does from the very same people who are now fiercely opposed to any current trade with the Communist countries. The basis of all trade is benefit to *both* parties. There is no need for the traders to like each other for each to gain by the trade. There is no reason, therefore, why the Communists, even if in charge of most of the world, would not be willing to trade with us, just as they are willing and eager to trade now.

A return to old-fashioned isolationism, then, is paradoxically the only really practical foreign policy that we have. It is precisely because we are living in the terrible technology of the nuclear age that we have a sound basis for a workable disarmament agreement with the Russians. And, with such an agreement, we would be back to the military realities of the prenuclear age when even our present right-wing interventionists agreed that isolationism *was* practical.

One thing I would like to make quite clear: I am *not* proposing a program of large-scale foreign aid to the Soviet government, or a joint UN slush fund for the backward nations. In fact, adoption of a true isolationist program would finally end, once and for all, the blackmail wheedling of foreign countries that they will go Communist if we don't come across with a suitable bribe. We can now tell the foreign nations to paddle their own canoes at last and to take full responsibility for their own actions.

There is, in short, an eminently sound alternative to the loudly trumpeted policies of either pro-Soviet or anti-Soviet interventionism. And that is a new policy of enlightened and realistic isolationism, sparked, as it needs to be in our day, by general nuclear disarmament of the world powers. Abandoning foreign meddling, we need neither continue the Cold War nor pretend that the Communist leaders are our "heroic allies." We need only adopt again that stance of splendid isolation that once made peaceful and free America the beacon of the world.

2. Review of Alan S. Whiting, *China Crosses the Yalu*

January 31, 1962

Mr. H. George Resch
William Volker Fund

Dear George:

Allen S. Whiting, *China Crosses the Yalu*[95] is a work of moderate revisionism on the Korean War, specifically on the reasons for the Chinese intervention in the Korean War as the U.S. troops advanced toward the Yalu border.

The conventional view is that Communist China helped to instigate a North Korean attack, was heavily involved in the war from the outset, and then lured the American troops up to the Yalu so as to counterattack. Dr. Whiting shows irrefutably that this is pure myth. Actually, China had had little to do with North Korea, which was much more Soviet Russia–oriented, and China made every possible step to avoid involvement in the war—sponsoring proposals for a negotiated peace, which the United States brusquely spurned; giving repeated warnings that it would intervene if the United States

---

[95] Macmillan, 1960

invaded North Korea and approached the Yalu—warnings the United States waved away as pure bluff; and, even after it had decided to intervene as U.S. troops approached the border, intervening in cautious and piecemeal fashion. Whiting shows, for example, that after the Chinese troops had crossed the border and beaten the U.S. troops away from the Yalu, they deliberately withdrew and disengaged themselves from any fight, from November 7, 1950 on. The implication, as Whiting points out, was that the Chinese might have been content to continue on this line, with the North Korean government left with token territory and the Yalu border protected. But General MacArthur was not content with such a settlement and blithely set out on a "final," "win the war," "home by Christmas" offensive against the Chinese. It was only then that the Chinese counterattacked in force, a counterattack that took place with no more troops than the Chinese had had before. It is, incidentally, an apt commentary on the American generalship that the Chinese were able to sweep the American-ROK[96] troops back despite the fact that the former were no more numerous, were considerably inferior in firepower, and were poorly trained.

Furthermore, Whiting makes clear that China only opted for military intervention when (1) its efforts for peaceful negotiations were rebuffed, (2) it was refused its seat in the United Nations, and (3) the Indian proposal for a ceasefire at the thirty-eighth parallel—eventually adopted after two and a half more years of bloody war—was shelved in favor of an aggressive American policy of compulsory unification of all Korea by American-ROK arms.

Two particularly important conclusions emerge from Whiting's data: (1) that China's policy in Korea was essentially peaceful and nonaggressive, and that even the intervention, when it came, was cautious and defensive; and (2) that the "tough" American policy of firmness, aggressiveness, etc., presumably designed to scare off the Chinese, simply didn't work.

Other valuable aspects of the work are these:

---

[96] Editor's note: Republic of Korea.

- Whiting points out that the postwar Chinese "expansion-ism," which has horrified so many, is simply a continuation of traditional Chinese imperialism and expansionism—an expansionism which was pursued by Chiang Kai-shek as well: e.g., over Tibet, portions of northern India (where China's, or rather Tibet's, case is excellent), northern Burma, Vietnam, Mongolia, etc.

- Whiting shows that the United States, soon after the end of the war, began violating agreements it had made with the Chinese Communists, in favor of discriminatory help for the Kuomintang. Whiting indicates the importance—which again the West tends to forget—of Chinese fears of a possible resumption of Japanese militarism and expansionism.

- He marshals a great deal of evidence to show that the Chinese were not involved in the Korean War at the start, including a study of Chinese troop movements and a severe cutback in Chinese military budget and troops.

- He shows that part of the reason for Chinese entrance into the war was the repeated American air and strafing attacks against Chinese villages across the Yalu.

- He shows the folly of American political and military leaders in blithely ignoring repeated Chinese warnings that China would enter the war if U.S. troops invaded North Korea and approached the Yalu. Various errors of General Whitney, apolo-gizing for MacArthur's grievous mistakes, including his wild speculation that China had discovered that we would not use the A-Bomb by espionage, are properly deprecated.

On the other hand, there are several important weaknesses in the book. The most fundamental stems from what we might call the "RAND Corporation approach" to the writing (the author is a staff member at RAND). The RAND emphasis on sociologizing and "game theory" often lead Whiting to engage in far-flung flights of sociological and psychological speculation: about Chinese motives;

about its reasons for various acts; about the weighing that the Chinese did about advantages and disadvantages of actions, which are not at all based on the historical evidence. In short, too often Whiting abandons history for flights of sociopsychological fancy. Happily, the above valuable conclusions are not particularly affected by this, but other conclusions and statements are.

In specific content, there are various errors, some connected with Whiting's frequent penchant for sociologizing.

For one thing, Whiting blithely assumes that North Korea launched the original attack, without even mentioning, much less considering, the considerable evidence that calls this into question—evidence backed by the fact that Russia's boycott of the Security Council made time propitious for a South, not North, Korean attack. Secondly, Whiting, again without evidence, simply assumes that North Korea was a puppet satellite of Soviet Russia. Certainly, the "People's Democratic Republic of Korea" was closely oriented to Soviet Russia; but, there is not sufficient evidence, certainly not supplied by Whiting, that Russia totally controlled North Korean actions. (The North Korean Communist Party, for example, now favors the Chinese over the Khrushchev line in the interparty dispute.) The fact, pointed out by Whiting himself, that Soviet Russia pursued a conciliatory line in the United Nations would, in fact, tend to point the other way. At any rate, the absence of any evidence or discussion of the Soviet position is a large gap in the book.

Similarly, I would like to have seen some fuller discussion of American positions and reactions on the Korean question, both in government and out—but there is very little on it. Moreover, there is a large gap in the discussion: when the tide of war was just beginning to turn, at Pusan, the British proposed that the United Nations forces stop at the thirty-eighth parallel, and this was vehemently opposed by the United States; yet, a month or so later, when the UN forces arrived back at the border, the British had meekly shifted their position, and acquiesced to the US-UN invasion of North Korea, leaving the Indians almost alone as conciliators. Why the shift? What had happened? There is no mention of this problem in the book.

Other defects and biases of Whiting:

- Whiting, weak on Communist theory, assumes that the aggressive, "tough," "two-camp" position of the Chinese *is* the Marxist-Leninist position, thereby ignoring that other tendency in Marxism-Leninism which has been particularly developed by Khrushchev: "peaceful co-existence" and a recognition that "neutralists" are not "tools of Western imperialism."

- Also, Whiting defends the American refusal to recognize Communist China or to admit it into the United Nations, even before the Korean War, as having "little choice" because a few minor irritations that occurred with consular officials when the Communists came to power. Surely this is superficial and overdrawn; further, here Whiting adopts the unfortunate Wilsonian theory of recognition of a country as a moral device and instrument of international sanctions—thereby violating the traditional American (and libertarian, nineteenth-century) position of a government recognizing any other government on the basis of its existence, and not on the basis of approval or disapproval of that government.

- Whiting also refers rather blithely to Soviet "obstructionist tactics" in delaying a peace treaty with Germany, which is hardly a careful description of the problems there.

- As one of the few "proofs" that Korea was a Soviet-controlled satellite, Whiting points out that many key North Korean officials were ex-Soviet citizens of Korean descent. He fails to explain that these were, of course, exiles from Japanese oppression who had taken refuge in Soviet Russia and then returned. Their presence in the North Korean government can hardly be called proof of Soviet domination.

- Another flaw in the book is Whiting's failure to mention the highly significant fact that the U.S. decision to intervene in the Korean War was made in *advance* of UN sanction, which was just used as a convenient excuse by the Truman administration;

Whiting makes it appear that it was a UN decision. Whiting also denies that the Korean conflict was a civil war, between Koreans, which it obviously was, rather than a true international conflict, in inception.

- There is also not enough material on who in the United States government believed, or did not believe, the Chinese warnings that they would intervene. Further, if Soviet Russia had been running the North Korean policy, how is it that the Chinese had no Russian arms, and that—at least from Whiting's skimpy data—Russian-arms aid only seems to have come in force after China and America had come to grips?

- Finally, although this is happily only a hint in the book and plays no major role, Whiting indicates that he favored a U.S. policy of war on behalf of China against Japan in the 1930s.

Because of these defects, the Whiting volume is hardly a great work; but despite them, its net positive contribution is highly valuable, especially because very little rational and objective historical work has been done about the Korean conflict. The mythology about the Korean War is so widespread that a pioneering work like this performs a valuable, even if limited, service.

3. Review of Frank S. Meyer, *The Moulding of Communists*

October 28, 1961

Mr. H. George Resch
William Volker Fund

Dear George:

One reason why a rather detailed report on Frank S. Meyer's *The Moulding of Communists: The Training of the Communist Cadre* is important is that it starkly raises a crucial issue that has, in recent years, been dividing proponents of individual liberty.[97] That issue concerns the nature of "the enemy" the advocates of liberty face in the modern world.

One school of thought identifies that "enemy" as socialism or statism in all its forms. To this school, Communism is simply one wing of socialism, and a wing that, certainly in the United States, is of almost zero political importance. Since socialism and statism, in numerous forms, has been greatly on the rise in this century and is indeed dominant in the modern world, this school of thought tends to regard the "battle" as being largely if not wholly ideological: as an effort to turn men's minds from an acceptance of statism to one of liberty. For purposes of simplification, though a negative is not sufficient description, we may call this school "anti-socialist."

The second school of thought, on the contrary, believes that *in addition to and over and above* the problem of socialism is the problem of Communism, that the world Communist movement (or "conspiracy" as they like to call it) poses a uniquely diabolic threat which must be met, and which must be given even greater priority than the problem of socialism. It is important to realize that this school shifts the priority of focus from ideas to *persons*, for the persons of Communists now take on a Luciferian quality which must be combated in a physical more than an ideological way. This school, which we may call "anti-Communist," concentrates, then, on a specific group of persons, and therefore on a physical rather than an ideological battle. The solution tends to be *not* ideological education for men's minds, but taking up arms and liquidating Communists wherever they may be found, at home and abroad.

Note the problem that the "anti-Communist" faces. He cannot, like the anti-socialist, simply concentrate on the *ends* toward which the Communists are aspiring, for these ends are simply socialism, and the Communist variety of socialism is obviously of negligible importance in the United States as compared to, say, the Americans

---

[97] Frank S. Meyer, *The Moulding of Communists: The Training of the Communist Cadre* (New York: Harcourt, Brace, 1961).

for Democratic Action or "modern Republican" variety. Any concentration on ends would, for Americans, virtually eliminate concern about Communism *per se*. To establish his thesis of unique diabolism, then, the anti-Communist must concentrate on the means or the persons or the structure of the Communist movement itself. For if he concentrates only on ends, the Communist wing of socialism would sink into insignificance. The importance of Frank's book is that he specifically focuses *not* on the Communists' ends—socialism—but on the means that they use: on them as persons, on the Communist Party as uniquely diabolic people, etc. In doing so, Frank is, perhaps unwittingly, putting his finger on the nub of the central issue.[98]

Before going further, it must be clear that there is no hope of "reconciling" the anti-Communist and the anti-socialist positions as I have described them. The emphasis, the outlook, the conclusions are totally incompatible.

The central and almost total thesis of Frank's book, in fact, is precisely the unique diabolism of the Communist movement and the Communists as persons: this is reiterated time and again. We read of the "profoundly different character of Communist consciousness—different from anything with which we are acquainted"; "for the Communist *is* different. He thinks differently. Reality looks different to him."

The personality of the Communist is, says Frank, totally transformed, transformed by the "training process that moulds the Communist cadre." He becomes a new man—a "Bolshevik"—and this new type is the same throughout the Communist movement, *regardless* of the country involved. (This transcendence of any national or cultural boundaries is important for Frank to establish, for otherwise he would have to admit that not all Communists are uniquely diabolic "Bolshevik" types). As a result of this training, he declares, "they acquire a strength and confidence which, like the fearful evil they bring into being, can only be described as Luciferian."

---

[98] Editor's note: Rothbard and Frank Meyer were colleagues at both *National Review* and the Volker Fund and were friends, despite their disagreements on foreign policy and political strategy.

"Luciferian" is the operative word, because the thesis of Frank's book is the radical difference between Communists and all other men, a difference that makes them nonhuman, in effect, that makes them agents of the Devil—cunning, almost always successful in the pursuit of their ends—and against which force and violence are called upon by Frank to extirpate them root and branch: "Against this vision . . . of Communist man, there is no recourse in compromise, reasonableness, peaceful coexistence. . . . Communist man poses two stark alternatives for us: victory or defeat"—kill or be killed. Except, of course, that modern weapons are such that killing and being killed are likely to occur together—a highly important fact that Frank, in his peroration for total war, neglects somehow to mention.

Frank's book, then, stands or falls on whether or not he establishes this thesis of unique diabolism, of the radical "difference" between Communists and other men. It is my firm conviction that he has established nothing of the sort.

Let us remember that, in judging Frank's success or failure, we must largely abstract from the *end* Communism wishes to pursue (socialism) and consider the Communist from the point of view of the type of man, the type of organization this is. The important point is this: Frank loads the dice throughout by speaking only of Communists and thus implying that their training and organization are unique. This is totally false, for most of the characteristics Frank mentions can be found in almost *any* organization (or, sometimes, even profession) of dedicated men, regardless of what that dedication is.

The major characteristic of the "Bolshevik" is absolute dedication and loyalty to the decision of the Communist Party, a party that takes on the right to run the members' lives for its benefit. And yet, this is not at all unique with Communists. This phenomenon exists in numerous organizations of any sort. We see much of this process, for example, in the typical Organization Man of our time. Take a rising young middle-rank executive at General Motors or IBM. He begins as an ordinary quasi-independent human being, an individual. As he works and goes up the rungs in IBM, his values begin to be transformed and molded into the Organization Man. He begins to believe that his own subjective values and pursuits must be subordinated to "loyalty to the company." And, as for his private affairs, he submits to the right of his boss to dictate his personal affairs: "this woman will *never do* as the wife of a rising and important executive"; "surely, you must move to a bigger house so that you can entertain important industry men in style," etc. Frank's assumption that only the Communist Party tends to dictate to its members and reduce them to "loyal" ciphers is total nonsense.

This phenomenon can be seen even more starkly in another organization—one that Frank is quite fond of—the Army, or, more specifically the CIA, Army Intelligence, or the FBI. Frank expresses shock that the Communist, through process of training, holds the good of the party above the good of his family, his friends, his private life, etc. And what of the "good CIA man"? Is he not taught the same thing? Is he not taught to lie, to cheat, *even to kill*, if the "interests of his country" as interpreted by his government bosses so demand? Isn't he taught to disregard his own interests, or his family's, in relation to these "larger" interests? Is he not taught to keep secrets from his own family, to lie to them for his "country's sake"? How does this differ from the Communist?

At one or two points, Frank comes close to this truth by pointing to the Communist as a sort of soldier in the ranks. Granted, but then what of all the *other* soldiers in this world? What of the American soldier? If Frank answers that the ends of the two are different, this would concede my total attack on the thesis of his book, for that thesis deals not with the Communist's end (socialism) but with his means and his personality and the structure of his organization. It is the latter that is supposed to make him "Luciferian" and peaceful coexistence with him impossible—while, apparently, peaceful coexistence with Walter Reuther or the ADA is eminently possible.[99]

---

[99]   Editor's note: Walter Reuther (1907–1970) was a prominent American labor-union figure and long-time president of the United Auto Workers (UAW). In the 1930s he was considered pro-Communist, but in 1947 he helped found the liberal Americans for Democratic Action (ADA).

If the Communist is taught that his end justifies any means to attain it, so is the American or British or German soldier, so is the intelligence officer—and so, after all, is the politician. Are we not told, again and again, that the State and its politicians cannot be bound by ordinary rules of individual morality? That "reasons of State" compel them to lie, to cheat, to kill, for the sake of the "national interest"? Every State, every government follows such a path. How does this differ from the Communist?[100]

The objection might be raised: if we say that Communists are not uniquely monsters, how can they justify such brutalities as Soviet slave labor camps, as the suppression of the Hungarian Revolution, etc.? Doesn't such justification make the Communists diabolic and uniquely inhuman, as Frank claims—and as Frank bolsters his claim with support from Whittaker Chambers, and his and Chambers's depictions of the "crises" faced by Communists as they wrestle with the problem of the "screams in the night," of those butchered by the Soviet government, etc.

Well, let us investigate this "screams in the night" problem. Here again, we shall see that the justification by Communists is not only not unique, but is almost universal and is engaged in by the supporters of *all* States, everywhere and at all times. For example, Harry S. Truman, Henry Stimson, et al. gave an order that deliberately and wantonly annihilated something like 400,000 Japanese civilians, including women and children, in A-bomb blasts at Hiroshima and Nagasaki. How many Americans have listened to their screams in the night? How many Americans have failed to "justify"—in the name of the "national interest" or whatever—this barbarous act? How many

---

[100] Editor's note: This paragraph was in the original text but appears to have been added in error. It has no relation to what precedes or follows it.

    Meyer does not inform the reader that the explanation for this is very simple and nonsinister. The reason is that the Communists follow the economics of Karl Marx, and Marx wrote at a time when *all* economics was called "political economy." Hence, the Communists still cleave to the name—just as do the Henry Georgists, and for similar reasons. The term "economics" only came in toward the end of the nineteenth century.

"cadre Americans"—either in the government or out—jumped off the American-State bandwagon because of this action? How many have even expressed remorse or indignation? And the same can be said of numerous American actions, including the bombing of hundreds of thousands of German refugees at Dresden, the sending of hundreds of thousands of refugees back to the Soviet zone, etc.

Coming closer to home, Frank Meyer's friend Dr. Medford Evans went so far as to write an article recently justifying the A-bombing of Hiroshima and Nagasaki. Justifications, rationalizations, for butchery and murder have been served up by every State and adopted by the overwhelming majority of their citizens. The United States has not lagged behind in this activity. One amusingly ironic example: the U.S. went to war against Spain ostensibly to free the Cuban people from the activities of such as "Butcher Weyler," the Spanish general who inaugurated the policy of the "concentration camp" for the native civilian population. Yet, only a few years later, in direct consequence of our conquest of the Philippines in the war with Spain, the *American Army* used the exact same tactics—to which were added the burning of native villages, along with all of their inhabitants—against the Filipinos who were fighting for their independence against our occupying forces. Who remonstrated? Who jumped off the cadre-American bandwagon?

The Russian suppression of the Hungarian Revolution needed no *special* justification by Communists; for *every* State in history, with no exception that I know of, has ruthlessly fought to suppress any revolution against its rule. The United States Army ruthlessly suppressed rioters and rebels a few years ago in the U.S. colony of Okinawa. The size of the revolt and its suppression may have been different from the Hungarian case; the principle was exactly the same. And, on a larger scale, the British, in their ruthless war against Malayans fighting for their independence, razed and burned whole villages to the ground, using the very principle of "collective guilt" for which Americans and British had denounced the Nazis at Lidice.

Who protested in the West? Did Frank Meyer? On the contrary—for Frank Meyer himself has an enormous number of anti-Communist "screams in the night" to account for and justify before the bar of morality. Frank for example, supports the French in the war to suppress the Algerian national revolution. In the course of this war, the French have used every barbarism of which the Soviet government can be accused: collective guilt, mass slaughter, torture of prisoners, etc. And yet, Frank S. Meyer, in the name of "Western Civilization" and "anti-Communism," wholeheartedly supports these moves.

Do not Frank Meyer and his fellow "anti-Communist men" have as many screams in the night to justify and alibi for, as have the Communist men? We can say, as a matter of fact, that they may have *more*: for Frank S. Meyer and his fellow anti-Communists look forward almost with enthusiasm to a nuclear holocaust against the Communist nations which would annihilate millions, if not hundreds of millions, of human beings. The devastation and suffering caused by nuclear war would bring about so many more "screams in the night" than Communism has ever done as to defy comparison. And yet Frank justifies such a war. Are Communists then, *unique* monsters, *unique* justifiers of criminality?

(And just as every State suppresses revolutions against its power, so do they jail enemies or suspected "subversives." The Soviets send anti-Communists to prison; the United States sends not only Communists to prison, but other enemies, including for example, giving life sentences to a whole group of Puerto Rican nationalists whose crime was conspiracy to agitate and work for Puerto Rican independence from the United States.)

If, then, Communists are dehumanized or brutalized by their fealty to their organization, or their justification of its actions, the same is true—even more so—for other groups and especially other States: for the soldier who is deliberately brutalized by his training to kill unquestioningly at the command of his officers, for the paratroopers who are especially brutalized by their army training, for CIA men and espionage agents, etc. The "anti-Communist man" and his organization can be—and is—just as brutal, just as inhuman as the Communist, if not more so.

And let us remember also that the typical "conservative" is usually to be found justifying, even glorifying (even apart from the problem of anti-Communism) military training and its brutalization as a good in itself: it "makes men out of men." Frank Meyer himself seems singularly unaware of the brutalization or inhumanity of military training or the military life.

Another favorite indictment of the Communists and a favorite indictment used by Frank Meyer in this book, to demonstrate their unique diabolism, is that Communism is a "conspiracy." How often have we read of the "international Communist conspiracy"! Other socialists are not so bad, the cry runs, because they are not "conspirators," whereas Communists are.

Meyer maintains that the world Communist movement is a monolith run by the Soviet Politburo, yet we have seen increasingly in recent years that this certainly is not true. That his statements are pure assertion unbacked by convincing evidence is shown, further, by his failure to cite any *sources* dealing with the Russian or Asian or other non–Western European parties. And there is another important consideration vis-à-vis the "Communist man" that Meyer fails to consider. In countries where the Communist movement is out of power, we can be sure that its members are eager, dedicated ideologues. But in countries where Communism is in power, the situation inevitably changes. For this means that the *only* way to rise in society, to rise above the level of ditch digger, is to join the Communist Party.

It is then inevitable that Communist Parties in Communist regimes will become heavily infected with the virus of "careerism," "opportunism," etc., men who will of course spout the slogans, but do so only ritualistically, and who will act increasingly as Russian (or Yugoslavian or whatnot) bureaucrats rather than ideologues. And as time goes on, this process is bound to accelerate. Yet, by omitting this element, Meyer's policy conclusions *vis-à-vis* Communist countries and their leaders become totally misleading.

We must conclude that Frank Meyer has not in the least established his thesis, that his discussion distorts the picture, and that one cannot concur in the special diabolism of the Communist organization. But if that is true, then the only thing really wrong about the Communists is their end: socialism, an end that is pursued by a great many more people, people who are far more influential in the direction of socialism or quasi-socialism than is the negligible and half-outlawed CPUSA. If the Communist is not uniquely diabolic, then what *is* he? I think we can pretty well summarize the Communist by saying that he is, in form, structure, and means an Intellectual *Organization Man*, and his end is socialism of the proletarian-Marxist variety. Like all other organization men, he is devotedly loyal to his organization, here his party. In the ranking of organizations, it is fair to say that he is *more* subservient than a General Motors executive, but far less brutalized than a soldier, a paratrooper, or a CIA man. If he rationalizes and justifies *brutality,* he does the same as the members or defenders of *every* State.

He is far more independent than the soldier, paratrooper, or CIA man, as witness the numerous schisms, defections, etc. that have occurred in the Communist Party, as compared to the scarcity of mutinies in the ranks of the armed forces. The Communist has many admirable qualities which other people would do well to emulate: the striving to be rational and objective, the striving to integrate all of man's knowledge and social philosophy into one great philosophic system, the wish to be serious and responsible, the striving for an ideal which (he thinks) will bring about a paradise on earth for the human race.

He has two main errors and vices: one is that the philosophic system that he has picked out for himself, Marxism, is incorrect; and as a consequence, that his goal of socialism is a tragic error. But we have seen that the *goal* (socialism) must be ruled out of this discussion, because there are lots of socialists, and Communism becomes no worse than the rest. His second error is that he is an Organization Man: that he tends to place the locus of science, of reason, of reality, in other persons: i.e., the ones who constitute the leadership of his organization. But while this is a vice, we have seen that it is a vice that the Communist shares with many millions of others today, in innumerable organizations of all types throughout the world. What we see here is *not* the compulsory bondage of the individual to the State, but the voluntary bondage of an individual to some external organization. It is, I believe, incumbent on libertarians and individualists to begin to give some profound attention to this problem; we have thought and written a good deal about the State; we have done very little in considering the problem of the individual and organizations.

Since there are Organization Men everywhere, and since the Communists are far better individualists than Army officers, etc., we must conclude that Communists are not uniquely diabolic, and that the main thing wrong with them is their end.

So much for the Communist man and his movement. As for Meyer's book, it should be noted that it is written in lively, even powerful fashion—but, again, that it is skimpy and ignores vast stretches of space and time in the record of the Communist movement. Finally, it is important to note a disquieting passage or two that indicate that *one* reason why Meyer is so fiercely opposed to Communism is that *it*, in turn, is opposed to the State (or, at least, the non-Communist state). Thus, Meyer, in the course of his anti-Communist philippic, says:

> Previously, the policeman on the corner has been for him, as for most Americans or Englishmen, a neutral symbol at the worst, at the best a source of information and ultimate protection against robbers and other malefactors. Now he is transformed into an immediate symbol of danger, an agent of the enemy, the bourgeois state, with whom one's only potential relations are those of warfare. An alienation from the mores of the society is being artificially created. . . .
>
> Through theory, through atmosphere, through interpreted experience in demonstration or picket line, the sense of community with the nation is shattered. Very concretely, the idea of a commonwealth within

the established commonwealth, and in bitter battle with it, is instilled.[101]

Let us note this passage very carefully. For what Meyer is doing is *identifying* "the society," "the nation," and "the commonwealth," *with* the State—with the "cop on the corner." Now this is the grievous error that has been made by every writer who has opposed liberty: this identification of the public, of the citizenry, with the State apparatus. It does not salvage Meyer's position to add his wish that the state be "the limited government of a constitutional republic"—the damage is done.[102] It is disquieting, but perhaps not astonishing, that Frank Meyer should reveal a deep-rooted and fundamental statism in his political philosophy; it is almost impossible to agitate for the State to kill Communists throughout the world without adopting statism at the root of one's social philosophy.

4. Critique of Frank S. Meyer's Memorandum[103]

March 1962

The first thing to note about Mr. Meyer's memorandum is his striking, almost remarkable, lack of foresight in evaluating the status of the world Communist movement. Presumably, the memorandum was written shortly after Khrushchev's report of January 6, 1961. Any perceptive and knowledgeable observer of world Communism knew, by early 1961, that the ideological stresses and strains between the Khrushchev and the Chinese-"Stalinist" wings of the movement were becoming ever greater and more intense; any such observer would have known that the seeming agreement expressed in the

---

[101] Meyer, *The Moulding of Communists*, pp. 127–28.
[102] Also see page 68, where Meyer is opposing the Communist view of the State as pure force—when that, of course, is exactly what the State is.
[103] Editor's note: Many of the points in Meyer's memorandum were incorporated into an article by Meyer, "Communist Doctrine, Strategy and Tactics," *Modern Age* (Summer 1961).

November 1960 conference of the Communist parties was a mere temporary papering over of these differences, and that a crucial split was soon to occur.

By the fall of 1961 and since, as the whole world knows, the split has come savagely into the open, as well as further splits within the numerous Communist parties, and more open drives toward a "revisionist" position. But Frank S. Meyer, in early 1961, saw none of this; no, for him, the Sino-Soviet disagreements had been minor and transitory, and they were, furthermore, successfully "resolved" (*not* just "compromised," states Meyer) at the 1960 Communist Party conference. A "unified policy" for international Communism had been "hewn out"; and the "ideological authority of Nikita Khrushchev as the leader of international Communism in all respects was confirmed."

Rarely has the analysis of a supposed expert on world Communism been more rapidly or more shatteringly disproved by the march of events. There are important reasons for this, as revealed by the memorandum, which go beyond the personal failings of the author. For the Meyer analysis was the only one that fit his preconceived worldview of the Communist movement as a single international "monolith." This monolith, in Meyer's analysis, is hardly composed of individual human beings, with ideologies and hopes and fears; instead, the world Communist movement is treated almost as if it were a "thing" from outer space, a diabolic monolith dedicated *solely* and simply to world conquest of power. The only time such an emotion as "fear" is indicated for Communists by Meyer is the supposed fear of the Communists of "awakening the West" to the creeping conquest of Communism; tactical moves of Communists are treated *simply* as diabolical ruses and thrusts in the conquest drive. Now, we submit that this sort of behavior—the only sort of behavior attributed to Communists by Meyer—has never been applicable to human beings on this Earth, but only to titillating monsters in science-fiction extravaganzas.

Totally absent from Meyer's purview is the possibility that the Communists might be frightened for their own skins. And yet this fear—the fear of a war launched upon them *by* the West—is probably the single most important guide to Communist views and policies since the advent of the Soviet revolution. In the first place, the Communists possess the ideology of Marxism-Leninism (barely mentioned by Meyer). This ideology tells them that while every effort should be bent toward making the socialist revolution a peaceful one, this effort will most probably fail, because the capitalist ruling class, when it sees itself threatened by socialist change, will itself turn to violence and—either by fascism, militarism, authoritarianism, or a mixture of these forms—stamp out the civil liberties and democratic processes that would bring about socialist change.

In short, Marxism-Leninism by no means advocates violent revolution; it prefers peaceful, democratic change; but, not being absolutely pacifist, it counsels the working class to prepare to fight defensively against offensive and fascistic suppressions by the bourgeoisie. (Let us note that in *no* democratic country, where free speech and free elections have prevailed, has the Communist movement turned toward either violent revolution or guerrilla warfare; that the latter have occurred only in dictatorial countries—Cuba, China, Vietnam, etc.—where peaceful methods were not open to the Communist Party.)

As in domestic affairs, so in foreign; the Communists believe that Western imperialism, which they consider to be run by the upper bourgeoisie, will not permit socialism to thrive peacefully and will not permit each country to decide and resolve its own "class struggle" in its own way without foreign intervention. The Communists believe that Western imperialism, concerned over the spread of socialism, will turn to *international violence* in an attempt to crush socialism and to prevent socialist states from coming into being.

There is a great deal of sense in both of these expectations by the Communists, who conclude that no ruling class will abide peacefully at its own displacement. In the *international* sphere, in which we are interested in this memorandum, Communist expectations have been more than fulfilled since the birth of the Soviet Union. No sooner had the Soviet Union been born than the United States and other Western powers fiercely invaded Soviet Russia and for several years gave armed support to the Czarist counterrevolution. Several years of this joint invasion were enough to confirm (and certainly reasonably so) the ingrained suspicion among the Communists that, given half a chance, Western imperialism would invade and attempt to stamp out socialism in the Soviet Union or in any other Communist lands.

Frank S. Meyer, in his odd terminology, says that, before World War II, Soviet Russia took the "strategic defensive" (for more on Meyer's fallacious methodology, see below); indeed it did, for it was scared out of its boots that the West would invade again. "Capitalist encirclement" it saw as a reality, not a slogan; this was confirmed by the failure of the United States to recognize the existence of the Soviet Union for sixteen years, until 1933; and then by the evident desire on the part of many Westerners to encourage Hitler to have a go at conquest of the Soviet Union. The "strategic defensive" was, then, not adopted for some sort of diabolic reason, or to "lull the West," or any similar "outer space" motivation; it was adopted simply and candidly because the Soviet Union was afraid of Western invasion, and its main and perfectly logical objective was—and always shall be—"defense of the socialist fatherland."

During this pre–World War II period, claims Frank S. Meyer, the Communists adopted a "tactical offensive." Where are the "offensive tactics"? The Soviet Union conducted itself, throughout these years, in a way so admirably defensive as to be worthy of emulation by the other great powers; when and where did it aggress against other nations? Indeed, Lenin, at the Treaty of Brest-Litovsk in 1918, rammed through the greatest "appeasement peace" in modern history, turning over to German control almost the entire Western Russia, and Lenin drove home this appeasement settlement over the determined opposition not only of all the other parties in Russia but also of the bulk of the leadership and rank-and-file of the Bolshevik Party itself.

Where are the offensive tactics? Indeed, no offensive tactics were pursued by the Soviet Union; here again, Meyer can only make out any sort of case by switching reference from the Soviet Union to other domestic Communist parties. But here, too, the Communist parties were simply pursuing their adopted ideology. In the early 1920s, the Communists believed, *a priori*, that Germany and other European countries were ripe for internal revolution, and indeed Germany was not far from going Communist in these years. But later on, these hopes died, and Stalin, particularly after the ouster of the fanatic Trotsky, who always wanted immediate revolutions everywhere, settled down to calm concentration on "socialism in one country."

Indeed, insofar as Stalin was able to influence the Communist parties abroad (and they were never the absolute monolith conceived of by Frank Meyer and the Sunday supplements), his influence—before, during, *and* after World War II—was always in the direction of moderation, of abstaining from violent revolutionary change. And *this* critical fact is one of the basic reasons for the current worldwide split in the Communist movement; ever since Stalin's ouster of Trotsky, the "left wing" of the Communist movement has been accusing Stalin and the Soviet leadership of "betraying" the world revolution, of inducing Communist parties to collaborate with the "class enemy."

This accusation of the Left is essentially correct, and the continued record of dampening of world Communism by the cautious and moderate Kremlin leadership has finally led to unbridgeable gulfs in the Communist movement. As early as the 1920s, Stalin tried to prevail on the Chinese party to form coalition governments with Chiang against the Japanese; and it was against Stalin's advice that Mao Tse-tung went into the hills to form his revolutionary guerrilla army. During the middle and late 1930s, the Litvinov line—guided again by defense of the Soviet Union against the rising threat of Nazi aggression—was to promote "collective security" and popular fronts with the bourgeoisie against the Nazi-Fascist threat. During World War II—again to Trotskyite and "leftist" chagrin—this policy of class collaboration with the bourgeoisie against the Nazi-Fascist threat continued.

World War II made another deep imprint on the Communist psyche. On the one hand, there was the savage and massive assault launched against the Soviet Union by Hitler, an assault in which 20,000,000 Russians lost their lives. On the other hand, Stalin and the Russian leaders saw that it was *possible* to engage in an alliance with *some* "bourgeois," capitalist leaders in the West, most notably

Franklin D. Roosevelt. From World War II, two important lessons were learned by Stalin and the Communist leaders: (1) a great (and rational) fear of German militarism, and (2) a recognition that *some* capitalists were not implacable enemies, out to destroy the Soviet Union (e.g., FDR).

Mr. Meyer maintains that, during and after World War II, Communist strategy shifted to "offensive strategy—defensive tactics," as compared to the reverse condition before the war. This is a wholesale fallacy; actually, the strategy *and* tactics of the Soviet Union *continued*, after the war, to be defensive. The really critical and important dichotomy is not between "strategy" and "tactics"; it is between the international, military position of the Soviet Russian state and the various domestic, internal policies of the Communist parties. The position of the Soviet Union has always, since 1917 and since Brest-Litovsk, been defensive; the position of the various Communist parties has always been "offensive" in the sense that they, like *any other party*, try to advance to power as best they can.

But there is nothing diabolic or mysterious about the process or the dichotomy. As a matter of fact, as we have indicated above, the influence of the Soviet Union on the various Communist parties has always been a moderating one. This was particularly true during and after World War II. So impressed was Stalin with the friendship of FDR, and so impressed was he with the need to maintain the "Grand Alliance" with the West, that Stalin went to great lengths to try to induce the various Communist parties throughout the world *not* to revolt and not to seize power where they were able.

We must remember the conditions that obtained in Europe and Asia during and immediately after World War II. The so-called Soviet "expansion" into Eastern Europe occurred as the inevitable and natural consequence of the rollback of the German armies. Russia could only defeat Germany by occupying Eastern Europe and part of Germany; most of Eastern Europe was not only occupied by Germany but had had governments allied with Hitler in the attack on Russia. But in addition, as the German armies fell back from occupied Europe, and the Japanese armies fell back from China and

Southeast Asia, a natural power vacuum *remained* in these countries. This vacuum naturally tended to be filled by the guerrilla armies that had been rebelling against Nazi or Japanese occupation. Now, in those countries where guerrilla armies existed, the guerrillas were invariably led by Communists. This was *not* the result of some sort of diabolic Communist plot; it was the simple result of the fact that it was generally only the Communists who were anti-Nazi enough, and determined enough, to form guerrilla rebel bands.

In Asia, the Chinese Communists profited enough by the Japanese defeat to move forward to eventual conquest of China. Ho Chi Minh had occupied *all* of Indochina immediately after the Japanese defeat. In Europe, Communist guerrilla armies were in a position to take over the following countries: Greece, France, Belgium, Italy, Yugoslavia, and Albania. Yugoslavia and Albania were taken over by Communist guerrilla troops.

But in the other countries, Stalin "sold out" the Communist movement; in the interests of what was later to be called "peaceful coexistence," in the interests of preserving the Big Three alliance for lasting peace, Stalin induced the Communist parties and guerilla bands of France and Italy to *refrain* from seizing power and to join coalition governments; in Greece, where the Communist guerillas (with strong "left" tendencies) refused to do likewise, Stalin consented to the British reinvasion of Greece and the imposition of a conservative government. (The Greek Communists were able to continue the struggle against the imposed Anglo-American counterrevolutionary government, because the independent Marshal Tito continued, despite Stalin, to supply the Greek Communist troops.) And in Indochina, Stalin consented to the reinvasion of the country by French imperialism, which beat back Ho Chi Minh. In China, Stalin tried many times to induce the Chinese Communists to enter coalition government with Chiang, but the angry Chinese Reds refused and went on to victory.

It is this record of what many dedicated Communists considered to be Stalin's base betrayal of the world Communist movement that has set the indispensable background for the Soviet-Chinese split of today. Stalin, therefore, began the conscious policy of "betraying" the interests of the world class struggle on behalf of a policy of what was later termed "peaceful coexistence" with the capitalist West.

At the conclusion of World War II, the Soviet Union faced some new world conditions. As the natural and inevitable result of the defeat of the German aggression, Soviet Russia found itself in occupation of Eastern Europe. Its primary object in Eastern Europe was, from the beginning, to satisfy its fear of a future German aggression; it therefore wished to guard against any resumption of German militarism and revanchism, and, in the other East European countries, to see to it that East Europe is never again used as a high road for an attack on the Soviet Union. Its primary object in these countries, then, was to insure, not so much *Communist* control of the East European countries, but a control by governments which would *not* be anti-Soviet. At the Yalta and other Big Three conferences, recognition by the West of the legitimacy of this Soviet desire was the capstone of the wartime agreements. To keep the good will of the West, as we have seen, Stalin in effect scuttled the prospects of immediate Communist takeover in many countries in Europe and Asia.

The crucial fact of the aftermath of World War II was the aggressive rupturing by the West of the Big Three alliance, and the principles hammered out at Teheran, Yalta, and Potsdam. Even before Roosevelt's death, the Allied occupation forces reneged on an agreement with the Russians to share occupation duties with each other in *every* country in Europe; instead, in the first European countries occupied by the Allies (Italy, Southern France), the Allies established their own occupation authority and regimes with little or no consultation with the Russians.

After the death of FDR, the West began immediately an intensified and aggressive pressure against the Soviet Union, particularly attempting to roll back Soviet and Communist power out of Eastern Europe. This aggressive pressure, launched by Churchill, Truman, Byrnes, Vandenberg, et al., refused to be satisfied with either the Yalta concept of coalition governments in the occupied countries, or with the several free elections that the Russians permitted in Eastern Europe (e.g., in Hungary, in 1944–1945 and 1947). Inexorably from

1945–1947, the United States launched the policy of an American empire. Military bases were constructed circling the Soviet Union, continual pressure was placed for a rollback in Eastern Europe, the German four-power occupation agreement was cut and the West German state established, and the United States assumed the old British role in Greece and Turkey. By 1948, Stalin, in despair of ending the Cold War that had been launched by the West, ended the coalition policy in Eastern Europe, and fastened complete Communist governments on the countries of Eastern Europe. The Soviet policy can only be considered defensive, and the Russian troop withdrawal, in the postwar era, from Iran, from Austria, from Finland, and from Manchuria, can only be considered as part of this defensive policy.

Another new condition faced by the Soviet Union after the war was the expansion of the Communist community as a result of the successful revolution in China, as well as the new wave of "national liberation" movements against Western imperialism in the underdeveloped countries of Asia and Africa.

The American policy of "containment" was *not* a defensive policy, as it may superficially seem to be. In the first place, this policy extends the American commitment from its own borders to the borders of all non-Communist nations, which constitutes, as Garet Garrett pointed out, the shift from "Republic to Empire." Secondly, the containment program was *not only* directed against any prospects of Soviet military aggression; it was and is directed also against *internal*, domestic Communist movements in every country. The fallacy here is common to Frank Meyer and many other writers: the melding together, as if they were one and the same band on the same plane, of Russian military movements and actions, and internal Communist growth or uprisings within other countries. Yet here is precisely the difference between a policy of peace in the nineteenth-century tradition, and a policy of imperialism. The American commitment, therefore, not only by Communist standards but also by any standards of nineteenth-century international law, is one of an imperialist propping up of unpopular dictatorial governments throughout the world, even in defiance of the will of the indigenous population.

Hence, the aggressiveness of American-imperialist actions in Greece, in Vietnam, in Laos. Hence the aggressiveness of the frankly CIA-directed coup against Mossadegh in Iran, and the CIA-directed coup against a *democratically elected* pro-Communist government in Guatemala. It was the Guatemalan coup that also helped to precipitate the Kremlin-Chinese-Albanian split; for the official Communists, moderate as always, had insisted that, in Guatemala, as in other underdeveloped countries, the first aim of the Communists should be to form a "national liberation front" with the "national bourgeoisie," in the fight against imperialism. The Left Communists came to the conclusion that more radical measures were necessary: viz., in dictatorial countries, immediate guerrilla uprisings based on the peasantry—thus skipping over the bourgeois-worker stages of orthodox Marxism. It is this Maoist-Trotskyite tradition of Left Communism that gave rise to Fidel Castro, and now in young Communist circles throughout the underdeveloped world, radical Maoist-Castroite groups are chafing bitterly against the Kremlin restraint. The fact that Khrushchev is attacking the "Stalinists" should not be permitted to obscure the fact that Stalin's policy was also one of moderation and peaceful coexistence, although he had not refined it to the extent of Khrushchev.

In the conditions of the postwar world, then, the Kremlin redoubled its older policy of defense and of peaceful coexistence with the West. Stalin made many retreats before the aggressive blows against his World War II–born position in Eastern Europe, but, finally, after the Cold War was fully under way, he could only consolidate his position in Eastern Europe, in the meantime launching a plea for peace, as embodied in the Stockholm Peace Appeal. Postwar conditions also saw an anti-imperialist movement (partly Communist, largely nationalist) in many underdeveloped countries, and here fissures developed, with the Kremlin still trying to exercise a restraining influence on the left-Maoist-Trotskyite-Castroite forces.

But another new condition appeared in the postwar world that Frank Meyer mentions not at all, but which has increasingly become dominant in Soviet thinking and in rational Soviet fears: this is the development of nuclear warfare. With the development of the air age—first of long-range heavy bombers, then of the atom bomb, next of the hydrogen bomb, and finally of missiles with hydrogen warheads—it has increasingly bccn borne home to the Soviet leaders, especially to Khrushchev (who acceded to power at about the beginning of the H-Bomb Era), that the *main* threat, not only to Communists and to the Soviets but to all men everywhere, is total nuclear annihilation. With the accelerating arms race, and the intensification of the nuclear annihilation threat, Soviet fear has become rampant.

Certainly, the Communist movement is much stronger than it was prewar; but it also must now face the threat of nuclear annihilation. And considering that the West has already invaded Russia once and Germany has invaded her once, considering the intensified anti-Soviet fanaticism building up in the United States and in West Germany, considering the number of military men and "strategic thinkers" in the West who perpetually mutter about a "preemptive strike," or "hit her now while we can," or "let's get this over with," or talk blandly about "only" "fifty megacorpses" (50 million deaths) in a nuclear war, no one can blame the Soviet Union and the Communist countries for greatly fearing a Western nuclear attack. *This* is the dominant consideration for the Communist movement, and it is to relieve this terrible fear that the Communists have genuinely propounded and elaborated their theory of "peaceful coexistence," of the necessity and prime importance of nuclear and general disarmament by all nations, as well as of rational peace settlements of matters left over from World War II (such as the Berlin-German questions.) The Communists, in short, have, as all members of the human race should, learned the lesson of the nuclear age. Has Frank Meyer?

The crucial difference between Khrushchev and the Maoist-Trotskyites is *not*, as the press has declared, that the Chinese "want war" while Khrushchev and the Soviets do not. The situation is a lot more complex than that. The point is this: the Maoist-Trotskyite Left believes, as did Marx and Lenin, that capitalist imperialism will *not* permit Communism to gain power within various countries, by guerrilla or even by legitimately democratic means. They believe, in short, that imperialism will one day launch a total war of aggression against the Communist bloc. Imperialism, say the Chinese, is an evil monolith; all the imperialists, whatever their country or nature, are alike. All wish only the conquest of the world and the destruction of the socialist countries.

There is no real difference between a Macmillan, a Kennedy, and a Robert Welch.[104] The seemingly "soft" imperialists like Macmillan, are simply lures trying to put the Communist militants to sleep while imperialism launches its attacks against the socialist bloc. (If you see a strong resemblance between the Chinese view and analysis of the world, and that of Frank S. Meyer, you are correct. Both refuse to recognize crucial distinctions in the world; both are infected with a diabolism approaching paranoia about the "enemy camp.")

Therefore, say the Chinese, since the imperialists will launch a war anyway, there is no point in all these negotiations, attempts to disarm, etc. They can only weaken the will of the socialist camp to resist imperialist attack. Above all Khrushchev must stop putting the damper on domestic Communist upsurges in the underdeveloped countries. Since imperialist aggression is inevitable, we must prepare to fight; and the only possible way of forestalling imperialist aggression is to push hard and ever harder, to launch continuing attacks on imperialism and to show it that it is only bluffing, that it is only a "paper tiger." (The Maoist concept of the "paper tiger"—one of Mao Tse-tung's famous articles is entitled "Imperialism and the Atom Bomb are Paper Tigers"—is, again, the equivalent of the Meyer-[Lloyd] Mallan-Medford Evans thesis that the Russians really don't have advanced weapons.) Besides, say the Chinese in an equivalent of the Herman Kahn-RAND Corp. "megacorpse" thesis,[105] in case of a nuclear war, there may not be any Russians or Americans left but there will probably be about 50 million rural Chinese remaining, to

---

[104] Harold Macmillan (1894–1986) British prime minister, 1957–1963. Robert H.W. Welch, Jr. (1899–1985), founder of the conservative John Birch Society.

[105] Editor's note: "Megacorpse" refers to calculations by Herman Kahn of the RAND Corporation, especially in his book *On Thermonuclear War* (1960). The term means one million deaths.

carry on—a viewpoint which is probably empirically far more accurate than the Herman Kahn wishful thinking about the United States.

So much for the Left Communist viewpoint. The Khrushchev viewpoint, which has been adopted by the Soviet party and by most other Communist parties, is considerably different. Khrushchev maintains that (a) since the Communist bloc is much stronger than before the war, and (b) because of the possibility of nuclear annihilation for *both* sides, this new technological fact, this changed world condition, renders obsolescent the gloomy Leninist view about the inevitability of imperialist aggression. Remembering the fruitful coalition with FDR, Khrushchevites believe that there *are* basic distinctions between various capitalists and imperialists, that there are substantial numbers of bourgeois who can listen to reason, and join in peaceful coexistence and disarmament agreements for their own mutual sakes. In short, the thermonuclear age renders both mandatory *and* possible the conclusion of peace agreements with the West. The Khrushchevites then see enormous distinctions between people like Adlai Stevenson or [Harold] Macmillan and people like [Nelson] Rockefeller or Robert Welch. The former can be brought to a reasonable agreement for mutual survival. The Khrushchevites, then, are able to see reality clearly and act upon it, while the Left is, as usual, "dogmatically" bound *a priori* by rigid Marxist-Leninist categories.

Faced with their rational fears of Western attack as well as the horror of nuclear weapons, the Khrushchevite Communists were confronted with the problem of how to have peace with the West, and still maintain the Communist movement, with its eventual aim of coming to power within each country, still intact. The resolution was certainly a sensible one; it is expressed in the concept of "peaceful coexistence." This concept is completely consistent with nineteenth-century ideals of "isolationism" and international law. It proposes the following: peaceful settlements of disputes and joint, inspected disarmament of nuclear and other weapons down to police levels—therefore, no country to aggress against the territory of any other country; and dismantling of foreign bases and of foreign occupying troops. In short, complete peace between the governments of all nations. And, also, a complete *non*-interventionist policy by each government in the affairs of other governments.

This means to let each country decide itself, within its own "domestic" borders, what social system it will adopt. There is to be no aid to any side by any of the major powers—as the Communists phrase it, "no export of revolution or of counterrevolution." In this way, since the Communists, as a basic part of their ideology, believe that every country will some day inevitably go Communist, they can genuinely and sincerely disarm and pursue a peaceful policy, in that way both (a) securing the defense and the survival of the Soviet Union and other Communist countries from the threat of nuclear annihilation, and (b) waiting for the "inevitable" time in each country as it decides to go Communist.

We have seen, however, that even in domestic affairs within each country, Stalin and Khrushchev have, if anything, tried to put a damper on militant Communist actions in underdeveloped countries, being thus often willing to sacrifice the class struggle for the sake of peaceful coexistence.

Now all this is a straightforward, sensible, candid, and nondiabolic policy, pursued eagerly and consistently, especially since Russia adopted the Western disarmament proposals (which we then quickly withdrew) in May 1955. The United States, on the other hand, has been most reluctant to engage in any honest disarmament negotiations, and one suspects that the reason is that we are unwilling to adopt the "isolationist" plan of leaving each country to its own fate and own decision. Certainly it is likely that many of the current "periphery" countries in Asia (Korea, Vietnam, Laos) would go Communist pretty quickly. We, in short, are reluctant to give up our "export of counterrevolution."

It might be—and has been—said, if Khrushchev is so honestly eager for peace, why doesn't he "call off" the Communist parties throughout the world? In the first place, it is unreasonable to make such a request; we can expect that the head of a government "call off" his own war preparations, but not that he "call off" ideologues in other countries allied to him. Would we wish to "call off" freedom fighters in Communist countries? Secondly, this question suffers from the delusion (held also by Frank Meyer in his memo) that the world Communist movement is essentially a mindless monolith directed by push button from Moscow. In actuality, these domestic Communists are not "things from outer space" "controlled" by push button from the Kremlin; they are not devil's agents, but living human beings. They have become Communists not to "take orders" but because they believe ideologically in certain ideals and principles. Khrushchev *could not*, even in the unlikely event that he wanted to, order these people to stop being Communists.

Already, we have seen the restiveness and the splitting of the Communist movement that has occurred in recent years precisely because of the alleged "betrayals" by Stalin and now Khrushchev; it should be evident even to Frank Meyer that now the world Communist movement is by no means a monolith; and if they are not now (and certainly were not in the *pre*-Stalin era), it is obvious that they were not even in Stalin's day, although they superficially acted as if they were.

This lengthy discussion has been, we believe, necessary to set forth the historical and current background for the Communist problem and for the Meyer memo. It is particularly necessary to set the record straight in order to show the alternative to the rigid diabolism categories assumed by Frank Meyer in his discussion of world Communism.

Let us now turn to the Meyer memorandum itself. In the first place, it should be noted that it is superficial and undocumented. It blithely assumes Communist diabolism and proceeds from there with no factual or theoretical analysis; it is no wonder that the author was so quickly proved wrong by the deep-seated split within the Communist world. Meyer's major methodological premise is his juggling of the concepts of "offensive strategy," "defensive tactics," etc. We confess that very little sense can be made of this approach. If Country X is aggressive, the theorist can either postulate (a) that X's "aggressive tactics" are masking long-term "defensive strategy," or he can say (b) that this is an example of "offensive strategy." By what possible rational method is the analyst or historian supposed to determine when a given action is to be "tactical" or "strategic," or "really in tune with" strategy, or a counter, "masking" strategy?

This whole approach impresses us as nonsense. How can Meyer or any other theorist prove, or collect evidence for, his theses? Is a defensive move a sign of defensive strategy, or is it only proof of truly offensive diabolism? All this is question begging and totally unscientific and unverifiable. Furthermore, the very concept of strategy and tactics diametrically opposed to each other makes little sense as well. Surely the long run and the short run must be basically in harmony; strategy and tactics must be in harmony for any sort of coherent policy to emerge. If, for example, the Soviet Union—or any other country—pursues, each month and each year, a continuing series of "defensive tactics," how in the world is it ever to implement its "long" or "medium" term "offensive strategy"? If *each year's* actions, in short, are to be defensive, how is an alleged five- or ten-year offensive ever to be launched, much less successfully completed?

We must conclude that this whole glib shuffling of "strategy" and "tactics" must be discarded as unverifiable and absurd on its face, and we must assume that both strategy and tactics will generally consist in the harmonious application to new conditions and events of the basic policy "line" of a country. It makes little sense, then, to say that "Communist documents cannot be considered as *ad hoc* reactions to current situations, but only as the continuing development of a major medium-term line"; let us simply say that Communist documents are applications of the basic line to changing world situations. There is no dichotomy here. And let us not try to camouflage the reality of Soviet defensive actions by saying that it only masks some sort of hidden "offensive strategy."

There is one crucial point made by Meyer in this second paragraph of his memo that deserves to be stressed: that we must realize that Communist documents are issued for the "guidance of Communists . . . they are understood as guides to action by the ruling circles of the Communist world." Very well; but let us see what this means; this means that we must not, as most "anti-Communists" do and as Frank Meyer does, pooh-pooh the documents as "masking" hidden aims, as "lulling the West," etc. The Communist movement is much too large to treat as a simple conspiracy; since it must indeed lay down guides for its many millions of members, and since Meyer admits that these documents serve as guides, then these documents must be carefully considered, and taken at face value—something Meyer does not do.

In Meyer's first paragraph, it is true that "Khrushchev's Report" must be given great weight (why is there such a stark absence of documentation on *what* that report was?), and that the Statement of the 81 Parties is equivalent to the old Communist International Congresses. And yet the general impression left by the paragraph is a false one; this is not simply a new tactical form of the old Comintern. The old Comintern movement permitted itself to be guided totally by the Kremlin; the new movement, as expressed in the November 1960 conference and also in the later 1961 congress, is one of substantial "polycentrism"; each Communist party functions as an autonomous unit, making its decisions and taking its stand; and then the various Communist parties make decisions in what is an approach to a world Communist parliament. Thus, in the 1961 congress, each Communist party took a stand on the Albanian issue: most joined Khrushchev; some joined with the Albanian-Chinese view; others abstained. Polycentrism has been growing inside the world Communist movement, even within the East European bloc, ever since Stalin's death in 1953, and particularly since Khrushchev's famous "secret speech," repudiating Stalin's tyrannical actions, in 1956.

As we have indicated, Soviet strategy and tactics were defensive before World War II. What, exactly, does Meyer mean by the statement that it aimed to "work by every means of subversion, conspiracy and diplomacy to secure the material base . . . from which to move forward"?

This sounds ominous enough, but is it rightly so? Securing the defense of the Soviet Union is certainly defensive policy, but what is the justification for the lumping of the terms "subversion, conspiracy, and diplomacy"? Diplomacy, in the first place, is a perfectly legitimate method used by every state; it is hardly proper, therefore, to lump it in with such alleged methods as "subversion" and "conspiracy."

What does "conspiracy" mean? If Communist A and Communist B put their heads together in private to carry out policy X, why is this any more a "conspiracy" than if socialists A and B or Democrats A and B, or Republicans A and B, or lodge members A and B put their heads together privately in the same way? Why is one "conspiracy" and the other not? No organization, be it business, labor, fraternal, or political, bares all of its deliberations and consultations to the public view. We must conclude that the use of the term "conspiracy" is totally unscientific and should be barred from political discourse; it is a "smear term" pure and simple.

If we then consider that the Communists publicize their aims and meetings relatively fully, it is clear that the Communist movement is *less* of a "conspiracy" than many other supposedly far more "legitimate" organizations. As for "subversion," this too is a meaningless "smear term." How is "subversion" to be defined? If government X is in existence, and party Y or group Y is in opposition to that government and wants to replace it, does this make it *ipso facto* "subversive"? For X's propaganda purposes it undoubtedly does, but the use of such a term as "subversive" is decidedly improper for a scientific political analyst.

The Meyer thesis that the *one* thing that might perturb the Communists is the awakening of the West to the Communist threat indicates that Meyer has a poor grasp of the realities of the present world situation. For the last fifteen years, and increasingly so, when has it ever been possible for an American to read a paper, listen to or watch a commentator, read an article or listen to a political speech, without having constantly drummed into his head the alleged imminent menace of the "international Communist conspiracy"?

Americans need to be "awakened" indeed! It might better be said that Americans need a good dose of tranquilizer, so concerned have they increasingly become about the supposed menace of Communism. What the Communists fear is not that the West will "awaken," but that its aggressive actions and words will culminate in the launching of all-out war. Meyer concedes this in a backhanded way when he talks of the Communist fear of the "consolidation in the West of a force dedicated to the destruction of Communism; the emergence in the West of a will which places the defeat of Communism as decisive"— i.e., the emergence of a determined drive for total nuclear war.

Communist defensive policies, in short, are not "tactics" but genuine policies, designed not to "disarm us" but to disarm all the big powers, the Communists included.

We have seen the total failure of analysis and perception implicit in Meyer's declaration that the 1960 Conference had "resolved" all the disagreements within the Communist movement, and "absorbed [them] into the main line." Equally important, Meyer's exegesis of *what* the essence of the three main positions (Left, Khrushchevist, and Titoist-revisionist) is totally false.

Meyer states that the Khrushchev line holds the concept of "peaceful coexistence" to be a *tactic* in the pursuit of a generally offensive strategy; that the Left (Chinese, etc.) are opposed even to the tactic of coexistence in this strategic offensive; and that the Right (Tito, etc.) are genuine believers in coexistence—i.e., that they believe in the long-range strategy of coexistence and peaceful transformation as the route to eventual Communism. Now this is a total misconception of the three positions, a misconception that fits into Meyer's biased *a priori* framework and diabolic view of the Communist movement.

On the contrary, the actual positions of the three groups must be shifted significant degrees "to the right." Namely, the Khrushchev line believes *genuinely* in peaceful coexistence as the "main line" of foreign policy, and denies that it is a "tactic"; the Chinese Left *does* believe in the tactic of peaceful coexistence, but *only* as a *tactic* and not as genuine long-run policy; the Right believes *not only* in peaceful coexistence but also in "peaceful transformation" internally, i.e., in virtual abandonment of any sort of militant class struggle *within* the various countries of the world. In short, no one (except perhaps the Trotskyites on the extreme Left) wishes to abandon peaceful coexistence even as a tactic; the Meyer version of the "Khrushchev position" is actually the *Chinese* position which has been repudiated by Khrushchev and the bulk of world Communism; the Meyer version of the "right-revisionist" position is, at least as regards peaceful coexistence, actually the central Khrushchev position. No wonder, then, that Khrushchev has been accused by the Chinese and old "Stalinists" of being "revisionist," and no wonder relations between Khrushchev and the revisionist leader Tito have continued to improve!

Before turning to documentation of this thesis, let us see what evidence Meyer offers for his. There is, in the first place, no documentation; there is the simple assertion that coexistence, prevention of war, and disarmament fall under the head of "defensive tactics," while the proclamation of Communist strength, the supposedly "aggressive position" on Berlin, Germany, and Cuba, and the assertion of a difference between "local wars" and "wars of national liberation," are all supposed to reflect the Soviet's "strategic offensive."

Now, for the objective observer, it is clear that the first set of proposals—disarmament, coexistence, etc.—are far more fundamental, basic, and long run, than a particular view on Berlin or Cuba. It therefore makes far more sense to say that Russia is revealing "defensive strategy" and "offensive tactics," but this of course would remove much of the aura of diabolism and imminent menace that Meyer tries to place on the Communist movement.

Secondly, let us consider these supposedly "aggressive" Soviet policies. The proclamation of Communist strength is hardly aggressive; it is a tactic being done by all major powers every day. Has any major power ever proclaimed its essential weakness? The position on Cuba and Latin America—how can it be called "aggressive"? As for Berlin and Germany, here too Soviet policy is far from aggressive; the Soviet Union has tolerated, for seventeen years now, a Western enclave deep inside its own territory, manned by Western troops, and it has tolerated the deliberate failure of the West to regularize in some way the Berlin and German problem and finally to conclude a peace treaty with Germany and thus liquidate World War II.

The Russians have, on the contrary, been remarkably patient about this failure to end World War II, and its wish to regularize permanently this peculiar situation resulting from the breakdown of four-power occupation is surely commendable rather than aggressive. Russia has proposed *either* a unified, neutralized, and disarmed Germany (again the threat of German militarism!) and a peace treaty with this single Germany, *or* separate peace treaties with two governments of East and West Germany, thus regularizing matters there. The West refuses to do one or the other. The West did it in the case of Austria, and nobody has called Soviet actions in Austria "aggressive"; why not a similar solution, then, for Germany? Is it, Russia asks itself, because the United States desperately wants to arm West Germany with nuclear weapons so that it can try to regain German territories lost in World War II by force?

The third example alleged by Meyer of Communist "aggressiveness" in the 1960 conference is the "assertion of a profound contrast between 'local wars' and 'wars of national liberation.'" This "assertion" is not "aggressiveness"; it is a simple and correct analysis of fact. Local wars are wars between great powers, such as the United States and Russia, meddling in domestic civil wars (e.g., Cuba, Korea, Vietnam) or revolutions; local wars, with their employment of transnational military force and foreign intervention, are condemned completely by the Communist policy.

Wars of "national liberation," on the other hand, do not require the participation of any outside armed forces; they are revolutions conducted by colonial peoples against their imperialist oppressors. Technically, indeed, they are not wars but revolutions; Communist distinction between them is the sort of distinction that any nineteenth-century upholder of international law would make also.

Furthermore, as we shall see documented below, the Communists do *not*, contrary to Meyer, believe in "all-out support for wars of national liberation." They believe only in *moral* support; they believe, as part of the theory of peaceful coexistence, in withholding *material* support for revolutionary wars of national liberation, *provided* that the United States and other Western powers *also* refrain from material support for counterrevolution against national liberation. This is certainly a fair position. Meyer, then, is totally wrong in calling "wars of national liberation" "aggressive local wars against the West."

They are revolutions against imperialist or imperialist-dominated governments.

Meyer also falsifies the other major points concluded by the 1960 Communist conference. He claims that one point was the "widest possible movement throughout the world for 'coexistence' and Western disarmament." On the contrary, the push is for general and complete disarmament in *all* countries, not just the West. The omission of "all countries" of course makes the Communist policy to be purely diabolic and insincere.

Similarly, another point mentioned by Meyer is to "capture Berlin" and the "neutralization of West Germany." Here again, Meyer distorts and falsifies the facts. The Soviet Union has proposed (in the Rapacki Plan) *not* simply the neutralization of West Germany, but of *all* Germany, West and East, *in addition to* the neutralization and disarmament of Poland and Czechoslovakia. The plan was angrily rejected by a West bent on rearming West Germany to the hilt. The "capture" of Berlin is excessively melodramatic. What the Soviets want is United States recognition of the existence of the East German government; in return for this, they are willing to agree to perpetual Western access in West Berlin, as well as West Berlin being a permanent free city guarded by UN troops. This reasonable proposal is hardly for the "capture" of Berlin.

For other criticisms of the Meyer memorandum see the discussion in part one of this paper.

Let us now turn from the specific Meyer memorandum to some documentation of our previous position and statements in this memo, documentation that in Meyer's memo is conspicuous by its almost total absence.

We have noted, for example, our important disagreement with Meyer, who claims that Khrushchev considers peaceful coexistence as a mere tactic, while the Chinese reject even that tactic. Let us turn to a critically important article that appeared in the American Communist publication, *New World Review,* for February 1962 (pp. 3–7). This article—really an editorial—is the first full-scale, open criticism of the Chinese position in an American Communist publication. The *New World Review* cites two authoritative sources; an article by the eminent theoretician Professor Fedor Konstantinov in the November 1961 issue of *Kommunist*, the major theoretical organ of the Communist Party of the Soviet Union, as well as an editorial in *Pravda* for December 14, 1961.

Says the *NWR:* "Professor Konstantinov charges that the Albanians regard peaceful coexistence mainly as a catchword and do not believe in the possibility of preventing war in our epoch."

Konstantinov then quoted Enver Hoxha, Albanian Communist leader, as asserting in a speech on November 7, 1961, "We do not object to the principle of peaceful coexistence, but we do not agree with those who regard peaceful coexistence as the basic line of the foreign policy of socialist countries."

In short, the Albanians-Chinese do *not* reject the concept of peaceful coexistence altogether; but they consider it as a mere tactic only, and not a genuine "main line" of foreign policy. The attack on this view is the nub of the Soviet-Khrushchevite difference with the Chinese-Albanians.

NWR then quotes from the aforementioned *Pravda* editorial:

> The question of peace and peaceful coexistence is the crucial problem of our times. There can be either peaceful coexistence or a devastating thermonuclear war, for there is no other way out. That is why it is quite obvious that those who come out against the policy of peaceful coexistence are playing into the hands of the most bellicose and adventurist imperialist circles, which are preparing a devastating thermonuclear war.

NWR reports that Konstantinov charges the Albanians with doing everything possible to discredit Soviet disarmament proposals as "counter to the interests of the socialist countries." The Albanians also fail to distinguish between the neutral countries and the imperialists, and consider all nonsocialist countries as being "in the imperialist camp." Also, "The Albanians disagree with the view of the USSR and other socialist countries that possibilities exist in some countries for peaceful transition to socialism and charge the Soviet government with 'revisionism'."

NWR then moves to the more painful problem of discussing the Chinese themselves. It first hails Communist China for its first explicit enunciation of the *Panch Shila*, "the five principles of peaceful coexistence," and for signing the statements of the 1957 and 1960 Communist conference—statements stressing the necessity for peaceful coexistence. Incidentally, Meyer, who does not deign to quote from the 1960 statement, certainly refrains from quoting its declaration that the possibility of averting war now exists, and that "peaceful coexistence of countries with different systems or destructive war—this is the alternative today. There is no other choice." But, warns *NWR*, the Chinese Communists keep quoting Mao's dictum that "imperialism and all reactionaries are paper tigers," that no one should be afraid of nuclear war.

Wrote Mao:

> The atom bomb is a paper tiger with which the U.S. reactionaries try to terrify the people. It looks terrible, but in fact is not. Of course, the atom bomb is a weapon of mass destruction, but the outcome of a war is decided by the people, not by one or two new weapons.

To this, the *NWR*, the American Communist monthly, replies sharply indeed:

> But when paper tigers have nuclear teeth whose bite could destroy the world it is necessary to seek all possibilities of dealing with them by means that avoid the risk of direct combat. . . . Did it [the atom bomb] only *look* terrible to the people of Hiroshima and Nagasaki? . . . Everyone in the world should be afraid of nuclear weapons and expend all their efforts on trying to get rid of them through disarmament and

peaceful coexistence and to prevent situations arising in which they might be used as long as they exist in the arsenals of nations.

Also, the Chinese believe that any top-level negotiations between socialist and capitalist countries are useless. Again, at the World Peace Council meeting, the Soviet delegates placed primary stress on peace and disarmament; the Chinese and Albanian delegates placed primary stress on the "liberation struggle of the colonial and semi-colonial peoples."

Again, the *NWR* returns to the pro-peace attack on the Communist Chinese position:

> In reading the *Peking Review* and other Chinese publications, we find the point of view frequently expressed that emphasis on the horrors of nuclear war only frightens people and disarms them in their resistance. We believe on the contrary that any glossing over of the mass deaths and destruction a nuclear war would bring, disarms the peace forces, weakens their efforts to insure that nuclear weapons will never be used.
>
> In taking the attitude that the socialist countries must be prepared to risk nuclear war, in belittling the strength of the forces armed with thermonuclear weapons, we believe the Chinese leaders underestimate all the factors involved—for there is not only the risk of a deliberate "preventive" or "preemptive" war which certain circles in our country have advocated, but the ever-present possibility of mischance, accident or madness which must be reckoned with, which makes the elimination of nuclear weapons from the arsenals of nations the first task of mankind.

There is no diabolism here; there is only a sincere opposition to war *versus* a tactical indifference. The evident similarity between the controversy carried on in the Soviet-versus-Chinese camp and that carried on between those in the United States today who wish for peaceful negotiations and those who are driving toward war, is too evident not to bear mention again.

Let us go back a few years for further exposition of the origins of the Soviet-Chinese split on the question of peaceful coexistence. At the Twenty-first Communist Party congress, of January 1959, Khrushchev proposed bilateral agreement with the United States to establish peaceful coexistence—for one thing, with the end of the danger of imperialist aggression, the Soviet Union could transform itself into complete communism and the withering away of the defensive functions of the State. Following this proposal came the visits of Mikoyan and Koslov to the United States in 1959, and Khrushchev's famous visit to the United States in September 1959, during which he came to believe at Camp David that Eisenhower was willing to make a reasonable settlement of the Berlin question. On his return from the United States, Khrushchev said at Peking, on September 30, "We on our part must do everything possible to preclude war as a means for settling outstanding questions. These questions must be solved through negotiations."

On April 26, 1960, however, the *Peking Review* (reported in the *New York Times*, May 26) implicitly attacked the Soviet position. It criticized those for whom "the peace movement is everything," and who seek peace which "may be acceptable to imperialists" but which would "destroy" the "revolutionary will" to socialism. The dangers of a general nuclear war, it added, are not great, since there would be some human beings (presumably particularly Chinese) left.

Added the *Peking Review*,

> War is an inevitable outcome of the system of exploitation. . . . The nearer they (the imperialists) approach their doom the more they will put up a frantic fight . . . on the debris of a dead imperialism, the victorious people would create very quickly a civilization thousands of times higher than the capitalist system and a truly beautiful future for themselves.

(*Pace* Herman Kahn!)

The *Peking Review* added that it is impossible for the imperialists ever to accept general and complete disarmament. The United States would be able to cheat under *any* system of controls. After the collapse of the summit, Khrushchev, on June 21, 1960, addressed a meeting of top officials of twelve communist countries; he declared that the socialist camp was now strong enough to prevent war by the imperialists. This is a duty since nuclear war would be disastrous for all people and for civilization. Coexistence of "different social systems" must therefore be established, and the class struggle must follow *non*-military lines only. Khrushchev accused the Chinese of failing to abide by the 1957 Conference declaration for peaceful coexistence.

On August 26, 1960, *Pravda* clarified the differences with the Chinese Left about the role of the colonial movements of national liberation. These movements, said *Pravda*, require support for *national bourgeois* leaders, and not immediate Communist revolt and conquest.

Furthermore, *Pravda* added,

> Marxism-Leninism regards as a reactionary utopia the attempts to export the revolution or to impose on other countries such social orders and institutions which are not the product of their internal development.

In short, hands off other countries, even to "export revolution"! The Chinese Communist Party answered with a circular letter to all other Communist parties on September 10, 1960, declaring that Soviet Russia had neglected its responsibilities as leader of the Communists, by failing to support revolutionary wars.

Next came the 1960 Communist conference discussed by Meyer. While supporting peaceful coexistence, and the possibility of peaceful negotiations with the capitalist countries, it also made concessions to the Chinese and Albanians and their desire for an aggressive strategy. The Chinese had apparently threatened to divert their four nuclear reactors to military uses if concessions to them were not made. Marshal Tito denounced the 1960 manifesto of the conference as a "rotten compromise" forced on the meeting by the Chinese and he pledged his continued good will to the Soviet Union.

Meyer concedes that great weight must be given to Khrushchev's report of January 1961. It is indicative and significant, then, that Meyer in no place documents his analysis by quoting or even paraphrasing that report. Khrushchev said in the report that the USSR would work unremittingly to prevent a general nuclear war because it would result in the deaths of hundreds of millions and the ruin of civilization. He was in favor of "wars of national liberation" (Algeria, Cuba), but opposed to local wars (Suez, Indochina) because the latter could lead to general nuclear war. Khrushchev (Meyer, please note!) emphasized that peaceful coexistence and general disarmament are "*not* a tactical move," for they would prevent both a nuclear war and any foreign intervention in wars of national liberation. The goals established by the 1960 conference would be achieved by *non*-military struggle.

On January 21, 1961, the Chinese Communist central committee apparently capitulated, accepting the noninevitability of war, and accepting the Soviet thesis that "revolution is the affair of the peoples in the various countries." But this was only papering over the split. On February 11–12, western papers contained documents from various Communist parties reporting on the severity of the Soviet-Chinese clash at the 1960 meeting. Chou En-lai had said that peaceful coexistence could not prevent a nuclear war between East and West. Khrushchev, rising eloquently to the occasion, had accused Mao Tse-tung of being a "megalomaniac war-monger"; in answer to the Chinese view that war was inevitable and that stress on the horrors of war would cause less of fighting nerve in the socialist camp, Khrushchev defended disarmament as "the dream of mankind . . . the only true humanism"; war, Khrushchev said, would mean the "destruction of the working class."

During the spring of 1961, Albania executed numerous pro-Soviet Albanians after a February 13 declaration by the Albanian Communist Party that coexistence was a failure because the United States was preparing for a third world war. On May 26, Russian submarines left permanently their Albanian bases. On July 13, Soviet Russia and Yugoslavia came to an accord on peace and the reduction of world tensions. On May 12, Khrushchev declared, at the fortieth anniversary of the founding of the Georgian Communist Party,

> I repeat that we do not need war to achieve domination of our ideas, the most progressive Marxist-Leninist ideas. War brings only harm. . . . We will create this victory because other peoples will follow our example.

On July 8 and 9, Chinese foreign minister Chen Yi again tried to deny a split by acceding to the "peaceful foreign policy of the Soviet Union," and reasserting the November 1960 stand that "revolution cannot be exported," and reaffirming support for "peaceful coexistence of countries with different social systems." But presumably this was superficial agreement only.

On July 2, Isaac Deutscher reported in the *Sunday Times* (London) that Khrushchev had sent a letter attacking Mao Tse-tung for advocating preventive war and for favoring an attack on Taiwan at the risk of causing a general nuclear war.

The next important document is the famous draft of the program of the Communist Party of the Soviet Union (CPSU) on June 19, 1961. This document criticized current welfare-state and social-democrat regimes as not being really "socialist," for they still pursue an aggressive, imperialist foreign policy and militarization:

> People suffer want in material goods, but imperialism is squandering them on war preparations. . . . State-monopoly capitalism stimulates militarism to an unheard-of degree. . . . While enriching some groups of the monopoly bourgeoisie, militarism leads to the exhaustion of nations, to the ruin of peoples languishing under an excessive tax burden, mounting inflation, and a high cost of living.

Now, in foreign affairs, said the CPSU statement,

United States imperialism is in effect performing the function of a world gendarme, supporting reactionary dictatorial regimes and decayed monarchies, opposing democratic, revolutionary changes and launching aggressions against peoples fighting for independence.

The CPSU maintains that forces capable of preserving and promoting world peace have arisen and are growing in the world. . . . Imperialism is the only source of the war danger. . . . The important thing is to ward off thermonuclear war, not to let it break out.

Peaceful coexistence of the socialist and capitalist countries is an objective necessity for the development of human society. . . . [It is] a mighty obstacle in the path of imperialist aggressions.

The CPSU added that its program can only be "fulfilled successfully under conditions of peace. . . . Aggravation of the international situation . . . may prevent realization of the plan for an upsurge of the well-being of the soviet people."

The CPSU also declared that

Peaceful coexistence serves as a basis for the peaceful competition between socialism and capitalism on an international scale and constitutes a specific form of class struggle between them.

Support for the principle of peaceful coexistence is also in keeping with the interests of that section of the bourgeoisie which realizes that thermonuclear war would not spare the ruling classes of capitalist society either.

The CPSU then pledged itself to the following foreign policy tasks:

- Use of "every means for preventing war and promoting conditions for the complete elimination of war from the life of society"
- "To work for the disbandment of all military blocs . . . the discontinuance of the 'Cold War' . . . and the abolition of all air, naval, rocket and other military bases from foreign territory"
- "To work for general and complete disarmament under international controls"
- To improve relations with capitalist countries to safeguard peace

It also expressed opposition to wars of conquest, wars between capitalist countries, and local wars against national liberation movements.

In an interview with the *New York Times* (September 7, 1961), Khrushchev further explained his foreign policy position: no country may fight even a war of liberation for another country, that country must fight its own war. The concept of peaceful coexistence, Khrushchev added, meant not just the absence of war, but also the rejection by all states of military intervention in each other's affairs, even when the social and economic systems of these states have antagonistic differences. Each state should respect and recognize each other's sovereignty and pursue friendly trade and cultural relations. The export of both revolution *and* counterrevolution were opposed by Khrushchev.

The happenings at the 22nd Congress of the Communist Party of the Soviet Union, held in Moscow on October 17, 1961, are widely known, including the resumption in depth by Khrushchev of the anti-Stalin campaign, and the attack on Albania, at which point Chou En-lai left the congress; and since then, the Soviet-Chinese split has come into the open at last. But we should emphasize that, at the twenty-second party congress, Khrushchev again stressed his concept of peaceful coexistence, including the refraining from intervening in support of even Communist revolution in other countries:

> We are convinced that in the end the socialist system will triumph everywhere. But this in no way implies that we will seek to achieve its triumph by intervention in the internal affairs of other countries. You cannot bring in ideas on bayonets . . . or on rockets.

And even Meyer concedes that Communist Party pronouncements and statements by Khrushchev must be taken with the utmost seriousness!

Fermentation within Communist parties of the world is now continuing apace. While Chinese leftism sprouts in Asian and Latin American parties, revisionism is spreading in other parties. Recently, the veteran leader of the Italian Communist Party, Palmiro Togliatti, went further in a pro-peace direction than any other official CP leader. He declared that "nuclear war must be avoided at any price." And this highly revisionist statement comes from the leader of the Italian CP, who occupies a *centrist* position within the Italian CP! The right wing of the Italian CP is growing steadily, and its leader, Giorgio Amendola, goes far beyond Togliatti in both foreign and domestic revision. The search for peace, as well as the growing internal campaigns against Stalinist tyranny, has caused a ferment within world Communism that makes all the more ludicrous Meyer's unsupported picture of the world Communist movement as a diabolic monolith.

We may conclude our critique of the Meyer memo by citing the wise cautionary words of Father John F. Cronin, in his recent pamphlet, "Communism: Threat to Freedom," published by the National Catholic Welfare Conference. Father Cronin writes:

> [T]here are three types of "experts" whose credentials should be scrutinized with care. They are former agents of the FBI, former informants for the FBI and persons who have had first-hand contact with the Communist party either as members or victims.[106]

---

[106] Editor's note: Frank Meyer had joined the British Communist party in 1931, while a student at Oxford. He abandoned communism sometime in the period 1945–1950.

5. Review of Walter Millis (ed.), *A World Without War*

August 23, 1962

Dr. Ivan R. Bierly
William Volker Fund

Dear Ivan:

A World Without War, edited by Walter Millis, is the first product of the Center for the Study of Democratic Institutions' Study of War and Democratic Institutions, of which Millis is the staff director.[107] It consists essentially of four pamphlets published in 1960 and 1961 by the center.

One essay, by Justice Douglas, may be dismissed quickly. A generally trivial collection of typically Douglasian clichés, its author apotheosizes the United Nations, gradually engaged in building up "world law," and praises such "wars against aggression" as the Korean War as an example of the UN's "alternative to force." Some of the clichés are true, as far as they go, such as the excursion into nineteenth-century international law theory, and its lessons for today (for one thing, this "law" was voluntarily created and came *without* institutions of world government), but generally it is a fuzzy, confused, and useless piece.

Dr. Harrison Brown and James Real's "Community of Fear" is certainly better than Douglas's article, but it is not very important. It is essentially an article stressing the havoc that nuclear war could wreak. There is a good critique of the proposals for mass shelters, and of the kind of moral nihilism and grotesque "optimism" of a Herman Kahn in contemplating all-out nuclear war. But unfortunately, in a factual piece dependent on the latest technology for its relevance, this article is already considerably out of date. We still read here, for example, of the supposed "missile gap" of the United States

---

[107] Walter Millis, ed., *A World Without War* (New York: Washington Square Press, 1961).

behind the Russians, etc., a myth that has been recently exploded by the Kennedy administration itself (originally so eager in broadcasting the concept). It has also been rendered obsolete by the new problem of the "counter-force" and "first strike" theories of the Air Force, which have been gaining ground in the administration, and render the discussion of "deterrence" theory quasi-obsolete; and it has also been superseded by the recent brilliant article of the British physicist P.M.S. Blackett dealing with the strategic significance of the Russian failure to exploit the theoretical "missile gap," as well as of the increasing adoption of "counterforce" strategy.

The heart and soul of this book—and by far the largest part of it, *and* the most important—is the contribution of Millis himself. This is particularly true of Millis's first pamphlet, originally also entitled "World Without War," which has had considerable impact in thought in this field. Millis, in contrasting his theoretical "peace game" to the "war games" of the Kahns and Kissingers, attempts to portray what a world would look like if it were totally disarmed down to police levels, and if, therefore, the "functions" of war had to be performed by other means. In refreshing contrast to almost all the utopian and fuzzy pacifist thinkers in this area, Millis recognizes (1) that, given human nature, a warless world would still have to face considerable struggles for political power, in numerous forms; and (2) the utter impracticality of any scheme of world government, *as well as* its undesirability in freezing all of the world into uniformity and tyranny. Millis, in short, recognizes the continuing need for revision of frontiers, readjustment of boundaries of state, etc. He recognizes that war, vicious as it has been, at least performed the "function" of such revision.

Millis's vision of a future disarmed world, then, is one that retains the inevitable power struggles and disdains the usual world government panaceas, propounded by the pacifists. It is a world in which political power struggles will continue through *domestic* struggles—both peaceful and ideological, and also through conflicts, ideological struggles, local rebellions, and riots, etc.—will still continue, but the world will be freed from the awesome threat of nuclear annihilation.

In showing that the world can be disarmed *without* assuming either (a) that all men will be angels, or (b) world government, Millis has made a highly significant contribution to peace research. He also states that international inspection of disarmament agreements is relatively easy, *especially* when that disarmament is general and complete.

It is almost always overlooked that arms inspection is far, far easier, and violations much easier to detect, when the disarmament is complete and general, than if a few missiles or machines are supposed to be scrapped.

There are various weaknesses in Millis's searching article. For one thing, Millis seems to have no conception of the Communist thesis of "peaceful coexistence" and precisely what it implies. Secondly, his vision of a world confined to guerilla warfare could easily be extended to interstate wars that are so small and local that they could be conducted *within* the framework of "police" instead of "army" units: e.g., India vs. Portugal in Goa, or Indonesia vs. Holland in Western New Guinea. These small, local wars could also continue.

Furthermore, Millis does not seem to realize that, to be *consistent* in rejecting world government, he is also obliged to reject the idea of a world police force to enforce the agreement. Furthermore, if such a world police force (which, most unfortunately, the United States has persistently insisted upon in its disarmament proposals) existed, there would be a mad scramble among the power blocs to grab control of it, with the terrible consequences that might ensue. In short, any world "police force" that is heavily armed would *negate* the very concept of a world disarmed down to local police levels. Millis also fails to deal with suggestions for Great Power policies in the peripheral or "underdeveloped" countries.

Millis also has a general tendency to overweight strictly power factors in international affairs, and to underweight both ideological and economic motivations.

But Millis's worst and most damaging foible is his view that war *also* performed certain *domestic* economic functions, for which there must also be substitutes in the peaceful world of the future. The domestic "function" consists of central planning, government control, government "investment," and "social cohesion" imposed by the State. To "perform these functions," Millis calls for a massive increase in statism, government planning, the "public sector" in nonmilitary areas, the government bureaucracy, etc. He also totally misinterprets the old Norman Angell proof that war was noneconomic. Sure, war is uneconomic for the various peoples *if* there is free trade and free markets (and, hopefully, freedom of migration); but if there is *not*, then war *can* confer national economic benefits in the sense of seizing raw material that would not otherwise be available due to tariff, quota, etc. barriers of national autarky.

And Millis absurdly does not realize that central and socialistic planning, far from bringing the world into a new age of harmony, would enormously exacerbate interstate and intercountry conflicts of interest; it is precisely the free market that minimizes such conflicts, and government planning that increases them. The economic part of Millis's theory is, therefore, totally fallacious and even the direct opposite of correct doctrine. Millis also has the thoroughly socialist view that leaving the labor market free means that "might makes right," "power rules," etc. instead of state law, as it presumably should be. Millis's bent is thus highly socialistic.

Millis's second part, "Permanent Peace," dealing with the present world setup, has many interesting insights, but is not as fundamental or challenging as the preceding. It is the application of Millis's analysis of the dangers of the arms race and of his view of power struggles to the current scene. He has a good critique of the popular "falling domino" theory, points out the nonexistence of the so-called "Congolese people," etc. Millis is hopeful that the present state can move toward the ideal by means of such tacit agreements not to make war as exist in Latin America.

He is, indeed, unduly pessimistic about the results of his world of guerilla warfare, etc., as he seems to feel that guerilla revolutions in Russia and East Europe would be unfortunate in making conditions less "stable," etc. Surely, if a people threw off the monstrous tyranny of Communism (and Millis recognizes that his system, for example, would not have enabled Russia to suppress the Hungarian Revolution), any succeeding system would most probably be a gain. Millis, further, tries to be objective about the disarmament positions of both sides, but clearly is poorly informed about exactly what they are, and thus misinterprets the situation.

All in all, a mixed potpourri, heavily biased in the direction of socialism and statism, but—in the case of Millis—engaged in a challenging inquiry into the implications of a disarmed world.

6. Review of George F. Kennan, *Russia and the West Under Lenin and Stalin*

August 23, 1962

Dr. Ivan R. Bierly
William Volker Fund

Dear Ivan:

George F. Kennan's *Russia and the West under Lenin and Stalin* suffers from what may be called a "split personality."[108] It is shot through with a basic inconsistency. On the one hand, in the bulk of his factual discussion and presentation of the history of the Russian Revolution and subsequent Soviet foreign relations with the West, Kennan stresses such themes as the culpability of the West for intervention in the Russian civil war, the desirability of a flexible and "realistic" approach to the Soviet Union, etc.

On the other hand, interspersed with this theme are numerous passages of hard-hitting anti-Soviet diatribes, which are strongly reminiscent of the "absolutists" in the United States who espouse a "tough" view toward the Soviet Union. Not only are these passages totally inconsistent and contradictory with the remainder, indeed

---

[108] George F. Kennan, *Russia and the West under Lenin and Stalin* (Boston: Little, Brown and Company, 1961).

the bulk, of the work, but they are irrelevant to the context in which they are placed, so that one gets the distinct impression that these passages have been inserted bodily into an alien organon, like so many raisins in a cake.

When we find that this book was composed in pieces over a period of several years—lectures at Oxford in 1957–58, lectures at Harvard in 1961, then, further additions to the book in 1961—the strong suspicion wells up that the different "levels" were composed for delivery at different times. Indeed, if we may speculate further, it would not be surprising if the bulk of the "flexible" lectures were composed for delivery in the congenial atmosphere of Oxford several years ago, and that the anti-Soviet diatribes were inserted in the final version to "appease" a much more strongly anti-Soviet American audience (especially the congressmen about to consider the Kennan appointment as ambassador to Yugoslavia).

Here are several examples of the inconsistency of the "two Kennans": early in the work he makes the flat statement that Communism is an international monolithic conspiracy directed by Moscow—and makes this as a general statement, not as a limited historical observation; and yet later in the work he stresses the non-monolithic nature of present-day Communism and the various internal conflicts between China and Russia, etc.

Another example: Kennan's fascinating discussion of the Allied intervention in the Russian civil war in its *details* consists of a vigorous attack on that intervention; and yet in his general statements summing up before and after, Kennan goes out of his way to justify failure of the Allies to have normal diplomatic relations with the Soviet Union.

Further, Kennan scoffs at the Soviet historians' conclusion that the Allied intervention was anti-Bolshevik in intent. Kennan ripostes that the purpose of the intervention was, rather, to bolster the war against Germany. This is very true as to the origin of the intervention, but what then was the reason for the *continued* Allied intervention from November 11, 1918 till early 1920, over a year after the war was over? The only possible logical reason is anti-Bolshevik intervention, and

Kennan grudgingly concedes this in his detailed discussion, though not in his general summary.

Even in detailed discussion, Kennan's "two faces" are revealed. Thus, the Allies at Versailles sent a note to both the Reds and the Whites proposing peace and normal relations on the basis of an immediate truce on both sides—a proposal, if anything, loaded against the Reds, who were steadily winning out in the civil war. Yet the Whites, with characteristic overoptimism, flatly rejected the note, while the Reds replied ambiguously. At this point, Kennan, who favored the peace offer, castigates the Reds for insults and evasion, and has nothing to say about the flat White rejection.

Kennan's confusions extend to other areas as well; thus, when dealing with World War I, Kennan is steadily and excellently "revisionist," attacking the idea of unconditional surrender, total victory, etc., whereas in dealing with Germany and World War II, Kennan's revisionism, "realism," etc. mysteriously fade away, and we see repeated the usual clichés about Hitler's aggression, of the shameful appeasement at Munich, of the cynical treachery of both sides in the Hitler-Stalin Pact, etc. Nowhere does Kennan show any sign of the sort of revisionism set forth in the brilliant work of A.J.P. Taylor, *The Origins of the Second World War.*

Further, Kennan has to walk a particularly fallacious line, in trying (a) to attack appeasement of Hitler, and (b) at the same time robbing the Soviets of the "credit" for launching the policy of "collective security" against Hitler in the 1930s.

Another typical example of Kennan's inconsistency is his flat general statement that the Communists consider *all* non-Communist governments as equally reprehensible; if that were so, of course, then there would have been no proposal for a "popular front" against fascism, as well as none of the recent recognition of the "superiority," from the Communist point of view, of "neutaralist" over "imperialist" governments. Indeed, Kennan himself recognizes the *dual* hostility of Communists toward capitalism and imperialism, which implies logically that Communists are less unfavorable to non-imperialist capitalist than to imperialist-capitalist states.

Also, at one point, Kennan points out that the Hungarian Communist government of Béla Kun, just after World War I, had no connection with Moscow, while, in one of his general attacks, he accuses Moscow of controlling this early Hungarian soviet.

For the discriminating reader, there is much interesting and even fascinating material in the Kennan book. This is particularly true of the period of Kennan's specialty, the Russian Revolution and civil war, although even here there is much material omitted—Kennan does not pretend to write here a definitive history, but rather to present some insights as an interpretive essay on the history of Soviet foreign policy. The story of the Allied intervention in Siberia, the incredible mishaps of the Czech legionnaires, and the regime of Admiral Kolchak is almost "worth the price of admission."

And the best feature of the book is its brilliant and graceful writing style, which undoubtedly accounts for its long stay on the best-seller lists. But these could not offset Kennan's theoretical confusions in deciding possible National Book Foundation distribution.

VI. Literature

1. Romanticism and Modern Fiction

1958

Belying their seemingly chaotic diversity, all of modern fiction and modern criticism unite on at least one point: rejection of romanticism. The characteristic literature—and, indeed, art in general—of the present century has been, broadly, either *naturalist* or *nonobjective*. Both schools were born in revolt against the romanticism of the nineteenth century. The aim of the naturalist, as of the historians of the school of Leopold von Ranke, is to "present life as it *really* is," to do an honest and competent reporting job on the people and places that the novelist has seen and heard. The old style "hero" or "villain," the dramatic plot, and the generally happy ending of the romantic novel here disappear, for, after all, there are precious few heroes among the people the novelist perceives, and precious little drama or climactic happiness in their daily lives. Instead, the novelist sets down, meticulously and minutely, the details of the world around him; and he writes in a characteristically deliberate, graceless, and plodding style, his pedestrian manner accurately matching the pedestrian theme and the drab characters. In the works of such writers as Theodore Dreiser and James T. Farrell, the straight naturalistic novel reached perhaps its apogee. Their technical and stylistic clumsiness was generally considered one of their strong points: for wasn't the honesty of their naturalism underscored by their very style's reflecting the clumsy groping of the characters?

The "symbolic" or nonobjective novel seems at first glance to be poles apart from the naturalistic, but, in reality, the two unite on fundamentals. While the naturalists reject romantic fiction as escapist sentimentality, the nonobjectivists and "higher critics"—in short, the *avant-garde*—reject it as hopelessly *simpliste* and unintelligent. While the naturalists reject drama, the *avant-garde*, in addition, spurn language and rational meaning. Instead of using the common language as an instrument of communication, the nonobjective writer tries to prove himself more intelligent than the common run of men by inventing or partially inventing a new language, replete with codes and "keys" to the "many levels of meaning" for the eager initiates. Both schools dismiss romanticism contemptuously as fit only for children and naïve adolescents, who, when they "grow up," are expected to realize that they are hopelessly bumptious and philistine, because (a) "in real life people don't act that way," and (b) without benefit of close textual exegesis by the New Criticism, how can they possibly understand *Finnegans Wake*?

In recent years, by a kind of logical progression, the naturalist and nonobjective schools have tended more and more to fuse. Old-fashioned naturalism had purged all drama from literature, and boredom was rapidly setting in. As a result, the naturalists tended more and more to depict not just the "average man" or the "girl next door," but the most grotesque and depraved of extant or conceivably extant characters. And this step seemed justified as the world noticed that, with the general breakdown in moral standards, more and more people *were* becoming depraved. With ever-greater intensity, novelists and playwrights have been cluttering their fiction with homosexuals, rapists, nymphomaniacs, narcotic addicts, etc. and proclaiming that this is the way people *really* are. Often, they will assert that this is the way people really are *down deep*, after the veneer of respectability has been stripped away. Freudian doctrine has been widely used to justify the claim that man, at the core, is a cesspool of iniquity, and that, therefore, these writers are being even more "realistic" about the world around them than were the Farrells and Dreisers of yesteryear.

And the grotesquerie of characterization has been matched by a growing obscurantism of language. Undoubtedly the apogee of this tendency was reached in the recent plays of Eugene Ionesco and of James Joyce's disciple Samuel Beckett, who have gone beyond even the Faulkners and the Tennessee Williamses and the Kerouacs to proclaim the meaninglessness of life by their absence of plot, depravity of *dramatis personae,* and virtual gibberish of their language.

Arriving in the midst of such a literary climate, it is no wonder that Ayn Rand's new novel *Atlas Shrugged* has struck the world as a puzzling phenomenon. For apart from her controversial ethical and political philosophy, Miss Rand has bewildered the critics by presenting the first important novel in decades to re-create—and, as we shall see, to advance beyond—the romantic tradition, a tradition that had for so long been driven underground into dime novels and costume dramas. In fact, one of *Atlas Shrugged*'s unique virtues as a novel is to make us aware once again of the romantic aesthetic.

What, then, is the fundamental romantic attitude toward art in general and the novel in particular? In answer, we may first ask the question, what is art anyway? Why do we not call "art" a block of stone as it comes from a quarry; yet why do we call it art when reshaped by a sculptor? And why do we *not* call it art if it is reshaped to serve as a bench or as part of a building? There can be only one answer: because the sculptor communicates *meaning* to the beholder, meaning *beyond* the fact that it is a block of stone or that it is now being used for some other consumers' object, such as a bench or a building. Since only aspects of objective reality can be meaningfully communicated, this means that art is the reshaping of reality by the artist and its subsequent communication to others.

We may, therefore, at once challenge the artistic credentials of the nonobjectivist, whether in painting, sculpture, or literature. For if art is necessarily *communication,* an objective medium is necessary in order to communicate. In literature, this medium is language. Hence, the importance in literature of precision and objectivity of language, and of *clarity* of style, for this clarity is the measure by which the artist is accurately and efficiently communicating his meaning.

Art is not only communication; it is necessarily also selection. No one, not even the von Ranke historian, can present *all* of reality as it really is. He *must* select some aspect of reality to communicate. But the moment this is conceded, it must also be granted that the artist or the historian can only select according to some *standard* of selection. And one of the functions of the critic is to judge that standard. The task of the historian or journalist is to capture the essence of the events of the day or of an age, and to select and present his facts accordingly. The standard is here set by the nature of the historical or journalistic discipline. But in fiction, or other art, there is no such evident standard; for in literature, the artist creates his *own* events. Since he is free to create his own events, the artist differs radically from the journalist, for if he tries to ape the journalist and record the events around him, we are free to ask, is this *art*? And if it is, may we not question the artist's purpose and standards of selection?

Any choice is necessarily determined by the *values* of the chooser. The artist's selection is therefore determined by his standards of value. We may now arrive at a definition of art: *the reshaping of reality in accordance with the artist's values and the communication of these values to the reader or beholder.*

In short, art is the *objectification*, the bringing into tangible reality, of an artist's values. We may now proceed at one stroke to answer the questions, why should the artist want to do what he does, and why should anyone else enjoy reading a novel or seeing a play or painting? Because the artist wishes to objectify his values in concrete reality, and the reader or onlooker enjoys seeing his own values objectified in reality. And the meanings and values can be communicated from one to the other by means of this objectification.

We all know that one of the prime characteristics of art is its ability to induce emotion in the beholder. This is particularly true of fiction, where the reader tends to identify with the central character. We are now in a position to explain this phenomenon. For emotions are *value-responses*, i.e., they are reactions determined by a person's values. If a man approves of something, he will feel a favorable emotion toward it; if he disapproves, he will experience an unfavorable reaction. The reader who likes and enjoys a novel so responds because he is seeing his own values objectified; the man who dislikes a novel is reacting to values that are opposed to his own. The process of communication between novelist and reader therefore operates as follows: the novelist selects and reshapes reality according to his values, and presents them in concrete form; the reader, experiencing the concrete forms, through them penetrates to an understanding of the writer's underlying values, and responds to the extent that he shares these values.

Since all art conveys values, all art is intimately bound up with morals. For values are either moral or immoral, good or bad. The novel, specifically, is also tied to morality in another way: it deals with the action of characters, and since men's actions are determined by their values, these actions can be judged as either moral or immoral.

Since the artist must choose, and therefore must choose according to his values, all artists are presenting reality not as it *is*, but as they believe it *ought* to be. Every novelist, whether he knows it or not, is a moral philosopher and teacher. The naturalist writers who *claim* to represent life as it really is, are misleading themselves; for when they present dreary human beings stumbling their way through meaningless lives, what they are telling their readers is this: life is dreary, men cannot achieve their goals, they are playthings in the hands of fate, or society, or of their id.

In short, these writers are conveying their basic values and premises, their philosophy of life. And when the extremists among them portray a world of dope addicts, homicidal maniacs, and other depraved persons, they are telling the world that *this* is the essence of life, that this is the true nature of man and all that man can attain.

The romanticist, on the other hand, realizes that he is presenting a world that ought to be, and by doing so he is saying that there are values and ideals that man can strive to achieve and which would make a better world than exists at present. What, specifically, are the means employed by the romantic novelist in communicating these values? The most important one is *plot*, and it is therefore not a coincidence that absence of an exciting plot is the prime characteristic of modern, and especially "high-brow" modern, fiction. For the plot is the objectification within the novel of the values and personalities of the characters. The plot is a purposeful logical progression of events, and it is through this progression of action that the author's values, and the personalities of his characters, take on concrete form. The author who presents characters without plot is not writing a *novel*, but a psychological casebook, which may or may not have value as psychology. Plot is therefore the critical distinguishing attribute of the novel.

The importance of the plot for the romantic novel was anticipated by Aristotle, in his *Poetics*:

> All human happiness or misery takes the form of action; the end for which we live is a certain kind of activity. . . . Character gives us qualities, but it is in our actions—what we do—that we are happy or the reverse. . . . So that it is the action in it, i.e., its Fable or Plot, that is the end and purpose of the tragedy.

A plot necessarily involves drama and conflict, and it is also a logical succession of events flowing out of the interplay of the novel's characters. A plot also implies that each individual has free will, that he is free to choose his values and to try purposefully to attain them. Since the romantic novelist is presenting a world that ought to be, his central character is a *hero*, i.e., a good man, a man with good and proper values, who struggles to achieve his values amid the conflict of the plot structure. The more intense this conflict, the more clearly will the hero's fight for his goals and values be emphasized and dramatized in action. And, if his struggle is with natural forces rather than with other men, much of the point of the story will be lost, for nature has no free will and can adopt no values, and is therefore not really an adversary. If, therefore, the hero is engaged in conflict with other human beings, and is trying to attain good values, his antagonists will necessarily be *villains* who are opposing him in order to realize bad or evil values. Hence the romantic novel will be a battle of heroes and heroines against villains.

The climax of the plot is of enormous importance, since this is the final resolution of the conflict, the final lesson, the concluding presentation of the author's implied philosophy of life, the ultimate impact on the reader. Hence the importance of the much-reviled "happy ending." For if the author is reshaping reality to objectify his values, then his good heroes will triumph over the villains, and thereby complete and crown the world he is presenting.

Apart from the rare case where the author's specific purpose is to show the *spirit* of the hero remaining unbroken, even when defeated physically, an unhappy ending displays a profoundly pessimistic conclusion that has no place in the proper novel, where a better world is being created. For such an ending conveys and attempts to inculcate in the reader the view that the good, in life, must in the end be vanquished, either by evil people or by blind chance. When Oscar Wilde bitingly lampooned the moral approach to fiction in *The Importance of Being Earnest*—"The good ended happily, and the bad unhappily. That is what Fiction means"—he writ more ironically than he knew. For what we have been saying is that Miss Prism was right.

It is, therefore, fallacious to criticize romantic novels for presenting neither events nor characters "as they occur in reality." The true romantic novelist does not try to set forth his characters as statistical averages or modal types of the people he sees around him; he molds them as *philosophical archetypes*, i.e., as concrete embodiments of certain sets of values, whether heroic, villainous, or definite mixtures of the two.

The romantic therefore presents the *essence* of his characters, and wastes little time in accumulating detail. In presenting his characters as essences, he raises them from the particular to the status of the universal, and carries a message to all readers regardless of time and space. The naturalistic novel, on the other hand, accumulates endless detail down to and even including, the brand names of clothes, thus diminishing the importance of the characters by rooting them ever deeper in particular concretes.

Now we can see the reason why issues and characters for the romantic novelist will be either "black" or "white," and why he will side strongly with the "whites." The more firmly a person holds values, the more strongly and openly he will be devoted to them. It is no coincidence that just as modern America is marked by a decay of belief in moral principle, so has the serious romantic novel all but disappeared from the literary scene.

Nothing about *Atlas Shrugged* has puzzled the critics more than its "blacks" and "whites," and small wonder: for the present age is a shifting inconstant sand of "middle-of-the-road" attitudes in all subjects: aesthetics, ethics, or politics—an age where the only firmly held moral principle is that no one may dare hold moral principles too strongly.

Romantic fiction has been denounced as "escapism," meaning that the housewife or the tired businessman is trying to escape from his daily cares into a world of enjoyment. But far from being philistinism, we have seen that such "escape"—the experiencing of a world where one's values have come true—is precisely the noblest function of fiction. And since *Atlas Shrugged* is our day's most striking example of important romantic fiction, we may say that just as Ayn Rand's explicit moral, political, and economic philosophy redeems the tired businessman from the weight of guilt he has long suffered for his productiveness and profit seeking, so her aesthetic principles redeem him from his "sin" of seeking in literature for values in action that he can admire and applaud—including noble heroes who vanquish villains and achieve their goals. In short, Miss Rand, by the construct of her novel, is saying that the modern intellectuals are just as wrong in condemning the tired businessman's "philistinism" as they are in attacking his method of livelihood.

Atlas Shrugged partakes of all the aspects of the romantic novel treated above. It has been accurately termed a "melodrama" by the reviewers, melodrama being defined by *Webster*'s as a "romantic and sensational drama, typically with a happy ending," in which "sensational" means "suited or intended to excite great interest or emotion."

How does *Atlas Shrugged* advance beyond the romantic tradition? In two main ways. One: it not only presents values in action, but portrays them as capable of being applied and achieved in daily life.

For the trouble with most romantic fiction has been that the authors have not believed their values to be applicable in the real world. They have therefore fled into such remote worlds as historical costume dramas or science fiction. *This* was their *illegitimate* form of "escapism." *Atlas Shrugged*, on the contrary, presents very clearly a world that not only *ought* to be, but *can* be, and its concrete relation to our world is evident. Hence, Miss Rand's own label for her aesthetics of "romantic realism," or perhaps, "realistic romanticism."

The second, and perhaps most important, departure of Miss Rand's is her creation of a new form of novel of ideas. A novel dealing explicitly with philosophical ideas is such a rarity in modern America that most reviewers dismissed *Atlas Shrugged* as scarcely a novel because it carries an explicit philosophical message. It has thereby violated a seemingly deep-seated American prejudice: what Irving Howe has called "the notion that abstract ideas invariably contaminate a work of art and should be kept at a safe distance from it."

But *Atlas Shrugged* has done far more. For previous novels of ideas have been essentially plotless and static. They have been books in which characters simply sit and discuss philosophy. A typical modern example is Thomas Mann's *The Magic Mountain*, where the device of a tubercular sanitarium is used to legitimatize the virtual dissolving of action into a series of philosophical conversations among the patients. Another is Simone de Beauvoir's *The Mandarins*, where the plot is essentially reduced to a series of parlor discussions on the principles and applications of existentialist philosophy.

Miss Rand, on the other hand, not only presents explicitly a far-ranging, comprehensive, and to a remarkable extent original, philosophical worldview, but also dramatizes that philosophy implicitly through her characters and her plot. In short, she fuses the novel of ideas with the best romantic form of the novel: a thoroughly exciting melodrama. Her characters are not only romantic archetypes; they are archetypes expressing her own explicit philosophical system. And since this system covers and integrates all aspects of human action—metaphysics, ethics, politics, economics, psychology, and sex—the breadth and scope of the work is enormous. For her characters are developed as philosophical archetypes in every aspect of their actions; and just as Miss Rand's philosophy is thoroughly integrated and interconnected, so are all of its concrete manifestations in the novel interconnected. Every theme, every character, every incident, every line of this 1,168-page novel has its function and purpose as part of the whole.

Setting aside, then, the specific content of Miss Rand's philosophy, the hostile and uncomprehending reaction to the aesthetics of *Atlas Shrugged* is a measure of the poverty and aridity of our literary and artistic scene. The disappearance of the serious romantic form is a measure of the extent to which we have lost our concern for values, which we all require as a guide to our actions; the absence of a novel of ideas is the measure of the sterility of our current intellectual endeavors, of our lack of concern for ideas themselves. It has been truly said that we are living in an Alexandrian age, an era not of original and profound thought but of taxonomic classifying, of living on the borrowed capital of the ideas of our predecessors. Perhaps the striking originality, in method and in content, of *Atlas Shrugged* will serve as a beacon for new and fresh literary and intellectual directions.

2. Letter on Recommended Novels

May 30, 1961

Mr. Kenneth S. Templeton

Dear Ken:

I have owed you for some time a letter about possible right-wing novels to suggest for schools. Literature is not my forte, but I have scouted my agents in the literature field, and have come up with at least a few suggestions.

I am assured that one of the most famous Italian novels ever written, Alessandro Manzoni's *The Betrothed*, just published in paperback by Dutton, is a great novel (it was on Eliot's original five-foot shelf), and also pro–free enterprise. Chapter 28 is supposed to be an excellent description of the sufferings brought on the poor by price control. Manzoni is also pro-religious, but anticlerical. He was a friend of Cavour.[109] In Italian, the novel is entitled *I promessi sposi*.

The founder of modern anarchism, William Godwin (unfortunately a left-wing anarchist, though not nearly as bad as Kropotkin, etc.) wrote about twenty novels of which the most famous, and still read sometimes, is *Caleb Williams*.

There is, of course, some acid anti-State material in Jonathan Swift's *Gulliver's Travels*.

For a "specialized" audience, the openly and avowed individualist-anarchist novel by John Henry Mackay, *The Anarchists*, would, I predict, warm the cockles of your heart. The climactic scene in Mackay's story is a great speech in which the hero, who had previously collaborated with the left-wing anarchists, breaks with them and espouses the Tuckerite cause of individualist anarchism.

The best novel by far on the causes of the Spanish Civil War, showing the monstrousness of the Left, is the two-volume work by José Maria Gironella, *The Cypresses Believe in God*.

There are, of course, the various Horatio Alger novels, and the "romances" of Harriet Martineau.

It is not well known, but the popular English woman novelist "Ouida" was a magnificent libertarian. Unfortunately, in her score or more of novels, I think the only work which was substantially libertarian was her short story, *A Village Commune* (1881), where Ouida attacked the network of crippling taxes which kept the Italian peasants, and all the other groups in Italy, in misery.

The strange young German writer of the early nineteenth century, Heinrich von Kleist, has just had his best stories translated into English and published as *The Marquise of O and Other Stories*.

---

[109] Editor's note: Camillo Benso, Count Cavour (1810–1861), was prime minister of Piedmont (1852–1861) and the first prime minister of Italy (1861). With Giuseppe Garibaldi (1807–1882), he was the principal figure of the Italian *Risorgimento* (Unification).

The most powerful—and rip-roaringly libertarian—of the lot is *Michael Kohlhaas*, the story of one man's private-army vengeance against the army and courts of "justice" of a German state that "did him wrong."

One time, I heard Ayn Rand commend an extremely obscure novel by Merwin and Webster, a writing team of the turn of the century, called *Calumet "K"*—a novel about the building of a grain elevator.

For current pro-business novels, there is Cameron Hawley's *Executive Suite* and especially Hawley's *Cash McCall* (which is also pro–speculator and anti–high taxation).

Everyone read John Dos Passos's first, left-wing trilogy *USA*, but few have read his later, anti–New Deal *District of Columbia* trilogy. I particularly commend an excellent one of the trilogy—*The Grand Design* is bitterly anti-FDR, both on domestic and on foreign issues, and with portraits of the New Deal dipped in acid. There is also Dos Passos's latest, anti-union novel, *Midcentury*.

There are countless "anti-Utopia," individualist science fiction stories and novels, of which one very famous individualist novel is Robert Heinlein, *Revolt in 2100*. Also see Eric Frank Russell's short story "And Then There Were None," a story of a libertarian, individualist-anarchist planet, that defeats, by Gandhian nonviolence, an American imperialist attempt to add it to its list of colonies.

George Orwell's *1984* is of course a classic anti-State novel; also good and witty is Aldous Huxley's *Brave New World*.

Taylor Caldwell has written various right-wing novels in recent years. The most hard-hitting is *The Devil's Advocate* (not to be confused, of course, with Morris West's famous recent novel of the same title.)

Dostoevsky was an authoritarian and a pan-Slavist, but his *The Possessed* is supposed to contain acid portraits of socialists and other leftists in action; also, of course, *The Brothers Karamazov* is valuable for its great sequence on "The Grand Inquisitor."

There is, finally, a host of antiwar novels of the 1920s and 1930s, which deserve to be resurrected. There are the multivolumes of Jules Romains; Erich Maria Remarque's *All Quiet on the Western Front*; *Paths of Glory*; and the grisly *Johnny Got His Gun* by Dalton Trumbo.

Of more recent vintage is Nevil Shute's *On The Beach* and Leonard Wibberley's magnificent comic spoof, *The Mouse That Roared*.

(Note: *Don't* recommend the war-mongering *Advise and Consent* by Allen Drury.)

This is only a foray into the literary field. I am sure that there must be other good novels.

I hope this has been helpful to you and Baldy.

3. Review of Edmund Fuller, *Man in Modern Fiction*

June 22, 1962

Dr. Ivan R. Bierly
William Volker Fund

Dear Ivan:

Edmund Fuller's *Man in Modern Fiction* is an important and interesting book; it transcends purely technical literary matters to discuss the philosophy of man that permeates modern fiction.[110] Not only is Fuller remarkable for his interest in the view of the nature of man expressed in fiction—rather than in literary symbolism or sociological reportage—but he has a philosophic viewpoint which is especially remarkable for today's literary critics.

While he doesn't precisely name it as such, Edmund Fuller speaks for the great classical tradition in aesthetics—the great tradition of Western civilization that brought us, in so many fields of aesthetics (painting, poetry, music, sculpture, and latterly fiction), the masterpieces of our heritage: especially in the Hellenic, Renaissance, Baroque, and nineteenth-century periods. As a classical aesthetician, Fuller stands out foursquare against the entire tradition of twentieth-century aesthetics, which, in the other art forms as in fiction, reflects in its

---

[110] Edmund Fuller, *Man in Modern Fiction: Some Minority Opinions on Contemporary American Writing* (New York: Vintage Books, 1958).

content a profoundly *antihuman* view of man. Fuller, in this excellent set of essays, points out again and again the assumption of modern novelists that man is *subhuman*, that he is a will-less, determined creature, little better than an animal, driven only by momentary sensation, and lacking purpose, values, free will, aspiration, heroism, or deep communication and love for others.

Fuller, in pinpointing the distorted and debased view in which man is held by the leading modern novelists, has written a far more important and significant work about fiction than almost any other, for he deals with the really crucial issues about a work of fiction—far more crucial than explaining some recondite symbol. The works of James Jones, Norman Mailer, Tennessee Williams, James Joyce, and Jack Kerouac are raked over the coals, and application made to others of their school as well.

We see the error of the sentimentalist view of "compassion" (compassion for the depraved and degraded, with corresponding hostility toward the "squares" who are not degraded—thus violating the classical-Christian view of compassion as only forthcoming *after* a person has repented since he or she arrived at his degradation by his own free will and has moved by his own effort and change of values toward redemption and rehabilitation).

We also see the error of these novelists' treating man as essentially depraved, sex as a clinical or psychological case history, with women as mere objects of men—instead of as passionate love between two people truly in communion with each other. Also criticized properly is James Joyce and the cult of obscurity and noncommunication—as well as derision at man's stature, and the insanities of "beatnik" writing and "philosophy."

In contrast to these morbid degraders of man, Fuller shows how the great classical novelists differed in their treatment of man, of moral problems, of love, etc., e.g., Dostoevsky and Tolstoy. When a modern novelist writes of criminals or rapists, they are considered guiltless, tragic victims of society or their environment, or "happy bums"; when Dostoevsky wrote of them he *took sides;* he showed that the criminals had tragically chosen, of free will and error, their own guilty path. Dostoevsky portrayed men with purposes, as choosing good or evil, etc.

The only serious error of Fuller's, in my view, is his defense of Herman Wouk's *The Caine Mutiny* as against the valid criticisms of William H. Whyte and others. Fuller lamely tries to defend Wouk against the charge of choosing the organization, and loyalty to the organization, as against individualism and individual responsibility. And curiously, while he praises Dostoevsky and the classical novelists for taking sides, he praises Wouk for *not* doing so, for treating the Captain Queeg problem as hopelessly muddled and two-sided. And Fuller even weakly tries to defend Wouk's conformist and anti-intellectual *Marjorie Morningstar*. However, the discussion of Wouk is the only real slip in the book. The rest is filled with insight. And not only does it, at last, bring classical (Hellenic-Judeo-Christian) philosophical attitudes to bear on modern fiction, but it does so with verve and wit.

Index